CONTENTIOUS REPUBLICANS

CONTENTIOUS REPUBLICANS

Popular Politics, Race, and Class in Nineteenth-Century Colombia

JAMES E. SANDERS

Duke University Press   Durham and London 2004

© 2004 Duke University Press
All rights reserved
Printed in the United States of America on acid-free paper ∞
Typeset in Quadraat by Keystone Typesetting, Inc.
Library of Congress Cataloging-in-Publication data
appear on the last printed page of this book.

for
MICHAEL FRANCIS JIMÉNEZ
1948–2001

Contents

Acknowledgments

I begin by thanking my wife, Jennifer Duncan, the most generous yet critical reader, always reminding me to follow the story. My family in Lake City, Florida, have always been supportive, even if what I do often seems a little strange; when I was a graduate student, my grandfather could never quite believe I was being paid to read books.

In Colombia, more people took an interest in my project and offered me more assistance than I ever expected. I thank especially Isabel Cristina Bermúdez, Beatriz Castro Carvajal, Guiomar Dueñas, José Escorcia, Margarita Garrido, Gary Long, Eduardo Mejía, Eduardo Sáenz, and Fabio Zambrano. My most heartfelt thanks go out to the eminent chronicler of the nineteenth-century Cauca, Alonso Valencia Llano, who generously helped my project along in numerous ways. I was always made to feel welcome in Colombia's wonderful archives. I salute the staffs of the Archivo Central del Cauca, the Archivo del Congreso, the Archivo General de la Nación, the Archivo Histórico Municipal de Cali, the Biblioteca Nacional, and the archive of INCORA. Special thanks go to María Leonilde Chirva, at the Biblioteca Nacional, Gladys Martínez and Martha Jeanet Sierra at the Biblioteca Luis Angel Arango, and Hedwig Hartmann Garcés at the Archivo Central del Cauca.

Along the way, I have met many other Colombianistas whose company and ideas enriched the research and writing process for me immensely. They include Nancy Appelbaum, Charles Bergquist, Hayley Froysland, Richard Goulet, Marixa Lasso, Catherine LeGrand, Frank Safford, David Sowell, and Brett Troyan. I first encountered Aims McGuinness in Bogotá, where we wasted much time over *chocolates*, bouncing ideas off each other and reworking our future books; we have continued our discussions, but mostly now over email and the phone, without, alas, the *chocolates*.

Research support was provided by University of Pittsburgh Mellon Fellowships and a Center for Latin American Studies Graduate Student Field Research Grant. Some material on indigenous groups first appeared in my "Belonging to the Great Granadan Family: Partisan Struggle and the Construction of Indigenous Identity and Politics in Southwestern Colombia, 1849–1890," in *Race and Nation in Modern Latin America*, ed. Nancy P. Appelbaum, Anne S. Macpherson, and Karin Alejandra Rosemblatt (Chapel Hill: University of North Carolina Press, 2003), 56–86. I would also like to thank all the staff at Duke University Press. The anonymous readers gave very careful readings and valuable advice. Likewise, Valerie Milholland has been a great editor. Natalie Hanemann at Duke helped with the maps, as did Wendy Mann-Eliot of Hillman Library. So many people helped me, especially those who read draft manuscripts, that I fear listing them for leaving someone out; nevertheless, thanks to Jennifer Belden-England, John Beverley, Seymour Drescher, Mike Ervin, Alejandro de la Fuente, K. C. Johnson, Shirley Kreger, Marcus Rediker, and Matilde Zimmermann. Of course, any faults and shortcomings are mine alone. Special thanks to Reid Andrews, who made this book (and me as a scholar) so much better through his rigorous critiques and trenchant suggestions. I hope I keep writing on topics that interest him so that I can continue asking him to read my work.

Finally, I dedicate this book to Michael Jiménez, my adviser and great friend. Michael is in so much of this work, both as an intellectual presence and as an inspiration. Whenever I reread these pages, they remind me of our conversations and debates and his expansive, wise counsel. So it saddens me to leave this work now for other things. I am not sure what we will do without him.

Map 1   United States of Colombia, 1863–85. Reprinted by permission of Louisiana State University Press from *Rafael Núñez and the Politics of Colombian Regionalism* by James William Park. © 1985 by Louisiana State University Press.

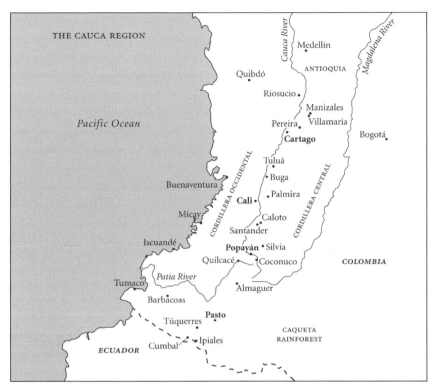

Map 2 Map of the Cauca region

1 Introduction:

A Social History of Politics

In a beautiful vale north of Cali, on 31 August 1876, at the Battle of Los Chancos, thousands of soldiers—only months before working as farmers, day laborers, and tenants—stared across a field at one another. Some carried banners supporting the church and the pope; others marched under the tricolor of "liberty." They would engage their opposing brethren for seven hours of brutal artillery fire and desperate charges, each force meting out death, each shedding blood, until finally one group broke and ran, watched by the tired but victorious eyes of fellows not so different from themselves. After the guns had fallen silent, hundreds of foot soldiers lay dead or dying on the field, having killed one another to secure the triumph of either the Conservative or the Liberal Party.[1] These same soldiers—back in their guise as plebeian workers—would also have voted many a time for Liberals or Conservatives in the multitudinous elections that punctuated the year. In those more tranquil times, candidates scoured the countryside, visiting the smallest hamlet and the most humble tavern, campaigning for support. On election day, people streamed into the cities from across the land to vote, to ensure that no fraud cost their side its victory, and to enjoy a respite from the demands of the soil.[2]

In mid-nineteenth-century Colombia, thousands of everyday people regularly cast ballots or fought in civil wars in the name of the new nation's Conservative and Liberal Parties. Why? Why did subalterns bother to vote in contests between political factions led by rich men? Why did they sacrifice their very lives in battles for economic and political doctrines about which they supposedly knew or cared little? Yet subalterns' words and deeds argue that they did know and they did care. When they went to war or exercised the suffrage, they understood what they were doing and usually acted for sound reasons. This book will explore these words and deeds to show the distinct ways in which popular groups understood and practiced politics in nineteenth-century Colombia.[3]

Traditional literature concerning nineteenth-century Colombian politics suggests that subalterns were politically ignorant, indifferent, or, simply, the clients of powerful patrons.[4] This approach—besides excluding plebeians from history and denying them agency—fails to explain the astonishing variety of subaltern political action and discourse in the nineteenth century and elites' continual efforts to come to terms with subaltern politics. Such assumptions also ascribe a power to elites that, at least in Colombia, they simply did not possess. A new historical literature has begun to explore the popular liberalism of plebeian groups in Latin America, recognizing subalterns' political participation and their contributions to nation and state building.[5] The popular liberals who shed their blood at Los Chancos were not just fighting against elite hacendados and merchants but also fighting against men of a social class very much like their own. Opposite them stood popular conservatives whose political ideology has received much less attention than has that of popular liberals. Popular republicanism often seems to be synonymous with popular liberalism, but, in Colombia, and I suspect elsewhere, popular liberalism was simply one possible variant, among many, of popular republicanism.

Conservatives as well as Liberals always enjoyed the support of at least some subaltern allies. These popular republicans—liberal and conservative—were not stooges, mindless peons, or bullied clients but often consciously allied with elites in the hopes of finding the political space in which to pursue their own agendas. Sometimes these alliances were short-lived and aimed at achieving immediate goals. Yet, over time, many subalterns came to identify with the two dominant political parties and to see these parties as their own. The most emotionally resonant explanation for this is that families inherited their partisan affiliation from past generations, whose loyalties to any faction were often the result of clientelism or serendipity.[6] However, subalterns often had very good reasons for supporting a specific political party, and these reasons changed over time. These motivations sprang from their own visions of popular republicanism and their particular social and economic situations.

In the Cauca region of southwestern Colombia, three distinct forms of popular republicanism emerged that I have denominated *popular liberalism, popular indigenous conservatism,* and *popular smallholder republicanism.* (These forms will be further explored in chapter 2.) Popular liberals tended to be landless workers or tenants on great haciendas in the central river valley. Many were Afro-Colombians—slaves or their descendants—who formed a strong alliance with the Liberal Party. Most studies of popular liberalism focus on mestizos or Indian peasants, but I hope to add Afro-Colombians' experiences to the debate.[7] Popular indigenous conservatives were Indians living on communal landholdings in the southern highlands. They felt threatened by Liberal economic and social policy and saw allies in the Conservative Party, whose language of tradition echoed Indians' own desires to protect their historically legitimated communities. Many popular smallholder republicans were small farmers, especially migrants coming into the area from the Antioquia region to the north. They supported both Liberals and Conservatives, their allegiances changing depending on their local situations and the parties' projects. The political history of the Cauca revolved around the complex relationships between these groups, the leaders of the two political parties, and party factions. While politics in Colombia is usually interpreted as the formation and breakdown of elite factions, the ebb and flow of elite-subaltern relations was often as, if not more, important.

Bargaining increasingly defined the relationship between subalterns and elites after Independence, intensifying after the Liberals took power in 1849. Elites in nineteenth-century Colombia were not all-powerful; they were internally divided into parties, and the state that they controlled was quite weak. They regularly turned to subaltern allies to pursue political projects; indeed, without these alliances, any such project was doomed to fail. The great landholding and merchant class certainly did not exercise political hegemony over most Colombians. Bargaining mediated between the notables' need for allies and subalterns' claimsmaking concerning their social, political, and economic lives.

Of course, bargaining is always an aspect of politics, except in moments of savage conquest or repression. In the colonial period, economic bargaining took place every day on plantations, mines, and haciendas. Subalterns, especially Indians, at times found support in the church and the crown, whom they played off local hacendados. Save for some important exceptions such as the 1781 Comuneros' revolt, bargaining rarely extended beyond the site of production, rarely entered the broader political realm.

I am proposing that a new postcolonial or national form of bargaining emerged after Independence. Chapter 3 will more fully explicate this new form of bargaining, whose most salient features were that it was less personalistic, more public, more programmatic, and, most important, republican.[8] During the nineteenth century, bargaining became less personalistic, less limited by the face-to-face negotiations of landlord and tenant, master and slave, patrician and plebeian. Patron-client relations would continue to be important in the Cauca, but, after midcentury, most bargaining took place beyond those relationships, often between individuals and groups who had little or no personal connection.

As bargaining was less personalistic, it was correspondingly more public. Negotiations continued on the sites of production but swelled beyond them to dominate the public sphere. Plebeians' access to public space was quite limited in the colonial era, but, after Independence, subalterns could enter the public realm and did so with increasing frequency. Bargaining followed subalterns into the public sphere, and, as a consequence, negotiations were not limited to the conditions on any single site of production but began to concern themselves with the whole of society's economic, social, and political life.

Bargaining also became programmatic. Bargaining was frequent in the colonial era, but it was ad hoc and unsustained, becoming most intense in periods of social stress. In the Cauca after 1848, the two dominant political parties began to negotiate with their plebeian allies in a sustained and planned manner over time. Although popular groups had been trying to break into public, political life since Independence, only with the Liberals' ascension to national power in 1848 did an opportunity arise for subalterns to change the nature of Colombian politics, the story of chapters 3 and 4. Bargaining ceased to be evanescent but became a constant, potent force in the Cauca's political life. Successful politicians knew that they would need to negotiate with subalterns. Bargaining became the way politics worked in the Cauca, the program that everyone had to follow.

This new style of bargaining was not a sharp break with the past but an evolution that retained many older aspects of negotiation from the colonial era while incorporating new ones, especially the ideas and practices of republicanism. Republicanism offered new and powerful ways of talking about and engaging in politics that plebeians appropriated. Subalterns used bargaining to reframe elite republicanism, often significantly democratizing it to better suit the needs and visions of Colombia's lower classes. Republican bargaining became hegemonic in the Cauca, the way everyone—elites and subalterns, Conservatives and Liberals, Indians, Afro-Colombians, and Antioqueño migrants—practiced politics.[9]

Hegemony is a tricky and often ill-defined concept, but it is nonetheless useful. I employ it here in a very limited sense to help explicate why bargaining was so prevalent in the Cauca and why republicanism dominated Caucanos' political language and actions. I utilize *hegemony* to mean the reigning shared terrain in which politics operates—the current limits of what political actors can say or do. Following E. P. Thompson and William Roseberry, hegemony is most efficacious in understanding, not consent, but struggle. Hegemony defines the political and ideological terrain on which contention takes place. Roseberry notes: "What hegemony constructs, then, is not a shared ideology but a common material and meaningful framework for living through, talking about, and acting upon social orders characterized by domination."[10] In the Cauca, republicanism became this common framework.

Bargaining was the primary way in which subalterns and elites contended within republican politics. Florencia Mallon argues that the use of hegemony as the shared arena of social and political struggle allows scholars to pay more attention to the ground-level interactions between rulers and ruled.[11] The Cauca's political history is a story of the continual negotiation between three distinct subaltern groups and the divided elite that attempted to rule over them. This negotiation and bargaining took place within a contentious republicanism that provided the framework for elites' and subalterns' discourse and practice of politics.

Republican bargaining became the only way in which both elites and subalterns could talk about and practice politics publicly.[12] Yet, of course, both elites and plebeians have their own private discourses and conceptions of politics, although those of plebeians are often completely inaccessible to the historian, except by means of risky, and often insubstantial, inferences. In a sense, these private discourses are enticing as they are what people "really thought," but I would argue that, often, they are less important than the shared public discourse of politics.[13] This public discourse is what sets the boundaries of what can be said and, more important, what can be done.

The hegemonic political culture does not just limit or engender discourse, but also action. Transgressive action—gross repression or revolutionary revolt— grabs the imagination, and justifiably so. These moments often mark when a hegemonic political and social system is breaking down and being overtly challenged. These moments can reaffirm an existing system or lead to vast changes in the political and social compact between those above and those below. The Mexican Revolution is the preeminent example of this phenomenon in Latin America's long nineteenth century. However, a political system also changes through the shared political and social negotiations of elite and popular groups. Moments of intense social and political bargaining reframe the discursive and political public realm. In the rough-and-tumble of negotiation, the ways of thinking, speaking, and conducting politics change. When a group decides that the hegemonic system is too limiting (or too liberating for some) and feels that bargaining is futile or too sluggish, then it must withdraw into the realms of raw force, violent repression, or desperate revolt.

In contrast to most of nineteenth-century Latin America, Colombia experienced the relative absence of both mass violent repression by elites and desperate revolt by plebeians. Popular claimsmaking occurred across the Americas, but, in Colombia, it usually manifested itself as republican bargaining instead of open revolt. Most violence was channeled through the republican system—legitimated so to speak—in the form of civil wars or partisan attacks. Let me be clear. I am not saying that elites did not engage in often-horrific violence to secure their hold on wealth and power and that everyday violence, against men and especially women, was not de rigueur for nineteenth-century Colombia. Yet elites never had to, or were never able to, marshal massive projects of violent repression to bend the masses to their will or violently eliminate whole recalcitrant populations. Likewise, plebeians did not engage in do-or-die revolts on a large scale, be they slave revolts, millennial movements, or peasant jacqueries. Whatever their secret desires, elites and subalterns had to play by the rules—rules continually under negotiation—of republican politics. However, the possibilities of republican politics were rather expansive (the subject of chapter 5), and Colombian subalterns often successfully appropriated and manipulated republicanism to suit their own ends.[14] In the late 1870s and the 1880s, Colombian elites did try to close down the political culture of republican bargaining that had flourished since the 1850s through a movement called the Regeneration, but they could attempt this only by recruiting significant subaltern support for their project, the denouement of the story, which I relate in chapter 6.

Although subalterns in Colombia shared a broad vision of popular republicanism, distinct subaltern groups had distinct political discourses and objectives. A focus on only one relatively homogeneous subaltern group—be it of slaves, peasants, Indians, unionized workers, or the urban poor—can, at times, miscast the workings of politics and hegemony. By looking at only one group, especially a group about to be defeated, politics may seem only a struggle between the mighty and the weak. Close examination often reveals that many of the weak are allied with the mighty. This relationship could be interpreted in one conception as hegemony—some popular groups internalize the beguiling discourse and ideology of elites and then repress the brethren with whom they should be allied. Or, if looking only at the repressed group, hegemony seems not to exist at all, to be a myth created by the powerful for their psychological comfort. In this second conception, hegemony does not exist: look at the slaves rising up, the peasants revolting, the workers striking! I would argue that both these conceptions are limited. Neither explains why elites so often find subaltern allies for their projects: the first considers such allies dupes; the second ignores their existence altogether. Neither explains how a particular practice of politics originally came into being. Analyzing various subaltern groups makes the complexity of subaltern politics more evident and illuminates the power and limits of republican bargaining's hegemony. This strategy brings to the fore negotiations between the various factions, negotiations that take place within the hegemonic public sphere of politics. Now subaltern allies of the powerful no longer seem like dupes; similarly, brave rebels no longer appear as completely isolated and unaffected by (and not affecting) the dominant discourse in society.

Liberal or Conservative, hacendado or peasant, elite or subaltern, none alone exercised what Gramsci called the "intellectual and moral leadership" necessary to change society or control politics.[15] Yet the republican political system that emerged in Colombia was hegemonic; by midcentury, hardly anyone challenged its power or legitimacy. However, the meanings of republicanism, the role that subalterns could make for themselves in politics, and the nature of Colombian democracy were all open to debate.

What I mean by *popular politics* in this book's subtitle should by now be clear, but what about *race* and *class*? Politics was not divorced from but, rather, intimately tied to social and economic relations—hence a social history of politics. Race and class were the two most powerful factors influencing the political interactions between elites and plebeians and between different groups of subalterns.

My views on hegemony and my insistence that the divisions among popular groups are central to understanding history may make a focus on class seem somewhat strange. Most often, I refer to class, not to automatically convey a sense of class conflict (or class consciousness), but to underline the importance of subalterns' economic and material lives. I would stress here two important aspects of subalterns' class position. First, subalterns' political concerns never strayed far from the goal of trying to secure some modicum of economic independence and security in a rural world still dominated by great landlords. Second, the members of Colombia's lower class often occupied strikingly different economic positions.[16] Some subalterns, while perhaps poor, nevertheless owned their own small plots of land and enjoyed a certain degree of security and well-being. Others owned no land whatsoever and endured the grueling and precarious life of the tenant, sharecropper, or day laborer. Still others, especially Indians, owned land communally, with all the promises and frustrations that communalism entailed. However, all subalterns lived in a world of uncertainty and threat, sometimes from other subalterns, but usually from the intentions of the landed. Popular politics sought to make life a little less uncertain and to right the imbalance of wealth and power that defines social class. Yet their lives' material differences ensured that subaltern groups would pursue this common goal in distinct ways.

Race is, of course, a historically constructed identity, but it is, nevertheless, an incredibly powerful one. Not only did race mark the difference between a "white" ruling class and the Indian, black, mulatto, and mestizo middling and working classes, but it also divided subalterns from one another. Conversely, groups formed alliances across the supposedly rigid racial (and class) boundaries of the nineteenth-century Atlantic World. Indeed, perhaps surprisingly, upper-class Liberals and lower-class Afro-Colombians formed a potent alliance in the Cauca, defeating Conservatives and their allies in numerous civil wars. However, the very success of this alliance frightened many other subalterns, who saw popular liberals as a threat to their families, culture, and properties. Part of this story is how the increasing racism and racial fears of both elites and plebeians divided Caucano society and strengthened Conservative and reactionary political programs.

However, race and class are also proxies for all the material, ideological, and historical factors that affected popular politics: subalterns' historical experiences, geographic location, cultural lives (especially relations to the church), social status, market relations, and so on. Gender was also extremely important; while women were formally excluded from republican politics, gender roles were crucial in constructing popular and elite republicanism. These divisions of race, class, and gender also account for my use of the term *subaltern*. In one sense, it is a synonym for *lower class, the poor, the pueblo, popular,* or *plebeian* (these last three commonly employed in nineteenth-century Colombia). Beside avoiding repetition of these designations, *subaltern* more accurately captures the heterogeneity of the social groups under study. *Working class, whites, blacks, peasants, laborers, men*—these all fail to capture the political alliances that developed in the Cauca and historical actors' varied social lives. The region's social movements, at times, united (or divided) black and white, worker and peasant, men and women, the poor and the middling. *Subaltern* captures this variety and hybridity while also suggesting the various forms of power and oppression exercised or endured, without privileging any analytic category.[17] Race, class, and gender all combined to influence subalterns' political visions, practices, and objectives. In general, I propose that politics cannot be understood without examining the material and social situations of historical actors, whose quotidian lives determined their possibilities and constraints for making history.

Exploring the social history of politics requires an intensive investigation of local, regional, and national conditions—local, to grasp the everyday realities and choices that people faced, and national, as actors were influenced by and influenced politics beyond their region. Nationally, from the 1840s until the 1880s, Liberals' and Conservatives' fortunes in the Cauca either greatly influenced or determined national political life. Locally, the Cauca region of southwestern Colombia had an interesting mix of Liberals, Conservatives, Indians, Afro-Colombians, and Antioqueño migrants, which makes the area particularly interesting for study. By 1848, two of the groups, Indians and Afro-Colombians, had been living in the Cauca for centuries; the third group was Antioqueño migrants, just beginning their journeys south from their homeland into the frontier along the region's northern border. The three variants of popular republicanism—popular liberalism, popular indigenous conservatism, and popular smallholder republicanism—emerged out of the identities and historical experiences of the Cauca's various social groups and, along with the region's history, can be understood only in the context of the Cauca's physical and social life.

The region centers around the Cauca River, running north from the mountains around Popayán through a broad tropical valley, bordered by the Cordillera Occidental to the west and the higher Cordillera Central to the east. The river flows on into Antioquia, eventually joining the Magdalena River, but is not navigable at times (and, thus, not an outlet to the sea). The Patía River forms the other major valley (although smaller and less populated than the Cauca Valley), running south and west from Popayán. The Cauca Valley rises toward Popayán, which enjoys a more temperate climate, and the land becomes more elevated as the two mountain chains unite (along with the Cordillera Oriental) in the south around Pasto to form the southern highlands. To the north of the valley is the hilly region called the Quindío (the area north of Cartago), a frontier between the two colonially settled areas of Cauca and Antioquia. Finally, the long Pacific Coast runs from Ecuador to Panama, cut by hundreds of streams and rivers, and blanketed by dense tropical rain forest. The Cauca also controlled the vast Caquetá jungle, Colombia's part of the Amazon rain forest, although this administration was often more theoretical than real.

The mountainous terrain physically isolated the region from the outside world during the nineteenth century. Two principal routes connected the coast with the interior. The most important began at the port of Buenaventura, proceeded up the river Dagua to the mountains, and then continued as a mule path to Cali. Traversing this course could take from eight to twenty days. The Dagua route was treacherous, as boatmen in canoes ferried goods and passengers up and down the river, whose current ran very swift. One traveler exclaimed: "If Dante had navigated the Dagua, many of his damned would have made the terrible trip through the regions of hell by that way."[18] Another route (slower yet) went from Tumaco, via Barbacoas, to Túquerres and on to Pasto and Popayán. As poor as the routes to the sea were, overland travel to other parts of Colombia was even slower. Many of the roads were only mule paths, and other cart roads became impassible in the rainy season.[19] As one Caucano noted: "The immense Andes Mountains . . . suffocate and oppress us with their gigantic arms, isolating us from ports and the foci of civilization."[20] Schemes to build a true wagon-bearing road connecting the valley and the coast, or better yet a railroad, dominated Caucanos' imaginations throughout this period.

Before 1857, the region was divided into seven provinces; afterward, the entire region was consolidated into Cauca State—until the 1886 constitution eliminated the states. Local administrative boundaries further subdivided the region, jurisdictions that engendered long-running parochial rivalries. The central valley and the highlands were reasonably populated, while, along the coast and high in the mountains, inhabitants were more scarce.[21] The 1843 census counted 268,607 people in the Cauca. The total population stood at 435,078 in 1870.[22] The region was decidedly rural. By 1868, including the immediately surrounding countryside, Cali counted only 8,282 people, Popayán 7,603, Pasto 11,701, and Cartago 5,211.[23] Almost all studies of nineteenth-century Colombian politics have focused on urban life (usually Bogotá), but the Cauca, like Colombia as a whole, was dominated, not by its cities, but by its countryside.[24] Political debates focused more often on rural concerns (especially land) than on urban ones (e.g., tariff issues).

Racially, the region was very diverse. The 1851 census and Tomás Mosquera's 1852 estimates provide some clues to the area's racial composition, as shown in table 1. The U.S. consul in Buenaventura thought that the racial composition of the Cauca was five-sixths black and mulatto and one-sixth white, not including "the Indians in the mountains."[25] These numbers are problematic, as racial categories were quite fluid and politically charged, but they do provide a rough guide to the Caucano elite's racial thinking.

Different racial groups tended to reside in different areas. Indians, whose ancestors the Spanish had initially encountered during the Conquest, along with other groups of Native Americans who had moved into the region during the colonial era, mainly lived in the mountain highlands around the colonial towns

Table 1 The Racial Composition of the Cauca Region, Early 1850s

	1851[a]	1852[b]
Caucasian whites	19.4	17.7
Civilized Americans	7.9	9.1
Ethiopian blacks	13.0	13.7
Quatroons	—	5.3
Mestizos	37.3	12.0
Mulattos	21.8	41.4
Zambos	.6	.8

Note: Racial labels are taken from Mosquera, *Memoria*. A *zambo* is a person of African and Indian descent.
[a] Safford and Palacios, *Colombia*, 261.
[b] Mosquera, *Memoria*, 96.

of Popayán and Pasto.[26] A few small groups of Indians lived in the valley, but most of these populations had disappeared owing to the colonial legacy of land grabbing, exploitation, and disease. However, in the northern hills, some *resguardos* (communal landholdings from the colonial period) still remained along the northwestern border with Antioquia, around Riosucio. "Whites" and "mestizos" considered the Cauca's Indians very Hispanicized (many had lost their indigenous language and spoke only Spanish), as opposed to the so-called "savage" Indians of the Amazon jungle or the Darién region along the border with Panama.[27]

Along the Pacific Coast lived mostly Afro-Colombians, their ancestors brought to the region as slaves in the colonial period to work the gold mines. Some Indians also resided there, along with whites and mestizos, who were more likely to be found in the towns.[28] The Cauca and Patía Valleys were the other central areas of Afro-Colombians' residence and slavery; there they worked in the mines in the surrounding hills and on the valleys' haciendas.[29] Slavery was in decline as an institution, owing to many slaves' winning their freedom in the Wars of Independence, the general economic stagnation, a prohibition on the slave trade, and the 1821 law of free birth.[30] In 1843, the Cauca counted 15,212 slaves. By 1850–51, there were 10,621 slaves and over 7,614 children of slaves, who, while nominally free, had to live and serve their parents' masters until the age of eighteen (and then had to work for low pay until age twenty-five).[31] While in decline, slavery was still very important to the region's hacendados and mineowners. The Cauca, where a majority of the nation's enslaved toiled, remained the center of slavery in Colombia.[32] However, most Afro-Colombians were not slaves. Indeed, if we accept Mosquera's dubious figures (see table 1 above), people of some African descent made up well over half of all Caucanos.

In the early 1850s, migrants from Antioquia began to move south both onto the forested slopes of the Quindío region, north of Cartago, and into the northwestern Cauca around Riosucio. The northern Quindío was largely a wilderness, the Indian population having disappeared before the settlers' arrival. While the temperate slopes of the Quindío were extremely rugged, they were also incredibly fertile, and settlers flocked there in search of land. The situation around Riosucio was different, as Indians and other Caucanos were already living there. Competition for land in both areas would become ferocious and violent. The migration started in the early 1850s and accelerated over time. Between 1860 and 1877, an estimated twenty-seven thousand Antioqueños settled in the state, most to the north of Cartago in the Quindío region.[33] While probably classified as whites or mestizos, the Antioqueños actually considered themselves a different race—la raza antioqueña—superior to Caucanos, especially blacks, mulattoes, and Indians.[34]

Indians, Afro-Colobians, and Antioqueños did not constitute the entire population of the Cauca. There were, of course, Caucano mestizos and whites, who lived throughout the state, but especially in the towns, the large central valley, and other smaller valleys throughout the southern highlands.[35]

In spite of the important local differences in economic structures, a similar class system permeated everyday life in the Cauca. A small, inbred elite class—composed of hacendados, planters, large merchants, and the upper levels of the bureaucracy and the clergy—dominated society. A very small middling class consisted of more prosperous artisans, professionals (lawyers, doctors, professors), tinterillos (untrained country lawyers), overseers, shopkeepers, more prosperous small ranchers and farmers, and lesser bureaucrats and priests. This was hardly a middle class, certainly not a bourgeoisie, and it was not really much larger in size than (just not as well off as) the elite, but these middling actors often served as interlocutors (social, economic, and political) between rich and poor. Finally, the vast majority of Caucanos were poor, although the nature and extremity of their poverty differed greatly, from mendicants, apprentices, and servants in the cities, to landless day laborers, tenants, sharecroppers, slaves, miners, and peasant farmers in the countryside.[36] In Cali—an urban center where a middle class was more likely to reside than elsewhere—for purposes of a tax on personal service, adult men were divided into three categories determined by wealth: only 55 (4 percent) made the first class, 98 (7 percent) the second, and 1,197 (89 percent) the third.[37] Caucano society was extremely hierarchical but, nonetheless, fairly spatially intimate, with little physical separation between rich and poor.

Within the mass of the lower class, however, the conditions of life could vary widely from one area (or family) to another, largely determined by access to land. In the southern highlands around Pasto, haciendas sat alongside a large smallholding class, including numerous Indian resguardos.[38] Around Popayán, all the valley land was in private hands, and, in the densely populated lower slopes of the Cordillera Central, only very small and isolated areas high in the mountains were still baldíos (unclaimed public lands).[39] Northeast of Popayán, important mines and haciendas dominated the districts of Silvia, Santander, and Caloto, interspersed at higher elevations with Indians' resguardos.

In the valley proper, from the south of Cali north to Cartago, there were no unclaimed public lands. The only lands not privately owned were the cities' ejidos, or commons, and land high in the neighboring mountains.[40] Large haciendas dominated most of the valley and even laid claim to the mountains beyond their immediate borders, leaving little for those seeking their own soil.[41] Small farmers and ranchers worked the land on the margins—the only property not owned by the great estates. Farther north in the valley, haciendas became less prevalent and middling farms and ranches somewhat more numerous.[42]

However, to the north of Cartago, in the densely forested hills of the Quindío region, much good, arable land remained unclaimed and unsettled. Further north and west, around the town of Riosucio, there were also some baldíos in the hills, but much less than directly north of Cartago.[43] Unlike the Quindío hills, this area had long been settled, and Indians still maintained their resguardos, although struggles would erupt between them and immigrants over access to land. Along the coast, almost all the land in the tropical rain forests, except for widely scattered gold mines, remained unclaimed and with a very low population density.[44]

Most Indian communities owned some land in the form of resguardos, even if greatly reduced over the years, and many had substantial holdings.[45] They mostly farmed potatoes, wheat, corn, ocas, and barley. Indian communities were somewhat insular and enjoyed partial independence from outsiders and their own governing structures. Parcialidades were divisions, more or less villages, within a resguardo, although some resguardos had only one parcialidad. Each parcialidad had a cabildo pequeño (also referred to as a cabildo de indígenas), a council chosen or elected by the male Indians of a parcialidad to govern its affairs. Finally, an Indian governor led the cabildo and usually conducted the resguardo's business with outsiders.

Most Indian communities existed in uneasy relation with large haciendas nearby, which tended to control the lower, more productive valleys.[46] Indians would often work on the haciendas as day laborers to earn some specie. However, disputes between the communalists, large hacendados, and other whites or mestizos were continuous. Sometimes, smallholder whites—often sandwiched between large haciendas and the resguardos and not daring to confront the hacendados—described the resguardos as unproductive and entered into long-running disputes with Indians over land. At other times, Indians would rent parts of their resguardos to farmers who lacked their own land.[47]

Afro-Colombians' situations varied greatly depending on whether they were slave or free and whether they lived on the coast or in the central valley. In the valley, most worked on haciendas, as day laborers, tenants, or slaves, or worked in the mines. There were also numerous maroon communities along the coast and in the interior, especially in the Palo River region around Santander. After the Wars of Independence, maroon communities expanded, further weakening the slave system.[48]

After abolition in 1852, Afro-Colombians tried to break ties with their former masters whenever they could. In the tropical forests of the coast they succeeded, largely abandoning the mines to work their own plots of land along the hundreds of rivers running to the sea. However, the Afro-Colombian population in the Cauca River Valley had no such options, as almost all arable land was held by hacendados and small farmers or ranchers. Unable to own their own farms, most either found work in cities as best they could, particularly in Cali, or remained on the haciendas as day laborers and tenants, growing corn, rice, plantains, yuca, and beans, with a little cacao, tobacco, and sugarcane for their own use and to sell in local markets.[49]

Life was somewhat easier along the coast. Given the low population density there, families could exploit the rain forest's abundance, much to the chagrin of potential capitalists who hoped to exploit workers' labor. The coast's inhabitants had little need for wages. Land was abundant, plantains proliferated, corn grew rapidly in small clearings, and hunting and fishing freely supplemented the diet. One observer thought that only harsh police laws and the immigration of Antioqueños would induce people to labor in the mines.[50] The geographer Felipe Pérez had a more ecologically based plan: he urged the clear-cutting of all the jungle's trees, thus creating open farmland, ending the miasmal heat and humidity, and forcing inhabitants deprived of nature's bounty to work.[51]

In the Quindío hills, land was available if one had the resources to clear and settle it. The Antioqueño migrants quickly established homesteads, although they faced continual land disputes with speculators. Corn and beans were the major crops grown by the settlers, supplemented with wheat, potatoes, vegetables, and sugarcane. Some experimentation with the coffee bush would begin, although not in earnest until the 1880s. The settlers also had considerable livestock, especially swine.[52]

While not producing exports, subalterns did engage in a continual petty commerce, selling their few crops and buying with wages from day labor or other work.[53] Before 1848, much activity was clandestine, as the unlicensed selling of tobacco and *aguardiente* (cane liquor) was forbidden or heavily taxed. In the valley, women dominated the important activity of small-scale distilling and vending of aguardiente. A black market existed for many items, and haciendas were on constant guard lest their bamboo (used by the poor for construction), wood, cacao, cane, or even livestock turn up in Cali for sale.[54]

The artisan class was large if one considers all the weaving and other handicrafts done by women on their farms—but very small if one considers only urban craftspeople engaged full-time in such work. In the south, much housework was done in weaving, and the local industry was relatively famous, although poor roads prevented much growth.[55] Popayán boasted an established artisan class, which existed to serve the regional capital's aspirations, but, elsewhere, such a class was not very significant.[56] The Cauca imported most of its manufactured goods, much clothing, and some foodstuffs.[57]

In spite of the great diversity in their lives, most plebeians lived in the shadow of economic domination by the wealthy and powerful.[58] In the colonial period, the Cauca had been one of the wealthiest regions of Colombia, with an economy fueled by gold mines and haciendas, both worked by slaves.[59] The church, especially powerful in the region, owned a good deal of land, both rural and urban, including property set aside by rich and poor alike (especially, it seems, Indians) to support religious obligations.[60] By the nineteenth century, haciendas controlled almost all the region's most productive agricultural land. In spite of their vast estates, elites had yet to discover an export crop for the Cauca that would make their fortunes. The only truly successful plantations— around Palmira and in the northern valley—farmed tobacco and cacao, the former exported abroad, the latter mainly consumed in Colombia, especially in Antioquia.[61] However, while Caucano tobacco was considered good quality, planters produced little compared to eastern Colombia, the center of the tobacco boom until the mid-1870s. Before 1850, tobacco was a government monopoly for which a growing permit was needed. Some peasants planted the crop clandestinely; the maroon communities of escaped slaves around Santander, against

A Social History of Politics   15

which the government occasionally sent punitive expeditions, especially favored it. Unlike in Cuba, in Colombia almost all tobacco exported came from large plantations rather than smaller farms.[62]

The central activity of most haciendas was ranching, especially of cattle, but also of goats, pigs, horses, and mules.[63] Usually, the value of livestock far surpassed that of agricultural production in the valley and around Popayán.[64] Haciendas made money from livestock, rents from tenants, food crops, the distillation of aguardiente, and, sometimes, cacao, tobacco, coffee, and cinchona bark (the source of quinine). In general, however, livestock and land rents produced most income. Haciendas leased plots to the landless, not just for the rents, but also to obtain a captive labor force. Some, especially in the central valley around Cali, relied mainly on day laborers (many of them Afro-Colombian).[65] Others had slaves, who also worked their own plots of land (often selling food at local markets) and would hotly contest the ownership of those parcels after abolition.[66] Labor, at least at the pittances that hacendados wanted to pay, was a constant problem; therefore, most activities, especially ranching, were land extensive rather than labor intensive.[67]

Except for the cacao and tobacco plantations, most haciendas were fairly unenterprising. The central valley was prime land for growing sugarcane, the stalks maturing in only ten months' time, but lack of a submissive labor force, capital, and transportation links with the Pacific limited production to regional needs.[68] Farmers began experimenting with coffee only in the 1860s, with cultivation enjoying some small expansion in the 1870s; as with tobacco production, the center of coffee production (before the 1890s) was further east. The coffee boom in Antioquia and the Cauca took place in the late 1880s and 1890s.[69]

Most other exports from the Cauca were not farmed but extracted from natural resources. Mining, once the region's economic engine, had sunk into a state of long collapse—as had, arguably, the Cauca's economy in general. The Wars of Independence had devastated mines along the coast and in the mountains bordering the central valley.[70] After abolition, especially along the Pacific littoral, workers abandoned mines in droves for the freedom of the rain forests, where land was plentiful and independence guaranteed by the vastness of the jungle.[71] Rubber and other resins, especially from the tagua palm, formed another fairly important commodity along the coast. Merchants were usually content to buy the resins from poor gatherers, although, at times, speculators tried to control the forests in order to monopolize production completely.[72] The other mini–economic boom—in, again, a gathered rather than farmed product—came in the 1850s (continuing until the late 1870s, when prices collapsed) as a market for cinchona bark beckoned.[73] Any capitalist development that did prosper was almost certainly in Colombian hands given that there was relatively little foreign investment in the region.[74]

In 1857, despite mining's precipitous decline, gold still dominated the region's exports, followed by tobacco; other exports (although in limited values compared to gold and tobacco) included livestock, hides, cacao, quina (cinchona bark), resins, and rubber.[75] By 1874–75, official gold production had further stagnated, and tobacco and quina dominated exports, along with hides, resins, and a little coffee. Total exports from the Cauca's ports of Buenaventura and Tumaco in 1875–76 were only 8.6 percent of the national total, while the Cauca counted 16 percent of the national population in 1870—a testament to decades of failed schemes to enter the Atlantic economy.[76]

At first glance, the Cauca would appear an isolated, undeveloped region, or what some would call a backwater; however, Colombia's political culture did not differ so much from that of other republican societies in the Atlantic World. While Caucanos largely failed to enter the Atlantic economy (and this failure would have dire political consequences), they dramatically succeeded in creating a political culture in the Atlantic revolutionary tradition. Many Colombians saw their own battles, such as that of Los Chancos (described above), as no different than those of Gettysburg or Puebla City. They viewed their elections as no less legitimate than those occurring in Europe or the United States. Certainly, the Cauca's elites saw themselves in the current of modernity, if not at its vanguard. Indeed, Colombia's political culture, whether measured by suffrage rights, popular participation, or republican discourse, was as innovative and democratic as any in the Atlantic World. In the nineteenth century, the vast majority of the world's republics were in Latin America, yet the region's history is usually ignored in favor of developments in the North Atlantic. Latin American republicanism and nineteenth-century democracy are often dismissed as hollow facades masking corrupt oligarchies that ruled omnipotently. Yet Colombia's subalterns continuously fought to make their societies more democratic, and they won much, practicing a republican politics quite similar to that of their more studied counterparts elsewhere in the Atlantic World. If we are to understand the history of the Atlantic World, must we not explore the words and deeds of those millions in Latin America who claimed republicanism and democracy as their own?

2 "We the Undersigned, Citizens of the State": Three Forms of Popular Republicanism

> Liberty, equality and fraternity may not be precise slogans, but poor and modest people confronted with rich and powerful ones know what they mean.
> —ERIC HOBSBAWM, *The Age of Capital*

By the mid-nineteenth century, almost everyone in Colombia was a republican.[1] No one championed monarchy as a viable political option, and even the most reactionary of the newly emerging Conservative Party proclaimed themselves proud republicans. However, republicanism was not monolithic. Elite Liberals and Conservatives differed in their views of what a republican society entailed, as did their lower-class allies and retainers. In civil wars, elections, and daily life, the Cauca's subalterns actively participated in politics alongside the region's ruling class. What was the political thought of these plebeians? I will argue that subalterns were neither simply coerced pawns nor blind, enthusiastic followers of the region's notables. Instead, the Cauca's subalterns reframed elite republicanism to suit their own needs.

After first briefly reviewing the Cauca's experience with independence and the introduction of republicanism to Colombia, I will explore three different forms of popular republicanism in the Cauca region during the second half of the nineteenth century. Plebeians were not a homogeneous mass, and their understandings of politics varied greatly. Hobsbawm is wonderfully evocative when he writes of poor and modest people's comprehension of the famous slogan "liberty, equality, fraternity," but the poor and modest were not one people, and these words meant very different things to different groups of the Cauca's lower classes. Three distinct forms of popular republicanism developed in the region: popular liberalism; popular smallholder republicanism; and popular indigenous conservatism. These three variants of popular republicanism emerged out of the identities and historical experiences of the Cauca's different social groups (introduced in the last chapter)—Afro-Colombians, Antioqueño migrants, and Indians—and these groups' encounter with a multifaceted and heterogeneous discourse of republicanism that had spread across the Atlantic World beginning in the eighteenth century, entering into the consciousness of Colombians, to arise with force in the Wars of Independence.

A New Republic

The Cauca, along with the rest of Colombia, secured independence from Spain in 1821, after years of grueling fighting.[2] During the war, many of the most powerful families in the region had supported the patriots, although others were royalists. While, in the valley, the patriots enjoyed some popular support, many Indians and slaves sided with Spain. Given that their masters and landlords were patriots and that the crown and the church had provided some little protection against the local elites' use and abuse of power, these allegiances were not so surprising.[3]

The state that emerged from the Wars of Independence was decidedly weak and physically nonexistent throughout most of the country. It had little direct reach into the countryside and very little revenue. In 1869, the national government owned only seven buildings in the whole of the Cauca, one in a state of ruin and three others rented out.[4] Similarly, local and regional governments in the Cauca commanded very little revenue, even when compared to other parts of Colombia.[5] The taxes that were levied fell heavily on the poor, although, as state officials continually lamented, the total amount collected was pitifully small. The most common taxes were consumption or sales taxes, tolls, and—the tax that the poor hated most—the personal service tax, which required labor on state roads or other projects (unless one could pay to get out of it).

The new state's tranquility was soon shattered by the War of the Supremes (1839–42). The conflict started in the southwest, ostensibly as a protest against the closure of some convents (upsetting to many, especially Indians). Under the leadership of José María Obando, the war became an outlet for popular discontent, with many Indians and Afro-Colombians joining Obando's forces. Obando, who had been a royalist for much of the Wars of Independence, offered slaves their freedom if they joined him.[6] Although crushed, the movement was an important precursor of events that would later transform the Cauca, as elites made more open appeals to those below for political support.

The two political parties that would dominate Colombia's future slowly emerged over the first half of the nineteenth century out of groups vying to control the weak state. Given that the Liberal and Conservative Parties were only loosely organized and not monolithic entities, we should exercise care in generalizing about their makeup and programs; nevertheless, by the late 1840s, when politicians and their adherents began to call themselves Liberals and Conservatives, distinct differences existed between the two parties in the southwest.[7] Large landholders, who would become members of the Conservative Party, dominated the Cauca. This powerful aristocratic class also recruited middling allies through patronage and control of the conservative Universidad del Cauca.[8] Unlike in other parts of Colombia, where regional concerns, family connections, and social status—but not economic interests—tended to determine political affiliation, in the Cauca most (but not all) of the powerful land- and slaveholding class of the region affiliated themselves with the Conservative Party. Elements opposed to the powerful clans—who eventually denominated themselves Liberals—were mainly from the middle class, those with education and prospects but not much property.[9] Independent and republican Cauca was still a center of tradition, slavery, and church power.

By 1848, Conservatives—although the party under that name was just emerging—were comfortably ensconced in the Cauca. One of their own, the Caucano Tomás Cipriano de Mosquera (one of the region's largest land- and slaveowners), held the national presidency. Despite the region's economic stagnation, the elite class had apparently weathered the transition from monarchy to republic with its local power intact. Conservatives and many Liberals envisioned an elite-oriented republicanism, with modest and carefully managed participation from those below. The 1843 constitution limited citizenship to those male Colombians over twenty-one years of age with either property worth 300 pesos or an annual income of 150 pesos. Literacy was another requirement, although this only took effect in 1850.[10] Indeed, plebeians were considered too ignorant to practice politics, and they were largely excluded. For the ruling class, republicanism signified representative government for a propertied and restricted citizen class, personal freedom from tyranny, and legal equality—except for those not educated or "civilized" enough to appreciate it.[11] Elite republicanism legally, institutionally, and discursively excluded the poor in general, but especially slaves and Indians.

Afro-Colombians had tried again and again since the struggles for national independence to break open the segregated colonial society and find a sustained political voice. They had fought for both royalists and patriots during the wars, hoping that their service would hasten their freedom, and had used the chaos of war to abandon the haciendas and mines.[12] Slaves revolted in the region in 1813 and 1843.[13] Afro-Colombians fought in the first major civil war, the War of the Supremes. However, the unity of an elite class determined to continue slavery and control access to citizenship and formal politics limited the effectiveness of Afro-Colombians' struggles.[14] Their brave resistance and their hopes for political and social inclusion awaited some broader opening in Caucano politics that they could exploit.

Commentators often compared the Cauca in the first decades of independence to a feudal realm, in spite of the republican facade.[15] "A beautiful hell" was how one observer expressed his inability to separate the pleasing vistas of the Cauca's natural beauty from the brutality that the rich and powerful exercised against slaves and the poor before 1848.[16] Some Caucanos would look back on the time prior to the Liberals' ascendance in 1849 and the tumultuous events that followed as one of peace and tranquility, when subalterns knew their place and elites' prerogatives were not so easily questioned. While this memory was, of course, largely a fantasy, it did contain some truth, as the lower classes had very few options for challenging the status quo after the Wars of Independence (the War of the Supremes being the notable exception). However, this order was paid for with the poor's sweat and blood, and one Liberal reminded his fellows that the tranquility of the past was "the peace of slavery, . . . the menacing silence of misery."[17]

This silence would soon end. New ideas and political possibilities had emerged in the Cauca since Independence. While isolated economically, the region still had frequent contacts with the outside world. Between 1869 and 1874, for instance, Buenaventura hosted 378 arrivals of merchant ships.[18] There was much communication with, shared business with, and travel to the international hub in Panama, including the practice of sending plebeian prisoners there for periods of forced labor.[19] People moved around more than one might think, especially slaves; in 1851, slaves now in the Cauca had spent part of their lives on the Caribbean Coast and in Bogotá, Panama, Ecuador, and Peru.[20] International events did not pass unnoticed, filtered by local concerns; for example, Afro-Colombians interpreted the Haitian Revolution as, not just a slave revolt, but a republican revolution.[21] The extended Wars of Independence had forced elites to turn to the poor for their armies and even make concessions to them. The War of the Supremes continued this process, as rebel leaders bargained with subalterns for their support. Republicanism's language, as elitist as it was, permeated the air, evident in local government, elections, and the explosion of newspapers.[22] Plebeians appropriated much of this language from their elite allies and neighbors, but they also learned from other subalterns—slaves, sailors, soldiers, and muleteers, to name a few—who carried ideas with them in the course of their travels.

Despite the wishes of hacendado, merchant, bishop, and planter, plebeians were not quiescent. Subalterns were acutely aware of the political situation and the new opportunities that republicanism had engendered. Elites had created the political system for their own purposes, but plebeians were learning to exploit it, use it, appropriate it to their own ends, often guided by political attitudes from the colonial period.[23] Subalterns would take elite republicanism and make it their own, reframing it to suit their needs and social visions.

Exploring Popular Republicanisms

Three subaltern groups—Afro-Colombians, Antioqueño migrants, and Indians —developed their own particular forms of republican discourse that I have labeled *popular liberalism, popular smallholder republicanism,* and *popular indigenous conservatism.* Needless to say, these three groups did not make up the entire population of the Cauca. There were, of course, Caucano mestizos and whites, who lived throughout the state, yet their distinct discourses do not emerge in the historical record. Unlike Afro-Colombians, Antioqueño migrants, and Indians, the mestizo and white populations employed a variety of republican discourses, both liberal and conservative, although most mestizos leaned toward a popular conservatism of some kind, similar in many ways to popular smallholder republicanism. Poor and middling mestizos and whites' republican discourse was never as coherent or as organized as that of the more defined social groups, possibly because they were never as united politically.

Popular republican discourses were not historically immutable, although, for the time period of this study, 1848–86, they remained largely stable. The one exception is popular indigenous conservatism, which experienced major changes in the 1870s. Fortuitously, the generally static nature of the discourses over this time period makes their study more feasible since the difficulty of recovering plebeian discourse from the historical record requires pulling information from various places and time periods to create a coherent explication.

A lasting record of plebeians' discourse is found in the petitions that they sent to local, regional, and national authorities. While petitions are certainly multivocal, in that they reflect both the writer and the people the writer is representing, plebeian intentions emerge strongly in many of the texts.

First, there did not exist a generic petition template that everyone used and into which writers simply inserted subalterns' individual concerns. Some petitions were very straightforward, although these were rare in the Cauca. Most contained strategies and styles particular to each group and its preoccupations. Second, three distinct discourses emerge from the petitions; there was not one language that the writers forced onto their plebeian clients. To assign the entire content to the scribes' consciousness would be to make them omnipotent, possessing conspiratorial plans to design a specific discourse that they would impose on the various social groups. Third, we cannot assume that writers were members of the elite or had no inkling of popular concerns. Typically, middling types—poor country lawyers or local priests—penned the documents. The writers' varied backgrounds and the span of this discourse across at least two generations make it unlikely that only the literate decided the language of petitions.[24] Most important, many petitions seem to have been written by local intellectuals who were members of the communities that they represented, such as Indian governors or the leaders of migrants' village councils. Literacy was more widespread in the Cauca than might be expected.[25] Fourth, while this chapter deals with language, plebeian actions also reveal their political thoughts and motivations. The bulk of this book concerns those actions, and the discourses presented in this chapter will, I hope, resonate throughout the rest of the work.

I should note that these three variants of popular republicanism were the political discourse that plebeians employed when they entered the public sphere. The three discourses were not necessarily the mirrored reflections of plebeians' consciousness, which may be unrecoverable. Whether plebeians truly believed these discourses or merely used them is open to debate. But use them they did and to great effect, both as a form of discourse and as a form of political action (although many, especially women, had fewer options). I do not want to overly privilege public discourse over private, but this public discourse, not the private, was how plebeians engaged in politics in the Cauca. Subalterns did speak. Perhaps not in their "authentic" voice, but in a public discourse that they developed that sometimes strengthened, but more often challenged, elite republicanism.[26]

Popular Smallholder Republicanism

When Antioqueño migrants began to move south and west from their homeland into the wilderness of the north Cauca frontier during the 1850s, they brought with them a distinct form of popular republicanism that I call *popular smallholder republicanism*. As this variant more closely resembled elite republicanism than did popular liberalism or popular indigenous conservatism, I will treat it first. A laundry list of the important ideas, or tropes, of the migrants' discourse would include labor, community, equality, family, authority, and religion. However, the central tenet of smallholder republican discourse was liberty or, stated differently, independence. Liberty defined male migrants' identity as free citizens who ruled over their own families and plots of land.

For male Antioqueño settlers, independence and liberty meant land. They migrated in search of land, and they understood landholding to mean possessing individual parcels of ground that the owner could exploit more or less any way he saw fit. Land of one's own allowed independence from the landlord's authority and rule. It offered the settler a chance to prosper with the surplus that he produced by the sweat of his brow and also the opportunity to protect and control his family. Like other aspects of popular republicanism, much of this ideology emerged out of the colonial era, now cannibalized into a republican discourse. Finally, landholding established a migrant's political self as an independent citizen, free to decide his own fate and participate in the governance of his village, state, and nation.

Land was available in the forested mountains in the frontier area between the Cauca Valley and Antioquia, and migrants often succeeded in obtaining it.[27] The situation in central Antioquia, from whence they came, was quite different. There, large landholders, allied with a powerful merchant class in Medellín, dominated much of the countryside, both economically and politically. Also, Antioquia was experiencing strong, sustained population growth, which put even more pressure on independent smallholders. Migrants complained bitterly about the dismal economic and social situation that reigned in their beloved homeland. As migrants in Riosucio noted in a petition for land: "A large part of those who signed [this petition] are sons of the state of Antioquia, from where, blocked and impeded from being able to procure from the land bread for our children, . . . we have had to come to this very extensive and powerful state to solicit that element of life [land] so inexhaustible in this state, but so limited and scarce in that one."[28]

They were fleeing not just economic tenancy but social subordination as well. Settlers asking for land in what would become the village of San Francisco explained: "We are Antioqueños who have emigrated from that state in order to find in this one the liberty that there they so unjustly deny the poor worker."[29] Tenancy implied social deference; a family was beholden to the landlord for its survival and depended on his good graces. It also meant political subordination. A dependent tenant hardly fit the description of the free republican citizen. Until 1853, Colombian constitutions recognized this as well.[30]

Independence from authority and personal liberty, both social and economic, formed the core of smallholder republicanism. Settlers in the village of Salento asserted that they needed more land to attract even more migrants: "They come to us in search of the precious fruits of social liberty and of the means to satisfy their strong and industrious aspirations."[31] It is not that smallholders did not recognize authority or that they abhorred the idea of authority. They wanted to be the authorities, at least as far as their personal lives and their village governance were concerned. They recognized hierarchy to some extent; that is, they were willing to acknowledge claims from above that they saw as legitimate as long as their rights and claims were, in turn, acknowledged.

Liberty, obtained through landholding, formed one aspect of smallholder republicanism. Land was crucial to other aspects of smallholder republicanism as well, especially the ideas of fraternity and equality. Migrants imagined land to be held individually, but their idea of property did not mirror the atomistic liberal vision of Colombia's elites, in which landholding was unrelated to the larger community. For the settlers, while each family would possess its own parcel, migration and settlement were a fraternal affair. While many settlers emigrated individually, that is, accompanied only by their families, many also traveled in groups, especially when founding a new settlement. Settlement thus was a communal enterprise, as were some aspects of landholding. Each migrant received his or her plot of land as private property, but a village held much of its land in common or in reserve. Migrants exploited this land to gather firewood, hunt game, and obtain sundry other items; they also used it as forage for their pigs and cows. Perhaps more important, the commons served as a reserve both for the children of current villagers and for the newly arriving emigrants, who would expand the size and importance of the settlement.

Land was not, as in the liberal conception, a product to be disposed of, to be freely traded—like, say, a sack of potatoes. Migrant communities established their own rules and accepted government regulations defining their rights to land, regulations often suggested by the settlers themselves. For example, in the new town of Pereira, the state proposed that each "head of a family" receive thirty-two hectares provided that the family stayed resident in the village. They could neither mortgage the land nor sell any unless they had already built a house and cultivated four hectares, and even then they could not sell land to anyone in the community who already owned thirty-two hectares.[32] In another migrant village, Chinchiná, the state established similar rules, some proposed in a petition from the migrants themselves. Settlers could receive only thirty-seven hectares, all of which had to be cleared in eight years, except for a reserve for timber. The village could not sell the commons, only give parts of it to new arrivals. Finally, the villagers needed to set aside land for a church, a plaza, a town hall, a jail, schools for boys and girls, and a poorhouse.[33]

Migrants had a moral economy of landholding. Hardworking men and their families should own land and expand their holdings as necessary. Land should not, however, be dominated by a few, especially those who did not work it. The ordinances cited above expressed a disposition toward equality within the villages by establishing a limit to the amount of land that any one family could own. Migrants were wary that a handful of large landowners would come to dominate villages, as in Antioquia. Discussing a land conflict around Salento, one settler argued that migrants "flock here to convert themselves from slavish renters into propertyholders and men independent in their dealings." The writer further pointed out that concentrated landholding "does not satisfy the needs of farmers, nor of society in general, because those lands divided into huge lots paralyze industry and hold back the wealth that soon thousands of working arms would develop."[34] Throughout the nineteenth and twentieth centuries, settlers on Colombia's internal frontiers fought continuously to retain their land in the face of claims by land speculators.[35] In the Cauca, *especulador* (speculator) became a dirty word to the migrants.[36] Settlers vociferously denounced wealthy speculators who had unfair access to legal power through the state and recourse to extralegal violence. Ideally, migrants obtained a reasonable amount of land legally by title and morally through their labor.

Labor was another critical aspect of liberty. References to the settlers' struggles, their hard work, and their industriousness crop up almost without fail in the petitions that they wrote to the state and national governments, demanding recognition of their land claims. Work was central to their discourse for two reasons, one legal, the other sociopolitical.

First, the state recognized claims to public lands primarily two ways: through purchase (often by swapping government bonds for land) or by effective settlement (e.g., establishing a homestead). Poor migrants obviously opted for the latter. Although national law changed frequently, most of the time settlers could claim the land that they had under cultivation and a little extra.[37] Laws granting lands to specific communities restated these conditions. The migrants had a legal and economic incentive to portray themselves as hard workers. Time and again, when asking for land, they described themselves as "a population of hardworking men," or as "animated by the spirit of laboring," or simply as "poor and hardworking farmers."[38]

Again, the migrants contrasted themselves with the speculators and land barons who had also moved into the Cauca/Antioquia frontier. In a land dispute around Pereira, settlers protested a speculator's legal maneuvering to seize their property: "Because individual vecinos [residents] today freely possess and cultivate those lands from which comes their families' subsistence and have settled their possessions there, those poor people cannot be evicted who have worked and have tamed those sterile and desolate fields."[39] Migrants worked the land and, therefore, deserved it; speculators had no right to it, not having sweated for it, no matter the technicalities of the law. Labor moralized and legitimated landholding.

Yet migrants had another motive for emphasizing their work ethic beyond land acquisition: proving themselves good citizens. Migrants saw themselves as different from the poor of the Cauca, both racially and culturally. They were industrious, in comparison to the mulattoes, blacks, Indians, and Caucano mestizos who became the Other against whom the settlers defined themselves. Most of the migrants thought of themselves as part of la raza antioqueña, an identity that largely disavowed the Indians and Afro-Colombians who also lived in Antioquia.[40] When residents from the Aldea de María petitioned for their own judicial circuit, separate from that of Cartago, which counted a large Afro-Colombian population, they noted: "Heterogeneous races of distinct disposition demand special procedures for their ways of life." Having their own independent court circuit would encourage the further immigration of "hardworking" families from Antioquia and would fill the land with "robust generations of their prolific and vigorous race."[41] In Riosucio, townspeople, some migrants and others native Caucanos, lauded the Antioqueños as "hardworking by nature, vigorous and active, oppressed in their country by the growth of population and the little free land," while they derided the nearby Indians as having an "aversion to work."[42]

The migrants felt that they deserved land and attention from the state, not only because it was their right as citizens or residents of the country, but also because they had earned such favors through their own sweat and blood. Their labor made them good citizens. The others deserved nothing; they had not worked for it. Migrants brandished their work ethic before them like a talisman against their descent into the dark masses of Indians and Afro-Colombians whose land they had invaded. Therefore, settlers' strong support of equality was circumscribed. Equality was not a given. Migrants earned their right to equality through their labor and perceived cultural superiority.

Finally, labor was closely tied to the migrants' attitude toward progress and development, which forms another facet of smallholder republicanism. Migrants had a moral economy of landholding and economics, but they did not celebrate stasis. They believed in progress. Settlers wanted their villages to grow in size and prosper. They conflated their own desire for progress with the nation's economic well-being, thereby gaining the attention of liberal-minded elites and claiming a place for themselves in the nation at the same time. Smallholders in Cerillos claimed that with their "noble and constant exertions" they could fulfill "the duty that every citizen has to promote, by whatever means possible, the moral and material progress of the nation."[43] In yet another petition, the Maríans echoed such feelings, asserting that their settlement would "augment public wealth, converting the wilderness into a countryside that feels the welcome adoption of industry, civilization, and commerce."[44] The settlers did not behave like "typical" peasants, if such people exist, and did not seem to fear destructive progress, perhaps because the vast tracts of land in the Quindío region appeared to promise enough land for all smallholders' prosperity. Migrants asked for roads to be built, connecting them to other regions and to markets.[45] While most migrants focused their agricultural efforts on subsistence crops and some livestock, they also began to experiment with other crops, which would one day lead them to their aromatic gold, coffee. The migrants wanted, and expected, to prosper.

The settlers were proud of their achievements. They created productive farms and brought social life to the wilderness, "fighting the elements with Christian abnegation and bringing to these ancient forests comforts and civilization."[46] Progress was not just material but also cultural. They brought their "healthy" families and culture of work to the wilderness, civilizing both the landscape and the "barbarians" found therein. When settlers of the new town of Finlandia asked for land, they not only promised to help maintain the road and protect travelers but also asserted that their village would lead to "moral and material progress," echoing a petition made by Cerillos's settlers over thirty years earlier.[47] The socioeconomic situation that the migrants had left in Antioquia still influenced their discourse. Settlers challenged their subordination by emigrating to obtain land, but landholding remained a marker of social and political status. So, while migrants harbored suspicions about the wealth and greed of large landholders, they had their own idea of progress and development, an idea based on their family farms and homogeneous villages. Although certainly not synonymous with the liberal dream of development, the migrants' economic thinking did cherish a notion of progress and material gain, but one imagined on the relatively small scale of their thirty-two-hectare farms.

As the complexities of these attitudes suggest, land was not simply an economic resource but a social and political resource as well. Land ownership formed one base of the male republican citizen by providing the economic means to make him independent. On that land, the migrants imagined, they would nurture the other element of smallholder republicanism's foundation: the family.

Land allowed one to form a family, but the family was also the basis of landholding. Many of the laws regulating the distribution of land in new settlements assigned the property to the "padres de familia."[48] While communities gave women land if they were single parents (usually the law assumed that they would be widows), the ideal recipient was the husband and father. Single men got land, with the expectation that they would form families, but, often, they received a smaller allotment than their married comrades, who, if they had children, sometimes got even more acreage.[49]

More important, the status of *padre de familia* cemented a settler's place in the political life of the community. If being a landholder was the economic base of citizenship, being a padre de familia was the social base. The ideal citizen was a propertied man with a family. National and local constitutions recognized this in a small way, often eliminating the minimum age for citizenship for married men.[50] While the state would recognize much more democratic requirements for citizenship after 1853, it seems that the migrants held a more restricted view, emphasizing property and family. The association of all the padres de familia was the governing body of a settlement until more formal institutions took its place. The padres de familia assumed many roles in the village, from direct governance, to educational decisions, to the all-important question of land distribution.[51]

The importance of the family was intimately connected with religion. Migrants, and Antioqueños in general, were dedicated to the Catholic Church. The support of the faith against perceived Liberal attacks defined many migrant communities' politics. Settlers often boasted of having marshaled their scarce resources to build a church in their newly founded village and as often pleaded with the government to intercede on their behalf with ecclesiastical authorities to have a priest sent.[52] Religion was both a bulwark against the degeneracy of the feared Other, *negros* and *indígenas*, and, through the rite of marriage, the basis of the family. But priests were hard to come by, regardless of settlers' devotion and best efforts, and migrants lamented the lack. The residents of Boquía found themselves to be "70 padres de familia that do not have anyone to baptize our children, nor to conduct a marriage, absolve the dying or bless our cemetery. All of us residents are proletarians, but, in spite of our poverty, we have united to raise a chapel."[53] The family supported the dual identity of the proud male settler: padre de familia and landowner.

Padre de familia, with its emphasis on the local preoccupations of work and family, was often the identity that migrants assumed as public political actors. This is not to say, however, that their concerns were purely local or that they were not interested in regional or national political life. On the contrary, migrants evinced great confidence—much more so than did Afro-Colombians and Indians —in their place in the region and nation. Their confidence sprang in part from their strongly felt cultural superiority over the rest of the Caucanos. It also arose from the assumption that they contributed mightily to the improvement and progress of the nation. In petitions, the settlers did not hesitate to assert the usefulness of their villages to the nation. The residents of Santa Rosa, after noting how they and their families had sacrificed to create a village, and had even built a church, out of a "miserable wilderness," wanted the state to recognize their claim to the land over that of a speculator. They noted that before their arrival the land did not give "any benefit to the nation," but they would "give to the nation the benefit of a civilized and religious village." The state agreed and gave them the land.[54]

Migrants turned to the state in order to validate their claims and to obtain recognition for what they had won through their labor and resourcefulness. Settlers in Salento petitioned the national government in 1883, concerned about a group of speculators who had tried to exchange government bonds for large tracts of land around the village. The migrants reminded the government that they had "abandoned our native soil (Antioquia) hoping, as we have said, that we would enjoy the guarantees that the national government promises."[55] They did not always see the state as an intrusive force that must be repelled and kept at bay; at times, they saw it as a source of order and legitimate authority, something that they themselves tried to pull into their lives in order to counter those who abused authority and power. In this way, the migrants participated in "everyday forms of state formation."[56] The state and, of course, the nation were not solely the products of elite machinations and projects but also the result of more modest folks' efforts and imagination.

In their petitions, migrants rarely displayed overt hostility to the state, but they certainly expected the state to act fairly. The indomitable Maríans, in one of their numerous conflicts with speculators, demanded that the state do the right thing: "We cannot, with justice, be deprived of our rights without openly trampling the rights that a government owes to its members." They assumed that legitimate authority would support their reasonable requests, at least beyond the taint of local interest and the corruption of speculators' lucre. Of course—and this aspect of petitioning was common to all three variants of popular republicanism—migrants often subtly threatened dire consequences if a request was denied. Thus, the Marians announced: "We would find ourselves in the difficult situation of resorting to force in order to defend our homes."[57] In the petition from Boquía asking for land cited earlier, the settlers wrote "demanding protection" and "demanding justice." They closed their petition with a reminder that they were in some sense the legislators' equals and with a subtle threat: "Citizen Deputies, perhaps our humble proposition does not have the importance that we suppose. But remember that 350 of your compatriots are claiming protection, justice, and the exact fulfillment of a law. Remember that, if our supplication is denied, we will find ourselves obliged to abandon these fields and Quindío will return to be what it was before: the dread of the traveler."[58] Settlers always lived in fear that the state would betray them to land speculators. Therefore, they sought to remind the state what moral, productive citizens they were. In general, migrants held an ambivalent attitude toward the state. They worried that it would take away what they had worked so hard for, while, at the same time, they displayed a high level of confidence in their place in the nation, both economically and politically, and expected the state to accede to their modest demands.

As an abstract political discourse, and in the Antioqueños' actual political practice, smallholder republicanism appropriated aspects of both liberalism and conservatism. Migrants were above all republicans, calling for a place in the nation independent from the powerful. Their republicanism shared with liberalism a faith in progress and development and an emphasis on liberty and independence. However, conservatism—with its emphasis on family, hierarchy, religion, and order—appealed to the migrants as well. As subsequent chapters will show, the migrants formed alliances with both Liberals and Conservatives, depending on the local political situation and what each party had to offer at any given time. However, individual villages were not completely autarkic; they shared both an imagined community as Antioqueños in a strange land and a recognizable discourse. At times, many of these villages would unite politically to protect their perceived shared interests.

Independence and liberty formed the core of smallholder republicanism, emerging from many of the settlers' experiences in Antioquia. Land and family gave male migrants their economic and social position as both padres de familia and citizens. While the migrants' commitment to equality did not often extend beyond the village and their own position in the village resulted from a firmly patriarchal structure, they strongly challenged elite republican notions of economy and politics. Their hamlets championed a more democratic society that rejected the economic and political dominance of the few, favoring land and liberty for the many. They refused to submit to the role of pliant tenant or dutiful hanger-on at the margins of the great estate. While migrants embraced landed property, most, if lucky, possessed barely enough land to feed their families. They were not a comfortable peasant petite bourgeoisie. Although poor, they nonetheless insisted on their place as citizens in the new construct of the republican nation and demanded that the state recognize and respect their efforts. A petition from the Aldea de Chinchiná reveals both the confidence of the migrants and their determination to take a place at the table of the nation. The settlers of Chinchiná wrote to get their village named head of a district so that voting would be easier, thus assuring "the complete exercise of sovereignty that the constitution delegates to citizens." They closed by reminding the legislators that "liberty and independence are found in the cabin of the peasant too."[59]

Popular Indigenous Conservatism

If the liberty and independence of the migrant's frontier homestead formed the foundation of smallholder republicanism, the fraternity of the Indian village lay at the core of popular indigenous conservatism. More so than that of popular liberalism or popular smallholder republicanism, the discourse of indigenous conservatism focused on one goal: protecting resguardos—Indians' communal landholdings—from being transformed into private property. Indians' best hope to do this seemed to be recognizing local, regional, and national authorities while exhorting those authorities to utilize their power in a just and legal manner. Authority—both the acceptance of it and the demands placed on it—was the central trope of popular indigenous conservatism.

The most striking and constant aspect of Indians' petitions is the humble and self-denigrating language that they employed. The parcialidad of Pitayó declared itself "the most wretched and helpless class of society": "We are the mine that everyone exploits."[60] Villagers of Toribio, San Francisco, and Tacueyó described themselves as "wretched Indians" who "remain in a state of misery."[61] The Túquerres cabildo's officers identified themselves as a "wretched and hapless class."[62] In one petition, several communities in the south noted that "the indigenous class is wretched and has very little sense."[63] Harsher still was the judgment of a similar coalition of southern cabildos made two years earlier: "Civilization and culture are very underdeveloped among all the Indians of the south, without exception"; "as all the Indians are imbeciles, wretched, and ignorant, it is very easy for the astute to trick them and acquire dominion over their property indirectly."[64]

The understandable temptation is to dismiss this idiom as a fairly simple fabrication designed to play on the sympathies and expectations of the ruling class.[65] Certainly it would seem a mistake to ascribe this discourse to Indians' "true," if hidden, political ideology or even to take it as anything other than cleverly manipulated rhetoric. Did the self-denigrating language of this public discourse have any meaning at all for its producers, or does it prove that indigenous petitions were largely crafted by and for others?

A close examination of this language reveals a certain inner logic that extends beyond a simple "public transcript" of what the powerful wanted to hear. As the last example given above suggests, Indians used this discourse to justify maintaining resguardos, a communal institution that, from a liberal economic point of view, blocked the progress that individual propertyholding would foment. Playing up their supposed ignorance, guilelessness, and even stupidity allowed Indians to keep their property legally entailed. While Indians were certainly not the simpletons that they portrayed themselves as, they knew that their white and mestizo neighbors would soon start snapping up their property if the communalists received the legal faculty to dispose of it. Indians understood that their neighbors had more money and greater access to power; without the legal protection of the resguardo, land would be lost through litigation, seizure for debt, or sale by Indians desperate for money. Also, less stalwart members of the community, not as committed to maintaining the resguardo, could, after disentailment, sell their new "private property," and the other Indians would have no legal recourse. With the great risk of having their land stolen out from under them, Indians employed a discourse of misery and helplessness in the face of authority as a justification for preserving entailment.

Indians' concept of authority reveals this language to be, not simply a fabrication, but a coherent discourse designed to protect their resguardos and, therefore, their way of life. They did not only prostrate themselves and beg for mercy but also invoked authority to do its duty and provide justice. At its base, their idea of authority was one of mutual obligation. Indians from Guachucal and Muellamuez wrote to ask the government not to order the division of resguardos, "convinced of the good disposition that the government has to favor the Indians of this province." Then they added: "All of us Indians of this district are ready, and always will be ready, to lend our services that the government requires; we have the indispensable disposition to complete this duty, as it is the most sacred of all duties."[66] Indians would recognize and serve a legitimate power, be it state or patron, but on the condition that said power fulfill its duties toward them, namely, upholding the law and respecting their historical right to the land and the community that this land represented.

Popular Republicanism   33

Popular indigenous conservatism imagined state authorities as protectors. In 1869, Indians from around Riosucio asked that the state governor listen to their "weak voice" and act "as our protector."[67] Six years earlier, communalists from the same area had addressed Tomás Mosquera, president of both the nation and Cauca State numerous times, as "leader, republican, and protector."[68] However, if the protectors failed to do their duty, unfortunate consequences could follow. The Indians of Túquerres noted that, if they lost their land, "they would throw themselves into excesses, idleness would spread, and those that no longer could count on the land that they had owned would become rebels . . . and would corrupt the rest."[69] Whether subtle or not so subtle, such threats—which Indians rarely made—were, nevertheless, an important aspect of Colombian popular republicanism in general, as we have seen with the migrants.

Along with calls for protection, Indians pleaded, or, in some cases, demanded, that justice be done. Juan Ipia, the alcalde of the village of Paniquitá, asked for the "protection" owed to "wretched Indians," citing "rightness and justice" as reasons for help in a land dispute with the parish priest.[70] While asking for justice and protection, Indians were much more careful than migrants or popular liberals to state their respect for the authority they were petitioning. Caldono Indians opened their 1853 "just" appeal for aid in a land dispute "with moderation and respect."[71] Similarly, Indians from the northern part of the state, writing sixteen years later, began a petition by noting that they acted with "due moderation and respect."[72]

This language of self-denigration, respect for authority, and calls for protection and justice was not wholly, or even primarily, a republican discourse. It arose out of the sociopolitical experience of the colonial era. After the Conquest, Indians came to regard royal authority as often their only recourse against a rapacious aristocracy and corrupt local administration. During this era, a language of humility, suffering, and calls for a higher power to dispense justice arose. This discourse did not disappear with independence.[73]

However, neither would the discourse remain static. Indians in southwestern Colombia adapted colonial rhetoric to the new republican political institutions. While they kept a subservient relation to authority, they used a republican language of rights and duties to strengthen their case. The cornerstone of this adaptation was Indians assuming their rights as members of the nation and claiming that the state had a duty toward them. Returning to the petition from Caldono, we find that the Indians played on these themes of authority, duty, and belonging to the nation: "But now since that has occurred [a claim brought against their resguardo, stating that it was public land], Sir, it leaves us no choice but to implore protection from the relevant authority so that they order the appropriate remedy to impede a wrong that has put in conflict an entire population, worthy of a better fate owing to the simple fact of belonging to the great Granadan family [Colombia was known as Nueva Granada from 1830 to 1858].”[74] Similarly, the Indians from Paniquitá, also cited above, asked the governor, not just for protection, but for the “protection that you dispense to all the citizens.”[75]

The most important adaptation that the Indians made to their colonial inheritance was the assumption of the republican mantle of the citizen. Contrary to the way in which some scholars have traditionally portrayed them,[76] Indians were very assertive—perhaps even more so than the migrants—of their place as citizens. A common opening to petitions was some variation of “using the right to petition that the constitution conceded to every Granadan.”[77] Bautista Pechene, the governor of a parcialidad near Silvia, testified in a court case on voter fraud that, despite their “being citizens,” Indians from his village “were not able to deposit their votes in the ballot box.”[78] Indians from Jambaló, Pitayó, and Quichaya combined the discourse of citizenry, misery, and patriarchy when they wrote “you are the father of us unfortunate citizens” to the new governor, hoping for a more sympathetic treatment of their case.[79]

Duty and humility mark the citizen found in indigenous conservatism—not so much a citizen demanding his rights as a citizen requesting that the state fulfill its duties toward him. As Indians from the village of Sibundoy claimed: “We are free citizens, like any other civilized Caucano, and, therefore, we are confident that you will not ignore our just and well-founded claim.”[80] Similarly, Indians from Santiago ended a petition by declaring: “We, as citizens of Cauca, are confident that you will hear our pleas.”[81]

As the requests for aid cited above suggest, one reason that Indians so arduously sought to place themselves in the nation as citizens was the corruption and self-interest of local power. In part, Indians turned to regional and national authorities to counter the designs of local authority, thereby creating a new metalocal identity for themselves. Writing to the governor of Popayán Province, Indians from Quichaya pleaded: “We do not have any authority before whom we can protest or direct any action because the authorities of the district to which we belong do nothing else than the will of our oppressor.”[82]

When the state failed in its role, Indians questioned its legitimacy. In Cumbal, after local authorities had endlessly refused to honor the demands of various regional and national courts to turn over some land to the resguardo, the cabildo pequeño derided the Caucano state president: “As we explained, we believe that you, Mister President, are impotent to make them [local authorities] comply with the sentence of the judicial power, the constitution, and the law; therefore, we ask that you return to us our court records that we have sent to your office. . . . Perhaps one day good people will govern that will not give protection to criminals."[83] Indians questioned why regional and national governments would let local bumpkins so gratuitously challenge their authority. The Indians of Caldono noted that, if local powers succeeded in taking their land, "the right of property recognized by our constitution would become a joke in this miserable wilderness."[84] In such a way, Indians created a place for themselves in the nation and simultaneously pulled the state, as weak as it was, into the nooks and crannies of the Colombian countryside. The nation of Colombia, or Nueva Granada, existed in the minds of Indians when they imagined themselves as citizens of this new political entity, long before the feeble power of the national or even the regional state made its presence felt in rural areas—and, even then, often only at Indians' request. Popular indigenous conservatism helped both create a nation and legitimize a state.

Nonetheless, Indians did not imagine their new metalocal citizenship swallowing up their other, older identity as Indians. This identity arose in the colonial era through their classification at that time as both a separate caste and a separate race. It was not a primordial identity or even purely "Indian," even if such a thing existed. Indians in the southwest often spoke Spanish and were careful to differentiate themselves from the "savage" Indians of Tierradentro and the Caquetá jungle. The aforementioned Indians of Santiago requested that their village be made part of the municipality of Caldas and not the territory of Caquetá, noting that they were "citizens," unlike the Indians of the nearby village of Descancé, who had "entirely savage language and customs."[85] These so-called savage Indians, who were often not settled in villages, were the only (male) nonrepublicans in the state of Cauca, preferring their autonomy to the charms of citizenship.

In their public discourse, Indians never identified themselves by "tribe" or by any grouping larger than the village, although villages did work together and large pan-village coalitions were sometimes formed, as some of the petitions cited above attest.[86] And, when local villages described themselves as Indians, they did claim "Indianness," which other Indians, hundreds of miles away across the state, also claimed. The communalists even had a preferred appellation, indígena, as opposed to the derogatory indio, the latter signifying either "savage" Indians or extreme misery.[87]

While some Liberals sought to eliminate these apparently nonrepublican categories, Indians carefully differentiated themselves from their white neighbors. Indians from Pancitará, involved in a dispute with the town of La Vega, complained that "the white residents of La Vega" do not respect them and that "they do not look upon us as citizens but as slaves."[88] A petition from the governors of Pitayó, Jambaló, and Quichaya protested that their constituents "have been treated like savage Indians [indios] and slaves" by the "whites."[89] The Antioqueños' Others were the Afro-Colombians and Indians they imagined or actually encountered in their drive south; the Indians' Others were their blanco neighbors and slaves. Indians in Coconuco complained bitterly about the abuses of local authorities, especially the conscription of Indians—but not mestizos— into the army. After identifying themselves as "we Indians," they recognized that "we are subjects of the government but not slaves of those mestizos."[90] The Indians of Sibundoy lamented that the local prefect forced them to work without pay and treated them "like vile slaves."[91] For Indians, the gravest insult was to conflate their status with that of slaves, a discursive trope that continued long after slavery disappeared from Colombia in 1852. Differentiating themselves from slaves reinforced their own, freer status as "Indians" and consolidated their communities around what they were not.

One petition from Guachucal and Colimba sums up several of the themes developed thus far. The cabildo pequeño declared that "thousands of citizens of the indigenous class" were the "defenseless victims of the abuses and outrages of the whites, both public employees and private individuals," who were seizing resguardo lands to expand nearby white towns. The cabildo members combined assertions of citizenship in the same sentence with cries of victimization; they simultaneously claimed the "universal" identity of citizen while marking off a particular identity of Indian in contrast to the whites. Further, they noted that dividing the resguardo into private property would be the ruin of "our miserable villages." The Indians would quickly lose their land and "return again to servitude, to ruin, and to misery." "Do the legislators of 1873 want this?"[92] Yet again the Indians asserted their lowly and humble condition and called on the state to do its duty.

Why did Indians insist on differentiating themselves from whites and slaves and not want to follow the Liberals by exclusively taking up the supposedly universal category citizen? One reason was their pre-Columbian and colonial traditions and customs, their culture, which they felt would be threatened. They had a more immediate motive, however, and, again, the link to the resguardos was paramount. Since resguardos violated liberal economic notions of productivity and utility, they were exceptions granted to a special group of people, the

Indians. Therefore, the loss of their identity as Indians also meant the loss of the right to communal landholding.

Indians had good reason to fear the notion of equality introduced by republicanism and, especially, liberalism. Equality before the law was often cited by people interested in dividing Indians' resguardos since, for most Colombians, communal landholding was illegal. In 1852, in the village of Silvia, approximately forty-five people sought to have the nearby resguardos divided. They claimed that division was in the interest of "equality" and argued that, after Independence, laws were passed that "demand that the Indians become citizens and propertyholders; . . . but to the embarrassment of N.G. [Nueva Granada] within its own territory there today exist, forty-two years after Independence, groups of men with the name *communities of Indians*."[93] Native Caucanos and migrants around Riosucio declared that "a complete fusion of the indigenous race with the white and mestizo race has occurred" and, therefore, that everyone had a right to resguardo land, not just the Indians.[94] Indians had good reason to fear a concept that made them equal only after they had denied their community, their Indianness, and their rights to land. The cabildos of Guachucal and Muellamuez asserted that "to authorize Indians to be able to dispose of their properties in the same way, and by the same titles, as other Granadans will not result in any other thing than to complete our ultimate and absolute ruin."[95]

This is not to say that Indians rejected the idea of equality, just that they had a more nuanced idea than Liberals, allowing for legal categories that gave certain groups distinct rights and responsibilities. However, the centrality of law to their idea of landholding and their status as citizens ensured that some idea of equality before the law was a key component of indigenous republicanism. The *cabildo de indígenas* of Ipiales asserted: "The law is not only for some but, rather, for all."[96] Indians were republicans and, despite some government officials' desires, never really expressed any intention of returning to their former status as legal minors. Thus, laws that applied to all should be enforced consistently, but not all laws applied to every citizen.

Just as Indians' idea of equality was different than migrants' and very different than popular liberals', so too was their idea of landholding. For the migrants, landholding was justified by labor first, legal niceties second. For the Indians, however, legal ownership of the land reigned supreme. By *legal*, I do not mean land title as understood by the liberal vision of disposable property (which Indians often did not have) but a more traditional and historical sense of the law. Indians had a right to the land, not because they worked it, but because they had possessed it historically. Indians from Riosucio begged that the governor protect them from the encroachments of Antioqueño migrants, who wanted the resguardos that the Indians had been "granted by the king." They asserted: "Since the time of our ancestors [the resguardos] have been cultivated freely."[97] Indians from Cumbal complained about a local hacendado's seizure of their land; they claimed: the seizure took away the "enjoyment of our land that for the space of three centuries and with just titles we have possessed."[98] Indians of Túquerres noted: "[We possess] our lands following the statutes, customs, and uses that we have inherited from our ancestors."[99] In sharp contrast to the migrants, the communalists almost never made any mention of labor or productivity in their petitions and, in fact, were often accused by those coveting their land of sloth and mismanagement. Instead, they cited their historical ownership and entitlement to the land under Spanish law and the fact that their ancestors had lived and worked on the land for generations. Historical possession and historical titles, not labor or current titles, justified landholding.

Furthermore, for Indians, equality was a relation, not with outsiders, but with members of their own community. From a village near Pasto, the cabildo pequeño explained:

> Since patriarchal times, we have possessed our lands communally, and we have enjoyed them with the most complete peace and harmony; we do not desire private property because we make use of communal property with equality and order. We desire that the equality of our rights consist, not in the equal portion of land that we would have, but, rather, in the equal rights in the community that we all possess; in that way there is justice, and from justice flows equality.[100]

Equality sprang from community and was located within it.

Indians employed the discourse of authority and mutual obligation between citizens and the state to protect this community. Resguardos were not simply communal lands but economic, social, and political institutions that defined Indian life. While authority was the most important discursive weapon of indigenous conservatism, ultimately Indians fought for fraternity. The maintenance of community was both the goal in employing republican discourse and the base of that discourse. The Indians of Obando asserted the centrality of the resguardo for their community: "On the other hand, there is the reason of public order and a general positive good in the Indians maintaining in communal possession their resguardos because that way they conserve and respect their ancient moral and religious traditions handed down by their elders; they conserve their habits of obedience and submission to the political authorities, whose service they are at every day; and they also conserve among themselves harmony, good customs, good relations, and true fraternity."[101] Resguardos maintained Indians' moral sensibilities, their respect for authority, and the community as a whole, just as the community's cohesiveness was necessary in the struggle to maintain the resguardos. The fraternity of the resguardo community overrode any other consideration, be it liberty or equality, in popular indigenous conservatism.

The construction of this fraternity was in many ways similar to that of smallholder republicanism in that it was based on land—but communally held land—and on the family. The Indian *alcaldes mayores* of Túquerres and Ipiales, who represented all the parcialidades of the area, explicitly linked their resguardos with family life: "Communal property in our class is not prejudicial but, rather, advantageous because, by conserving it, one also conserves our domestic relations, so that there never will appear among us the horrible monster of discord. On the contrary, our union is known and sustained by our habits and by our customs."[102] Like the migrants, although not as frequently, Indians identified themselves as padres de familia and often cited the future impoverishment of their families as one reason why their resguardos should remain entailed.[103]

As in popular smallholder republicanism, in popular indigenous conservatism religion played a role in sustaining the community by sanctifying marriage and the family. Indians supported the church monetarily, and priests at times acted as interlocutors with the larger world. Villages carefully maintained their churches.[104] While their relation to the church was often difficult, Indians strongly supported the faith. However, important as religion proved to be for Indians' political action and alliances, it was not as prominent in their discourse as it was in the smallholders'.

The centrality of the family as the basis of both the community and male Indians' political personas was an important similarity between smallholder republicanism and indigenous conservatism; but, for the communalists, authority emanated more from the village as a whole than from the individual family. While the migrant entered the public sphere as the individual padre de familia maintaining the purity of his family and the productivity of his fields, the Indian entered the public realm as the elected officeholder of the parcialidad. While migrants acted communally when writing petitions, they did so as individuals, and, often, their petitions gave no indication whatsoever of the leadership structure with the community, except inferentially, by the order of the signatories. Titles were not often evident. Indian petitions, by contrast, almost always began with the signatures of the governor, alcaldes, and officials of the cabildo pequeño. While most migrant petitions bore the signatures of as many males as the community could muster, indigenous petitions usually bore only the signatures of the parcialidad's officers. Each migrant homestead was in some sense independent, but an indigenous village was a legal corporate body, with its members under the authority of the cabildo pequeño.

Like the father of the individual family, the cabildo pequeño assumed patriarchal power over the "family" of the Indian community as a whole. A coalition of Indians from the south explained the link between patriarchy and their resguardos in a metaphor: "Our parcialidades, Honorable Deputies, are like a family that lives under one father," and they follow the rules and customs that they "have received from our ancestors."[105] This metaphor of the patriarchal family extended beyond the level of the village leaders to include metalocal authority figures. The Indians of Guachicono referred to the governor of the province as the "father of the miserable people."[106] As with the migrants, patriarchal power and political subjectivity were tied together. When the village of Guachavéz lost its status as a parish and, therefore, its men lost leadership positions, the moral life of the village declined as "the immediate weight of authority is not felt." Before their power was taken away, they noted the good order of their village, "all the inhabitants respecting the lowliest constable as much as the ultimate local authority."[107] Of course, Indians would want their village to be designated a parish for many reasons, but they framed their argument around the notion of patriarchal authority. Indeed, while it seems that officeholders were often elected by the men of the community, once in office they wielded great power. They concerned themselves, not just with the maintenance of land, but also with the moral life of the village as a whole. As Nicolás Quilindo, governor of Polindará, noted: "Cabildos care for the regulation, morality, and good order of their respective indigenous populations."[108]

Community was not, as scholars have come to recognize, something that simply sprang fully formed from traditional villages.[109] Maintenance of the village's fraternity was a daily affair and not without its difficulties and social cost. Beneath the calm surface of popular indigenous conservatism's fraternity simmered the tension of individual Indians' desire to sell their resguardo land. The cabildos de indígenas's patriarchal power held together communities whose members did not always share the same goals. As the Indian leaders of Obando Province noted, if the resguardos were divided, "without the authority of their governors, their regidores, and their alcaldes who incessantly and daily keep vigil over each house, each family, each individual Indian, they would lose themselves in their passions, and, very soon, the customary links of union, order, and obedience broken, they would commit the most atrocious crimes."[110] From Túquerres, the *alcalde mayor* noted that Indians were loyal to their cabildo leaders "out of fear of losing the use of their lands," which the cabildo distributed, with "the condition that they be ready to serve the government and the church."[111] Submission to this type of domination was the antithesis of the smallholder republican ideal.

But recalcitrant members of a parcialidad were not the only threat from within to the community of indigenous republicanism. Leaders of the cabildos de indígenas also faced the temptation to have the resguardos divided, with the largest portions destined for themselves, and, thereby, join the ranks of liberal propertyholders. While this was more likely in the more divided, "racially" and culturally mixed resguardos of the north, problems of this sort occasionally appeared in the south as well.[112] In these cases, it took the efforts of the community as a whole to marshal its forces in defense of fraternity and to reestablish the cabildo under new leaders. While rare in the south, these examples of community defense were important as they reveal that the resguardos' maintenance was not just the effort of "rich" Indians who governed the cabildos to maintain themselves in power, as outsiders often suggested. Village patriarchal democracy seemed to enjoy high levels of support from the communities, as the almost interminable saga of each parcialidad's struggle to maintain its resguardo demonstrates. The continual commitment of resources in defense of fraternity shows the sacrifices that Indians were willing to make to maintain their way of life.

Throughout most of the region, and for most of the time span covered by this study, popular indigenous conservatism was, in some senses, a variation on elite conservatism. I denote it as conservative because of its strong orientation toward the past. Indians rarely spoke of progress, the hallmark of nineteenth-century liberalism, and explicitly justified their land ownership with an appeal to past laws and historical possession. While the discourse itself was profoundly republican, it was built on a base of a colonial language of self-denigration, respect for authority, and appeals for protection. Authority especially was central to both indigenous and elite conservatism, although the former emphasized authority's responsibilities, the latter its prerogatives. Also like elite conservatism, indigenous conservatism was corporative.[113] Indians acted as a corporate body with special rights and responsibilities, much like a guild. Also, Indians' allegiance to their resguardos basically supported a division of society into various groups that resisted a strict equality, the bugbear of conservatism. Similarly, their discourse was implicitly hierarchical, assuming a continuing chain of authority ascending from the cabildos, through local officials, to the president of the nation. They exercised this hierarchy in their communities and understood society beyond their parcialidades in much the same way. Finally, the supremacy of fraternity, defended at all costs, over liberty and equality marks the discourse as conservative. Indians' notion of authority is basically a fraternal one: the shared rights and responsibilities of imagined family members.

That said, I must emphasize that this was a *popular* conservatism. The ends of Indians' language and politics did not serve elite interests and were certainly not a form of false consciousness. While there is no doubt truth to the assertion that resguardos survived in the south because they had a functional relationship with nearby haciendas, it is also true that many elites and middling figures greedily coveted Indians' lands.[114] The discourse of popular indigenous conservatism developed to preserve these lands within the new republican political system in which Indians found themselves and in which they proceeded to create a place for themselves as citizens. Indians vigorously claimed their place as members of the nation while reconceptualizing citizenship along lines more to their liking. Their demands for justice and for authorities to fulfill their duties reframed the language of elites and turned it back on itself, forcing the powerful to live up to their own rhetoric or to expose the whole imagined republican system as a hollow shell. Their desire to maintain an independent life in their communities cannot be denigrated as "false consciousness" or a simple deferential acceptance of the socioeconomic situation. As Indians from Mocondino put it, their great fear was the disentailment of their resguardos, as "in a very short time our land would form a hacienda of some rich man or the town of people of the white race" and they would have to become "miserable day laborers."[115] Given the odds, Indians succeeded remarkably in keeping that grim future from coming to pass.

Popular Liberalism

Most Afro-Colombians of the Cauca Valley, along with many of their poor mestizo neighbors, were popular liberals. While most Afro-Caucanos had never been slaves, the idea of slavery and its memory defined their popular liberalism. The desire to escape from and destroy the almost all-encompassing social, political, and economic subordination of enslavement and its legacy underlay their politics and discourse. Therefore, the linchpin of popular liberalism was equality, the most troublesome element of the republican trinity.

An analysis of popular liberalism is problematic, however, for a variety of reasons. Perhaps most important, unlike migrants and Indians, Afro-Colombians controlled no institutional or corporate body through which to represent themselves. Large haciendas dominated the landscape of the central valley carved by the Cauca River. Unlike Indians, the poor residents of the valley had no traditional landholdings, and there were few, if any, public lands available for settlement, as in the north. Therefore, popular liberals did not often control villages or cabildos pequeños from which to draft petitions and represent themselves directly to the state.

However, the valley's residents had somewhat less need to represent themselves alone, as they often had middle-class and middling allies willing to help them. Instead of through the council of padres de familia or the cabildo pequeño, popular liberals often acted through Democratic Societies, political clubs founded by middling or even elite Liberals.[116] Often, the Democratic Societies' leaders employed a language of radical liberalism, emphasizing popular rights and political mobilization. These alliances significantly influenced popular liberals' discourse; conversely, their discourse and action affected their elite compatriots' politics too.

Afro-Colombians shared their discourse, not just with middling groups, but also with a large section of mestizo poor, with whom they often allied themselves politically. As there were some differences in Afro-Caucanos' and poor mestizos' versions of popular liberalism, for clarity's sake I will focus primarily on the Afro-Caucanos' discourse. However, many of the Afro-Caucanos' contemporaries did not make such distinctions. Conservatives often simply grouped all the valley's poor into one category of "negros" or blacks. Many of these "negros" were not of African descent, but, owing to their poverty and their proximity to and political alliance with Afro-Colombians, elites often labeled them black. Much like the race of the Antioqueño migrants, the race of popular liberals was based, not simply on phenotypic attributes, but also on region, culture, class, and politics. I do not want to overly racialize popular liberalism as being the domain of Afro-Colombians only. Much more so than smallholder republicanism or indigenous conservatism, popular liberalism did not define itself against a racial Other and, thus, was not as racially circumscribed.

Nonetheless, popular liberalism's Other was linked to race, a result of the Cauca's history of racial slavery. Slavery became the identity against which Afro-Colombians defined themselves, and it was one of the most prominent tropes of popular liberalism. Two Caleños wrote asking for land in the ejidos (commons owned by the city) since they had none after "having left the degrading condition of slavery."[117] Former slaves of the San Julián hacienda noted "that since we ceased to depend on the man that they called our master, and we entered, owing to the majesty of the law, into the category of free men," the leaders of the town of Caloto harassed them continually, assigning them unfair duties and taxes. The

Afro-Caucanos declared that Caloto's parochial government "wanted to convert us into slaves again, of a worse nature than what we were before."[118]

The overarching goal of Afro-Colombians' discourse and politics was to prevent their return to slavery. They abhorred, not only legal slavery, but also slavelike conditions suffered by free people—the lack of control over their lives, the arbitrary power of the master, the complete absence of liberty and equality. A Conservative official noted this when he wrote about former slaves' attitudes toward a new tax affecting them. He commented that they were convinced "that they are oppressed, that they are tyrannized, and that through these means [the taxes] we want to return them to slavery, which is the magic word that they employ in these situations."[119] For Afro-Caucanos, slavery was, indeed, a "magic word," evoking the nightmare against which they constructed popular liberalism.

One element of republicanism that Afro-Colombians embraced to counter attempts to return them to a slavish condition was liberty. Hilario Hurtado had been a slave on Rafael Hurtado's hacienda but claimed to be free, having served in the army for two years. His former master, however, had captured him as a maroon. Hilario protested that he had "acquired my liberty; now they want to deprive me of that inestimable possession."[120] Hundreds of ex-slaves from around Barbacoas wrote to the president of the nation thanking him for their freedom: "Owing to your efforts, the most degraded part of society, which today represents itself to you, has obtained the possession of liberty that we now enjoy."[121] Residents from around Micay, another coastal town, involved in various land disputes, noted that "more than two thousand inhabitants that breathed the marvelous air of liberty" had used the land since their "political emancipation."[122] From the coastal village of San Juan, ex-slaves wrote to the national congress, thanking them for abolition: "We enjoy the precious possession of liberty, so long usurped, and with it all the other rights and prerogatives of citizens."[123]

Liberty was only one of slavery's possible foils. Equality was even more important. Afro-Colombians esteemed equality so highly, not just because they or their ancestors had been enslaved, but also because, under colonial caste laws, free blacks and mulattoes had been categorized as inferior to whites. Slaves obtained their liberty with emancipation, but they also gained the equality of rights so long denied them. As the last petition cited above attests, this equality manifested itself most powerfully in the ex-slaves' new identity as citizens. Migrants seemed sure enough of their utility to the nation not to need to claim citizenship very frequently. Indians often claimed it, perhaps eager to dispel the liberal myth that, since they had special rights to their resguardos, they were not really true citizens but still the legal minors of the colonial era. Afro-Caucanos and other popular liberals claimed citizenship vociferously, much more so than did the other groups. The boatmen of the river Dagua, who ferried passengers and goods from the Pacific Coast to the central valley, asserted their place as citizens in a labor dispute: "We should be treated like citizens of a republic and not like the slaves of a sultan."[124] Over a quarter of a century after emancipation, Afro-Caucanos still knew the power of the metaphor of slavery. For them, equality meant never returning to that degraded position.

In the aforementioned petition from the residents of the San Julián hacienda, the residents not only noted that they were "free men" who should not be treated as slaves but also asserted their new status in the opening line: "The undersigned residents of the parochial district of Caloto, and inhabitants of the San Julián hacienda to which once we belonged as slaves, before you in the use of our rights as citizens. . . ."[125] The petitioners contrasted their former condition with their new identity as citizens and, even better, as citizens with rights.

Equality was intricately linked with both citizenship and rights. Unlike popular indigenous conservatives and popular smallholder republicans, who often justified their claims by asserting their goodness, their hard work, or historical precedent, popular liberals simply claimed their rights. When residents of Cali protested liquor monopolies that robbed the "poor part of the nation" of the faculty to produce and sell liquor, they derided such restrictions and police efforts to enforce them as "violating the most dear and sacred rights."[126] The right to distill and sell alcohol without taxation was nowhere evident in any law or constitution; popular liberals simply created it. In the same spirit, they also claimed themselves as citizens and as part of the nation, although, in 1849, when the Cali petition was written, most of them would not have been considered as such legally since they did not possess sufficient property.

In the Pacific Coast lowlands, residents of a small town identified themselves as "Colombian citizens," invoked their "right" to petition, and then reported that local authorities had "deprived us of our right" by threatening to kick them off some land unless they paid rents to the state. The villagers believed that they were entitled to use the land because of "our right as cultivators." In one short petition, these popular liberals asserted three distinct rights—the right to petition, the right to use land without paying rents, and the right to hold land if one worked it—with only the right to petition being legally guaranteed by the Colombian constitution.[127] The residents of Tumaco, another coastal town, also demanded their rights while involved in a land dispute with some merchants who were attempting to limit the extraction of resins from the surrounding forests. The Tumacanos derided these efforts as an attempt to reestablish "a wretched feudalism" and demanded that the national government protect their "equality of rights."[128] By claiming citizenship and rights, Afro-Caucanos asserted their equality with all the other members of the Colombian national polity. For popular liberals, the identity of citizenship both produced and guaranteed equality.

Equality symbolized many things to popular liberals. First, along with liberty, it denoted emancipation from slavery. Second, equality guaranteed the poor and people of color the same rights as the rich and white. Finally, equality signified social equality. Social equality was more complex than abolition or equal rights before the law. It meant an end to the deference owed to the master or others of the powerful class. It meant the death of the economic dependence that forced deference on the poor.

Popular liberals reacted in disgust to the social deference that the old master class demanded. In a broadside that circulated on the streets of Cali, the city's Democratic Society sought to justify the increasing number of violent attacks on outlying haciendas and their owners, noting that the attacks were due to the "multitude of insults" that Conservatives inflicted on Liberals and their popular followers.[129] Not only did popular liberals resent the haughty attitude of the elite, but they also refused to play the role of the pliant servant. A writer urging the expansion of export agriculture complained about the problems plaguing planters in the Cauca, problems due to the "perversion of the sentiment of personal independence of our workers."[130]

The tenants of a hacienda near Quilcacé, owned by the San Camilo religious order, asked for land for a new town to be cut out of the hacienda and given to them since the state was disentailing and selling land that religious orders owned. They claimed that their petition was a "just demand for the rights of this village." They worried about being the retainers of a new hacendado as now they "are vulnerable to becoming the tenant and feudal serf of any buyer of the hacienda."[131] Unlike most Afro-Caucanos who lived in the Cauca Valley, the Quilcasereños had the chance to acquire land of their own and escape the domination of the hacendado while not abandoning their homes. The Colegio Mayor of Popayán, which felt that it now owned the hacienda, disputed the residents' claim, the writer of its petition noting that they had once been the hacienda's "slaves." He complained that the "blacks" thought that the land was theirs, "enjoying to their satisfaction the hacienda, building their houses where they want, giving permission so that the most immoral people of other districts come to live with them, and they refuse to pay the land rent for where they live and have their animals and fields."[132] Quilcacé seemed a haven for Afro-Caucanos seeking to escape the continued dominance of the old master class. While migrants also sought to escape from tenancy's dependence, they did seem to accept ideas of appropriate, legitimate authority and deference within their villages. Popular liberals more completely rejected elite expectations of the social deference of the poor and weak.

The economic base of dependence and independence was land, a concern shared by all the Cauca's popular republicans. Unlike the migrants, however, the Afro-Caucanos who lived in the central valley generally had no empty public land readily available. An exception was those living in the rain forests of the Pacific Coast, where land was abundant and, to the capitalist at least, of little value. There, Afro-Caucanos could acquire land, and they employed a discourse similar to that of the migrants concerning landholding. In the central valley, however, most Afro-Caucanos were not as lucky as the Quilcasereños. Untitled land was not available; therefore, popular liberal discourse focused not so much on legal landholding as on the right to work and to enjoy the fruits of one's labor.

The Dagua River boatmen complained about merchants trying to impose conditions on them and control their labor: "You well understand, Señor, that we, like any other worker, artisan, or laborer in this or any other industry or profession, have the perfect right to put on our labor the price that seems to us the most just. There is not a law in Colombia that prescribes or fixes the sum with which the labor and fatigue of a citizen should be remunerated."[133] The boatmen, as in the previous quote when they asserted their identity as citizens, rejected what they saw as an attempt to return them to the status of a slave, without rights. Citizens of a republic had the right to control their labor, even if they had nothing else.

In a continuing dispute with elites and the government, popular liberals defended their right to produce and sell liquor and other products on which the state had declared a monopoly or over which it had established prohibitive taxes. Especially since they lacked land, popular liberals thought that they deserved to be able to engage in these industries. Residents of the town of Bolívar complained about tax farmers' attempts to enforce a law concerning liquor production. The moonshiners asserted: "In our state there is complete liberty of industry," and "republicans have difficulty viewing with calm and indifference those who try to wrest away our rights."[134] A few days later, the inhabitants of the nearby village of La Cruz joined them, complaining that the tax farmers "believed themselves owners of the industry of the citizens, although we have complete liberty concerning it."[135]

Little in elite or middling republicanism immediately addressed the poor valley residents' concerns about land. They were not claiming state land, as were the migrants; nor were they protecting land that historically had belonged to them and had been illegally usurped, as were the Indians. Hacendados held legal title to the land, as they had for generations. Since elite republicanism did not suggest a solution to this problem, Afro-Caucanos adapted republicanism in two ways. First, they focused on the question of rights, inherently republican, and emphasized their right to labor. Second, and more revolutionary, they claimed the right to the land itself, as their due as citizens, transmogrifying the republican discourse in a way most elites found unimaginable.

Afro-Caucanos rejected liberal notions of private property that gave exclusive rights to the owner. They asserted their right to gather wood and other products from forests, regardless of legal title, as we saw with the resin gatherers around Tumaco. Cali's elites rejected these claims, stating that the wood thieves "do not have any right" to exploit their forests, noting that the perpetrators used to be miners but now invaded private lands for a living. The landowners warned that these incursions threatened respect for private property.[136] The gatherers saw it differently. Fermín Pretel complained about a hacendado's efforts to prevent the gathering of firewood on a hacienda near Cali. Pretel asserted that the land was really ejidos, the city's commons, and that Manuel Collazos, the hacendado, "seeks to impede the work and civilization of the popular masses." He continued by claiming that "Mr. Collazos does not have the right to impede us from cutting firewood on the aforementioned mountainsides, nor, I believe, the right to enjoy our labor by taking the firewood that we have cut on the slopes." He closed by noting that such a state of affairs violated the "philanthropic sentiments of Liberty, Equality, and Fraternity."[137]

Surely, for elite Liberals and Conservatives the republican trinity had nothing whatsoever to do with cutting firewood on their property. Yet popular liberals would further radicalize their ideas about land, ideas that were linked to their conception of free labor. Their earliest efforts involved protecting various cities' common lands, often the only land not held privately in the central valley, from being taken over by haciendas. These struggles would culminate in calls for an end to land rents in general and demands for land redistribution in the central valley, as the petition that closes this section attests, and would eventually, in the 1870s, rend the alliance between Liberals and their plebeian allies. However, popular liberals first put forward their claims to hacienda land long before that time.

Hacendados complained bitterly about the attitudes of their former slaves, who often seemed to think that, along with their freedom, emancipation gave them the right to the land that they had worked as bondsmen. In 1855, Vicente

Arboleda griped that the ex-slaves believed that "they had a right to the properties where they were living" and that all the present tenants of the region "have become insolent, do not pay rent, yet nor will they leave the property."[138] Years later, a manager of the famed La Bolsa hacienda exclaimed that the "blacks . . . now do not recognize in the slightest the rights of owners of those lands and threaten with death those of us who administer the hacienda."[139] For perhaps obvious reasons, popular liberals generally could not express in petitions to the government desires to counter liberal property laws and elite interests; however, their actions spoke very loudly.

Still, as noted above, popular liberals could at certain times give voice to a radical discourse concerning land rights. The Palmira Democratic Society petitioned the national government in 1868 on behalf of its poor constituents, whom hacendados had forbidden to gather firewood and were trying to force to pay rents on the marginal land bordering the haciendas. The Democratic Society claimed that those marginal lands did not belong to the hacendados and that the poor had a "natural right" to exploit such lands. The petitioners noted that the nation was in a "glorious era of natural equality . . . with the fall and overturning of all those tyrannies of which the weak have been victims, here as everywhere; [land] is the exclusive benefit of a few, who present themselves as powerful, and usurp everything and exploit the weak, from their essential individual rights to the free gifts that God has apportioned." The use of the land was a natural right given by God to the poor, a right that perhaps overrode questions of legal title. The Palmira Democratic Society did not, however, rely on natural rights or appeals to religion alone to justify its claims. The Society reminded the president that "the poor class" has made "the very valuable contribution of their blood in order to defend our institutions, public order, and national independence and integrity." It continued: "These individuals have, at the very least, an unquestionable right to be protected by a liberal government."[140] Popular liberals made constant reminders of their past services to the state and the Liberal Party.

The Quilcasereños similarly reminded state officials of what the nation owed them for their past support, recalling "the services the village made to the cause of the federation [in the 1860–63 war] and . . . the bloody sufferings that it endured because of its adhesion to that cause."[141] By the 1860s, the cause of federalism for which the Quilcasereños and many Afro-Colombians fought was more or less equated with the cause of liberalism. Now it was time for the state to proffer some reward for their trials and tribulations.

In 1878, local conservatives in the municipality of Caldas accused former Liberal soldiers from areas including Quilcacé and Afro-Caucano-dominated

Patía Valley of banditry. The accused wrote to the Liberal state president to remind him of their past loyalty: "You know, Citizen President, what are the causes that motivate the said charges [of banditry] since one of them is having sustained in the civil war of '76 and '77 the dignity of the government, of the Cauca, and of the rule of the constitution of the republic."[142] Not only had these popular liberals not received any reward for their sacrifices for the Liberal cause, but they now faced punishment as a result of their fealty. This must have seemed the cruelest of treacheries, to be hounded by the same Conservatives that they had defeated in war.

The Dagua boatmen also cited their partisanship in the 1876–77 civil war: "In our profession we have lent great services to the Liberal cause, and more than a few times we have set aside the punting poles and oars in order to take up the gun. . . . Loyal to our opinions, we did not relent to [Conservatives'] demands for our services [during the war], and we continued serving in every way possible the Liberal cause, the cause of our sympathies."[143] Even though the Conservatives had threatened them during the war, ordering them to ferry supplies up the river, the boatmen had refused. They viewed themselves as good Liberals, loyal to the cause, but now it was time for the cause to be loyal to them. Now they sought the support of the state in their current dispute, support they saw as their due.

The boatmen made clear that they had volunteered their favors. The petition of two conscripts in jail in Cali, from decades earlier, expressed a similar sentiment. Local officials had consigned the men to the army for being vagrants. The pair contested their fate, pleading with the governor for "liberty, the first necessity of man," and expressing bewilderment how this could happen "where equality and justice reign." The two wanted to make clear that they did not oppose armed service in general: "Not for that [reason], Mister Governor, do we want to be exempted from the service we owe to the fatherland. No, a thousand times no. On the contrary, when it, in its conflicts, would call us as armed citizens in its defense, we would quickly prove with our actions the love and gratitude that we profess to a philanthropic and humanitarian government."[144] The two men would serve, not as forced underlings, but as proud citizens.

All popular republicans engaged in a continual bargaining with elites, claiming that the state owed them for their past services at the ballot box or on the battlefield. However, as opposed to smallholder republicanism or indigenous conservatism, popular liberalism made these claims of service central. One reason that the valley's residents needed a closer relation to the state was that they often relied on commons land, which state authorities distributed. Popular liberals also asserted that the government owed them for their support as it was all they had to offer. Unlike the claims of Indians, based on their traditional communities, or those of migrants, based on the prosperity that their villages would bring, the claims of popular liberals usually had no such foundations with which to buttress their arguments. Popular liberals based their claimsmaking on the simple fact of their citizenship and their past sacrifices for their nation and party. They fought in wars or voted because they believed in the cause, although, of course, their cause was not synonymous with the cause of Liberal leaders. In their discourse, they did not serve because of coercion or threats, as the patsies of their landlords or patrons, against whom they usually fought anyway. They served as free citizens. They served as equals.

Citizenship was important to the accused vagabonds in the Cali jail as it provided them an identity. They did not have to represent themselves as Caleños, or good farmers, or miserable wretches deserving of protection. They simply claimed to be citizens. Citizenship was the most important aspect of popular liberals' identity, as the various petitions cited above attest. However, their citizenship and, thus, their identity did not exist in a vacuum; like the identity of migrants and Indians, the identity of liberals was often defined by what it was not. The popular liberals' Other was—besides slavery—all the forces opposing their standing as free, nondeferential, independent citizens. Most powerfully, the slave master personified this Other, but so too did the aristocrat, the hacendado, the Conservative, or simply the rich.[145]

Sergio Arboleda, ex-slaveholder and Conservative hacendado, received an anonymous letter, signed only by the "the Masked Ones," protesting his attempts to enforce his monopoly contract to produce liquor. The writers constantly invoked Arboleda's past actions as a Conservative leader in civil wars. They complained: "It is a scandal that a man like you that has so many ways of making a living takes away from wretched women the industry that they now practice in order to survive and that is the only work that remains for them since all of our possessions that we had you, your brother, and friends stole from us in the last revolution." They warned that the "people . . . are free and sovereign" and that Arboldea was no longer "chief of the army of the godos [Conservatives] and able to rob and kill like you did in 1861."[146] For the Masked Ones, Arboleda was everything that they were not—rich, Conservative, a great landowner. His efforts to steal from the poor—especially from poor women—their only means of subsistence only strengthened popular liberals' discourse concerning the vileness and treachery of their enemies.

In the petition from Tumaco cited above, the resin gatherers characterized the land speculators who harassed them, not just as greedy, but as "three bad citizens" whose plans were an "inhuman and unpatriotic concoction."[147] The speculators' designs were not simply wrong or unfair but not republican. Similarly, the Dagua boatmen identified their opponents as "rich Conservatives" trying to impose "a corrupt tyranny."[148] Good citizens should not have to endure such treatment at the hands of bad citizens. During times of war or disorder, when popular liberals could more freely express such sentiments, Cali and other cities were filled with shouts of "Death to the godos [Conservatives]!"[149]

Popular liberalism grounded its notion of the good citizen much less on patriarchy than did indigenous conservatism or smallholder republicanism. Women participated in some popular liberal petitions, a situation found only rarely among Indians and never among the migrants. In one petition, a number of women were among the signatories asserting themselves to be "Colombian citizens."[150] In another, even more startling petition, a group of women acting alone assumed the mantle of citizenship: "We the undersigned, citizens [ciudadanas] of Colombia. . . ." They were protesting taxes on the sale of aguardiente in small establishments, accusing the local government of the "most fierce despotism."[151] By state and national law, women were not citizens. Yet these women claimed to be so, possibly bolstered by the independent status that being barkeeps gave them.

For popular liberals (although not, I should note, for elite Liberals), citizenship was not constructed on the backs of the family. Popular liberals mentioned families in their discourse much less often than did migrants or Indians. The good citizen did not have to be married, as did the migrants' padre de familia, and no patriarchal figure controlled the community, as in Indian villages. While I do not want to enter into the debate on the slave family, popular liberal men seemed somewhat unable or unwilling to exercise control over popular liberal women. Since most popular liberals did not own land, or at least not enough to support a family, male land ownership did not lend itself to gender control. Also, some Afro-Colombian women had an independent economic resource in small-scale liquor production and sale, a resource that popular liberal men were more than willing to defend. Finally, although the evidence is far from conclusive, women seemed to control a goodly amount of the land on the city commons that popular liberals did exploit, often heading their own households.[152] Popular liberal women had much more independence than other subaltern women did and, correspondingly, participated more overtly and regularly in the Cauca's political life.[153]

However, popular liberalism still envisioned a male political subject.[154] As noted above, service to the state and the party created the good citizen, and women could rarely perform such service. Legally, women were not citizens, and they did not, therefore, have the suffrage. Possibly more important from the standpoint of popular liberalism, men, not women, shed their blood in wars against the rich, the conservative, and the other bad citizens. By defining citizenship and service in such terms, popular liberal men excluded women from the equality that they themselves held so dear. By investing so much in their identity as citizens, defined by elites legally as available only to men, male popular republicans gained a powerful discursive tool in their political struggles. However, this discursive strategy also greatly limited the public, political role that popular liberal women could play.

Popular liberals continually struggled to gain the equality so long denied them. In an amazing petition that encapsulates the themes of land, equality, and service, the Cali Democratic Society demanded land redistribution, the right to gather wood from forests, and the elimination of tenancy. Its members, and the people of the valley generally, deserved these reforms because of their service to the Liberal Party in the recent civil war:

> Although this may seem an extravagant request, it is not, if one weighs the criterion of justice, considering that those individuals, born here or elsewhere, who have promptly presented themselves to defend their country have the perfect right to live in the Cauca under the expressed terms [i.e., without tenancy and with their own land]. How can one think it just that those who have come every time to defend this soil that saw them born against the repeated and unjust invasions from Antioquia, invasions aided by those who call themselves the owners of the greater part of the Cauca's land, live without a home?[155]

Again, popular liberals and their supporters stressed the service of the valley's poor, the right of all men who served to land and liberty, and the unfairness of the domination of the land by a few who were traitors to the cause of right. Note the difference from similar claims for land made by migrants and Indians; here, valor and sacrifice, not labor, gave one a right to land. The domination of the earth by a few was not wrong because it was economically unsound or others had labored on the soil (à la smallholder republicanism) or because others had an ancient legal claim on the land (à la indigenous conservatism). No, the unfaithful rich should not dominate the land because they had helped the enemy of liberty and their domination of the land prevented the equality of all citizens. Popular liberals deserved the land simply because they were citizens and, especially, citizen soldiers.

The veterans in the Democratic Society closed their petition by evoking the horrible consequence of the denial of their requests: a return to the status of the slave, a fate whose avoidance animated the discourse of popular liberalism. They railed against the obligation of deference and the loss of liberty that such an outcome entailed: "Land cannot be occupied to such an extent that the other members of the community are deprived of the means of subsistence or are obligated to be the slaves of those feudal lords who do not admit onto their supposed properties any but those individuals who implicitly sell their personal independence, that is to say, their conscience and liberty, in order to be the peons and tributaries of an individual and to cease to be citizens of a free people."[156]

Coherence and Divergence within the Cauca's Popular Republicanism

Popular republicans in the Cauca voiced, not one homogeneous discourse, but, rather, several distinct discourses. Three of these discourses appear consistently in the historical record, although others most probably existed, such as popular mestizo liberalism, its conservative counterpart, and women's popular liberalism. While each discourse had its own specific tropes—such as labor, resguardos, or slavery—all shared an emphasis on liberty, equality, and fraternity. Yet the three variants framed these ideas in their own particular manners.

Liberty was the central trope of smallholder republicanism as settlers hoped to gain their independence from domineering hacendados. Popular smallholder republicans thus defined liberty as the establishment of their own authority and the absence of oppressive authority controlling them. Liberty held a similar connotation for popular liberals owing to its connection with slavery and emancipation and Afro-Colombians' continuing struggles with hacendados over access to land, except it was more suspect of authority. Indians interpreted liberty quite differently. They saw it as the freedom and the right to maintain their communal landholdings and their own patriarchal authority while being treated as free citizens.

Fraternity was most important for popular indigenous conservatism as it linked republicanism with Indians' colonial resguardos and communities. The fraternity of the village acting together produced the political actor of the parcialidad officer. For migrants, fraternity was the settler village where fathers worked together to carve out individual farms and came together to secure their lands and liberty in the face of outside threats. Afro-Caucanos envisioned fraternity much more broadly, as a union of all good citizens protecting the republic from the treacherous bad citizen.

Equality lay at the core of popular liberalism. Afro-Caucanos understood equality as signifying both an end to old patterns of deference and the possibility of economic independence for all good people. For Afro-Caucanos, citizenship produced equality. Migrants saw equality as more limited. Equality was based on labor, and only the hardworking and moral deserved its fruits. Indians' principal concern was the equality of the members of their own villages. Equality was not a relation with outsiders but created by the sustenance of their communities. All popular republicans' definitions of equality went beyond a limited conception of equal standing before the law.

While the whole of subalterns' quotidian lives and histories shaped these discourses, how each group's relation to land influenced its interpretations of republicanism merits special attention. Popular smallholder republicanism developed around the need to legitimize tenuous settlements on frontier lands in the face of powerful speculators. Popular indigenous conservatism concentrated on the necessity of protecting inherited resguardos. Popular liberalism promoted a radically democratic vision of rights—a result of Afro-Colombians' confrontation with the haciendas' land monopoly—a vision in which citizenship meant entitlement to the soil. These distinct ties to land would fuel and shape the politics of all the Cauca's subalterns in the partisan struggles of the latter nineteenth century.

While the differences between the three visions of popular republicanism were important, I do not want to neglect their similarities. Each of the three discourses challenged the ideology and economic position of the powerful. Each contested the right of the wealthy to control the lives of the poor. All popular republicans sought to carve out an independent social and economic space for themselves away from the landlord, political boss, or overseer.

All the discourses were republican. Probably their most important republican aspect was their assumption of identities beyond the local and the colonial. Partisans of all three variants claimed to be citizens, with varying degrees of vehemence. Beyond those direct claims, popular republicans sought to place themselves in the larger region and the nation. They did this by dragging the weak Colombian state into their conflicts. Much more so than bureaucrats in chilly Bogotá or even Popayán, plotting to exert state authority, popular groups pulled the Colombian state into their localities. By claiming that the nation and the region concerned them too and that they had a right to be heard by both, subalterns made a place for themselves at the table of the new Colombian nation. The nineteenth-century Colombian state, if by that we mean institutions, was decidedly weak.[157] Yet the Colombian nation, if by that we mean something along the lines of Benedict Anderson's "imagined community," was very strong.[158] Unlike in Anderson's work, however, not only elites imagined this community. Settlers, Indians, and Afro-Caucanos envisioned a new, republican community too. Perhaps the most important imaginings of the Colombian nation were not those of bureaucrats and politicians but those of a more poor and humble folk.

This chapter has dealt mainly with the discourses and visions of the three forms of popular republicanism. These discourses reveal many Caucano plebeians' fears and hopes. The remaining chapters treat subalterns' actions and how popular groups invoked these discourses as means of entering the political realm and bargaining with elites. I noted earlier that plebeians' discourse was not a mirror of their consciousness or even of their ideology. However, subalterns' political participation may, perhaps, reveal what their discourse could not. For popular republicans not only imagined a new place for themselves but also acted to secure it.

3 A New Politics:

The Emergence of Republican Bargaining,

1848–1853

Nueva Granada will have the reality of the representative system, and the
government will be of the pueblo and for the pueblo.
—PRESIDENT JOSÉ HILARIO LÓPEZ (1849)[1]

Throughout the turbulent years of 1850 and 1851, the Afro-Colombians of Cartago gathered at the local Democratic Society when the mails from the capital would arrive, anticipating the news that Congress had finally abolished slavery.[2] By the summer of 1851, after over two years of unfulfilled expectations, President José Hilario López and his Liberal Party seemed ready to fulfill their promises and end the ownership of human bodies in Colombia. The Cartaganos, a mixture of slave and free whose ancestors had borne the brunt of the lash or whose relatives still toiled as chattel, waited to see whether the new words that they kept hearing since the Liberals' ascension to power in 1849—*liberty, equality, republic, democracy*—would mean anything for them.

The Cauca Valley's Afro-Colombians had entered into a bargain, a political bargain, even though they were not legal citizens of the nation, most not meeting the property and literacy requirements set by the 1843 constitution. They had thrown their support behind the Liberals—in spite of the fact that some prominent members of the party were themselves slaveowners—with the expectation that these wealthy men would emancipate them and their brethren. Since few Afro-Colombians could vote at the time, their political bargaining involved a form of barter more complicated than but still fundamentally the same as the modern political expectation that politicians trade promises of favorable policies, programs, and the state's largesse for support at the ballot box. If they had good reason to support the Liberals, the Liberals did not push for abolition simply out of altruism, or to spite Conservative slave masters, or to fulfill their own economic and philosophical program, which saw slavery as archaic and incongruous with the modern Atlantic World. No, the Liberals pushed for abolition not just for these reasons, although they would cite each in due course and, no doubt, some or all affected the lawmakers. They also bargained for political support, perhaps at the ballot box, but certainly on the battlefield, the terrain on which so many of Colombia's contests for power had been decided.

The Afro-Colombians, those of Cartago and the rest of the Cauca, did not disappoint. When Conservatives launched a civil war in 1851, blacks and mulattoes quickly rallied to the Liberal banner. They volunteered to do battle with the Conservatives, and even the Liberals most active in securing the alliance between Afro-Colombians and the Liberal Party seemed stunned by their response:

> I saw them, during those solemn days, arm themselves spontaneously and march to the campaign to defend the legitimacy and the regeneration of democracy, old men of eighty years, half naked, trembling with age, but strong because of their faith in and enthusiasm for the Republic; I saw hundreds of young men and adolescents abandon their homes, their wives, their children, their possessions, in order to go and offer their lives in a sacrifice for the holy cause. . . . I have seen, finally, entire pueblos offer all— their blood, their souls, their little property—their bread and the life of their children—in order to contribute to the triumph of democracy and the redemption of the pueblo.[3]

Thus wrote Ramón Mercado, the Liberal governor of Buenaventura Province during those heady times. Mercado, no doubt a romantic (as any good young nineteenth-century Colombian Liberal would have been), waxed grandiose about the masses and their support. His exuberance, however, should not be dismissed as either an overactive poetic sense or the more mundane desire of the powerful to feel the respect, and even the love, of those below. What Mercado saw, and what perhaps saved him from wasting in a Conservative jail, was the sealing of a pact establishing an alliance that would endure in the Cauca for the next three decades. With the law of 21 June 1851, Liberals had finally delivered on their promise to end slavery. Afro-Colombians repaid them with their blood.

This bargaining disturbed most Conservatives and many Liberals. They looked on it with apprehension at best, revulsion at worst, and a good deal of confusion at all times. Many simply did not understand what was transpiring. Politics, of course, had always involved the masses, even during colonial times, but especially after Independence. Conservatives could play the old game as well as, if not better than, Liberals. They knew how to marshal images of religion and order to excite their followers; knew how to encourage their retainers and peons to enlist in their ranks; knew how to manipulate the subtle exchange of favors and deference between patrons and clients; knew how to dragoon those peons who seemed less than eager to fight for the patron's cause. This was not what the Liberals were doing, however. They seemed to be actually campaigning for popular support, not on the merits of their persons or on the customary debts of allegiance that their followers owed them, but by promising certain programs and actions that they would implement once in power.

Conservatives simply did not know how to play this new political game in 1851 and, therefore, suffered a humiliating defeat in their rebellion of the same year. By the early 1850s, Liberals in the Cauca, both elite and popular, had forged a new type of politics, one based on republican bargaining, that was at the vanguard of democratic development in the Atlantic World. In the process, they reframed both how politics worked and what it meant to be a citizen. However, this political negotiation took hold in the Cauca Valley only because of the convergence of certain aspects of the Liberal program with the concerns and struggles of the valley's poor residents, particularly over slavery, common lands, liquor and tobacco production, and questions of deference. Also, both Liberals and Afro-Caucanos needed allies if either hoped to confront the powerful Conservative Party successfully. More so than other areas of the Cauca or Colombia as a whole, the Cauca Valley simmered with tension between those above and those below, between the masters and the slaves.

Oligarchs and the Pueblo

When the Liberals came to power in 1849, they encountered a situation in the Cauca that they could describe only as feudalism.[4] A small group of powerful families, primarily members of the new Conservative Party, controlled the region's economy and politics. Large haciendas dominated the floor of the Cauca Valley, most devoted to cattle, but some engaged in the more labor-intensive cultivation of cacao and tobacco. There were few people left in the valley who considered themselves Indians, but the remaining population was a heterogeneous mix of blacks, whites, mestizos, and mulattoes. The hacienda complex created both economic and political pressures on the valley's poor—the pueblo. The near monopolization of landholding and ranching's low demand for labor made it very difficult for them to eke out any sort of living, and what opportunities existed, such as tenancy, often came accompanied by political and social submission to a patron. Therefore, land and labor played a large role in the concerns of the valley's poor. The land question centered on access to ejidos, or old commons, that haciendas had been encroaching on since Independence. Subalterns also struggled against liquor and tobacco monopolies that excluded them from producing and selling those "necessities." All these struggles intertwined with the question of deference and the social debt that plebeians owed to the elite, especially their patrons. Almost all the valley's poor shared some of these concerns, but, for Afro-Colombians, by far the most pressing problem was the persistence of slavery.

Slavery dominated the lives of many of the valley's poor. Slaves had been struggling for freedom since their arrival in the New World, of course, but Independence gave them greater hopes and more possibilities to act on their desires. Some slaves secured their liberty by joining Bolívar's army; many others simply took their freedom by abandoning mines and haciendas during the chaos of war. The 1821 law of free birth promised freedom for future generations and gave hope to those presently enslaved. By the 1830s, however, initial expectations that abolition was nigh had dimmed, and slavery seemed unlikely to disappear soon. So, when the Liberals came to power in 1849, Afro-Colombians had renewed reasons to hope.

While Congress endlessly debated abolition and the details of the master class's reimbursement for the loss of their human property, slaves and their families took what initiative the law gave them. Congress had established *juntas de manumisión*, whose duties included enforcing laws concerning slave treatment, freeing the children of slaves who had reached adulthood, and raising money to manumit slaves. The law also allowed slaves to buy their own freedom (often with money from their relatives).[5] Caucano Afro-Colombians took advantage of the juntas, and, while the statistical evidence is very incomplete, it seems that, beginning in the summer of 1851, well before the 1852 general abolition, more slaves bought their freedom than were freed by their masters.[6] Slaves continued to buy their freedom even though they hoped and expected the state to liberate them soon anyway. Their noble efforts were an enormous drain on their few resources, reducing Afro-Colombians' ability to buy land after slavery or purchase the tools, food, and seeds necessary for migration to public lands to the north or along the coast after emancipation. Ironically, Afro-Colombians' self-purchase further enriched the master class, whom the freedpeople would now have to confront as tenants and day laborers.

The juntas proved largely ineffective at raising funds to free slaves. In Cali's province, the junta managed to free no slaves in the first year of its existence.[7] When the juntas did act, they rewarded masters handsomely, reimbursing them well above the market value; of course, these artificially high prices hindered slaves' ability to buy their own freedom. The Barbacoas junta paid out two thousand reales for slaves when the market price would have been sixteen hundred at most and probably far less.[8]

Afro-Colombians hoped that sympathetic Liberals, after coming to power in 1849, would enforce the existing laws on slavery. The law of free birth of 21 July 1821 made all children of slaves born after that date free, but these children had to live with and serve their parents' master until the age of eighteen. This requirement was odious enough. Worse, the authorities often selectively enforced the law of free birth. If slaves could not prove their age or that they had been born after 1821 when the law of free birth came into effect, they could not secure their freedom on reaching maturity. Afro-Colombians' suspicions of the Catholic Church were strengthened by the laxness or corruption of many priests responsible for parish birth records and, hence, the reckoning of to whom the law of free birth applied. In Micay's parish, a mining and slaveholding center, the priest recorded no slave births from 1821 to 1831.[9] José Esteban Raposeño, a slave of the Conservative leader Sergio Arboleda, protested that the priest of Caloto refused to give him his baptism record so that he could prove that he was born after the law of free birth and, therefore, was now free.[10]

Even more abhorrent than problems of proving one's age to secure freedom under the law of free birth were the provisions regarding children of slaves. While slavery would officially end on 1 January 1852, emancipation was decidedly incomplete, at least from many Afro-Colombians' point of view. The law left children born to slave parents before emancipation under the power of their former masters until the age of eighteen. Although not officially slaves, the children were bought and sold, their price at first rising as they grew older but then falling off as they neared eighteen years of age.[11] In the Conservative paper *Ariete*, one advertisement, next to another selling a horse, asked if any reader had a ten- to twelve-year-old *manumiso*—the term for the child of a slave held by a master—for sale.[12]

After turning eighteen, manumisos were not truly free; the state forced *libertos* (freedpersons) to contract themselves to someone for seven years. Although they would now be paid (but far, far below the market rate), the contract system basically ensured that forced labor would continue. Theoretically, libertos could contract with anyone, but corrupt local authorities and the threat of physical violence forced many to contract with their old masters. As sympathetic observers noted, the libertos often suffered worse than slaves, as masters now had no incentive whatsoever to protect their property. Libertos received the worst work assignments and even less food than slaves.[13] This titular freedom brought no new liberty.

Of course, as some Afro-Colombians struggled against the master class to ameliorate the brutality of slavery or secure their freedom through institutional means, others simply emancipated themselves. The Cauca, along with the area around Cartagena on the north coast, had long been a center of maroon activity. Conservatives, including the Borrero family, which dominated local politics in Cali, used the police to hunt down runaways.[14] *Marronnage* was a problem in all the Cauca's provinces, but the Palo region northeast of Popayán had become the most notorious haven for runaway slaves. Heavy forests and rugged terrain covered the Palo region near Caloto and the mammoth Japio and Quintero haciendas of the feared Arboledas. Runaway slaves were a serious problem in themselves, but the Palo maroons further angered the ruling class by engaging in fairly large-scale tobacco production and trade. Production and sale of tobacco, an official monopoly of the state, was permitted only by an auctioned permit. The poor particularly resented the monopoly on tobacco, as it was a crop that fetched good prices and required little capital investment.

Popayán's Conservative provincial government spent a great deal of its resources trying to destroy the contraband tobacco producers in the Palo region. The provincial authorities sent a small army into the mountains, hoping to destroy the illegally grown tobacco and return runaway slaves to their masters. In the summer of 1848, eleven sorties invaded the area, burning the dwellings and tobacco plants that they found. The troops did capture two maroons and two escaped prisoners while arresting two Indian contraband dealers and four others, including two women. More important, they claimed to have burned over fifty thousand tobacco plants, although that number is likely an exaggeration invented to make an operation that failed to reenslave the maroon community seem like a success.[15] While the material effects of the operation were questionable, certainly it further angered the Palo's contrabandists toward Conservatives.

Tobacco was not the only item produced by the poor that elites could pay the state to monopolize. Even more important was the monopoly on aguardiente (cane liquor). The contractholder had two options: forbid anyone else to produce or sell the liquor except for himself (or herself, as wealthy women invested in aguardiente too), or collect taxes on other producers. Small-scale distillation, using clay stills, was one of the few industries that plebeians could enter. Afro-Colombians relied heavily on moonshining and liquor sales, especially the valley's poor women, who dominated small-scale vending and production.[16] Plebeians had always detested the system, but the situation worsened significantly in 1848, when Rafael Troyano and his partners, who owned the contract in Popayán and Buenaventura Provinces, sought to raise the fee for small producers from three pesos annually to between twelve and fifty pesos. Worse, in Cali, Troyano forced vendors to buy from his own factory, but the liquor that he sold was contaminated with lead, which reputedly caused several fatalities. As with slaveholding, Conservatives dominated the aguardiente monopolies; Troyano was a Conservative, and one of his partners was the powerful hacendado Julio Arboleda.[17] The poor reacted to these monopolies by boycotting Troyano's liquor and tobacco, protesting police raids on their stills, and attacking and burning Troyano's stores. Troyano complained that the state needed to help him enforce his rights, while the poor resented the brutal methods used to enforce the monopolista's privilege.[18]

Not just economic privilege, but social privilege as well, galled subalterns. Equality was the most important element in popular liberalism, but, in the early 1850s, slavery, tenancy, and Conservatives' control of politics and society ensured, not only that most of the valley's poor were economically unequal, but also that they were often under the social control of others. Creditors and landlords could have their debtors thrown into jail at a moment's notice, and harsh laws punished vagrants and fleeing contract workers.[19] Hacendados could declare men or women vagrants and force them to contract themselves.[20] Contracted workers, by law, had the "duty to obey and respect the person with whom they agreed to serve, given that, by placing themselves under his dependence, they understand that they are now immediately subordinate."[21] Ramón Mercado lamented the total power that masters had over their human property, turning the slave quarters into "harems."[22] He and other Liberals described the social situation as no different than an aristocracy, with Conservatives expecting the rights and privileges due to their class.[23] Plebeians resented the haughtiness and arrogance of the valley's elite, their presumed dominance of the public sphere.

Land, however, sparked the most violent confrontations between elites and subalterns. As noted earlier, large haciendas dominated the Cauca Valley. In the early 1850s, the cantón of Cali had 140 square leagues of land, of which only twelve square leagues were baldíos (public land), these located in the hills above the town, not in the fertile valley below. While the county counted 19,277 residents, it had 56,000 cattle, which grazed on the great haciendas.[24] This situation made Cali's traditional ejidos (commons) crucial to the survival of many of the poor; indeed, Mercado claimed that over a thousand people used the land to graze their milk cows, sheep, and goats. Some actually lived on the ejidos and farmed small plots; many more gathered firewood there.[25] However, since Independence, neighboring hacendados had been seizing the ejidos and fencing them in, claiming the lands as their private property. By 1848, before the Liberals came to power, the situation reached the boiling point, and groups of men and women began destroying the fences that hacendados had erected in the ejidos.[26] The ejido dispute continued after the Liberal ascension when, in 1850 and 1851, popular liberals began openly to attack the powerful hacendados who coveted the commons—a violent eruption called the zurriago.

In all these struggles, a powerful slaveholding quasi aristocracy confronted the valley's subalterns. Along with Popayán's even more wealthy and powerful hacendados, such as the Mosquera and Arboleda clans, these oligarchs constituted the backbone of the Cauca's powerful Conservative Party. While the poor endured the brunt of Conservative rule, middling groups and even some wealthy families excluded from influence also chafed under the Conservatives' monopoly of power and state positions. In 1849, Liberals took power nationally, largely owing to division among Conservatives (called Ministeriales at this time) and the maneuvering in eastern Colombia of a potent group of young lawyers and hacendados eager to seize power and liberalize Colombia's economic and political life.[27] When José Hilario López took over the presidency, the centralized administration allowed him to appoint provincial governors, and the Cauca's own weak Liberals suddenly found themselves in power.

Most of the economically and politically influential families were Conservatives, a fact pointed out with pride by Conservative writers and grudgingly acknowledged by Liberals.[28] A Liberal writer noted how the opposition party held most of the land, land on which many poor people and slaves lived.[29] Although Liberals held national power by 1849, Conservatives, especially the extended Borrero clan, or those with conservative sympathies, dominated most local elected offices and owned most of the haciendas that surrounded the city. A few powerful landholders were Liberals; however, most of the Liberal Party's supporters were drawn from young men, who, while often highly educated, many being lawyers and professors, had less wealth.[30] Like their counterparts in Bogotá, these young professionals were inspired by the 1848 revolutions in Europe and hoped to refashion their society so as finally to escape colonialism's legacies. These men—such as Ramón Mercado, Eliseo Payán, and David Peña— sought to loosen the hacendados' grip on local politics and society.[31]

However, to do so, they would need some allies to counter the Conservatives' huge advantage in wealth and power. While I do not wish to slight the democratic, egalitarian, and romantic motives of many of the young Liberals, they also had a more prosaic incentive to reach out to the region's subalterns. The Cauca Valley's poor certainly had enough reasons to fear and hate prominent Conservatives. Liberals needed allies, allies they hoped they could marshal from among the poor of the city and its outlying areas, rallying them with a discourse of rights and citizenship. Liberals would pursue their risky strategy by creating a number of political clubs called Democratic Societies that would forever change the face of Caucano politics.

The Democratic Society of Cali

The Democratic Societies had begun in Bogotá but quickly sprang up around the country as the Liberal Party coalesced in the late 1840s. Cali's club started innocuously enough, as a vehicle to promote the election of the Liberal presidential candidate José Hilario López in the 1848 elections. Little in its beginning suggested the role that it would play in the mobilization of the Cauca's popular classes and in the history of Colombian democracy as a whole. The society began as an elite affair, as such clubs always had been. Men of liberal sympathies met on behalf of their candidate; most Colombians probably thought that this contest would be much like others in the past, fundamentally the concern of the powerful, the outcome possibly preordained. However, in Colombian society, a group of like-minded thinkers calling themselves Liberals had emerged, men who wished to gain power—for power's sake, of course, but also to institute a particular program. They had a plan, one that they viewed as eminently republican and democratic, that would break the old regime and position the Colombian nation at the forefront of the Atlantic World.

The Liberals' program consisted of many reforms, most based on what they saw as extending individual freedoms throughout Colombian society and, finally, decisively breaking with the colonial past.[32] They wanted to end economic monopolies and protections for domestic production, liberate large plots of land from religious and communal control, and, importantly, abolish slavery, all of which they thought would stimulate the economy. They sought political changes as well, planning to decentralize government, return power to municipalities, and increase the role that common people—common men to be exact—could play in society. In other words, they envisioned citizenship quite differently than the powerful in Colombia had imagined it before.

If electoral committees were not new, what the Liberals did when the elections ended was novel. After López won, the young Caleño Liberals did not dissolve their club; instead, they expanded it, with the intention of furthering the Liberal program. They imagined themselves creating a new society out of the colonial past that Independence had not fully vanquished. To build this new Colombia, they would first need to build new citizens, to break the powerful hold that centuries of colonial repression had on the minds of the poor. They would teach Cali's poor about their program, about liberalism, republicanism, and democracy. They would make the masses citizens.

They christened their club the Democratic Society of Cali, after a similar political club founded by artisans in Bogotá, and opened wide its doors, inviting one and all, by which, of course, they meant men. Perhaps to their surprise, certainly to the surprise of outside observers, the pueblo decided to attend. However, unlike in Bogotá and other Colombian regions, in Cali not just artisans but the poor in general and the workers on the surrounding haciendas of the countryside joined the club.[33] Ramón Mercado (a fiery orator and Buenaventura's appointed governor) noted that the Liberal Party was "composed almost exclusively of the scorned masses."[34] Conservatives delighted in noting that the club, and the Liberal Party in general, counted many blacks and mulattoes as members.[35]

The Liberals began a program of political education for the club's members. Orators expounded on the problems of the day. The literate read newspapers aloud. Every week, middling and elite Liberals held courses on the meaning of the constitution, the nature of democracy, the laws concerning elections, and the rights and duties of citizens.[36]

While Cali's Democratic Society was the most active and powerful of the political clubs, Liberals began to found new associations throughout the Cauca, especially in the valley. In Buga in 1850, Liberals established a Republican Society with an initial three hundred associates.[37] By 1851, Liberals had founded clubs in the valley towns and hamlets of Candelaria, Cartago (with over 350 members), Cerrito, Florida, Guacarí, Palmira, Roldanillo, San Pedro (with over 160 members), and Toro.[38] The size of the membership in the small village of San Pedro demonstrates that these were not just elite gatherings. In the southern highlands, clubs held meetings in Popayán, Puracé, and Pasto. In addition, artisans founded their own Liberal society in Popayán.[39]

Liberals did not rely on the Democratic Societies alone to diffuse their new ideas to their lower-class pupils. They also employed an institution closely linked to the Societies, the National Guard (regional militia). Members of the National Guard received, not just military training, but also what Ramón Mercado called "doctrinal exercises."[40] In order to join Cali's Democratic Society, one also had to be a member of the National Guard. After emancipation, Conservatives accused

Liberals of signing up "indiscriminately" all the freedmen for the militia.[41] The National Guard was doubly important to Liberals as a means of political mobilization: first, it served as a means of education, but, more important, it acted as a way of mobilizing supporters in the eventuality that politics extended to the battlefield.

Liberals also sought to turn the traditional power of public ceremonies—in the colonial period dominated by the church—to their advantage. On 7 March 1850, to celebrate the first year of López's administration and their party's triumph, Liberals around the Cauca organized grand public festivities. These fiestas included artillery salutes, music, parades by the National Guard carrying the national flag (or the tricolor, as Liberals liked to call it), religious ceremonies, and speeches. While elites organized the ceremonies, plebeians participated, especially those who were members of the National Guard. Suddenly, subalterns could take a very public place in the social life of the city. Liberals took advantage of their audience, and the centerpiece of these ceremonies left no doubt about the Liberal program and their hoped-for relationship with the pueblo. In Cali and Buga, the festivals' finales were ceremonies of manumission, during which masters freed their slaves.[42]

While, no doubt, Afro-Colombians were not particularly impressed by one or two slaves gaining their liberty while the majority still endured the whip, the ceremonies did begin to reinforce the idea that emancipation would be a Liberal accomplishment. As the juntas de manumisión collected more funds, they freed more slaves, and Liberals made sure that Afro-Colombians knew who was responsible for their emancipation. These ceremonies took place, not simply on the Liberals' new holiday, but whenever a number of slaves were to gain their freedom, throughout the Cauca and Colombia more generally.[43] In Micay, the junta coordinated the freedom of seventeen slaves, although two had paid their own price and others were free as they had reached the age of seventy. Again, there were parades, speeches about liberty, fraternity, and equality, and shouts of Libertad![44]

A similar spectacle in Cali was even more lavish and the symbolism even more obvious. Sunday, 2 February, began with a cannonade and the ringing of every church bell in town. Bands then marched through the city to call townspeople to the celebration. A parade began at the meeting hall of the Democratic Society; everyone of importance was to attend. The march left the hall, made up of the National Guard, carrying the flag, and the forty-six slaves who awaited their freedom. On arrival in the plaza, after more music and cannon fire, three chosen slaves, each bearing a standard with liberty, equality, or fraternity emblazoned on it, came forward to a table where the junta de manumisión presented them their certificates of freedom. As each new freedperson left the table, Liberal women placed a garland of flowers on his or her head. Then there were the requisite speeches celebrating the Liberal Party, followed by another parade back to the Democratic Society for more speeches. A fiesta in the central plaza closed the day.[45]

When, in October 1850 in Popayán, thirty-two slaves gained their freedom with the junta's funds, a similar public ceremony took place in the main plaza. Again, music, artillery salutes, and speeches enlivened the proceedings, all under the watchful eye of a portrait of President López brought out for the occasion. Afterward, the libertos (freedpeople) marched arm in arm with Liberal officials shouting vivas to the government while Conservatives looked on in horror.[46] Popayán—the center of the old colonial mining aristocracy and a stronghold of Conservative families and the church—was considered one of the most traditional cities in Colombia. Yet, in this bastion of power, built with lucre from mines worked by slaves, whites marched alongside blacks through the town. An alliance was developing, and Conservatives were not sure how to respond.

The Democratic Societies served as an important catalyst for the development of the alliance between lower- and upper-class Liberals. The clubs provided elites and plebeians with the terrain on which they could meet to build a shared discourse out of their respective popular and elite languages of republicanism, democracy, and rights. As Liberals were to discover, it would take more than language to gain the allegiance of the valley's poor. The Democratic Societies did establish a common ground on which the culture of republican bargaining might develop. However, the main reason for the Liberals' success was their willingness to negotiate with their popular allies over such concrete issues as slavery, monopolies, taxes, deference, and land.

Everyday Forms of Party Formation

Liberals' attempts to recruit subaltern allies and redefine republicanism began with the elections of 1848. These contests were not quite like elections in the past, at least for some Liberals. The partisans of Joaquín José Gori, the Ministerial aspirant (the Ministerials were embryonic Conservatives), stressed their candidate's personal merits and especially his piety as well as the danger that the election of General López would pose to religion and civilian rule. Conservatives also relied on the tried-and-true methods of political persuasion, patron-client ties, and plying supporters with food and drink—traditional electioneering.[47]

However, López's adherents not only stressed the qualities of their man but also spoke out about what he would do while in office. His followers promised such generalities as progress and equality but also went beyond those generalities to offer specifics, especially noting that they would ensure the poor's access to ejidos. An observer of the time noted that, in speeches, López's adherents claimed that their candidate would "break the chains with which the oligarchy has oppressed the pueblo."[48] This statement could be interpreted in many different ways by many different sorts of people, but such language would have been of particular interest to slaves.

Many elites reacted in horror to the Liberals' new campaign style. As early as the presidential campaign of 1848, the newspaper El Ciudadano complained that López's supporters had promised "the ignorant people of Cali" that, if elected, their candidate would return the ejidos to the people. The writer viewed this as basically unfair and dirty politics: "Such a way to influence elections is not appropriate for honorable citizens; . . . it shows that whoever uses it does not have the good of the country in mind, nor the glory of their candidate, but, rather, his own personal gain."[49] Campaigns should be run on the basis of undefined goals for the country and the personal merits of the candidates, not on the basis of specific promises made to individual interest groups (beyond, of course, the elite). The same paper also worried about the disorderliness of political parties in general and hoped that the new government would abolish them.[50] Such protests aside, López won, and he and the Liberal Party began to attract the interest of many of the valley's poor residents.

The debacle of the 1848 elections was bad enough, but Conservatives worried even more about the Liberals' disgraceful politicking after their victory. The newly founded Democratic Societies that began to pop up all over the region particularly dismayed Conservatives. Most Conservatives, however, lacked a plan to respond. Some, such as Julio Arboleda, simply refused to participate in this new form of politics. Arboleda wrote to the ex-president, Tomás Mosquera, a relative of his, expressing his bitterness about the new situation—"the spirit of the mob"—in which, to his thinking, the two of them would never participate.[51] But Arboleda was wrong. Mosquera, more astute than most Conservatives to the changes happening both inside and outside Colombia, understood the Liberal program, and he acted to counter it by imitating Liberal politics.

Mosquera suggested that the Caleños establish a society to counter the Liberals' Democratic Society. But the Conservative doyens still either would not or could not accept the new politics. As Mosquera suggested, they established the Society of Friends of the People, but Vicente Borrero noted that "all the men of order and that are worth something" had joined it. He added that the "manifest object of that society is to educate the masses and foment industry . . . but we have had as our principal goal to assure success in the elections." Borrero thought that the education of the masses was just for show. The Conservative society was basically an old-fashioned political machine, designed principally to prevent divisions among the Conservative elite.[52]

Borrero rather smugly noted that the Liberals "have not spared any means in order to gain followers and attract the pueblo to their designs." But he went on to assure Mosquera: "The men of influence and quality are with us."[53] Politics had been a gentleman's game, and no doubt Borrero thought that having a majority of the powerful and wealthy was sufficient to win any political contest; after all, it had been that way in the past. In Buga, the Conservatives also established a club to counter that town's Democratic Society, but, again, the organizers stressed that many of the ninety men who attended the first meeting were "the most notable of the cantón," along with "a few artisans and honorable laborers."[54] Soon, however, Conservatives would not be so dismissive of the pueblo or of Liberals' success at gaining the masses' allegiance.

Other Conservatives realized that they had to act "to end the influence over the masses" that the Liberals seemed to have.[55] Popayán's Conservatives sought to distribute money from government coffers to the poor after a fire swept through a neighborhood, an action that Liberals viewed as a cynical manipulation to gain supporters.[56] Charity, and the unequal give-and-take between patron and client, was a traditional method used by all politicians to maintain their retainers' loyalty. Conservatives seemed unable to understand, or unwilling to implement, the Liberals' strategy of educating the masses (establishing a common, shared discourse) while presenting their program to them in an open bid for support.

The theoretical foundation for this republican bargaining was that some Liberals had to some degree accepted that, at times, as elected representatives they must, not just rule as they thought best, but also govern as the people thought best, at least concerning some issues particularly important to the people. Liberal newspapers began to suggest that elected representatives could not simply do as they wanted but must also follow the will of the pueblo.[57] Indeed, some plebeians pressed this point, as did the petitioner who, asking for ejido land, noted that, now that Cali's cabildo was made up of "citizen patriots," it would "never betray the confidence" of the pueblo.[58] Conservatives reacted with disgust to a broadside that circulated in Cali stating similar ideas, sneering that, of those who had signed it, many were illiterate and had to have others sign for them. Conservatives asserted that representative democracy was not the same thing as pure democracy, which could never work in a society of conflicting interests.[59]

While Liberals did mainly govern for themselves and for those of their class, they now sometimes took into account their plebeian allies' desires, not just out of a sense of benevolence or charity, but because they felt that they theoretically should (in the republican system) and that they had to (or they would lose their allies' support). The blossoming of this new political culture, although incomplete and halting, resoundingly changed old understandings of politics, both those of Colombia's elites and those of its plebeians, as it altered the conception of whose interests should be considered important in the body politic. Also, perhaps fortuitously, many of the Liberals' concerns—abolishing slavery, freeing industry from monopolies, ending old forms of deference—coincided with many of the concerns of the valley's poor.

The Democratic Societies were the place where the theoretical program of elite Liberals and the struggles of popular liberals came together. In the clubs' meetings, Liberals began to make promises of what their administration would do and to listen to the concerns of the society's members. In short, the societies provided the locale where the Liberals hoped to implement their program. Ramón Mercado wrote to his president to report the progress that he had made in strengthening the Liberal Party and assure him that the masses were still under control. He urged López to push Congress to pass several key reforms, stressing the need to abolish slavery, increase the importance of the National Guard, end monopolies, make the judiciary more fair, "strengthen the principle of equality," and "procure land and industry for the poor classes."[60] Mercado more or less summed up the Liberal program to win over the masses of the central valley, especially Afro-Colombians: emancipation; aguardiente; equality; land. All were central preoccupations of popular liberals. Liberals then acted on many of these concerns, as the region's provincial governments, along with the national government, began to pass legislation concerning slavery, monopolies, taxes, and the role of the poor in society and politics in general.

From the time of Cali's Democratic Society's founding, its members heatedly discussed the aguardiente monopoly. The club particularly objected to how the liquor monopoly hurt "our women."[61] Five hundred of the club's members signed a petition demanding the dismantling of Buenaventura Province's monopoly system. They complained, not only that the tax hurt "the poor part of the nation" most, but that the violent methods used to enforce it—hired goons burst into poor women's homes looking for clandestine stills—violated their "most sacred rights." The signatories suggested that new taxes should apply to "citizens in proportion to their fortune."[62]

Liberals had long complained of abuses by the monopolistas. As early as 1848, a Liberal paper had suggested that small producers band together to confront Rafael Troyano in his efforts to raise the price of production permits.[63] By 1851, the national government had decentralized the national aguardiente monopoly, returning the tax to provincial control, with the expectation that many areas would abolish the tax. Compelled by the events of the zurriago and plebeians' staunch resistance to the liquor monopoly, the coastal and valley provinces began to eliminate the tax. The national government completely eliminated the tobacco monopoly.[64] The pueblo's desire to control their own livelihoods coincided with the Liberals' goal of "freedom of industry."[65]

Even after the Liberal regime had ended monopolies, the poor still faced harassment by unsympathetic authorities. Six residents of the mining town of Buenos Aires complained, not only that the parish alcalde had prevented them from selling their liquor to the workers at a local mine, but also that he had broken many of their jars and arrested a "poor woman."[66] The alcalde protested that he was only helping the mine administrator enforce order, noting that the "blacks" drank the aguardiente in "excessive quantities." It was a question, not just of trade, but of deference: the overseer had to maintain his authority. The alcalde added that, since the sale of aguardiente had been restricted, the miners worked harder and paid their rents on time.[67] His protestations fell on deaf ears; his boss, the *jefe político*, told him to allow the commerce and reminded him that his job was "to favor and protect the citizens in every class of industry throughout the district."[68] As in the petition from Cali's Democratic Society cited above, poor liquor vendors were now citizens, deserving of protection.

Liberals attacked, not just the monopoly system, but the whole method of taxation in the region. Most of the existing taxes were based on consumption (either sales taxes or monopolies), and, thus, the poor felt them considerably. Cali's Democratic Society sought to replace taxes on salt, meat, aguardiente, and tobacco with a progressive direct tax.[69] In 1852, Cali's provincial legislature established a new progressive direct contribution based on property, with nineteen different tax brackets, beginning with those who owned property worth 250 pesos.[70] Liberals in Popayán had tried to pass a similar law in 1850, but the Conservative legislature had defeated it.[71] Liberals had more success in ending many of the harshest statutes concerning vagrancy, often simply wiping old police laws off the books.[72]

Liberals used the Democratic Societies, not just to promote their own program, but also to lambaste the Conservatives and ensure that the pueblo knew their enemy. Liberals regularly contrasted the moral bankruptcy of the rich with the rectitude of the poor. In the Democratic Society, Liberals claimed that Conservatives believed that "the black and mulatto are not their equals."[73] They also said that Conservatives sought to limit public education to the rich only.

Some Liberals even embraced a discourse celebrating those of the "ruana" (poncho) versus those of the "casaca" (dress coat). Such open discussion of class and its prerogatives showed that some Liberals were at least sympathetic to the questions of deference that so concerned the poor.[74] Liberal papers also virulently opposed the law allowing imprisonment for debt. El Pensamiento Popular employed an explicit language of class, complaining that the hombre de casaca could go bankrupt with impunity but that "the poor hombre de ruana has wasted away in the jails for insignificant sums."[75] And Liberals blasted the taxation system, claiming that the poor paid proportionately more in taxes while the "aristocracy" enjoyed various "privileges" and paid less. They demanded a progressive system that would bring "equality." However, unlike the equality of classical liberalism, this equality was not just equality before the law. Liberals wanted a progressive taxation system under which the rich would pay more. They viewed their plan as establishing a "real equality."[76]

Such language raised plebeians' expectations concerning the all-important land question. Progress on the question of ejidos, however, was slow, although Cali's Democratic Society was generally supportive. By 1852—propelled by the events of the zurriago (described below)—an agreement had been reached, over the opposition of the Conservative Borrero family, that the haciendas in and near the old ejidos would give up one-third of their land to form new ejidos.[77] Plebeians began to send petitions to Liberals expressing their desire for land. Residents of Cali said that they had a "right to enjoy" the ejidos, citing "liberty, equality, and fraternity" in one petition.[78] While the question of ejidos was by no means settled, some plebeians did receive the right to farm the commons. Plebeians, including ex-slaves, pressed Liberals to enforce the agreement with the hacendados to turn over one-third of their haciendas. One petitioner noted that, now that the "cabildo is made up of residents directly named by the pueblo," it should ensure that the hacendados hand over the land.[79]

However, by 1852, the restoration of Cali's ejidos had still not been completed, owing to problems with the surveying. An official warned that the city should do whatever necessary to resolve "such a hazardous question and thus avoid it becoming the apple of discord that will produce immense problems in the future and engender eternal hatreds."[80] Liberals knew that the ejidos were a problem, yet their ideological program had little to say about such an issue. Indeed, Liberals, especially at the national level, generally sought to eliminate ejidos, viewing them as premodern communal landholdings, like Indians' resguardos.[81] Yet popular liberals were obsessed with ejidos and, apparently, discussed them frequently in the clubs. A Conservative noted that the "plebes" continually talked of "the possibility of taking over lands from the current propertyholders."[82] The Liberal paper El Pensamiento Popular suggested that any practice that increased inequality was unjust but that any that aspired "to divide between all men with more equality the common inheritance is divine."[83] Such talk raised the hopes of popular liberals, but elite Liberals had little chance of satisfying popular desires, even if that had been their goal. Nevertheless, despite the complete variance between elite Liberals' philosophy of landholding and the existence of ejidos, many of the valley's Liberals supported the continued existence of the commons. Popular concerns had forced Liberals to adapt their philosophy in order to satisfy their lower-class allies. Land would always be the most difficult point of contention between elite and popular Liberals, eventually shattering the alliance between them, but, by 1852, some of the Caleño subalterns' most immediate concerns over the ejidos had been addressed.

If not with the land questions, Liberals did succeed most spectacularly in satisfying popular desires with the question of abolition. Before emancipation was achieved, ending slavery gave Liberals the most concern, as it was the centerpiece of their program, both ideologically and practically, that is, as a means of securing alliances with the poor. Congress's failure to abolish human bondage and the increasing militancy of the valley's masses by 1851 worried Liberals with ties to subaltern allies and those sympathetic to the slaves' plight.[84] These men, like Ramón Mercado, fretted over their position as interlocutors with the pueblo. They had made certain promises, and the people seemed inclined to hold them to their word. Perhaps more important, the increasingly bold attacks on Conservatives, and property in general, risked alienating many moderate Liberals. Mercado and his friends needed something to reassure the masses that progress was being made and that the leaders had not betrayed the followers, or perhaps the Liberals would no longer lead. Mercado knew that the valley's residents were particularly anxious about abolition, as they had now been waiting for the Liberals to act since 1849, three long years.[85]

Liberal leaders did their best to reassure Afro-Colombians. José María Obando, a rebel leader in an earlier civil war that had developed antislavery connotations, spoke in Buga at a Liberal political rally. A Conservative paper mocked the greeting that the pueblo gave him, noting: "At the entrance to the city a great number of blacks and vagrants waited for Obando." (The paper sneered that "a loathsome and despicable black women named la Maravilla" hugged him on his arrival and further insinuated that la Maravilla entered Obando's lodging that night.) Obando promised the assembled that he was working so that the current Congress would finally pass the law to abolish slavery.[86] López himself urged Congress to act in March 1851, noting that slaves "craved the liberty so many times sensed in the republican atmosphere."[87]

The Liberals' program was conscious and premeditated, and their plan to ally with the lower classes was not simply conducted by a few middling radicals or on a whim. Not all middling and elite Liberals grasped this new politics (the political parties were not formally organized at this time, and members' views were not necessarily uniform); in more traditional Popayán and further south, many Liberals confined their political activity to the elites or building patron-client ties.[88] But a core group of Liberals, especially in the valley, seemed much more willing to engage with the pueblo and hoped to unite many of the poor behind them. They arrogantly viewed the Indians as too barbarous and religious for an alliance and noted that many poor mestizos had close personal, clientelist ties to Conservatives. One group already hated Conservatives, the Afro-Colombians, as most (but certainly not all) of the great slaveowners were Conservatives. The Liberals thought that, if they could take credit for ending slavery, they could secure a large number of allies for future electoral or military struggles. The Liberal priest and politician Manuel María Alaix remarked: "The slaves who lose their chains bring to society gratitude for the government that has lifted the yoke off them."[89]

Alaix, however, did not just imagine some indefinite support and goodwill. He had more immediate concerns in mind, such as the upcoming elections. He wrote to President López: "The complete extinction of slavery is the magnum work to which we must consecrate all our efforts: twenty-seven thousand men who become citizens weigh something in the electoral balance."[90] While most freedmen would not be able to vote under the literacy and property requirements, some would. More important, along with ending slavery, many Liberals hoped to amend the constitution and redefine citizenship to include all men, regardless of literacy, property, or social standing. Alaix and his fellow Liberals imagined a dedicated voting bloc to counter Conservatives' traditional electoral advantage.

Even after abolition, many Liberals were eager to attend to Afro-Colombians' concerns. As described above, 1 January 1852 did not find all slaves freed. The manumisos (children of slaves) were still under the masters' power. Afro-Colombian parents turned to Liberal authorities to try to secure freedom for their children.[91] A Liberal Caleño wrote to López, urging him to free the "slaves called manumisos," adding that such action would "strengthen public opinion."[92] Not waiting on the national government, Ramón Mercado decided that, since the law recognized the power of fathers over their children, that right superseded the law concerning slave children. Therefore, legitimate children would be free of their masters, which unfortunately affected only a few (while showing again Liberal commitment to the family as a basis for citizenship).[93] On the coast, the Liberal governor J. N. Montero pleaded with the national government to alleviate the plight of the manumisos and return them to their parents, noting that, by such action, the Congress would "form citizens truly free and addicted to the regenerating principles of the epoch."[94] For Caucano Liberals, emancipation equaled political support.

Liberals also sought to end the practice of forcing libertos to contract themselves from the age of eighteen to the age of twenty-five. They asserted that, as free men were citizens at the age of twenty-one, libertos should not be subject to this forced contract labor.[95] Liberals in Barbacoas also maintained that the overly steep rents that freedpeople had to pay to keep using the mines and the surrounding lands were akin to slavery. They tried to claim that the land around the mines did not really belong to the titular mineowners as they had only colonial use rights to the land granted by the Spanish king, which meant that the land now belonged to the nation. Needless to say, the owners were outraged, calling such a ploy *socialism and communism*.[96] Conservatives accused Barbacoas's governor of telling slaves that they did not have to pay rents on the lands that they worked.[97] Similar disputes took place in the mines near Almaguer, with the former slaves appealing to Liberal officials for aid.[98]

After the civil war, when abolition finally occurred, Liberals did not risk subtlety when they informed the freedpeople to whom they owed thanks for their liberty. At a ceremony in Almaguer, the local official noted that "there could not be a true republic where slavery exists." He went on to ask the crowd: "Who is it that made you equal before the law? The government, the democratic government of Nueva Granada."[99] In Barbacoas, three thousand people gathered for a ceremony of mass emancipation. Governor J. N. Montero told the assembled that they owed their respect to the "citizen general José Hilario López, who had fought so tenaciously and with such dedication to assure for them their liberty and to return to them their rights as free men." Montero applauded the crowd's shouts of approval, basking in "the sentiment of gratitude [that] has been established in all hearts and how one finds everyone disposed to the defense and sustenance of the government under whose regime they obtained the long-dreamt-of good of liberty." The ceremony ended with vivas to liberty, the president, and the governor.[100]

Ramón Orejuela grimly acknowledged the Liberal strategy to win over Afro-Colombians. First, Liberals had promised to end slavery. Then they had voided the forced contracts between masters and ex-slaves, as such contracts "gave some influence to the landowners." Now the Liberals had offered the freedpeople "division of the lands, and they [the masses] are so persuaded by this promise that now they considered themselves absolute owners of the lands."[101]

Conservatives feared the Liberal program but generally reacted to Liberal activities simply with disgust. As they did the Liberals' election strategy, Conservatives viewed this republican bargaining as extremely unstable. In Popayán, Conservatives also disdainfully noted how the Liberals worked "to pervert the people of the pueblo," by showing concern and attempting to gratify the interests of the masses.[102] Other Conservatives acknowledged Liberal success but denigrated the race and class of their opponents' new allies. Julio Arboleda ridiculed popular liberals as "blacks that run around armed through the streets of Cali." He insultingly referred to them as *barbarians* and *criminals*.[103]

The cleric Alaix defended the Liberals' plebian allies while issuing a prescient warning to Conservatives about their increasingly open plans to test the Liberals in armed struggle. Responding to Arboleda's ridicule of popular liberals as ex-slaves, criminals, and uneducated savages, Alaix responded: "Those manumitted blacks, those ignorant men, are the best National Guards that the Republic counts as members because they will not flee on the day of danger."[104] The next year, 1851, would prove Alaix correct.

Popular Liberals' Offensive

In the course of only a few years, popular and elite Liberals had redefined the nature of politics in the Cauca. Through the venue of the Democratic Societies, elites and subalterns had begun to negotiate openly over the future of the region's society, politics, and even economy. They had transformed bargaining from a private, sporadic, and largely local way of working out conditions on sites of production to a public and sustained experiment in republican politics. The success of republican bargaining and the Liberals' impassioned democratic rhetoric greatly inflated the expectations of the valley's poor. By 1850, many of the important gains noted above, especially the abolition of slavery, had not yet come to pass. Yet popular liberals felt their own growing power and sensed that, with their Liberal allies controlling the state, they need not wait for others to guide them; instead, they took the initiative and attacked the master class in a movement known as the zurriago.

Initially, elite Liberals did not worry about their new allies pursuing independent action. They were confident that they would be able to mold the masses into a political force, one that they would lead. The newspaper El Pensamiento Popular commented on the new politics, noting that "all attempts to excite the masses emotionally are futile because each citizen now knows how to think and discuss" and that the masses will follow those that promise "to work for [their] emancipation."[105] Before 1848, Liberals had seen the masses as a problem—stupid, illiterate, gullible. The paper's writers saw the new politics as a result of the masses' new political savvy, inculcated by people like themselves. While Liberals thought that the masses finally had learned to resist the enticements of the clergy and the aristocracy in favor of their own interests, popular liberals' enthusiasm may, instead, have been a reflection of Liberals' own changing style of political mobilization. I do not want to deny that, in those few years around 1850, subalterns did internalize a great deal of new ideas in the Democratic Societies. However, beyond the supposedly new commitment of the masses to liberty, equality, and fraternity lay the new, and surprisingly successful, efforts of middling and elite Liberals to mobilize those masses in support of a (somewhat) shared political project. Subalterns responded so eagerly because they now sensed an opening that would allow them to enter politics and because the new language of liberal republicanism that both popular and elite Liberals had created together resonated so strongly with plebeians' social visions and hopes.

Liberals generally were sure that they could control their newly mobilized plebeian allies, but Conservatives were not so sanguine. Conservatives knew the dangers of exciting subalterns with talk of liberty and equality; after all, they would be the ones feeling the sting of the whip if the Liberals lost control. They feared the repercussions of the Democratic Societies' lessons about democracy, especially rights talk. One Conservative writer claimed that Liberals were corrupting the pueblo, "filling them with exaggerated ideas of their legitimate rights."[106] Another worried about the consequences of the Democratic Societies' definition of the pueblo. He complained that, instead of teaching that the pueblo includes all members of society, "they [the clubs] make them [their members] believe that the pueblo is only the most poor, uneducated, miserable, and abject class of society; that the rest of the citizens are not the pueblo, but, rather, enemies against whom it is necessary to make war."[107] Conservatives worried that, owing to the Liberals' teachings, and with the Liberal state and party as allies, the valley's subalterns might act to impose their own views of equality and democracy. They were right.

Cali's poor took the opportunity that the Liberals' victory provided in order to gain revenge on Conservatives, whom they viewed as arrogant and haughty slaveowners who sought to monopolize any hope that the poor had for a better life—be it tobacco, moonshine, or the ejidos. With sympathetic Liberals occupying at least some of the important local offices, the valley's subalterns began to realize that the poor need not fear the rich quite so much. Conservatives angrily commented on the decline in respect showed them by their social inferiors, complaining that plebeians openly insulted them in Cali's streets.[108] The pueblo had begun to claim public space as their right too, inspired by the Liberals' parades. Now demonstrators regularly marched through town at night, shouting vivas to Liberals and insulting Conservatives.[109] Part of popular liberals' newfound assertiveness came from their alliance with the ruling Liberals, the strength of the Democratic Societies, and the lessons learned at the clubs. However, there was also a more material factor. Many of the valley's poor now had firearms. Subalterns had particular interest in joining the National Guard as they often got to keep their assigned weapons. Elites, both Conservative and Liberal, would rail for years about the need to recover the state's arms from the people, but it was too late.[110] Peasants who seemed so deferential to the armed gentleman on his charger one day seemed much less so the next when toting a rifle.

During 1850, attacks on Conservatives increased from mere insults to physical assaults. Conservatives blamed the attacks on Liberal demagogy, this new politics that Liberals employed to rally the masses and inflame their passions with unbridled talk of democracy and rights. Liberals had perverted the poor with their political clubs, the Democratic Societies.[111] The modern historian has an entrée into the meetings of the Democratic Societies since their middling and elite leaders wrote about them. However, the new politics and ideas spread through much more ordinary contact as well, of which only hints survive. Common sense tells us that surely subalterns discussed all that they had heard at the clubs once back at home, at work, and, of course, in the bars and gaming halls that they frequented.[112] Perhaps not surprisingly, Cali's Democratic Society sometimes met in the cockfighting house.[113] Beyond the discourse of republicanism, what plebeians heard in the clubs were direct challenges to the economic and political system that existed in the Cauca, particularly the system of landholding.[114] With this discursive support, popular liberals thought that they could implement their own ideas of equality and contest the hacienda system. Ramón Mercado noted that just because the people could not always eloquently express their political ideology did not mean that they did not have one: "The pueblo has a prodigious instinct to comprehend its fears and inclinations, but not to explain them, except through action."[115] Cali's poor were ready to act, ready to challenge the authority of the hacendados, to try to turn the world upside down.

In late 1850 and early 1851, the nightmare of every slaveowner exploded out of elites' fears into reality: former slaves turned the lash on their old masters, whipping them in the very streets of Cali. Those same elites called this eruption the zurriago or perrero after the symbol of slavery they had wielded so long—the whip. The zurriago began in December 1850 with another round of fence destruction in Cali's ejidos. Soon, however, plebeians became more violent, flogging Conservatives whom they found out at night. The zurriago spread throughout the valley, centered around Cali and Palmira, but extending as far north as Cartago and to the south around Caloto and Santander.[116] The immediate goal was the reclaiming of Cali's and other cities' commons, but the perreristas (participants in the zurriago) also seemed eager to challenge the distribution of landed property in general. Perhaps eight hundred to a thousand people joined in destroying the fences of Cali's ejidos; women also participated, seizing what little political space they could in that moment of crisis.[117] Conservatives claimed that the destruction of fences extended nine leagues from the city.[118] The question of ejidos and the question of slavery were not distinct in the minds of many popular liberals. In Palmira, the groups that destroyed the fences of nearby haciendas also called for abolition.[119]

Perreristas probably were a cross section of Cali's poor, but commentators noted that many were former slaves.[120] One observer blamed the depredations on "the black race, who are so abundant and cruel in this country." This same individual noted that the weapons distributed by the government, both firearms and lances, had made the marauders even bolder as now they ventured out during the day.[121] Hacendados hid indoors at night, but often this did no good. Conservatives and some Liberals deliriously reported the increasingly violent actions of the roving bands of perreristas. They accused the perreristas of murder, robbery, and arson. Perreristas broke fences, destroyed property, and laid waste to the countryside, even ransacking the hacienda of the Conservative leader Vicente Borrero. Commentators reported that the perreristas whipped and beat anyone whom they identified as opposing them, including young children, and that armed men broke into houses and raped the daughters of Conservatives in the presence of their families.[122] For former slaveholders, the whippings and physical assaults must have been the most dreadful. A group of Caleños, begging ex-president Mosquera to come to their aid, bitterly reported that the "vandals" attacked them "with the lash and club as if we were beasts."[123]

Even radical Liberals expressed outrage at such events. Some worried that

Republican Bargaining 81

the Democratic Societies spent too much time talking about rights and not enough time emphasizing "law and authority."[124] Other Liberals denied responsibility for the zurriago, claiming that it was not organized attacks of popular liberals against Conservatives but only personal vendettas, the perpetrators of which the government would attempt to prosecute.[125] In particular, they denied that the gangs had raped anyone and challenged victims to come forward, doubtless confident that the mores of honor would prevent any woman from doing so.[126] When Liberals did admit that crimes had been committed, they absolved the government of any responsibility and promised that they were working hard to restore order.[127]

Yet, even when Liberal officials made attempts to suppress the bands, the results were counterproductive, at least from the Conservative point of view. In late March 1851, Antonio Matéus led a patrol to pacify the countryside around Palmira, where roving perreristas had destroyed many fences and flogged hacendados and their families. He first ran into vigilantes trying to defend their property, whom he ordered dispersed as they had not been called up by the government. The company marched around the countryside for a few days, finding nothing, but imposing themselves on the nearby haciendas for victuals. Matéus, with no little embarrassment, had to report that his own troops contributed to the zurriago as one night they caught and whipped a Conservative whom they accused of planning to poison them![128] Matéus could not even control his own troops, let alone stop the zurriago. Despite Liberals' protestations to the contrary, officials throughout the valley arrested few people, and sympathetic comrades quickly broke the accused out of jail.[129]

However, many Liberals did not totally separate themselves from events. Some acknowledged the destruction of fences but blamed Conservative resistance at returning the ejidos to the people, correctly noting that disputes over the ejidos had existed long before the Liberal Party had come to power.[130] One observer went further, arguing that Conservatives now reaped what they had sown, attributing the zurriago to "the division of property" and the history of slavery in the region. This observer noted that the "theory of equality" had caused the pueblo to remember the long history of abuse suffered and to lash out.[131] Mercado and the Democratic Society blamed the numerous insults heaped on the masses by the "oligarchs" and the threats made by the Conservative Society of the Friends of the People against the Liberal administration.[132] Mercado presented a list of reasons for the disturbances—the ejidos, the aguardiente monopoly (especially the recent arrest of two poor women for contraband), anxiety over whether and when abolition would occur, taxes, old resentments, and the general cruelty of hacendados to their tenants.[133]

Mercado's analysis of events was prescient, correctly divining, not just the economic, but also the social roots of the popular uprising. If we can "read in reverse" Conservatives' interpretations, it seems that the poor wanted to create a communal landholding situation along with a radical social leveling.[134] The actions of the perreristas certainly reflect a moment that they thought opportune for implementing their ideas of a truly democratic republican system in which equality reigned. Of course, the perreristas sought revenge for the centuries of terror that they had endured at the hands of master and hacendado. But, beyond settling old scores, they sought land and economic livelihood through liquor and tobacco production, which would give them economic, political, and social liberty. They sought to assert that, in their republic, the hacendado would not so carelessly lord it over those below. They sought to end the slave system, not just the direct enslavement of some of their brethren, but the whole hacienda slave complex of economic dependency and social deference. Across Colombia, the poor, especially Afro-Colombians, shared similar dreams, yet the zurriago was unique to the Cauca. In the southwest, popular liberals had some hope of success, sensing the changed political atmosphere that they had created via their alliance with elite Liberals in the Democratic Societies.

The situation became intolerable for many elite Conservatives. Contrabandists ignored Conservatives' dearly bought monopolies, almost openly peddling home brews. Hooligans knocked down their fences and set ablaze their country homes. Plebeians whom they met in the street paid them no heed, no respect, or, even worse, they insulted them. More distressing, the streets—streets that they had once owned—seemed no longer to be theirs; blacks and mulattoes regularly took them over, shouting vile slogans. Plebeians marched in parades to celebrate the Liberal Party or fete manumitted slaves. But most horrible were those new freedpeople and the threat that they posed. The unbearable scenes of their fellow gentleman, or, almost unimaginable, "their" women, being whipped by black men, whom Conservatives no doubt imagined as their former slaves, was simply too much to bear. The hacendado Ramón Orejuela cried: "We are in the epoch of the terror, and our throats are threatened with our slaves' knives."[135] Ironically, in their "slave" tormentors, Conservatives found their own rallying cry. They would rather die free than live as slaves to the terror.[136] They rose in revolt.

The 1851 Civil War

In April 1851, Conservatives around the Cauca and the nation entered into armed revolt, often in piecemeal fashion, against López's government. In the Cauca, they were easily and decisively defeated by troops made up of Liberal partisans, mostly, it seems, volunteers. The lengthy quote from Ramón Mercado offered early in this chapter is from this period, a grateful homage to the people who had come to the Liberals' rescue. Conservatives had dominated Caucano politics and society for years, yet popular and elite Liberals vanquished them with surprising ease. How did this come to pass?

The zurriago had frightened Conservatives like nothing in their living memory; it seemed to them as if the world had turned upside down. It was not just the perreristas' actions, as terrible as those were, that drove Conservatives to revolt. The attitude of many Liberal officials was equally worrisome as these representatives of the state seemed decidedly nonchalant in the face of the attacks, or perhaps even implicated in them. They certainly did not seem to be vigorously pursuing the perreristas. Worse, the contest over ejidos and the hacienda system threatened their very idea of landed property; meanwhile, the state now intended to take away their human property through abolition, with perhaps only the promise of indemnification, a promise not worth much given the Colombian treasury's pathetic pecuniary resources. In a word, they feared communism.

While modern observers can easily dismiss this talk as hysterical rhetoric, the Colombian state and the Liberal Party seemed not to be following the tenets of nineteenth-century liberalism at all but, instead, to be intent on seizing and redistributing property. Conservatives did suffer massive capital loss after abolition. Mosquera noted that one mine near Popayán was worth fifty thousand pesos before emancipation but only twelve thousand after, as thirty-eight thousand of the capital had been in slaves.[137] Ex-slaves refused to work for their former masters or to pay rents on the lands that they now thought they owned on the hacienda. Vicente Arboleda railed that Liberals had filled the heads of "blacks" with "the ideas of communism of the land."[138] Many elites also understood the attacks on ejidos as the poor desiring "communism of the land."[139] They saw the drive for abolition in much the same terms.[140] The state was going to take their property, the slaves, and give that property to others, namely, the slaves themselves. Conservatives feared that they would be ruined if Congress passed a law freeing slaves without indemnification for slaveowners.[141] Conservatives cited the terror of the zurriago, particularly the destruction of fences and whippings, as the reason for their revolt, which they saw simply as a necessary move to protect their property and persons. After the rebellion, many Conservatives' legal defense was that they had organized to prevent the perreristas from attacking them, not in revolt against the government.[142]

In their efforts to mobilize followers sympathetic to their cause, Conservatives did not put forward a program of their own but simply attempted to instill in the masses a fear of Liberals' intentions. When Conservatives did talk about recruiting the pueblo and instructing them, they tended to do so only as an immediate response to Liberals. The newspaper *Ariete* noted that Buga's Society of Friends of Order would teach the pueblo "the true meaning of the words liberty, equality, and democracy." It would "combat the antisocial principles of communism, immorality, and impiety in religious matters."[143] The society's founders would have to instruct the pueblo, if only in order to counter Liberal heresies. They also promised to work against vagrancy and drunkenness. Conservatives would reveal Liberals' enticements and lies and discipline the pueblo at the same time. While the choice of Friends of Order as the name for the society reflected mainly elite Conservatives' fears of popular liberals' growing assertiveness, order would come to be very attractive to many popular groups, even if in the early 1850s its appeal was limited.

In the southern highlands, however, Conservatives benefited from the Liberals' arrogance and racism. The Indians of the south greatly feared Liberals' attempts to divide their resguardos and convert their lands into private property, a tenet of the Liberal program, following the theory that disentailment would stimulate land markets and free property for productive uses. In 1848, Indian villages began to send petitions begging local and national authorities not to implement plans to divide resguardos. Indians feared that, with division, their lands would be snapped up owing to the "ambition of the whites."[144] They argued that, while perhaps not right for all, the "community of goods" fit their habits and customs and protected their families. They also pledged to support the government if called on.[145] The Liberals, however, confident in their program, were not interested.

Governors appointed by López seemed to have little sympathy for Indians' resguardos and traditions. Joaquín Garcés, the governor of Túquerres, complained that Indians came to his office every day to protest abuses. He asserted that only the rich Indians benefited from the resguardos as they allotted all the good land to themselves, implying that only those wealthy Indians opposed the division of the communal lands. The next year, Garcés went further and called for the partition of the resguardos and the redistribution of the land to the Indians as private plots. He noted that this would free from "slavery" those Indians who had to work as contract laborers on haciendas while the rich Indians controlled all the good land; further, some of the divided land would go to support primary education.[146] The governor of Pasto proposed a scheme that would have immediately divided the resguardos, chopping off 20 percent of the land, half awarded to the surveyor and half to support schools.[147] The governor of Popayán supported dividing the resguardos as well; he claimed that this would end the rivalry "between whites and Indians."[148] Also, Liberals supported a law codifying a principle similar to eminent domain that allowed towns to seize lands from Indians if doing so was necessary for the town's growth. Many villages around Popayán quickly took advantage of this opportunity and seized parts of the resguardos.[149] While Liberals made exceptions for the valley's ejidos because of their bargaining with popular liberals, they insisted that the Indians' resguardos become modern, individual private property.

When the Conservatives were in power, they had made at least cosmetic efforts to prevent Indians' exploitation by their neighbors.[150] Conservatives accepted, as they did not with Afro-Colombians, that Indians were an important part of society, if not yet always as citizens. In the dispute over land around coastal mines mentioned above, Conservatives chastised Liberals for their obsessive pandering to the blacks. They noted that the Liberals should be more concerned with the welfare of Indians, who "are Granadinos and deserve more than the Africans."[151]

By early 1851, many Conservative leaders were plotting to revolt. Julio Arboleda's hacienda La Bolsa was the center of the intrigue.[152] Conservatives around the Cauca began trying to marshal as much support as possible for their coming uprising. If, by 1851, the republican bargaining between Liberals and their plebeian allies had cemented their alliance in the Cauca Valley, in the southern highlands Conservative elites still relied on more traditional methods of mobilization. Conservatives focused on Liberals' attacks on religion, marriage, and property. While elite Conservatives rebelled for many reasons—to regain power, to keep their slaves, to limit the opening of politics, and to protect religion—in their attempts to mobilize the masses they mostly focused on the Liberals' godlessness; beyond the Cauca, religion may have been the most important motivation for Conservatives.[153] This strategy had been a traditional method of mobilizing popular conservatives, and there seemed to be no reason why it should fail now. Led by the archconservative slaveowner Julio Arboleda, the Conservatives went from village to village throughout the highlands seeking recruits for their planned rebellion. In Indian villages, they spoke out against the godless *rojos* (reds [Liberals]), who had expelled the Jesuits, would destroy the church, and planned to profane the sacrament of marriage.[154] López's expulsion of the Jesuits had angered many Conservatives and equally dismayed many Indians. Conservative southerners drew up massive petitions, signed by over sixteen hundred people, begging López not to expel the Society of Jesus.[155]

Liberals fulminated against what they saw as Conservatives' slander and feared that Indians would see them as profaning religion. Liberals, whose writings were filled with allusions to the sacred, may have thought of themselves as anticlerical but certainly not antireligious. Nevertheless, Liberals continually ranted about Indians' simpleminded faith and obedience to the church, an obedience that Conservatives perhaps took for granted. Even though Liberals had the support of some priests, many Caucanos viewed the activities of Liberal clerics with suspicion in the south: two priests who supported the Liberal Party earned the nicknames "Calvino" and "Lutero" among the Pastusos.[156]

The Indians of the south were alarmed by the increasingly hostile debate over religion and the role of the church in Colombian society. Throughout the colonial epoch, the church had been an ally—if often unreliable—against the designs of the hacendados. López's expulsion of the Jesuits no doubt shocked them. However, some Liberals' desire to secularize marriage struck even closer to the Indians' concerns. Conservatives took any opportunity to impugn Liberals' views on marriage and the family, reporting that a Liberal official in Puracé had raided a dance and stolen off with some of the young girls. Referring to the incident, one newspaper sarcastically exclaimed: "¡¡¡Viva el comunismo!!!"[157] Marriage and the family—sanctified by religion—were the bases of popular indigenous conservatism, undergirding the communalists' identity as Indians and, therefore, both their culture and their holding of communal lands. While elite Conservatives simply hoped that Indians would be righteously enraged by Liberals' disrespect of the church, Indians themselves saw in Liberals' actions much more than that. Liberals seemed to them to be assailing, not just the church, but the whole ideological and structural system on which their society rested. Conservatives warned that Liberals wanted to end all religion and raze all the churches and threatened that the Liberals' communism would affect not just the rich, that they would take the livestock of even the smallest farmers and redistribute it to those that had none.[158] Indians' resguardos, always legally precarious, now seemed threatened again. As one Liberal succinctly put it, clerics had motivated the south's masses, "preaching the defense of religion, of their women, and of their properties."[159]

Conservatives did not need to bargain directly with their Indian allies. Perhaps without exactly understanding why, Arboleda and his cronies succeeded in mobilizing many Indians by stressing Liberals' attacks on religion and property. Both these threats would have been supremely effective in animating Indians against the Liberals. Conservatives seemed to have some support in the south among Indians and other smallholders, but, more important, they thought that the zurriago had made all the wealthy class sympathetic to their cause. With emancipation drawing near, in April 1851 they revolted.

Conservatives were unhappily surprised, however. The reaction of the valley's plebeians amazed even the most militant Liberals. Popular liberals rushed to the Liberal standard with a zeal that shocked most observers in the valley. Liberals made sure that their popular allies knew the Conservative rebels' designs, namely, to roll back all the gains made in the past few years. The newspaper published by Cali's Democratic Society proclaimed that the Conservative rebels wanted to eliminate plebeians from politics and ensure that tobacco and aguardiente remained monopolies. It added that all the rebels were slaveholders too.[160] J. N. Montero noted: "The blacks knew that the revolution had, in part, the object of impeding their liberty, and they let it be known that they were ready at any moment to go and fight for their freedom and that of their children."[161] Liberals also reminded the poor of the Conservative Julio Arboleda's bloodthirstiness in the last civil war (1839–42), when he had hung many Afro-Colombian soldiers who had enlisted in rebel armies hoping for a chance at freedom.[162]

Liberal volunteers quickly assembled as rumors of the revolt spread. When the call went out to defend the government, the response was quick: two thousand men assembled in Cali, six hundred in Palmira, five hundred in Santander, two hundred in Celandia.[163] The areas where Liberals enjoyed the most support and that provided the most volunteers were the areas where Afro-Colombians lived, areas where the zurriago had raged, areas where Liberals' success with the abolition of slavery and monopolies, of changing traditional power relations, was most appreciated. The political clubs served the Liberals well; Mercado noted that the "Democratic Societies serve as the base for the organization of the National Guards."[164]

In the valley, the Conservative rebellion centered on Caloto, a conservative town and rival of the nearby liberal Santander.[165] After defeating the first Conservative forays into the valley, six hundred Liberal volunteers went south to confront Conservatives in the highlands. After reaching Popayán, about half left the camps and returned home, having been ordered to Pasto, too far away for many popular liberals. Liberals did not control their troops, often having to rely on soldiers' willingness to fight. Luckily, over two hundred new volunteers replaced the deserters.[166]

By July, Conservatives had once again tried to invade the valley, but Liberals had one thousand men under arms, including the "blacks of the Dagua," and handily defeated the rebels—no mean feat since, even though the rebels numbered only four hundred, most were mounted. When the Conservatives attacked Palmira with around 250 men, Liberal defenders again counted on over a thousand troops. More volunteers then went north to put down the revolt in Antioquia, the heartland of Conservatism, where the hated Caleño slaveowner Eusebio Borrero directed rebel forces.[167]

In the closing days of the war, Liberal armies occupied the Arboledas' massive Japio hacienda, a symbol of the Cauca oligarchy's landed power. Earlier that same year, the hacienda counted 242 "slaves," as the overseer described them, although some were the children of slaves or those under obligatory contracts (all still property in the master's eye).[168] Local plebeians particularly hated Julio Arboleda, considered by many to be extraordinarily bloodthirsty (today his ghost is rumored to roam the mountains near Japio, seeking absolution for his many sins).[169] Troops from the valley and from the nearby town of Santander took control of the plantation, and, for the Afro-Colombians in the army, some from that very region, having the run of the place, as much a symbol of slavery in the Cauca as the whip and the chain, must have been very sweet indeed.[170] Ironically, the Conservatives who used the metaphor of slavery—they would rather die free than live as slaves—failed to imagine that their slaves thought the same thing.

The outcome of the 1851 civil war revealed that, while Conservatives enjoyed broad support throughout the Cauca, Liberals could marshal a level of dedication that their opponents simply would not or could not match. Conservatives relied on dragooning troops, even the Indians, who might have been more willing supporters if given the opportunity. Nevertheless, some Indians mistrusted Liberal intentions concerning marriage and their resguardos enough that they voluntarily enlisted in Conservative ranks.[171] In the valley, where Liberal support was strongest and most evident, Conservatives seemed to have had little success in rallying subalterns. Conservatives did attract some support from mestizo smallholders in the valley, who feared the perreristas' attacks on property as well.[172] However, Liberals reported that most of the Conservative rebels were mounted and, therefore, of a higher station, and that "very few peons" accompanied them.[173]

Conservatives did not actively bargain with Indians. While many Indians and other smallholders feared the Liberal program, Conservatives never actively engaged them with anything more than exposing the Liberals' nefarious schemes. Conservatives relied on traditional methods of making war and marshaling troops: forced conscription and reliance on patron-client ties. An anonymous Conservative diarist regretfully noted that almost all the people of the southern highlands supported the rebels, but Conservatives did not have time to rally them, and, consequently, their army was made up almost entirely of conscripts. After initial defeats, volunteers did begin to stream into the Conservative camp, but by then it was too late.[174] Even then, some Liberals with strong patron-client ties to Indians, especially the charismatic José María Obando, convinced many Indians to lay down their arms.[175]

Liberals had much more success with popular groups, as the anonymous diarist cited above realized, noting that the government could rely "on the proletarian classes that it has perverted."[176] During the war, Congress finally passed the law that set 1 January 1852 as the day of slavery's abolition (the children of slaves were released from their masters' control on 17 April 1852). Afro-Colombians did recognize that the Liberals had aided in their emancipation. Some ex-slaves and their relatives wrote to President López to ask for a pardon for J. N. Montero, Barbacoas's former governor, who was being tried for abuses of office during his term. They noted how Montero had supported them and, when they were still slaves, used the law to protect the "poor and helpless" when he could, to the point of poisoning his relations with "our masters." They opened the letter with a powerful appeal to López (and the Liberals in general): "You have worked arduously, and owing to your efforts the most degraded part of society, that today represents itself to you, has obtained the possession of liberty that we now enjoy. Your name, now sacred to us, will pass into posterity blessed and pronounced by our children's tender lips as the benefactor of their parents."[177] Another petition, sent by ex-slaves from the village of San Juan, similarly thanked Liberals: "Owing to the philanthropy of the citizens who compose the Honorable House and Senate, we enjoy the precious possession of liberty."[178] Later, even Conservatives would acknowledge that many Caucanos fought in the 1851 war to ensure slavery's abolition.[179]

Indeed, perhaps one way in which to understand Afro-Colombians' participation in the zurriago and the 1851 civil war is to view their actions as a successful slave revolt. Perhaps the true mind-set of subalterns is unrecoverable, but more evident is that the popular project to end slavery existed within the framework of the negotiated alliance between popular and elite Liberals. Certainly, Afro-Colombian volunteers were not automatons or just out for vengeance; they were fighting to create a just economic and political space for themselves in the nation. As Cali's Democratic Society announced, it had defeated the rebels thanks to "thousands of Liberal citizens armed in defense of the endangered Patria."[180]

The Expansion and Limits of Citizenship

Liberals succeeded in recruiting a large section of the valley's poor into a political alliance—through a complex bargaining process that redefined social, economic, and political relations in the Cauca. But, in order to do so, they needed to legitimize their new allies ideologically. They needed to turn the masses into citizens. The new politics went beyond simply educating and "civilizing" the masses, which had been the goal of all republicans since Independence. Some Liberals began to reframe the concept of citizenship and the lower classes' political role. Elite and middling Liberals expanded citizenship to include some elements of the poor, while popular liberals revalued citizenship as an important political tool.

Liberals' need for political support aligned nicely with their emerging more democratic conception of citizenship. While the accepted interpretation of nineteenth-century political history is that there were few important program-matic differences between the Conservative and the Liberal Parties, aside from their plans for the role of the Catholic Church, Marco Palacios recognizes that the two parties did not share similar visions of subalterns' political role.[181] Liberals were much more amenable to allowing subalterns some participation and seemed ready to expand the notion of citizenship to include their new allies.

Liberals were willing to embrace a broader vision of the citizen than were Conservatives. Although not, as they might claim, universal, this vision was less directly tied to property and literacy than was Conservatives'. Instead, their con-ception of the citizen relied heavily on reason, which the masses would gain through Liberal-directed education. The entire program of the Democratic So-cieties, along with the National Guard and Liberal ceremonies, was based on education. Colombia's Liberals and Conservatives mirrored European trends in their respective thoughts on citizenship, with Conservatives focusing more on place and tradition and Liberals more on reason.[182]

Cali's Democratic Society expressed its concern for education in a petition to the provincial legislature, signed by over three hundred of the society's mem-bers and other "padres de familia." The signatories asked that the province spend money, not on secondary education for a few, but on primary education for many. They noted: "One of the bases of republican government is the educa-tion of the pueblo so that they know their rights and their duties and will never be the instrument of the ambitious." With primary education, the people "would become citizens useful to the Patria, citizens of order, of good manners, inde-pendent citizens, citizens that think and that do not let themselves be moved like a machine by the ambitious nor servilcly obey tyrants."[183]

From the standpoint of elite Liberals, if the masses were to be included in politics as citizens, they had to be rational, able to see their own interests, freed from the obscuring veil of blind obedience to the priest or the hacendado. For now, teaching the pueblo their rights was the main concern. Years later, when it became all too clear that they knew their rights and, moreover, were creating new rights and interpreting old ones in ways worrisome to the wealthy, Liberals would turn their attention to the duties of the citizen and stress the disciplinary nature of education in order to control the populace. In the early 1850s, however, Liberals concentrated their efforts on creating new citizens to join them in the political realm.

The criterion of rationality was also the means by which Liberals excluded those whom they considered not yet ready for citizenship. Liberals' program of negotiation and bargaining required rational subalterns who understood their own needs and what they had to do to improve their own situation. The Cauca's Liberals thought that they could enlighten the valley's mestizo, mulatto, and black poor. They had no such faith in the other large racial group in the Cauca, the Indians. Generally, in the south, Liberals had a tough time proselytizing their gospel. A writer for one Liberal paper bleakly informed the masses that Conservatives referred to them as the "rabble and vile plebes" and denied that they possessed the capacity for reason. He warned that Conservatives would try to fool "citizens" by saying that Liberals threatened religion. However, while he claimed that Conservatives questioned the masses' reason, he also revealed his own doubts about the pueblo's reliability and intelligence. He whined that the people of Pasto were so filled with "fanaticism" and had so "little civilization" that they could not know their "rights."[184] Liberals complained that Indians' resguardos condemned them to "barbarism" and ensured the continuation of their "wild customs."[185] While Liberals had been remarkably successful in engaging the valley's residents with rights talk, such discourse seemed to fall on deaf ears in the southern highlands.

Conservatives' conception of citizenship had found expression in the 1843 constitution. Citizenship was limited to men over the age of twenty-one who had property worth 300 pesos or an income of 150 pesos; in addition, after 1850, prospective citizens had to be literate.[186] Literacy and property defined citizenship, property being viewed as generally hereditary. Julio Arboleda, the Cauca's leading Conservative intellectual, believed that, without property, wisdom was impossible.[187] Conservatives hoped for a two-house legislature, where the upper chamber would be a "conservative body," occupied by men of greater age and property. They felt that society should be divided into two groups, the wealthy and the rest of society, the former electing senators, the latter representatives. Both groups would have to pay a poll tax (thus excluding the poor), although the wealthy would pay more.[188] Other Conservatives had even more aristocratic visions. A Liberal observer described the 1843 constitution as a "truly monarchical" instrument that "put a monetary price even on citizenship."[189]

However elitist many Conservative conceptions of citizenship were, this mattered little in Conservatives' relations with plebeians since Conservatives did not privilege citizenship as the only entrée into political and public life. They accepted that everyone—and not just citizens—had some role to play in society and, thus, worried much less about the rationality of plebeians, especially Indians. They placed a higher value on received traditions and the importance of local relations for determining political worth than on the new "universal" and totalizing liberal citizenship. As discussed in the last chapter, this localized vision of political identity found reflection in popular conservatives' political imagination, although Indians did often insist that they too were citizens. For elite Conservatives, Indians might not yet be citizens, but they were still Granadans or Colombians with social rights and responsibilities.

The political role of elite conservative women best illustrates this conception of citizenship. After Liberals began mobilizing in 1849, it was patrician conservative women who seized much of the initiative in the new political arena that so confounded their husbands and fathers. The most forceful opposition to the Democratic Societies came, not from the fairly weak, hesitant attempts of Conservatives to form their own clubs that might include subalterns sympathetic to their cause, but from elite women. Conservative women formed their own societies and were not hampered by having to deal with the question of the masses' political role as only elite women constituted these assemblies. The women quickly used their social influence and control as a potent weapon, mocking Liberal officeholders and insulting the vile Democratic Societies.[190] They snubbed the wives of Liberal leaders and did not invite any Liberal too closely associated with the new regime to their soirees. They condemned a Liberal priest in Pasto by refusing to let him baptize their children, carting them off to another parish. Conservative women organized petition drives to protest the Jesuits' expulsion. One Conservative observer in Pasto even credited women with silencing the local Democratic Society, noting that, owing to the women's efforts, the club had not met in over six weeks. A Liberal paper in Popayán reported that conservative women had reportedly promised to attend the elections with their daggers, waiting to kill any Liberals. An exaggeration, of course, although conservative women did attend elections, as did popular liberals who similarly could not vote, to express support for their candidate.[191] Such talk, however, reflected the animosity that many Liberal men felt for women's political participation and interest in elections.[192]

Liberals reacted in shock to the activities of these women. In Pasto, a Liberal paper insultingly told the women to remain in their homes: "Your mission is the domestic life, the care of your husbands and children: listen, madres de familia, while you leave your homes to occupy yourselves in political conquests, perhaps your daughters, those delicate flowers, will hear the voice of the seducer." The paper further insinuated that, as women could never hope to convince a man through reason in a political discussion, they would inevitably be tempted to employ their more physical charms.[193]

Liberalism allowed no place in political life for women as women could not be citizens. Conservatism, not quite so bound, saw room for certain forms of participation for all members of society. Since Conservatives imagined society as inherently unequal, women could be allowed to participate in politics in certain ways since such participation would give them no grounds to claim equal standing with men. Liberal thought allowed political participation for citizens, but, since all citizens were theoretically equal, this created problems regarding women. Poor men had already asserted that, when lacking legal citizenship, they could seize effective citizenship through political action. Therefore, political participation made the citizen, not vice versa. This definition seemed to open the door to women, a door that Liberals promptly tried to shut. The new politics of subaltern men's role in public life was disconcerting enough. Women's participation threatened the viability of the whole republican system in two ways. First, it made republicanism seem simply too frightening and strange. Second, by making women equal, it removed them from their husbands and fathers' control, thus eroding the base of the citizen as a padre de familia. If masters could not rule over slaves or the rich over the poor politically, men must still rule over women.

It is not that Conservatives thought differently than Liberals regarding women's fitness as citizens, simply that, for them, women's participation in the political sphere did not suggest the same outcome. For Conservatives, citizenship was still an inherited, not an earned, right, and, at that time, women's political activity seemed not to pose a threat. Quite the contrary: it provided a valuable weapon against Liberal power. I would argue that Convervatives viewed the political activity of Indians and their other plebeian allies in much the same way.

While Conservatives saw citizenship as inherited and elite Liberals saw themselves as molding new citizens from the raw clay of the uneducated, irrational masses, popular liberals envisioned citizenship differently still. They did not simply wait for the mantle of citizenship to be officially placed on their shoulders. Already, as the zurriago and 1851 civil war revealed, they were acting like citizens, participating in politics, attending political meetings, and marching in street demonstrations. Citizenship always denoted more than simple suffrage rights, symbolically marking who had the right of full participation in politics. While seizing the right to enter the political sphere through action, popular liberals also sought formal recognition of their status and the obtainment of the right most associated with citizenship: the suffrage.

While the poor could enter the political realm in many ways without the direct blessing of the state, they needed the state's recognition to vote and, therefore, the recognition of the state's minions. In 1848, over two hundred men attempted to be inscribed on the list of voters and, hence, become state-recognized citizens. Their timing, coinciding with Liberal organizing, and their retention of the promising young Liberal Eliseo Payán to help write their petition strongly suggest that most, if not all, were popular liberals. However, while all these men surely thought of themselves as citizens, the electoral board thought otherwise. Only twenty-four would "enjoy the right of citizenship." The examining committee denied the rest for not having the necessary property or not having proved that they met all requirements for voting.[194]

Popular republicans fiercely contested the restricted notion of citizenship put forward by many elites and the constitution of 1843, attempting to force the state and the powerful in society to recognize their status. However, when these efforts failed, as they usually did before 1853, subalterns simply assumed the mantle of citizen. They joined the Democratic Societies, participated in political rallies and demonstrations, took up arms in the National Guard. They even participated in elections. If the state forbade them from voting, they could still arrive on election day, wait in the plaza, cheer their compatriots, and with their presence make it known that they would respond forcefully to any fraud. They seized their rights by knocking down the haciendas' fences that blocked their access to land and punished those Conservatives whom they saw as attempting to destroy the citizen body. They themselves became judges of who was a citizen and who was not. If the elite Conservatives and Liberals who sat on the electoral jury could deny their status as citizens for lack of property, popular liberals denied these same men the status of citizens when they caught them at night and whipped them. For the pueblo had their own idea of citizenship. They rejected these rich men's status in the public, political realm on the grounds that Conservatives were not good citizens but, instead, threatened the Republic and democracy. Popular liberals had earned their place in their nation by their participation as "armed citizens" in the defense of the Republic.[195] Popular liberals, as much as their elite counterparts, defined citizenship and made it meaningful.[196]

While Liberals' vision of citizenship excluded Indians and women and attracted few of the Cauca's poor mestizos, it succeeded spectacularly with Afro-

Colombians. The liberal version of citizenship so appealed to Afro-Colombians because it provided them with a new public and political identity that they did not have, coming as they did from the "social death" of slavery. Liberal citizenship demanded no special identity, history, or property beyond a willingness to support the Liberal cause. This definition alienated popular conservatives, with their devotion to their historical customs, identities, and properties, but enticed popular liberals. Thus, the armed citizen became central to popular liberals as it gave them a new public identity, one that elite Liberals recognized. Liberals implied that Indians could never be true citizens as long as they lived under the special laws of their resguardos and did not accept the "universal" identity of liberal citizenship. Likewise, the call for armed citizens removed many possibilities for popular liberal women to play a greater role in Liberal politics. That said, while elite Liberals did exclude their wives and daughters, popular liberal women (less under the control of fathers and husbands than other lower-class women owing to their men's lack of property and their own resources) participated in political life to a great degree. Women ran the taverns where popular liberals met and talked politics, joined the men in protesting the aguardiente monopolies, and tore down fences in the ejidos alongside men. Nonetheless, they remained ideologically excluded from the liberal conception of politics and public life.

As limited as Liberals' conception of citizenship was, and as distinct as it was from the conceptions of both Conservatives and popular liberals, Liberals in general worked for a new constitution that would expand citizenship rights and the suffrage.[197] Conservatives feared this mightily. Miguel Borrero noted that, while Liberals had won the last series of elections overall, Conservatives had triumphed wherever there was some degree of education and refinement. Accordingly, he thought that Conservatives had to ensure that the constitution "require a base of property in order to be a citizen." He also worried about the Liberal plan to extend the suffrage, noting: "The reds want the unruly rabble that do not have any property whatsoever, or those that they call the shirtless ones, to have the vote."[198] Eusebio Borrero was particularly concerned that the Liberals might try to extend "democratic liberty," by which he apparently meant an expansion of suffrage and citizenship.[199] He thought that the Liberals would not do so now that they were in power and, therefore, would not want to jeopardize their position. He thought wrong.

Liberals pushed through a new constitution in 1853 that declared: "Citizens are all male Granadans," married or over twenty-one years of age. All citizens could vote and be elected to any office. Granadans included all born in the nation, thus giving some status to everyone, but excluding many from citizenship: children; women; and the insane. The constitution also forbade slavery forever.[200] By October 1853, all adult males could vote. One Liberal wrote with pride about the changed face of election day: "In the electoral amphitheater, the classes and races into which society is divided mixed together; the slave, that yesterday shrank from the presence of his lord, today reclaims with dignity the part of sovereignty that the constitution has given him, in order to make use of it and to expect from the ballot box the verdict of his social future."[201]

The Establishment of Republican Bargaining

Most Liberals looked on the situation after the civil war of 1851 with satisfaction. In his letter of resignation to President López, Ramón Mercado dutifully recounted all the Liberal administration's achievements: the abolition of slavery; the end of monopolies; freedom of the press; the implementation of trial by jury; the decrease in size and strength of the professional army and the concomitant growth of the civilian National Guard; and the limiting of the death penalty. He bragged that theirs was the "first democratic administration of our nation" and that his most proud accomplishment was the "emancipation . . . of the popular masses from the tutelage of the oligarchy, from the prestige of fanaticism, and from the domination of the powerful." He further recalled how, during the civil war, the masses had supported him and the government.[202] Mercado saw the Liberals as first liberating the minds of the masses and then gaining their faith through a program of just policies and laws that favored subalterns. Finally, at the moment of truth, when Conservatives revolted, the masses sealed the bargain by supporting the Liberals, who easily triumphed. Of course, Liberals did not open the eyes of subalterns to their true interests for the very first time, but they did establish a common discourse with popular liberals, enabling an alliance to form. With this shared discourse, republican bargaining could, and did, take place.

I am not saying that at this time the pueblo learned their rights and discovered the true meaning of liberty and democracy or, even more erroneous, that middling and elite Liberals successfully taught the poor to understand politics and not be so deferential to their betters. The change in subalterns' political attitudes began in the late colonial period and accelerated immensely during Independence and the first years of the Republic. After 1848, a public, political space opened for the poor, especially Afro-Colombians, in the Cauca, allowing them to express and practice their political ideas in ways that had not been possible or efficacious before.

This opening, of course, did not just appear, nor did the Liberal regime automatically usher it in. People created it. Middling and elite Liberals turned to the poor out of a need to counter daunting Conservative power. Popular liberals responded, not simply to the elites, but with them. Subalterns around Cali, especially Afro-Colombians, seized the opportunity that elite Liberals offered. If popular liberals had not been waiting for such a moment, all the efforts of the Liberals would have been for naught. Elite Liberals had been contesting elite Conservatives in one guise or another for years. Popular groups had sought more power and more control over their lives and resources since the colonial era. In the late 1840s, however, these struggles came together, united by both immediate needs and new ways of talking about and practicing politics.

Middling and elite Liberals initiated this catalytic discourse, but popular liberals (and, later, other popular groups) altered it to suit their needs and pursued their own agendas, in the process dramatically altering their elite allies' politics. Middling and elite Liberals passed laws ending slavery, but popular liberals pushed them to do so. Middling and elite Liberals legally ended the monopolies over liquor, but only after popular liberals had ended them in reality by their actions. Middling and elite Liberals created the Democratic Societies, but popular liberals turned them into a political force. Middling and elite Liberals wrote the doctrinal exercises for the National Guard, but popular liberals transformed those militias into a force capable of defeating a Conservative reaction. Middling and elite Liberals certainly hoped to marshal the masses to their cause, but, in responding to the Liberals' call, the masses made the cause their own. The new politics was the offspring of both those above and those below, and both groups would fight bitterly over its future in the years to come.

Bargaining between those above and those below had always existed. The regular, sustained nature of this negotiation, however, was new. Before the early 1850s, elites and plebeians had bargained during times of stress or changing political or economic systems.[203] In contrast, by the 1850s, bargaining became the way in which both elites and plebeians normally conducted politics. Bargaining also became something not done solely in an ad hoc fashion; that is, it became a conscious political program pursued by political factions. Bargaining became more public and institutionalized as well, taking place in the open Democratic Societies instead of only on sites of production. Finally, republican discourse opened up whole new areas to negotiation, by allowing subalterns to redefine their political and social rights. Bargaining was eroding the old political hegemony of personalistic politics and patron-client relations with a new political culture based on republican negotiation, however unequal, between elites and subalterns.

Republican bargaining involved four major categories of Caucano life—the juridical, social, representative, and economic. Concerning juridical matters, Liberals ended or mitigated harsh vagrancy and police laws. In the representative realm, popular liberals redefined citizenship, and the new 1853 constitution recognized their efforts. Socially, popular and elite Liberals abandoned many older forms of deference, while Afro-Colombians found unprecedented space in the Cauca's public sphere. Economically, Liberals reduced some taxes, protected the ejidos, and ended the hated monopolies. Of course, the abolition of slavery, the most important achievement, involved all four aspects of bargaining. Negotiation would continue in all these areas, but economic issues would eventually prove the most difficult to resolve, the area with the least common ground between popular and elite concerns.

Beyond the abolition of slavery and the ending of monopolies—developments consistent with liberal political economy—popular and elite Liberals' economic visions diverged sharply. Subalterns' desire for land was the most taxing for their elite allies. While elite Liberals could to a certain extent support subalterns' efforts to regain the ejidos—after all, Conservatives controlled most of the land in question—they could not support subalterns' goals for a radical reconfiguration of property relations. As popular liberals began to pursue their own goals, exploiting the new politics in ways most Liberals had not imagined possible, some Liberals began to doubt the wisdom of the political experiment that they had helped initiate.

4 Fragmented Hegemony:

The Limits of Elite Power,

1853–1863

I would fain know what the soldier hath fought for all this while? He hath fought
to enslave himself, to give power to men of riches,
men of estates, to make him a perpetual slave.
—Sarcastic interjection of COLONEL THOMAS RAINBOROUGH,
arguing in defense of his soldiers' rights,
Putney, 29 October 1647[1]

The Liberals' victory in the 1851 civil war demonstrated the critical weight of subaltern allies in the struggle for political power in nineteenth-century Colombia. The subsequent decade's conflicts would confirm the importance of popular support. However, Liberals had little time to enjoy their success before events in distant Bogotá came to dominate the Cauca's political landscape in 1854. A military coup against the government (but in support of the Liberal president) shattered Liberal unity and led to Conservatives retaking control of both the nation and the southwest.

Conservatives—and a few Liberals—celebrated their unexpected triumph with plans to roll back the gains that popular liberals had made since 1849. Plebeians would return to their place in the social hierarchy under an orderly, conservative republican system. Yet, within the span of a few years, Conservatives' designs evaporated under the pressure of subalterns' insistence on entering the political sphere. Conservatives were unable to impose their will on Caucano society, and they failed to construct a political culture in which plebeians had limited access to the public, political world.

Despite Conservatives' efforts, republican bargaining had become commonplace in the Cauca. But no one social group controlled bargaining. Caucano elites, especially the powerful former president, Tomás Mosquera, schemed to dominate the nation as a whole by initiating the 1860–63 civil war; however, they had to turn to popular groups for support. Negotiation between elites and subalterns not only had survived the 1854 civil war but had become ingrained in the Cauca's political culture. No single faction of the powerful in Colombia (in the guise of political parties, the almost nonexistent state, or the economic elite) could dominate the midcentury political landscape. Any national or even regional project (be it a plan of reform or simply the pursuit of state power) required the recruitment of popular allies. The powerful in Colombia were not that powerful in the mid-nineteenth century, certainly not strong enough to impose their vision on society as a whole. Only the culture of republican bargaining could be considered hegemonic.

While in the early 1850s Liberals had succeeded remarkably well in recruiting Afro-Caucanos into their party, by the end of the decade other popular groups had also entered into political negotiations more fully. In the southern highlands, Indians continued their struggle to maintain their resguardos and now found much greater support in the halls of power. Unlike popular liberals, however, Indians could not find satisfactory allies in either political party. On the northern border, Antioqueño migrants pushed into the frontier, creating homesteads, new villages, and political alliances. Both these groups would find themselves courted by the two political parties and drawn into relations of republican bargaining.

The Liberals' Weakness

Liberals soon discovered that the new political system that they had helped construct in the Cauca would not function as smoothly as planned. Their drive to modernize the region's economic and social structure—by eliminating communal landholding (except for ejidos) and the special prerogatives of certain members of society—increasingly angered the indigenous communities. Furthermore, while Liberals had great support among Afro-Colombians, other subalterns viewed their designs with some suspicion. Many small farmers and Indians feared Afro-Colombians' political influence and Liberals' attacks on the church and property. Under the system of unrestricted adult male suffrage that they had initiated, Liberals as often as not found themselves on the losing side of elections in 1853.

After their victory in 1851, Liberals escalated their drive to liquidate the

Indians' resguardos and bring the communalists, kicking and screaming if necessary, into the modern world of individualistic equality before the law and nation.[2] Also, the Cauca had begun to feel the effects of the capitalistic Atlantic market more powerfully, as cinchona bark (the source of quinine), growing naturally in the mountains, found a market among malaria-ridden Europeans colonizing distant Africa and Asia. Suddenly, Indians' lands outside the valleys held appeal to their white neighbors; to save costs, speculators simply destroyed whole forests in the process of harvesting the bark, denuding hillsides. Indians from Quichaya and Caldono complained angrily about cinchona gatherers violently usurping their rights to the resguardos but found little support for their pleas.[3]

Even in areas not affected by the cinchona boomlet, Indians feared the intentions of the Liberal government. In eastern Colombia, under the Liberal resguardo legislation of 1850, many Indian communities were losing their land at a rapid pace.[4] By 1852, Indians' petitions, asking that they be allowed to keep their resguardos, had flooded in to governors' offices from villages across the south.[5] Indians even proposed that they would support the government—if only their resguardos were left intact. Communalists from Guachucal and Muellamuez begged the provincial governor not to support the resguardos' division, promising him "that all the Indians of this district are and will be ready to lend any services that the government demands of us."[6] However, Liberals did not take the opportunity to create an alliance with Indians as they had with Afro-Colombians. As expansive and "universal" as Liberals' view of citizenship was, it did not include the traditional and pious Indians. After the 1851 civil war, Liberals did not seem to need additional lower-class allies: the support of Afro-Colombians was so strong that they thought that they could alienate Indians with impunity. By the 1870s, some Liberals would regret that decision.

Other Indians warned Liberals of the dire consequences of dividing the resguardos. The cabildo of Cumbal threatened emigration if the division came to pass. Túquerres's cabildo was more bold; while not threatening rebellion directly, it noted that the community's members would be uncontrollable once the resguardos ceased to exist: "They would throw themselves into excess. . . . [T]hey would become rebellious."[7]

While Liberals were further alienating Indians, they had to organize for the first elections under the 1853 constitution and its provision of unrestricted adult male suffrage. Before the constitution went into effect, their candidate, the Caucano José María Obando, had already won the presidency. The decentralized constitution of 1853 ordered the local election of provincial governors, previously appointed by the president. Conservatives took advantage of their numerical superiority in the country and the Cauca to win control of many localities, including ardently Liberal Cali. Liberals lost Cali's 1853 elections for several reasons, not the least of which being that two Liberals ran against each other, dividing the vote. Enjoying the support of many small farmers who had felt threatened by the zurriago, Conservatives narrowly carried the day.[8]

Conservatives dominated elections in the south, winning the governorships of Popayán, Pasto, and Túquerres Provinces.[9] Now some Conservatives followed their enemy's lead and courted potential subaltern allies. In Túquerres, the legislature and governor passed a law in 1853 allowing resguardos to continue indefinitely (superseding a Liberal ordinance initiating division) unless the Indians themselves decided otherwise.[10] The new governor, Antonio Chaves, moved to strengthen his party's relations with Indians. He astutely showed his understanding of where power lay in the indigenous communities by supporting Indian governors and cabildos. Chaves ordered land that had been sold without the cabildos' approval returned to the resguardos, and he made it harder for outsiders to claim to be Indians in order to use resguardo land. He also made it easier and less expensive for Indians to present their claims to him.[11] Some Conservatives were ready to bargain too, at least over Indians' juridical and economic interests, if not over issues of deference and representation.

The 1854 Civil War

Events in Bogotá, however, soon overshadowed Conservatives' attempts at resurgence in the Cauca. Liberals across the nation had been divided into two camps: Gólgotas, elitists who adhered firmly to the principles of economic liberalism, and Draconianos, who favored tariffs and supposedly had more popular support, especially among Bogotá's artisans. Upset by Conservative victories in the 1853 elections and the declining influence of the professional army, the Draconianos, under General José María Melo, revolted against the government but in support of the Liberal president, Obando. They wanted the 1853 constitution discarded and Obando to assume total control over the state. Obando, however, rejected the coup—at least overtly—and refused to lead it. Viewing Melo's revolt as a dangerous lower-class uprising, many Liberals joined with the Conservatives in an attempt to defeat it, the combined forces coming to be known as the Constitutionalists.[12]

In the Cauca and other provincial regions, confusion reigned. Liberals, both elite and popular, had no idea whom to support: their Liberal president and their constitution or a revolt in the name of the president. Around Popayán, rumors ran rampant about the events in the capital—everything from the Arboledas having been killed in an attack on the Congress to Conservatives rebelling in Bogotá in an effort to assassinate Obando.[13]

The newspaper El Sur warned that Melo was no Liberal, seeing as he wanted to reinstate the conservative 1843 constitution, restrict the suffrage, reduce local power, reinstate the death penalty, and establish a dictatorship—none of which would have been popular with popular liberals.[14] While Bogotanos accused Melo of class warfare and communism, such rhetoric found less play in the Cauca. There, Melo's opponents focused on his suspect intentions, calling him a dictator. One broadsheet declared that he wanted to enslave the country and that those supporting his dictatorship were "not republicans."[15] Many Liberals and Conservatives cast Melo's revolt as antirepublican, greatly limiting its support among all social groups in the Cauca. Constitutionalists claimed that many of those in Melo's ranks had been tricked into thinking that they were really supporting Obando and the Liberal cause.[16]

Ex-president José Hilario López's actions exemplified the general confusion felt in the Cauca over Melo's revolt. López was the human symbol of national liberalism, his portrait presiding over the emancipation ceremonies. He addressed the Caleños, assuring them that he understood how some might think that supporting Melo meant supporting democracy, but at the same time warning them that nothing was further from the truth and that supporting the rebellion would "forge new chains of slavery."[17] López well knew how to manipulate the discourse of popular liberalism.

Local concerns having little to do with Bogotá or Melo (or Draconianos and Gólgotas) erupted during the chaos.[18] The pretext at least for an uprising in Popayán occurred when a government patrol stopped José Ramos, a black man, and proceeded to question him about a small amount of gold that he possessed. Some Liberals intervened, claiming that the patrol had violated the arrestee's "liberty." After much shouting, the patrol took Ramos to jail, and the Liberals went to the city's ejido and organized a company, which returned and attacked the patrol. Thus Melo's revolt began in Popayán.[19]

Melo generally found little support in the Cauca. Soldiers did rebel in Popayán, presumably because Melo promised to increase the prestige and importance of the military. To the south of Popayán, and along the coast, Melo found no sympathy among the Indians or other Caucanos. What revolts did spring up to the north were quickly and decisively put down, with help from Constitutionalist troops from Pasto and from the Indian villages around Silvia. While, because of their clientelist ties with Obando, some Indians did support the revolt, more sided with Conservatives. Rebellions did take place in areas of the Cauca Valley where Afro-Colombians lived. Blacks and mulattoes were suspicious of any Conservative mobilization, fearing reenslavement and partisan vengeance.[20] About the latter, they were not mistaken.

Liberals claimed that, after order had been restored, Conservatives insisted on exacting revenge and removing from office any Liberals of whom they did not approve. The feared Conservative commander Manuel Tejada (rumored to have killed a number of his own slaves in fits of violence) threatened to seize Cali unless the city was surrendered to him—even though Liberals in the city claimed that they were not in revolt. Antonio Matéus, the Liberal governor of Cauca Province, avowed that he had no intention of revolting, and supported the constitution, but would not allow Tejada to commit depredations against Cali. Thus, Conservatives' desire to restore their idea of order to the valley forced Matéus (later murdered in Palmira) and his popular liberal supporters, many of them Afro-Colombians, into the war. Disorganized, confused, and divided, Liberals could not organize a coherent response and quickly fell to defeat.[21]

After Tejada took control of Cali, Conservatives began to persecute the rebels, brutally killing many, including prisoners of war. Caleños wrote to López, begging him to secure a pardon for those who had rebelled, as most were men "without influence" and poor. One writer noted that four hundred people had died during the suppression of the rebels.[22] Another claimed that Conservatives slaughtered two hundred "citizens" in an attack on Palmira, recovering only eleven weapons from the supposed rebels.[23] López, outraged at the Conservatives' brutality, demanded that Acting President José de Obaldía (who had replaced Obando after the latter was implicated in Melo's revolt) put a stop to it. He claimed that Conservatives in the Cauca were shouting: "Death to all the blacks without a single exception!" Obaldía himself acknowledged that he had heard that prisoners in Cartago had been strangled, bayoneted, and shot. And, at first, he appeared to appease López, saying that he would put an end to the atrocities and planned a broad, although not universal, pardon.[24]

However, Obaldía turned on the general, revealing that his sympathies did not lie with Liberals who had links to the popular classes. He questioned whether any depredations had taken place at all, arguing that most of the prisoners died from fatigue in a forced march (the assumption being that there was nothing amiss in that). Obaldía then acknowledged that the murders had occurred but placed the blame on popular liberals. He cited the zurriago, asking how López could not expect vengeance for the whippings, property destruction, rapes, and assassinations of 1851. He said that many Liberals had blamed the zurriago on the understandable desire for revenge that "blacks and those of other tints" harbored against those "whites" who had been their masters under slavery—so those same Liberals could hardly complain if the tables were now turned. He assured López that those killed were certainly the "old whip wielders, arsonists, property destroyers, assassins, and rapists" of the past disturbances.[25] López was not the only one to bemoan the outcome of the revolt. Others, thinking that they were supporting a Liberal president and constitution, regretted that Conservatives had used them to regain power.[26]

The situation in the Cauca was quite distinct from that in Bogotá. In the capital, many Liberals had experienced a falling out with their numerous and organized artisan popular supporters over the tariff question. These artisans formed the backbone of Melo's forces. In the Cauca, however, popular and elite Liberals' alliance was still very strong in 1854, and the tariff debate was not much of an issue. Also, many of the young Liberals who had come to power in Bogotá had begun to make alliances with older, established families and had experienced both the taste of power and some material success with their investments.[27] For these men on the make, popular mobilization suddenly entailed much more risk. In the early 1850s, no such alliance had yet emerged in the Cauca, the economy stagnated, and Liberals still needed popular allies to counter Conservative strength. Unlike their compatriots in Bogotá and the eastern highlands, Cauca's Liberals had not yet become disillusioned with the effects of popular mobilization, even if they were unsure about the consequences of Melo's distant revolt.[28]

Taking advantage of Liberals' confusion, Cali's Conservatives rallied at the chance to restore the old order and quickly raised three thousand pesos to equip a division under the command of the brutal Manuel Tejada to hunt down any remaining rebels. As late as November, Governor Manuel María Mallarino was requesting funds for six hundred troops to pacify the areas around Cali and Palmira, claiming that roads and rural properties enjoyed no security.[29] Conservatives not so subtly redefined the conflict, not as a civil war with soldiers, but as a criminal action with "bandits," who had to be hunted down and "severely punished."[30] The national government had pardoned most regular soldiers, but vindictive prosecutors circumvented the pardon by accusing some popular liberals (including a number of women), not of rebellion, but of banditry.[31] As is the case in the present-day United States, those convicted of serious crimes lost their full citizenship. Many Liberals with strong connections to subalterns went into exile.[32]

Conservatives were overjoyed at their good fortune. Seemingly out of the blue, Liberals had vanquished themselves. The Conservative Party was back in power nationally and in control of the Cauca; many of the most troublesome Liberal leaders had been killed or exiled. Also, the war gave Conservatives the opportunity to put popular liberals back in their place, to take vengeance for the insults and abuses of the zurriago and the 1851 war, and to restore order and respect for their privileges. Never again, they thought, would those below so grossly challenge their betters. As one Conservative wrote to Sergio Arboleda: "I do not regret the disorder in the Cauca because it is only thus that this poor country can be cleansed so that it will be inhabitable in the future."[33]

A Conservative Bid for Social Control

After their victory and the brutal reprisals against popular liberals, especially Afro-Colombians, the Cauca's Conservatives sought to remake the region as a bastion of order and progress, to rein in popular liberals, and to reduce the political space open to plebeians. Provincial legislatures redrew police laws that the previous regime had liberalized, ordering officers to prevent vagrancy and enforce work contracts, including pursuing those who fled their obligations. They also reinstated debt peonage. On the coast, the police could force vagrants to work in the mines, largely abandoned after emancipation. Conservatives equated vagrancy, not just with sloth, but also with crime, including rape, casting vagrants as a threat to the sanctity of the family, a concern of many plebeians.[34]

Conservatives also tried to close down the Democratic Societies. In Túquerres, a new police law, not only outlawed vagrancy and ordered anyone without employment to work, but also forbade any public meeting that threatened "rebellions against public order" or any demonstrations at night, a favorite part of the clubs' repertoire.[35] Before the war, Cali's governor, Mallarino, had also ordered the police to prevent any night demonstrations or "tumultuous" meetings.[36] Conservatives blamed the societies for corrupting the pueblo and distracting the poor from their labors with politicized speeches and lessons. In Popayán, the governor ordered the Democratic Society's newspapers impounded. Conservative papers reminded their readers about the evils of the clubs, which, once established, caused everybody—artisans, farmers, and laborers—to abandon their work and devote themselves to politics.[37] The harassment seemed to work as, after 1854, the clubs became dormant for some time. Generally, while Conservatives had found some success by bargaining with their Indian allies in the south, they were more than willing to try to restrict political space and destroy popular liberalism. One observer claimed: "Demagogy in the Cauca has breathed its last breath."[38]

Conservatives did not just attack popular liberals; they also rewarded their Indian allies. In Pasto, an 1855 law assured Indians that their resguardos would not be divided.[39] Liberals accused Conservatives of enacting lower taxes in the south, a Conservative stronghold, while unduly taxing districts with Liberal sympathies.[40] Conservatives also sought to revive traditional charitable institutions, such as the hospitals in Popayán and Cali, in order to demonstrate their benevolence to the poor; elite women often sponsored these organizations. Conservative women also founded schools, especially for girls' primary education. In further support of the family, many hoped for the revocation of laws that allowed civil marriage or restricted the prerogatives of the church.[41]

Although individual Conservatives attempted to win Indians' sympathy, Conservatives generally had no overall project or design to do so. While Conservatives supported legislation favoring indigenous communities, individual landowners continued to covet particular plots of resguardo land. Without any public, sustained mechanism like the Democratic Societies to unite Indians and Conservatives institutionally, the extent of their alliance (and bargaining) was limited. Indians did not identify with Conservatives as Afro-Colombians did with Liberals.

In spite of their efforts to remake the Cauca, Conservatives found themselves challenged sooner than expected. In 1857, under a new national constitution, all the old provinces of the southwest became the Cauca State, with Popayán the capital. The formation of a constitutional assembly, charged with writing a new state constitution, gave many Liberals the opportunity to reenter politics.[42] Even though Liberals had lost many of the 1853 elections, the first with unrestricted male suffrage, most continued to support an open policy for citizenship. Some Conservatives, despite their past success, pushed for more restricted access to the franchise, proposing that, at the very least, citizens have property or an "honorable" profession; but others were buoyed by that same success and supported an expanded suffrage.[43]

Conservatives did manage to have General Tomás Cipriano de Mosquera, the ex-president, named acting governor of the state until elections could be held. However, despite the large Conservative majority, most of the assembly's constituents did not follow the hard line advocated by newspapers such as Cali's El Cauca. Most Conservatives were not ready to restrict the republican system dramatically, perhaps because they feared a new Liberal revolt.[44] The new constitution declared all men over twenty-one, or those married, "electors." Conservatives did manage to outlaw progressive taxes, which many Liberals had hoped would replace consumption taxes, unpopular with many plebeians.[45]

The constitutional assembly marked the end of Conservatives' bid for domination. The assembly issued another pardon to the 1854 rebels and to those fugitives accused of minor crimes since the war as well.[46] Until Mosquera could travel to the state to take his office, the Liberal Emigdio Palau served as interim governor. In his first speech, Palau praised the new constitution, assuring his audience that it confirmed the abolition of slavery and monopolies and made allowances for juries and freedom of association.[47] Despite some Conservatives' wishes, the new state constitution did not radically reduce the political space that popular liberals had opened.

However, far more serious than Liberals sharing institutional power was the aggressive attitude and actions of the region's poor. Small uprisings began to occur against Conservative rule. While not a serious threat, these disturbances further destabilized the order that Conservatives had hoped to nurture. Worse was the continued problem of banditry. In the Cauca Valley, and around Popayán, bandits eluded the authorities. Most of the gangs seem to have been made up of popular liberal partisans from the 1854 war.[48] During the nineteenth century, banditry was at times a fluid category. Men (and some women) moved between legitimacy as commanders during war and lawlessness as renegades during peacetime if their side lost. Cattle rustling also became endemic. The fear of bandits or larger revolts was pervasive by the summer of 1855, and rumors of a coming uprising ran rampant. Conservatives tried to recover arms distributed to plebeian combatants on all sides during both the 1851 and the 1854 wars, but success eluded them.[49]

Contrary to Conservative designs, crime seemed out of control, and order in the Cauca was more scarce now than ever. Conservatives were shocked to hear that Manuel Tejada, their strongman and leader in the 1854 war, was found murdered in 1856.[50] Four black men had ambushed and shot Tejada near Caloto. Debate erupted over the meaning of the murder, some claiming that the men killed Tejada because he was trying to evict them from some land owned by Julio Arboleda or at least force them to pay their rent. Others claimed that the murder was the result of a personal feud with other members of Caloto's elite, who had hired the accused as assassins.[51] Whatever the motive, the courts ordered the execution of the four assailants.

Crime did not affect only the rich, of course. As disorder spread, armed bands attacked not only large haciendas, which often were well guarded, but the small farms and ranches of peasants and Indian communalists as well. Complaints poured in, not just of missing livestock, but of the theft of all types of agricultural produce.[52]

Of perhaps even greater concern to Conservatives was the lack of control that hacendados exercised over their labor force, now all at least nominally free. Former slaves often simply refused to pay rents, asserting by their actions that, for them, abolition meant freedom, not just from the whip, but from the authority and purview of the landlord. Most Afro-Colombians fled the mines, but those who stayed tried to work for themselves, resisting the landlords' attempts to claim a share of any extracted gold.[53]

After their victory, Conservatives seemed bewildered by their former slaves' continued recalcitrance. Vicente Arboleda furiously complained to Mosquera that his hacienda was in ruins—the freedpeople believing that "they have a right to the part of the property where they lived" and refusing to work for him at all, except for one day a week, working poorly on that one day to boot. The situation was even worse around Santander, where the ex-slaves "had become insolent" and not only did not pay rents but also refused to leave the haciendas.[54] On the Arboledas' mammoth Japio hacienda, the overseers desperately tried to force the "black tenants" to work when called on and to stop them from stealing firewood.[55] In general, haciendas endured relentless incursions by scavengers, both their own tenants and outsiders, who gathered, not just firewood, but anything else of value, including rubber, resins, cinchona bark—whatever merchants would buy. On the Arboledas' other haciendas, similar problems existed, with the "blacks" refusing to pay rents, trying to open roads through the haciendas, and stealing plantains and other crops.[56] Hacendados could not comprehend how "insolent" their workers, people who should fear and respect their employers and patrons, had become.[57] Not only did Conservatives regret the economic blow that abolition had delivered, but they also pined for the days when they commanded social respect.

Conservatives hoped to resolve their labor dilemma by encouraging the immigration either of foreigners or of presumably docile Colombians from the central highlands around Bogotá. The Japio hacienda wished to attract "good mannered white peons" to settle on the hacienda in exchange for their labor.[58] Not surprisingly, these plans failed. Hacendados and mineowners also hoped that the forced contract labor of vagrants would fill their needs, but, while no doubt the laws created serious hardships for many plebeians, such legislation did not solve the problem of labor discipline or supply. Of course, hacendados employed all the judicial authority and extralegal violence at their disposal— including beating employees and burning their houses—but any control that they won was transitory.[59] While hacendados raged about the insolence of their tenants, they suffered serious economic setbacks as well. Rents were often the surest source of income for haciendas that lacked export commodities. In addition, tenants' recalcitrance to work when called on created severe labor shortages, bringing work to a dead stop on some haciendas. Around Cali, insecurity caused by bandits and a radicalized workforce decreased agricultural production dramatically.[60]

In general, Conservatives expressed disappointment at the failure of the national government and their own local efforts to remake politics and restore order.[61] The paper El Cauca fumed about renewed Liberal influence throughout the state.[62] Both on the haciendas and in the public sphere, plebeians still did not respect their old masters' authority. Conservatives had tried to control politics without securing alliances and active support among the region's lower classes; they did not take into account how significantly the political sphere had opened since they were last in power. Within two years of their victory, the Conservatives' bid for social control had failed.

Mosquera's Gambit

In spite of their disappointments, Conservatives had by 1857 some reason to hope that the orderly and hierarchical Cauca of which they dreamed might still come about. The former president, General Tomás Mosquera, took command of the newly defined Cauca State in 1857. Mosquera was the favorite son of one of Colombia's most powerful clans, known as the "Royal Family of New Granada."[63] His relatives had been important figures in the colonial government; his younger brother became archbishop of Bogotá, and his older brother had in 1830 briefly been president. Mosquera and his family were some of the Cauca's largest landholders, as they were slaveholders before emancipation, and had close ties with the other powerful Conservative dynasty, the Arboledas. The young Tomás had fought with Bolívar in the patriot armies and later served various proto-Conservative governments, becoming a mortal enemy of the Liberal José María Obando. He had assumed the national presidency in 1845 and, despite his strong ties to the Ministeriales (proto-Conservatives), had initiated a number of liberal economic reforms before being supplanted by the Liberal López in 1849.[64] As far as Conservatives were concerned, Mosquera had a number of worrisome personal quirks, including an almost rabid anticlericalism, but everything else in his past seemed to mark him as the man of order needed to restrain the unruly masses. Again, however, Cauca's Conservatives would be sorely disappointed.

Mosquera had his own designs, plans in which the Cauca served as no more than a stepping-stone. He hungered to regain national power, to seize control from the elected Conservative president, Mariano Ospina. While Mosquera was friendly with almost all major Conservative power brokers and assumed to be a staunch Conservative by most Caucanos, nevertheless he held many liberal ideas. As noted above, he promoted liberal economic reforms, invested in a variety of export-oriented business ventures, and despised the church. In addition, his own personal desire for power led him to challenge the national Conservative Party. As Mosquera's plotting grew increasingly obvious, it became apparent that the vast majority of the Cauca's Conservatives, both elite and popular, were less than eager to support a revolt against their own party.[65] Mosquera would not be denied, however, and cast about for other allies. He made overtures to most of the Cauca's social groups—Indians, the Antioqueño migrants, even popular liberals.

Mosquera first tried to create a new party, the National Party, under a federalist banner that would unite support across the Cauca's fractured political spectrum. He hesitated to make overt gestures to the Liberal Party, both for fear of alienating his Conservative friends and from reluctance to grant the concessions that he knew an alliance would demand. Initially, he encouraged his deputies to lure popular liberals into the fold of the new National Party, but they had little success. One lieutenant explained: "Almost everybody that belongs to the Liberal Party in the Cauca are people of the *pueblo bajo* [lower class] (as one generally says) and blacks, whom it is pointless to try to convince through reason as this class of people do not listen to anyone who is not of their party."[66] Afro-Colombians' devotion to the Liberal Party was strong, and they certainly were not going to join the new National Party without some serious enticement.

As it became clear that little support was to be found in the Conservative Party and that the Liberal Party was growing in strength, Mosquera turned more and more attention to his old enemies. Liberals began to win elections again. By 1859, they controlled the state legislature and quickly sought to reestablish ties with their popular allies. They prevented any new statewide taxes on aguardiente from being enacted. Indeed, in the atmosphere of the late 1850s, such taxes may have been unenforceable, at least in the valley, where collectors deemed a new tax on tobacco consumption basically nullified by the extent of contraband trafficking.[67]

In the valley, popular liberalism reemerged out of the ashes of the 1854 debacle. Conservatives worried that the Democratic Societies had returned clandestinely in Cali, Palmira, Buga, and Popayán and that Liberals had formed "latent Democratic Societies organized with the title *republican juntas*" in all the towns of any size in the Cauca.[68] In Cartago, Liberals organized a club whose membership, Conservatives claimed, was made up entirely of "blacks."[69] Conservatives denigrated the Liberals elected in Palmira as "an Indian, a black, and a half-white, tinterillos all."[70] Tinterillos, untrained scribes who acted as lawyers, had resumed their role as the middling figures uniting popular and elite liberalism. If not yet in name, the Democratic Societies had returned in fact. By July 1859, Cali's Democratic Society had officially reorganized.[71]

Liberals worked to get their own candidate, Emigdio Palau, elected state governor in 1859. Popular and middling Liberals traveled across the region, speaking at haciendas and farms, organizing support. The campaigners promised to work for land redistribution and lower taxes for the poor.[72] After the Liberals' electoral defeat, however, many began to look anew at Mosquera (the victor), who had started to challenge the Conservative national government.

In July 1859, while Mosquera schemed against President Mariano Ospina, he received an extraordinary petition from Cali. Over 750 men signed, or had their names signed for them, asking that Mosquera assign Cali's provincial governorship to a young professor named David Peña. Peña was a Liberal firebrand, already known for his oratory, and immensely popular with Cali's lower classes, perhaps, in part, because he was a mulatto. The signatories assured Mosquera of Peña's popularity in Cali, his intelligence, and his loyalty to the cause of federalism and Mosquera. Peña, they said, would enjoy great support and be able to carry out "ideas of progress and social welfare," by which they probably meant taxes and land distribution. Finally, they made an offer to Mosquera: "We will accompany him [Peña] in danger, and when you, Citizen Governor, need the residents of Cali Province, you will find more than two thousand soldiers resolved to sacrifice themselves in defense of the state."[73] An earlier letter from Cali's Democratic Society, under the name of David Peña as president, promised similar support against "the traitor Congress."[74]

Mosquera was not about to appoint the relatively unknown and possibly dangerous Peña to so sensitive a post as Cali's governorship, but he knew that many Caleños were anxious and ready to support someone willing to challenge national Conservative control. Surprisingly, Mosquera did appoint a new, moderate governor and named Peña as the governor's designated alternate, a move that worried moderate Liberals and appalled Conservatives.[75] Mosquera now had the promise of two thousand troops for any move that he might make against the national government.

Mosquera was still uneasy; after all, he had been one of the largest slaveowners in the Cauca, the leader of conservatism before 1848, and one of the most aristocratic of the aristocracy. Knowing a losing cause when he saw one, he wisely sat out the 1851 war, attending to his business in New York and Panama, despite pleas from his Conservative allies. He was also absent from the Cauca in 1854 and, thus, not tainted in the minds of popular liberals. However, he hesitated to ally himself fully with popular liberals, owing either to his racist reservations about Afro-Colombians or to his fears of losing control of a movement that might push for a radical reconfiguration of the Cauca's economic and political landscape. One Conservative grimly noted that the only thing that held Mosquera back from revolting was that he "fears to become one of the victims himself."[76] Nevertheless, Mosquera overcame his qualms, at least somewhat. Luckily for him, popular liberals, so desperate to end any vestige of Conservative rule, did not need much encouragement to support him.

Indeed, popular liberals imagined Mosquera to be their man. He became for them "a true republican," one who would fight alongside them for "the holy cause of liberty." Their politics became his politics, and, if his actions while governor did not suit them, they chalked it up to untrustworthy local agents' malfeasance.[77] The opportunity that Mosquera presented was too good to pass up, so, perhaps unconsciously, popular liberals reverted to the colonial habit of believing in the good king and the nefarious local official. They really had no choice; the opportunity to best the Conservatives once again, to avenge 1854, was too sweet.

Despite his qualms, Mosquera did bargain. Soon after receiving Cali's petition, he addressed the state legislature, expressing his dissatisfaction with the vagrancy law, calling it too draconian. "This question is of great social importance in the Cauca," he noted, in that the law was often much abused, not to pursue vagrants, but to "satisfy passions."[78] Afro-Colombians and others of the rural poor detested the harsh vagrancy laws that Conservatives enacted after 1854. Mosquera, the hacendado, now offered to repeal them.

Mosquera also sought to position himself as protector of Cali's ejidos, claiming that he had supported "the rights of the community" when he was president in 1848. He pushed for a law that strengthened municipal control over ejidos, in Cali and elsewhere, and that legally prevented landlords (or even the city) from charging rents on land whose ownership was being disputed in the courts.[79] Mosquera also began to appoint Liberal governors in many of the valley's provinces. The legislature, dominated by Liberals and Mosqueristas, also considered abolishing the death penalty and did lower consumption taxes on a variety of items—including imported salt, tolls, and raffles—across the state.[80]

Unlike most Conservatives, Mosquera was quite adept at the new politics of bargaining. He had urged Conservatives to establish closer relations with the poor in the early 1850s. He had also understood the importance of at least appearing to relate to the lower classes before his bid for power in the late 1850s. Once, in 1850, while passing through Cali, he was met by throngs of Conservatives who saw him as the savior who would deliver them from the increasingly bold Liberals and their plebeian allies. However, in spite of this, the Democratic Society invited Mosquera to address its next meeting. Perhaps surprisingly, the ex-president agreed, and he further shocked the crowd by giving a rousing speech declaring himself, in the recollection of one observer, "a friend of the popular cause" and a supporter of López's administration. Liberals were more confused the next night, when he spoke at the gathering of the Conservative Society of the Friends of the People and condemned the "reds."[81] Mosquera knew the importance of maintaining ties with the popular classes.

While one may surmise that Mosquera cynically used both popular and elite Liberals, that explanation is too simplistic. Indeed, some contemporary observers saw it differently, asserting that the Liberals were using Mosquera. One Conservative insultingly said: "[Mosquera] has become the toy of his enemies and his adulators, . . . [the] instrument of a party to which he does not belong."[82] I offer that Mosquera, elite Liberals, popular liberals, and smallholder republicans (see below) all, in a sense, used one another. Bargaining with each other, they understood that their interests and goals were different, but they were willing to set their differences aside in order to pursue the common aim of ending Conservative rule, even if the imagined result of obtaining that goal was strikingly different for all the parties involved. Mosquera duped neither popular nor elite Liberals into supporting him; rather, he openly bargained for their support (by softening vagrancy laws, reducing taxes, and protecting the ejidos), providing them with an avenue through which to challenge Conservative power. Mosquera had no ideological predisposition to aid the poor or even negotiate with them, but he recognized the new nature of republican politics.

Conservatives reacted first in confusion, then in disgust, at Mosquera's maneuvering. They reminded him that he had been elected by Conservatives. Some, sympathetic to Mosquera, worried about his alliance with popular liberals, fearing that, if he should win, it would mean the return of the zurriago.[83]

Mosquera did not rely only on popular liberals, however; he also courted the Cauca's indigenous peoples. On 19 October 1859, the legislature passed a law that would become famous among the communalists. That law—Law 90— explicitly recognized the authority of the cabildos pequeños to govern Indian life, officially granting them any powers that they had customarily enjoyed, save those that violated state law or their residents' rights as citizens, and giving the cabildo officers the duty to correct any "moral" transgressions of their charges. Moreover, the law explicitly stated that Indians would continue to enjoy their resguardos, with no timetable set for division. It also returned illegally sold or rented resguardo property to the control of the community. It did allow some meddling in Indians' affairs by outside (local and state) authorities—public officials must represent and aid Indians in disputes as *protectores de indíjenas*—but, generally, it recognized Indian prerogatives concerning resguardos and community governance. The legislation was an amazing about-face for many Liberals, basically ending their previous assaults on communal property. Mosquera and his allies hoped that these concessions would neutralize Indians' support for Conservatives, who would now have trouble saying that Liberals wanted to destroy the resguardos.[84]

Conservative Antioqueños Become Liberal Caucanos

Mosquera had made overtures to both popular liberals and Indians, but he also cast his eyes northward, toward the Conservative bastion of Antioquia and the thousands of migrants settling along the frontier between the two states. Caucanos, both Liberals and Conservatives, were eager to recruit the Antioqueños into their parties. Many saw the migrants as racially and culturally superior to most Caucanos, especially "lazy" blacks and Indians, and as hard workers with a regulated family life who would bring economic progress to the wilderness areas of the northern frontier.[85] Migrants to the Cauca settled in two areas. Around Riosucio, they found Caucano society already in place, with towns, Indians, and even Afro-Colombian peasants in old mining camps. There, migrants had to scramble for land, competing with many others; along with native Caucanos, they began to call for the division of the Indians' resguardos. In the mountains above Cartago (the Quindío region), however, the Antioqueños found a wilderness, open to settlement.[86]

During the 1850s, migrants moved down into the mountainous Quindío region, founding small villages and farms. As noted in chapter 2, many cited their Antioqueño origins proudly, but they also sought greater independence and opportunities for land than were available in their homeland (those opposed to the dominant Conservatives also sought greater political freedom).[87] Following the settlers were powerful speculators, intent on claiming huge tracts of land, and either basing their claims on ancient land grants or exchanging government bonds for titles to public lands.[88] The speculators actually hoped that migrants would settle on their properties so that they could charge them rents. Legal action inevitably ensued, punctuated by violence.[89]

In response, the settlers turned to state power to counter the speculators. However, the speculators had close ties to the Antioqueño state government, which, in turn, was a principal backer of the national government. Therefore, if migrants hoped to appeal to sympathetic state power, the only remaining option was the Cauca State. Some migrants began to look to Popayán for aid. While many hamlets engaged in similar struggles, no one village would be as successful, or cause as much contention, as a little settlement called María.

Around 1852, settlers from Antioquia founded a town across the river Chinchiná from the Antioqueño city of Manizales, calling it the Aldea de María. They made spectacular progress, quickly building a school, a bridge over the river, and a church while hewing homesteads out of the forests and working on a road heading south into the Cauca.[90] Almost immediately, speculators began to harass them. The Maríans became engaged in a bitter and long-running legal dispute with the land speculators González, Salazar, and Company.[91] The company claimed a huge land grant, thousands of acres, with its southern border on the river Chinchiná, which the speculators claimed was not the waterway that flowed between María and Manizales (they called this the Manizales River) but one that lay well to the south of María—making all the land that the Maríans had settled the property of González, Salazar, and Company. The Maríans for their part claimed that the southern stream was the Rio Claro, not the Chinchiná.[92] The dispute was, however, more than a matter of local importance, the Chinchiná marking, not only the terminus of González, Salazar, and Company's claim, but also the boundary between Cauca and Antioquia.

The villagers began to petition provincial, state, and national authorities, asking for aid against the speculators, citing their industriousness, their families, and their wish to enjoy the freedom and independence that the Cauca offered.[93] They found little support in Ospina's national government, however. Ospina, an Antioqueño, had close ties to many speculators and may even have served as a lawyer for González, Salazar, and Company.[94] The village began to suffer violent attacks, including assaults and arson.[95] The settlers' only remaining hope was an appeal to the Caucano authorities.

Ramón Arana, a representative hired by several villages involved in land disputes, wrote to Mosquera in June 1859 expressing the Maríans' plight. He noted that, if Mosquera aided the village, "you [Mosquera] could rely on the small influence that I have in the village of María and in other villages of Quindío Province." Arana asked Mosquera to pass a law affirming that the river that ran between Manizales and María was the river Chinchiná and, therefore, the state border.[96] A few months later, Arana was even more explicit, asking for help against "the villainous Ospina." Arana assured Mosquera that, in any coming confrontation with Ospina, favoring the Maríans "would help substantially in the present circumstances so that the settlers will voluntarily lend their support to the state government."[97]

Arana had laid his cards on the table, offering Mosquera soldiers in exchange for his support. The general did not hesitate long. Mosquera realized the strategic value of María, situated on the frontier into Antioquia, the Conservative heartland. He ordered his provincial governor to go and "whip up the enthusiasm of those in the village of María."[98] Mosquera did not rely on words alone but, with his Liberal allies in the legislature, passed laws protecting the Maríans against the speculators, affirming that the village lay in the Cauca and, therefore, that the company had no claim on the lands.[99]

Arana wrote to thank Mosquera for the law fixing the state boundary and nullifying González, Salazar, and Company's claims, crowing that "in this village we do not have any Ospinistas."[100] Shortly thereafter he requested arms for the coming conflagration.[101] María was not the only village that asked Mosquera for aid. The new town of Boquía (Nuevo Salento) petitioned for Mosquera's aid in securing land, claiming "to be very federalist and devoted and grateful to your person."[102]

In 1860, Ospina officially recognized González, Salazar, and Company's assertion of the river Chinchiná's location and the company's ownership of all the land between the Manizales and the Chinchiná Rivers, contradicting Mosquera and the Maríans. The resolution did set aside some land for the Maríans within this huge area, but they would be surrounded by the company.[103] Also, any settlers living on the company's grant would be forced to move or pay rents. The company asked for help from the national government to evict the squatters on the land that it had won.[104] Some local Conservatives urged Ospina to support smallholders during land conflicts, apparently worried about Mosquera's popularity with the migrants. But, as Mosquera's intention to revolt became obvious, the Centralists (as Ospina's supporters were known) had to acknowledge that, in towns confronted by speculators, especially strategic María, Mosquera had succeeded in wooing many settlers.[105] The battle lines had been drawn.

When the war finally came in 1860, the Maríans loyally backed the Liberals, even though their new hamlet, on the front lines between Cauca and Antioquia, suffered serious depredations by the opposing armies.[106] Other migrant villages, however, sided with the Conservative forces. Conservative Antioqueño armies invaded the Cauca, and some migrants enlisted in them, identifying with their homeland. Intervillage rivalries may also have played a role in wartime partisanship, as previous disputes between settlers found their way to the battlefield.[107]

In the northwest Cauca around Riosucio, where large land companies had much less of a presence given that the area was already populated, migrants had less reason to turn to the Caucano state and tended to side with Antioquia or Conservatives, who enjoyed considerable support from the existing Caucano mestizo peasantry.[108]

After the war, the victorious Liberals rewarded the Maríans for their efforts. Mosquera personally pressed the villagers' claims, calling them "citizens passionate for liberty who have fought during all the battles of these three years."[109] María, Santa Rosa, San Francisco, and Palestina all got land grants from the constitutional convention after the war; the relatives of "the citizens who have died in the civil war, defending the cause of federation," got additional acreage.[110] The state government recognized María as a "pueblo Liberal."[111] Perhaps more important, the residents of María thought the same way. The migrants, who had in 1854 described themselves as all "from old Antioquia," now in 1863 noted that Antioqueños hated the Maríans "because we are Liberals and Caucanos."[112]

The 1860–1863 Civil War

With support from many elite and middling Liberals, popular liberals, personal friends and clients, and some of the Antioqueño migrants, Mosquera was ready to act. By 1859, he began to oppose Ospina's government openly, issuing a call for federalism that united Liberals across Colombia behind him.[113] He criticized Ospina for seeking to centralize all power in Bogotá and interfering with the rights of the states to conduct their business. Of course, plebeians had their own reasons for supporting Mosquera, reasons that were only tangentially related to federalism.

Afro-Colombians had strong motivations to support any project, be it Mosquera's or another's, that sought to end Conservative rule. Although they may have been less than successful in restricting popular politics, Conservatives had, while in power, succeeded in tormenting many Afro-Colombians. Petty officials relished their ability to intimidate "blacks" once again, interfering in their private lives, as such authorities had during slavery. Supremely galling to the freedpeople were efforts forcibly to contract their children to work without pay in powerful families' homes. José Tomás del Carmen complained that his eight-year-old daughter had been forced into domestic service, violating his "rights" and returning him to a "worse condition than when we were slaves."[114] The local mayor responsible for the arrangement defended his actions, arguing that contracting "the blacks' children" into white families would "teach them morality and good customs." He claimed that the blacks were "ignorant men" who "hate our constitution," seek only to rebel, and "do not deserve the title of true Granadans."[115]

Such cases infuriated Afro-Colombians, not only because of the economic exploitation of their children, but also because of the appropriation of their parental authority and the denial of their equality as citizens. Again, Conservatives sought a return to a social and political order under which they ruled and the dignity and concerns of those below were of little import. Under Conservative rule, Afro-Colombians were no longer an accepted part of the body politic and, therefore, did not enjoy the rights of citizen or padre de familia.

Liberals began to rally their popular allies once again. Food prices had skyrocketed in Cali in 1859. Conservatives asserted that the disorder in the countryside that had ground agricultural production to a halt caused the inflation, but Liberals told their followers that the food shortage was the result of hacendados' refusal to allow the landless to cultivate haciendas' fallow lands. Conservatives claimed that Liberals promised redistribution of land after the revolt.[116] Liberals also pointed out how the Arboledas had muscled through a law reimbursing themselves handsomely for the damage done to their haciendas in 1851.[117] No doubt, the ex-slaves who had toiled under the Arboledas' whip wondered from where their reimbursement would come.

Conservatives also feared that popular liberals would seek vengeance for the brutal reprisals committed after the 1854 war.[118] As 1859 wore on, all semblance of Conservative control evaporated in the valley. The night marches, with insults shouted at Conservatives, the beatings, and the destruction of fences had all begun again. Rumors of revolts spread unchecked, and, by late 1859, Conservatives believed that Liberals awaited only the arrival of armaments to begin their assault.[119] By the spring of 1860, Mosquera felt that he had maneuvered his alliances as best he could and that it was time to act. On 8 May 1860, he formally declared the Cauca free from federal control until a legitimate government was installed in Bogotá.

As in 1851, the Democratic Societies, popular liberals, and Afro-Caucanos formed the heart of the federalist/Liberal armies.[120] A Conservative noted: "The blacks are those that make up the Democratic Societies of Buga, Palmira, and Cali."[121] Another commentator on the war described Mosquera's troops: "The majority of that army is composed of blacks, zambos, and mulattoes, assassins and thieves of the Cauca Valley."[122] A few blacks and mulattoes rose considerably in the ranks of the Liberal armies during the war; two of these men, David Peña and Manuel María Victoria, would come to play even more important roles in the

Cauca during subsequent years. While Democratic Societies in other parts of Colombia also organized for the war, Mosquera's Caucano troops played a central role in the Conservatives' defeat.[123]

Conservatives drew most of their troops from among the mestizo smallholders of the southern highlands and the Cauca Valley. As in past wars, in this conflict religious motivations spurred many plebeians to support the Conservative cause.[124] As mentioned above, some migrant villages also sided with Conservatives, following their home state of Antioquia, the Conservative heartland. President Ospina praised such troops, saying that his armies were "composed of propertyholders and hardworking padres de familia," implicitly contrasting them against Mosquera's army.[125]

As in 1851 and 1854, some Indians voluntarily sided with Conservatives.[126] Whatever sympathies Conservatives had enjoyed among Indians deteriorated in the 1860–63 war, however, as the conflict's imperatives forced Conservatives mercilessly to conscript Indians into their armies and castigate any who seemed to sympathize with the Liberals. The Centralist leader Julio Arboleda, who unlike many Conservatives did not seem to have many patron-client ties with Indians, harshly punished Indians, hanging twenty men from Tierradentro.[127] Conservatives' brutality and the new law protecting Indian lands effectively ended any possibility that Indians would become to Conservatives what Afro-Caucanos were to Liberals.

Perhaps owing to the 1859 law, Mosquera did receive some support from Indians, although most came from across the Cordillera Central in the land of the Páez Indians. At least some Indians from Jambaló and Pitayó supported Mosquera because of a land dispute with the Conservative Arboledas (after the war, Mosquera gave his allies the contested property).[128] However, most of his Indian troops seem to have been unwilling conscripts. Many indigenous communities stayed neutral, or at least tried to, resisting efforts by the armies to conscript their menfolk.[129]

The war was long and brutal, control over parts of the Cauca going back and forth between Conservatives and Liberals throughout its course. Each side's guerrillas (or bandits) continued the fighting when the regular armies of either side left the region in defeat. Afro-Caucano liberal guerrillas incited fear in popular and elite Conservatives alike.[130] The war caused widespread destruction, worsened by armies' looting. In reaction, Mosquera somewhat desperately tried to limit the political activities of popular liberals, but with little success.[131] Both armies carried out harsh reprisals against prisoners of war and suspected enemy sympathizers. Liberals protested that Conservatives brutalized Afro-Caucanos and other prisoners, torturing "black women" by hanging them in the air upside down, and forcing other prisoners to dig their own graves before being executed.[132] Finally, by 1862, Liberals secured the Cauca, remaining in control for the duration of the war, which ended in early 1863 with Mosquera assuming the presidency of the nation.

I have tried to show the various motivations that foot soldiers had for fighting, in both Conservative and Liberal ranks. Once war began, another consideration emerged for the volunteer or conscript: booty. Conservatives alleged that Liberals enticed troops to join their ranks by promising to allow the looting of Conservative property.[133] After the war, many complained about the extensive damage done to their haciendas. Indeed, many observers claimed that looting was plebeian soldiers' primary motivation.[134]

However, booty as a motivation cannot be so easily separated from popular liberals' desire to break the haciendas' control over land. During the war, Liberals expropriated the Arboledas' mammoth haciendas, Japio and Quintero. Sergio Arboleda claimed that some Liberals planned "to distribute them by lots between the members of the army that had served in certain campaigns."[135] Perhaps needless to say, such a massive and radical land-redistribution program was not carried out, but at least some Liberals had proposed it. Conservatives swore that desire for land drove many popular liberals to fight.[136]

Some historians have considered nineteenth-century troops cannon fodder, peons without motivation.[137] Generally, however, armies were made up both of volunteers and of unwilling recruits. Both Conservatives and Liberals made appeals for volunteers and claimed to enjoy popular support, although, of course, armies did not hesitate to conscript troops, often violently, when necessary. For commanding officers, there was nothing embarrassing about forced recruitment, although volunteers seemed to have been preferred.[138] Conscription did not guarantee control, however, and desertions were common. Commanders had to concern themselves with the conditions under which their troops lived, fretting over lacking money for pay or having enough food to prevent even more desertions.[139] As one officer described his troops: "They do not acknowledge their duties and assert that they are free, recognizing nothing but their own will."[140] It seems that, early on in the 1860–63 war, Liberals enjoyed a great deal of support and volunteers swelled their ranks but that, as the war dragged on and campaigns ranged far from the Cauca, forced conscriptions became more common.

The 1860–63 war should put to rest notions that most foot soldiers came to serve through patron-client relationships, peons serving under their hacendado. The reverse often seemed to be true. Tenants and sharecroppers, angered by years of abuse at the hands of their masters, sometimes joined the opposing side. Afro-Colombians from the Arboledas' hacienda, La Bolsa, were eager Liberal partisans.[141]

More than any other civil war in nineteenth-century Colombia, the 1860–63 civil war would seem to have no relation to popular concerns whatsoever, appearing as simply a squabble among power-hungry elites.[142] However, a close examination of the Cauca experience shows that popular groups had very good reasons to support Mosquera. Many migrants got their landholdings recognized. Popular liberals received a variety of concessions—from the abrogation of vagrancy laws to the abolition of the death penalty—not the least being the removal of hated Conservatives from power. Even the long-suffering indigenous peoples won strong legal recognition of their resguardos. Instead of being unthinking pawns, caught up in a war that to them had no meaning, subalterns used elites' power struggles to win important economic and political gains.

The Consolidation of Republican Bargaining

The 1854 and 1860–63 civil wars revealed the limits of elite power in the Cauca and in Colombia as a whole. At first glance, 1854 would seem directly to contradict this assertion as Conservatives and Liberals united to crush a "populist" rebellion in Bogotá. However, this victory came about in the Cauca only because popular liberals and their elite allies were confused about and divided over events in Bogotá and the meanings of a very contradictory military coup there. Soon thereafter, Conservatives' plans for the Cauca evaporated under the heat of popular liberals' resistance and elite Liberals' political resurgence. Conservatives failed to recognize the degree to which political culture had broadened since they had last ruled in the 1840s.

The 1854 war was not a turning point in the Cauca's political trajectory (as it may have been in other regions of Colombia); popular and elite Liberals maintained a strong alliance. If the conflict had any lasting effects in the region, it was the caution that the valley's poor would exercise in the future when they challenged the economic (less so the political) domination of the hacendados. Never again could they be so bold as during the zurriago, except in times of war. Conservatives managed to unleash, however briefly, something verging on social war. Even though Conservatives' broader project to restrict political space failed, in the future Afro-Colombians and their poor white and mestizo brethren would have to weigh the risks of reprisals carefully in any attack on the hacienda system. Popular liberals had sought vengeance on their tormentors in 1851, only to have that violence returned, manyfold, on them in 1854. After 1854, popular liberals would not again act as independently as they had during the zurriago. Just as elites needed popular allies, the lower classes needed the protection of upper-class supporters, who provided some shield against their enemies' unbridled fury.

The 1860–63 civil war demonstrates the importance of examining the role of popular groups in the making of political and military (as opposed to only social) history. Mosquera triumphed only by obtaining the support of the Cauca's popular liberals (while neutralizing many potential popular conservatives). Mosquera, or, for that matter, any single member or faction of Colombia's elite, simply lacked the power to enforce his will over anything beyond the smallest locality without some assistance from those below. Conservatives, with some Liberal sympathizers, had tried in 1854—and had failed spectacularly. Divided by class, race, and party affiliation, political power was fractured in mid-nineteenth-century Colombia. No one group of the elite could impose its own hegemonic project over society as a whole; any hoping to do so had to make alliances with and concessions to the lower classes.[143] Republican bargaining, which now even some Conservatives were attempting (albeit ineptly), had become hegemonic.

5 The Triumph of Democracy, 1863–1876

The Granadan people, if not as prosperous and powerful as others whose existence measures centuries, are without a doubt as free as any in the Old and New Worlds.
—PRESIDENT M. M. MALLARINO, Bogotá, 1 February 1857[1]

With the end of the 1860–63 civil war, Liberals found themselves securely commanding both national and regional power in the Cauca. They took advantage of their victory to complete what they thought was a total break with the decrepit colonial past, positioning Colombia where it belonged—in the forefront of the world's republics.[2] They had triumphed over the Conservatives and now sought to create a new, democratic society that was politically and, they hoped, economically as modern as any in the Atlantic World.

This chapter examines the republic that Liberals attempted to create and the political culture that emerged from the interactions of the Cauca's republicans, rich and poor alike. Liberals claimed that democracy had triumphed, but—like liberty, equality, and fraternity—democracy meant different things to different Caucanos. While democracy was often discussed and this discourse was not unimportant, how Caucanos actually practiced politics during this time also gave democracy meaning.

In spite of Liberals' success, all was not well. Racial tensions, always present in the Cauca, became more worrisome for the elite (and some popular actors) after the 1860–63 civil war. More generally, elites fretted about the lack of discipline in the lower classes over whom they designed to rule. For the Liberals' democracy to work, the citizen had to know, not only his rights (and this he did—they saw the success of this everywhere), but also his duties. The subaltern citizen might choose actively to participate in public life, but he must always be disciplined in his economic and social responsibilities as a good member of the republic. After the war, Liberals devoted much effort to educating and "moralizing" their followers. Meanwhile, popular and elite Conservatives, if committed to republicanism, became increasingly suspicious of democracy as practiced in the Cauca.

Elections

Liberals dominated the Cauca throughout the period from 1863 to 1875. During this period, Conservatives, both Caucanos and Antioqueño invaders, launched several small revolts (and, in 1865, one large one), all unsuccessful.[3] Triumphant on the battlefield thanks to its citizen soldiers, the Liberal Party also dominated statewide elections, controlling the Cauca throughout the period, much as it controlled Bogotá.

The national, federalist constitution that Liberals crafted after 1863 devolved much power to the states, including the responsibility for determining citizenship requirements. Eliseo Payán, the Liberal governor of Cauca State, urged his compatriots not to raise the requirements for voting but, rather, "to extend as much as possible the right of suffrage."[4] The legislature obliged, and, in spite of past electoral setbacks, Liberals kept faith with their lower-class allies by maintaining unrestricted adult male suffrage in the Cauca. All citizens, save priests, could also serve in any post if elected.[5]

Elections were commonplace affairs in the Liberal republic. After 1863, the state president, as well as judges and deputies to the unicameral state legislature, was elected every two years. Citizens also elected local municipal councils. In addition, there were elections for national president and congressmen, although the state legislature named national senators (in subsequent years various politicians proposed the popular election of this office as well).[6] Instead of taking place on a single election day, voting occurred throughout the year. The citizens of Cali exercised the suffrage six times in 1867: on 10 February for representatives to the national congress; on 17 February for deputies to the state legislature; on 3 March for state president; on 10 March for national president; on 27 October for judicial magistrates; and on 1 December for deputies of the municipality (i.e., the provincial council).[7]

While statistics are generally unreliable or unavailable for the period, the 1856 presidential election is an exception. David Bushnell found that, throughout Colombia, around 40 percent of eligible adult males voted in that election, which, given the poor communication and transportation networks, he considered impressive. In the Cauca region, the voting rate was, on average, even higher.[8] After 1863, most electoral questions were devolved to the states, and statistics are even harder to come by, but scattered evidence suggests that voting rates remained quite high. In the election of 1865 in Cali for national congressional representatives, at least 1,028 people voted (in 1869 the city counted 1,796 men over the age of twenty-one), which gives us a minimum participation rate of 57 percent, although this rate was probably higher in actuality.[9]

Many scholars have viewed most elections in nineteenth-century Latin America with suspicion, claiming that they were either elite affairs, with plebeians voting as their patrons dictated, or so contaminated by fraud as to be meaningless, except perhaps as a legitimating mechanism.[10] Fraud was common, with voters sympathetic to a particular candidate turned away by hostile electoral boards or having their votes thrown out. Partisans regularly accused their opponents both of signing up unqualified supporters (before 1853 people who were too poor or illiterate, after 1853 nonresidents, those under the voting age, and the insane) and of unfairly denying the suffrage to their adversaries.[11] While close examination of voting records broken down by electoral district does show one candidate winning all or almost all the ballots for some districts, other districts were quite competitive, with votes going to multiple candidates.[12] Outcomes were not always preordained; rather, elections were often seriously contested throughout the period, especially before the period of Liberal hegemony, 1862–75.[13] At times, numerous candidates clogged the field; in 1867, over two hundred aspirants vied for eight positions in the national congress.[14]

The history of apparently massive fraud carried out by the Liberal Party around Bogotá seems less applicable to the Cauca. Of course, accusations of fraud were legion, but the fact remains that the opposition often won elections. While Liberals certainly had the power to exclude Conservatives from all local offices during the 1860s and 1870s and at times did commit fraud to secure victories, they often allowed competitive local elections, some of which Conservatives won. While Liberals dominated statewide elections, regular transfers of power took place between the parties in local elections across the state, and Conservatives won seats in the state legislature.[15] Even when Conservatives abstained from voting (or Liberals denied them the opportunity), Liberals still turned out on election day.[16] Indeed, Conservatives' exclusion from the statehouse was a combination of Liberal control, a Conservative boycott of many elections, and an expression of the genuine electoral support that Liberals enjoyed among their popular allies. Elections were contested, and not just by powerful patrons who competed to see who could corral the most plebeians to the polls.

Of course, leaders of both parties worked tirelessly to manage elections as closely as possible, attempting to organize and control their subaltern allies.[17] Liberals even engaged in gerrymandering. Residents of Chinchiná, citing their service in the past war, asked that their electoral district be moved from Ansermanuevo to Cartago, as the latter was much closer to the village. However, the state government rejected their request, noting that the Cartago District was overwhelmingly Conservative and that their votes would, therefore, be wasted. Although the current districting might be inconvenient, the villagers' votes were crucial in keeping the Ansermanuevo District Liberal.[18]

While some of the politicians' activities might be considered clientelism, most seemed more like electioneering. Rarely could elites simply bully their supposed clients to do their bidding on election day. In 1859, one of Mosquera's henchmen complained about the strenuous efforts required to convince people to vote for the general, even among "the Indians" of his own hacienda. This retainer reported that Liberals were telling Indians that Mosquera would raise taxes if elected; he asked Mosquera to intervene personally to contradict this rumor since one of the Indian leaders was a tenant on Mosquera's hacienda.[19] Intense pressure could be brought to bear on tenants during elections, but the Cauca's political leaders did not assume that they could rely on their workers and clients automatically doing as they were told. Suasion, both threat and enticement, was required.

At the minimum, campaigners proffered food, alcohol, and other seductions as candidates sat down to drink with potential voters, frequently wearing peasant garb while on the stump.[20] Liberal candidates and their surrogates actually campaigned among, made promises to, and pleaded with the citizenry for their support. Pledges to cut taxes were ubiquitous, but campaigns promised action regarding all aspects of the Cauca's economic and political life.[21] Conservatives participated as best they could—Liberals groused about clerics instructing their flocks as to which was the correct slate come election day.[22] Elections were very much a part of the Cauca's culture of political bargaining.

Indeed, while statistics may be lacking, commentators regularly described the excitement that election days generated and the enthusiasm that subalterns brought to the polls. Subalterns were eager voters; before 1853 and universal male suffrage, many of the poor clamored to have their names inscribed on the electoral rolls, claiming that they indeed met the property and literacy requirements.[23] Subalterns often vociferously defended their right to the suffrage. Indians from Silvia argued that, in illegally denying them the "right to vote that the law allows Granadan citizens," Liberals "cheat the republic, rip apart our principles, [and] undermine republican truth."[24] Indians and Afro-Caucanos regularly participated in elections (which was striking compared with many parts of the Atlantic World at this time), and their exclusion, rare after 1853, was bitterly protested by themselves and their elite allies.[25]

Besides simply voting, popular republicans participated in elections more broadly. Both popular liberals and popular conservatives tended to believe that the leaders of the opposing parties would commit fraud and deny the popular will if given the chance. On the eve of elections, when the electoral boards compiled the lists of eligible voters, and on election days proper, subalterns would gather in town plazas to oversee the voting and the examination of the ballots as well as to show how much support their candidate enjoyed. Often these men (and women, who, if they could not exercise the suffrage, could at least swell the ranks of their party) carried arms and threatened the supporters of opposing candidates—claiming, of course, that they were protecting their own party's voters from intimidation. When not too disturbed by violence, people took advantage of the crowds to stage a fiesta.[26]

Election days were notoriously turbulent affairs. Over time, more and more of the Cauca's elites became disillusioned with the constant disorder that elections inevitably brought. However, at least in the 1860s and early 1870s, Liberals were more or less sanguine about such disturbances, considering them the price of republicanism.[27]

Repertoires of Politics

For many elites, republicanism was more or less synonymous with elections and representative government, but subalterns sought to participate in the political system by employing a much broader repertoire of political action. When adult male subalterns won the right to vote in 1853, the suffrage was added to an already extensive catalog of ways of participating in politics. Many of these forms of participation, such as petitions or riots, had their roots in the colonial period, but plebeians easily adapted them to the republican system. Over time, new activities were added to the repertoire, expanding the ways in which subalterns practiced politics much beyond the realm of the ballot box.

I will argue, following Charles Tilly's model for Europe, that Colombia's subalterns developed new forms of political action in the nineteenth century, forms as innovative as those in North Atlantic political systems. Tilly characterized eighteenth-century (or traditional) repertoires as being local and particular, concerned only with the immediate region, and utilizing particular types of political action—such as a food riot—that were tied specifically to certain problems. A new repertoire emerged in the nineteenth century that was national, modular, and autonomous. Subalterns directed their action toward regional and national power, used political tools—such as the demonstration—to address a variety of problems, and acted with more independence than before.[28]

In the Cauca, the range of plebeians' political activities was impressive, voting being just one facet. Subalterns did not forget about their representatives after elections either and often attended the meetings of provincial legislatures or town councils to make their voices heard. When Cali's town council discussed the destiny of the ejidos in 1851, over four hundred people attended the meeting. One elite commentator complained that the shouting and threats from the galleries prevented open and honest discussion of the problem.[29] Subalterns' idea of democracy was that their influence should endure past election day. This contrasted sharply with elites' view of the role of representatives in the republican system—that, once elected, representatives should not have to deal with their constituents.

I have already extensively discussed the petitions that subalterns sent to try to influence the state, one of the most common elements of their political repertoire. Petitioners concerned themselves with almost every aspect of Caucano political and economic life—land disputes, the suffrage, village jurisdictions, taxes, the quality of schools, religion, the conduct of elected officials, pensions, pardons, roads, requests for charity, and concerns about order. Voting, attending meetings of elected officials, and petitioning were all recognized (if grudgingly so) by most elites as perfectly legal; however, much of the other political activity in which plebeians engaged lay outside their officially recognized rights.

Subalterns engaged in boycotts, refusing to buy liquor or tobacco from licensed agents, before the monopolies on those products were overturned. Tenants regularly refused to pay their land rents, another type of boycott or strike. There is even evidence of one labor strike in the region.[30] More common were riots against the abuses of authorities. Whether protesting the persecution of priests or objecting to liquor taxes, subalterns took over the streets and jeered authorities until enough force could be mustered to disperse them. There was also a riot against imperial power. After the U.S. consul killed an employee of his tobacco plantation, a mob rioted outside the jail in which he was being held, demanding justice for the slain man as they tore down the American flag hoisted over the consul's house.[31] A series of riots broke out around Almaguer over aguardiente taxes. The rioters, who described themselves as "citizens," thought their actions appropriate in a republican system, saying that they were the direct result of "the difficulty that republicans have in calmly standing by and watching those who want to trample their rights."[32] Again, subalterns viewed their actions, not as crimes, but as part and parcel of the republican system.

Like riots, individual and collective acts that the state classified as crimes cannot be so easily separated from political action. While crime could be simply for personal gain and, in the 1870s, calls for order were very appealing to many plebeians fearful of the Cauca's lawlessness, much supposedly criminal action was also a critique of the region's socioeconomic system and power structure. For example, tenants on haciendas often refused to pay rents or stole crops from the hacendado. Some subalterns even articulated that they had squatters' rights on the land of haciendas or plantations and the right to gather wood and other products from privately owned forests.[33]

Some middling writers expressed their sympathy for those accused of certain crimes, especially involving land. The overseer of the Arboledas' La Bolsa hacienda accused some of the tenants of theft, usurpation of property, and threatening violence. A broadside that appeared in Cali lamented the persecution of the accused tenants: "This is the time of thieves, good for rich thieves, bad for poor ones."[34] When Manuel María Quintero faced prosecution for stealing a few ears of corn, his lawyer protested: "The value of the stolen item is less than the paper on which I am writing the defense, and everything about this strange case reveals the deficiency of our legislation." The judged freed Quintero.[35]

Then, of course, there were moments such as the zurriago when subalterns basically supplanted the judicial system, punishing those whom they considered malefactors and deciding questions of property rights as they saw fit. The events of 1851 stand out, but, in times of disorder, especially during war, similar episodes occurred. While such actions were seen as criminal by those above, they may well have looked like democracy in action to those below. Indeed, Conservative commentators called such actions *democratic*. Liberals and Conservatives in power often turned a blind eye to their subaltern allies' attacks on their enemies' persons or property, expanding again plebeians' ability to exert some power.

Banditry was also an endemic problem. Bandits moved in and out of legitimate society, decorated warlords one year and hunted criminals the next. Whether bandits or not, most plebeians were well armed. Firearms were easy to come by in the Cauca, a result of popular participation in the region's interminable civil conflicts. Whenever a disturbance loomed, the party in power would distribute the state's armaments to its supporters, which the officials usually failed to recover once the crisis had passed. A local official lamented that, after distributing arms to lower-class liberals to put down the 1865 revolt, he discovered that the returning soldiers "refused to turn in [the weapons] even after it was demanded of them."[36] Soldiering rounded out the violent elements of the repertoire. Especially for popular liberals, armed republicanism was a key component of their political repertoire.

The two most innovative aspects of subalterns' political repertoire—according to Tilly—were the demonstration and membership in political associations.[37] Popular republicans, both liberal and conservative, marched through their cities' streets in demonstrations. Demonstrations in the Cauca were collective action in public space designed to pressure authorities about a variety of concerns. Conservative women in Pasto marched against the new national constitution of 1853, calling it antireligious.[38] Whenever elections neared, partisans would try to rally support with demonstrations. Much more common were demonstrations in support of one political party or condemning the actions of the other.[39]

Even more important than demonstrations were the region's political associations. Beginning with the Democratic Societies in the late 1840s, political clubs that incorporated subalterns were an important force in the region's politics. Popular liberals were more active in the societies in the 1850s and 1860s, although Conservatives made some attempts at forming their own. However, by the 1870s, many plebeians rushed to join the Conservative Catholic Societies. From 1848 until 1885, at least 118 different societies appeared in the historical record in forty-six different towns in the region, from Ipiales on the Ecuadorian border to Riosucio in the north.

The most active of the clubs were the Liberals' Democratic Societies. The societies were sites of political education and debate and arenas in which political bargaining took place. At least some of the clubs served as limited mutual-aid societies as well. In the Palmira Democratic Society, if an associate were in particularly dire straits, the club would pass the hat to raise money (Cali's club also had a fund to buy medicine and food for the sick). More specifically, the society employed a lawyer to defend any of its fellows accused of a crime (as did Cali's club). As well as helping each other through life's travails, all members were expected to attend any associate's funeral, at which the club's orators would eulogize the departed.[40] Palmira's Democratic Society met every Sunday. Monthly dues were five cents. Members made decisions by majority rule, raising their hands to vote.[41] Membership in the societies varied wildly over time, but, at the largest clubs, meetings of hundreds of people were not uncommon.[42] While the societies were concerned with political education, they also worked on general education. Cali's Democratic Society expected its members "to teach one poor child to read and write."[43] Other clubs held special night classes in general and industrial education.[44]

The influence of the Democratic Societies extended beyond meetings as their members spread their ideas anywhere poor men and women gathered, be it the taverns and gaming halls of cities or the haciendas' fields. An overseer on the Arboledas' haciendas complained of Caleños traveling there and making the workers "believe that they can use and enjoy as their own the lands that they have occupied." The tenants "absolutely ignore the rights of the propertyholders to those lands and threaten with death all those who administer the hacienda." Also, the Caleños had helped the tenants write a petition to local authorities complaining of abuses. Finally, the overseer reported that these outside agitators had urged the tenants to enter a life of crime and that across the haciendas was now heard the dread cry of "tierras libres."[45]

Of course, the societies' main function was to influence high politics, and their full weight was evinced most dramatically during elections and times of war. When active, the clubs always involved themselves in the region's politics. The Democratic Societies regularly concerned themselves with local and national government, forwarding advice to authorities about their favored candidates for appointed positions, expressing their approval or disappointment with a given policy, or simply welcoming an ally into office.[46] Palmira's Democratic Society explicitly stated that its objective was to oversee elected officials' actions.[47] The societies' key role in political bargaining continued throughout the period of Liberal ascendance. As detailed throughout this book, the clubs lobbied on behalf of their members, concerning themselves with such issues as primary education, voting rights, pensions, slavery, aguardiente, access to commons land, and general land redistribution.

The Democratic Societies, along with demonstrations and other aspects of subalterns' repertoire, were decidedly innovative. Older forms of political activity, which Tilly would characterize as parochial and particular, still existed in the Cauca, but alongside new forms that he would characterize as national, modular, and autonomous.[48] Certainly, the struggles over slavery and campaigns to remove the Conservative Party from Bogotá were national concerns; Cali's Democratic Society was not obsessed with one single issue but instead offered a venue in which subalterns could air many problems; and, while some Democratic Societies may have been wholly controlled from above, in others subalterns played a much more equal role. In the nineteenth century, forms of political participation in the Cauca were not all that different from those in Europe; subalterns across the Atlantic World developed a shared repertoire of politics, albeit adapted to local needs.

In the Cauca, not just demonstrations and associations, but every aspect of subalterns' political repertoire was tied into the culture of republican bargaining. Certainly, subalterns knew of their power to influence those above and employed a variety of weapons to do so. Therefore, it is difficult to classify their actions as prepolitical. Subalterns' participation in politics, whatever the particular part of their repertoire they happened to be using, revealed the variance between their conception of republicanism and democracy and that of the region's elites.

Republicanism versus Democracy

Subalterns' active political participation was perhaps the most democratic aspect of Colombia's republican political system. Certainly, the poor's entrance into politics more fully after 1848 made many of the region's political thinkers concerned with defining the true nature of the republican system and subalterns' role in it. Republicanism, understood as rule by elected representatives, was never seriously questioned or worried over. However, its more troublesome sibling, democracy, caused no end of bedevilment for the region's elites.

For many elites, elections and representation were synonymous with republicanism and democracy. Certainly, the suffrage constituted a central component of citizenship and republicanism, if less so of democracy. Elections, lauded by elites as the paramount "ceremony of republican countries," defined republicanism and the appropriate moment for the pueblo to participate in governance.[49] Conservatives stressed that voting, and nothing more, constituted the heart of the republican system, implying that any activity beyond orderly plebes casting ballots was deleterious.[50] Unrestricted suffrage for all males was, however, more problematic; an elite Caucano warned: "The results of elections, since the establishment of universal, direct, and secret suffrage, are that the candidate that is adopted by the democratic masses has more votes and he of the propertied class and intelligent citizens has less."[51] Conservatives complained that electioneering corrupted the political system. By the 1870s, even some Liberals took pains to suggest that, while "true democracy" involved voting, it certainly did not signify candidates actively campaigning and bargaining with the poor, which stirred up dangerous "antisocial ideas."[52] Cauca's elites celebrated republicanism but found democratic republicanism extremely troublesome.

Even more problematic were questions of representation. Subalterns had the most opportunity to enter political office at the village level. Councils composed of all the padres de familia traditionally governed smaller villages. The 1857 constitution legally enshrined this system: in districts of fewer than three thousand people, instead of elected town councils, a council of male householders (not all citizens, notably) met to make decisions.[53] This direct participation in governance, as opposed to electing representatives, worried many elites. The Conservative paper El Cauca argued that, whereas elected officials would be literate and somewhat restrained, a meeting of several hundred ignorant men was liable to result in anything. The paper exclaimed: "What will happen to propertyholders if an assembly composed in its majority of tenants or owners of only a small farm is excited by a communist?" It accused the constitution of creating permanent democráticas—its word for Democratic Societies—in all the region's towns.[54] Direct rule by the people, equated here with democracy, was to be feared and suppressed.

Liberals apparently agreed as the councils were not mentioned in the 1863 state constitution, although perhaps they continued informally. Liberals had also long tried to end both Indians' communal landholding and the resguardos' local community governance. While Liberals were comfortable with republican elections, local democracy (which enjoyed a longer historical tradition in the Cauca) was decidedly more threatening.

The fact that few subalterns would actually be elected to higher office made the republican system much more comfortable for elites. Liberals usually elided the problem of representation, blithely asserting that elected representatives would follow the will of the people and that education would open political service to a wider spectrum of the Cauca's inhabitants.[55] Conservatives added that, in a "representative democracy," it was the duty of the elected to follow their own will and not the will of the people. The will of the people ruled only in a "pure democracy," an impossibility in a society divided by multiple and competing interests.[56]

However, some blacks and mulattoes did serve in local, regional, and even national offices. Others with very close ties to popular liberals and the Antioqueño migrants also held important local and regional positions. David Peña, a mulatto professor, was a sergeant major at the beginning of the 1860–63 civil war but, by the 1876–77 civil war, had become one of the most powerful Liberal generals.[57] President of Cali's Democratic Soceity and the executive of Cali's and Palmira's municipal governments in the 1860s and 1870s, he also served in the state and national legislatures and as a delegate to state constitutional conventions. He enjoyed widespread popular support, as petitions backing his candidacy for local office attest, and he repaid his allies by continually defending their interests, be it over aguardiente, pensions, or land.[58] Manuel María Victoria, probably "black," went from being hunted as a bandit, narrowly escaping the death penalty in 1855, to holding important local offices in Palmira, serving as president of that city's Democratic Society, and rising to the rank of colonel in the Liberal army.[59] Generally, however, subalterns did not hold many important positions, and we can therefore hypothesize that elections and representation did not exclusively define republicanism and democracy for them.

For popular republicans, bargaining—the expectation that their political support would merit some redress for their concerns—lay at the heart of republicanism and democracy. The bargaining described during the 1850s—now encompassing popular liberals, Antioqueño migrants, and Indians—continued in the 1860s and 1870s and centered more than ever on land: the Indians' resguardos; migrants versus speculators; and popular liberals desperate to break the haciendas' monopoly.

Older issues were still contentious as well. During the continued debate over taxation of small liquor producers, popular liberals expressed their vision of elected representatives' role in a democracy. Mindful of subalterns' political support, the state had at first refrained from taxing small distillers and producers of aguardiente in the valley after the ending of the monopolies in 1851. However, desperate for revenue, Liberals restored the tax in 1866. The resulting protests were quick and fierce, led by Cali's Democratic Society, which reminded the state president that all law is the "expression of the popular will." It asked him not to enforce the law, even though acknowledging that this was technically illegal and that the legislature could rebuke him for it: "When they do not approve it [the suspension of the law], you will still have an approbation that is more valuable, that of the sovereign people."[60] The state legislature revoked the tax the next year.

Nonetheless, land questions most occupied popular liberals, and land issues revealed the gap between elite and subaltern conceptions of democracy. Soon after the end of the 1860–63 civil war, some middling Liberals proposed a conception of citizenship more in line with popular liberals' ideas. Two Liberal professors, Manuel María Villaquirán Espada and David Peña, asked why people should love the Patria, follow its laws, fulfill their obligations, and even defend it with their lives. They questioned: "What good are rights that do not protect you against the avarice of the propertied on whose lands you live and exercise your labor?" Without land, one had to submit to the capriciousness of the landlord or perish from hunger: "Either of these choices is a death." The authors noted how much popular liberals had sacrificed in the past war, both their few properties and their very lives. They demanded reform of laws that gave all power to the landlord and none to the tenant but also hinted at a broader agenda: "We would like the liberty and independence of the individual complemented with the recognition of his right to the land."[61] The Democratic Society of Palmira also petitioned for unused land to be declared public and for the right of the poor to settle and gather wood there without paying rents to nearby hacendados.[62]

Peña and Villaquirán, both leaders of the Democratic Society, understood popular liberals' vision of citizenship and democracy better than most. Democracy was not just legal and representative rights but the right to enjoy the nation's bounty, especially land. Popular liberals knew that they would never be truly equal without their own economic independence, an independence possible only when one escaped the purview of the landlord. True equality (and, thus, land) was not free or available to all but only to those who had served and sacrificed as good citizens in defense of the nation and the Liberal Party. Failure to reform the hacienda system denied the compact of republican bargaining and vitiated true citizenship and equality, which, the writers warned, would lead to disorder and instability.[63] Most elite Liberals understood the notions of equality and republicanism quite differently. These diverging views of republicanism would begin to tear at the Liberal Party. The necessity of war and the fear of Conservatives papered over these breaches for a time, but, eventually, elite Liberals would have to decide whether they were willing radically to reconfigure the class system, while popular liberals wondered how long they would wait for the social justice that they saw as both the reward and the basis of citizenship.

I have already discussed the importance of citizenship in plebeians' conceptions of popular republicanism. For popular liberals and other subalterns, citizenship and democracy guaranteed more than just certain rights and duties. The poor often compared the denial of access to land to "feudalism," seeing it as opposed to the republican system that was supposed to govern the nation.[64] Indians assumed in their petitions that a "democratic" government would accede to their wishes and let them keep their resguardos.[65] Republicanism and democracy were not simply voting and representation; they also involved bargaining, popular will, justice, and equality. Of course, the exact understanding of these concepts varied greatly among subalterns. Equality especially evoked a broader, more holistic understanding of democracy.

Conservatives and many Liberals stressed that democracy had nothing to do with equality, one paper warning: "Democracy does not mean establishing an impossible equality."[66] Equality meant equal access and rights before the law and, for Liberals, the dismantling of the old aristocracy.[67] For subalterns, however, equality had much broader socioeconomic connotations. To Indians it meant keeping their resguardos, to migrants protection from land speculators and landlords, to popular liberals social dignity, the abolition of slavery, and land of their own. Although each plebeian group defined equality differently, all assumed that it was somehow involved with democracy and the republican system in a manner more substantial than simple legal definitions.

It is unlikely that subalterns drew many distinctions between democracy and republicanism. Both concepts implied greater access to power, greater responsiveness of the state to their concerns, and a place in the public, political sphere. Democracy and citizenship provided some hope for the possibility of participating more equally in the use and control of power in Caucano society. What is striking is how subalterns seized on citizenship and republicanism as political tools to create both a powerful discourse and practice of politics.

While Liberals and their subaltern allies disagreed over the meanings of equality, democracy, and republicanism, elite Liberals had no intention of abandoning the culture of bargaining during the 1860s and early 1870s. When needed, the Liberal heartland of Cali, Palmira, and Buga quickly supplied troops to put down Conservative rebellions. When a religious revolt threatened in the south, a Liberal paper remained calm: "Only a contingent of the state's Democratic Societies will suffice to make the government invincible."[68] The Cauca's Liberals might have had trouble managing their popular allies, but, as aggravating as subalterns might be, they guaranteed the electoral and military dominance of the party.

Indeed, Caucano Liberals criticized the national government for offering the poor merely a flowery language of liberty and equality while its actual projects seemed to benefit only financial speculators.[69] Many Liberals knew that they needed to act to improve their allies' economic and social condition, yet the national government seemed to think that political rights and talk of democracy alone would be sufficient to satisfy the poor. Many of the Cauca's Liberals knew that, for better or worse, "true democracy" was entangled with bargaining and that their allies expected the democratic, republican system to better their lives.[70]

Many Liberals embraced a republican system that not only included significant participation by the poor but also implied a broader definition of democracy as well. Liberals referred to López's regime as the "first democratic administration" because he freed men (by abolishing slavery), their thoughts, and their labor (by ending monopolies).[71] Democracy involved acting to increase liberty (i.e., economic and personal freedom), distinct from mere republicanism, which was related to representation. Liberals called their vision of politics—in which they would ally with popular sectors, represent them, and act to increase their well-being and freedom—"radical, democratic republicanism."[72]

Conservatives embraced republicanism, but they generally feared democracy. The zurriago of 1851, and other disturbances like it, became known as the period of "democratic tumults" or the "democratic zurriago."[73] Conservatives sarcastically described robbed houses and ransacked haciendas as having been "democratized."[74] As passions built in the Cauca in 1859 before the Liberal revolt, a Conservative fretted that he and his fellows were "waiting for the democratic explosion."[75] In general, many elites considered excess political participation—especially through the popular political associations—by liberal subalterns as "democratic" or, more evocatively, "savage democracy."[76] A Conservative writer warned about the dangers of "pure democracy," which "would give predominance to the barbarous element."[77]

Almost everyone in nineteenth-century Colombia was a republican. While Liberals tried at various times to paint their enemies as monarchists, Conservatives never really seriously considered abandoning the republican system. However, no such consensus existed about democracy. As in nineteenth-century Europe, the relation between liberalism and democracy was often contentious.[78] However, in the 1860s and early 1870s, most Liberals still felt confident that they could control their allies' democratic impulses and still welcomed popular political participation. They chided Conservatives, saying that they wanted "to establish a repressive regime . . . believing that only through repression and the weakening of popular action one can achieve order in society."[79] This would change, however, in the late 1870s as Liberals had more and more trouble reconciling their vision of republicanism with that of their popular supporters.

Republicanism and Race

Complicating elites' conception of democracy was race, something that they rarely wrote about but that was nevertheless central to the Cauca's political culture. The region's political elites and middling newspapermen expended surprisingly little time or energy overtly worrying about race before the late 1870s. Before this time, the ideology of scientific racism had not yet been widely disseminated; many hazily conceived of race as a combination of regional, biological, legal, political, and cultural attributes.[80] Racial categories were often fluid—mulattoes especially had some degree of social mobility. In a broad sense, many elite Caucanos, like the Conservative leader Sergio Arboleda, thought that there were basically three races—white, Indian, and African—the latter two being "inferior."[81] However, the Cauca's racial system was quite complex in its quotidian workings: mulatto, mestizo, zambo, and many other racialized categories formed a complex racial typography.

Conservatives were much more openly racist and more likely to view nonwhites or mestizos as a serious threat to the Cauca's political and economic future. As mentioned above, Conservatives decried making democracy synonymous with equality—since they deemed equality an impossible goal in a Cauca with different (and unequal) races.[82] Sergio Arboleda went further than most, denying the utility of even legal equality: "I see another obstacle to industrial progress in the titular absolute equality with which the three races that form our pueblo should obey the same legislation."[83] However, other Conservatives denied, at least publicly, believing that race should be the basis of legal discrimination, but they did claim that racial differences indicated a natural social inequality.[84] The newspaper Ariete noted that God had created inequality among men and that "never will the color black be equal to the color white." It warned of the danger of teaching "the black, the rogue, the vagrant, the stupid, and the criminal to be jealous of and to be insolent and discourteous enemies with the white, the honorable, the hard worker, the talented, and the virtuous."[85] Privately, Conservatives denigrated Indians and especially blacks, calling the latter an "ignorant and bestial race that is the mortal enemy of whites."[86] Conservatives, and some Liberals, often fretted over the possibility of a "race war."[87] In reality, however, Conservative whites engaged in the closest approximation to a race war when they persecuted and murdered many blacks and mulattoes during and after the 1854 civil war.

Especially problematic for Conservatives was the inclusion of Afro-Caucanos, their former slaves, in the republican system. Conservatives were horrified that their elected representatives would not be white, one complaining that, in Palmira, "an Indian, a black, and a half-white" had won offices.[88] Another Conservative reported to Mosquera (before the latter's opportune political conversion) that the Conservatives had lost elections in Palmira because of the sixteen hundred votes of the "blacks." He complained that blacks voted more than once (claiming that the white electoral board could not tell them apart) and that Marat himself would have laughed at the proceedings. He sarcastically asked Mosquera: "How does this democratic republic seem to you?"[89] Democracy, problematized enough by class, was doubly threatening to Conservatives given the Cauca's racial diversity.

Liberals exploited Conservatives' overt racism to solidify their relations with Afro-Colombians, reminding their allies that the "Goth Party"—Liberals' moniker for reactionary Conservatives—still had "pretensions to dominate those whom they call people of color."[90] As late as 1876, a newspaper accused Liberals of telling Afro-Caucanos that Conservatives "are going to enslave them."[91] Liberals proudly trumpeted the region's racial equality, calling Colombia the "Vanguard of America" in regard to freedoms of all kinds: "Men of color are as esteemed as whites, and all enjoy the same rights and guarantees."[92] One Liberal paper declared that equality meant denying race as a meaningful category, declaring that all people were of similar origin and that races were just "based on ridiculous accidents."[93]

This is not to deny Liberals' racism; they certainly were racists, although usually they exercised care in any public discourse. Following the tenets of liberalism and their reliance on citizenship as a universalizing social identity, Liberals simply did not talk about race much. Regardless of their discourse (or lack thereof), many Liberals were willing to politically embrace those whom they viewed as racially different (and perhaps racially inferior). Despite public acclamations to the contrary, many Liberals did not believe that blacks, and certainly not Indians, were their intellectual or social equals, but they did assert that they could be political equals, or at least political participants (with Liberals in the vanguard). The Liberal paper El Pueblo argued in 1850 that all should be equal before the law; on Julio Arboleda's arrest for sedition, it noted: "We believe that the governor was right to send Mr. Julio Arboleda to jail, just as he would have sent a black who had committed similar offenses; because we believe that Mr. Julio Arboleda with his poetic talent and his chests filled with gold is, before the law, equal to a black man, equal to the most stupid and miserable plebe."[94] This passage reveals the boundaries of Liberals' commitment to racial equality. They saw Afro-Colombians as potential political allies, and even potential citizens, but also brute citizens who required their lead, and ignorant citizens who required education and discipline. From the Liberals' point of view, education and discipline would solve any problem that recalcitrant or culturally backward races posed for the Cauca's political or economic modernity.

Liberals' accusations, alliances with Afro-Colombians, and public protestations of racial equality angered Conservatives. During the 1860–63 civil war, Conservatives imprisoned wealthy white Liberals in the same cells with their poor Afro-Caucano allies, all of whom were dying of hunger, telling their elite enemies that this would "teach them democracy."[95] For Conservatives, democracy signified the unhealthy breakdown of class and racial barriers to political participation. However, in spite of Conservatives' derision, many Liberals seemed more than willing to form political alliances with Afro-Caucanos.

The extent of alliance between Liberals and Afro-Caucanos was such that, in at least a small way, it altered how Caucanos thought about race. While some blacks and mulattoes were Conservatives, the overwhelming majority were Liberals. By the 1860s, if not earlier, popular liberalism became closely associated, especially for Conservatives, with Afro-Caucanos, and a discourse linking liberalism with blackness was well established. The connection began with abolition and the zurriago, which Conservatives blamed on Liberals and the "black race."[96] By the 1860–63 civil war, the idea had solidified. Conservatives contemptuously derided Mosquera's troops as "ferocious gangs of blacks."[97] When Conservatives called all Liberal troops "black," they included many mulattoes, mestizos, and poor whites, but, since the soldiers were poor and Liberal, they became black in Conservative eyes.[98] Ramón Mercado, who was white or mestizo, was described as being black or mulatto because of his association with popular liberals.[99] David Peña, who was a mulatto, was denigrated in private letters for belonging to the "African race."[100] One Conservative was confident that his party could triumph over "the blacks and all who call themselves Liberals."[101] Liberalism, especially popular liberalism, became synonymous with blackness.[102]

Liberals and Conservatives' ideas about race and the relations between race and republicanism are much easier to examine than are Afro-Caucanos'. In the Cauca at this time, blacks and mulattoes hardly referred to themselves as such; unlike Indians or Antioqueños, they rarely claimed a specific racial identity in their public discourse.[103] Their private beliefs, largely inaccessible to the historian, were another matter. Generally, the region's elites did not directly target Afro-Caucanos' cultural and social existence at this time (at least compared to the attacks on Indians' culture). Perhaps, therefore, Afro-Caucanos had less reason to assert an identity as "blacks" or "mulattoes." We can hypothesize that many were much more concerned about securing the identity of citizen and equality with whites, both denied them so long, than about protecting a specific racial or cultural identity (again, the contrast with Indians is striking). Of course, racism no doubt forced many either to deny a racialized identity or to fear asserting it.[104]

In sharp contrast were Liberals attitudes toward Indians. Liberals would champion the downtrodden, but only those who relinquished colonial or racial identities that stood between the citizen and the nation-state. Liberals warned that, until Indians ceased to be governed by special legislation, "they will never be able to become free citizens and active members of the democratic republic."[105] Most Liberals still considered Indians inferior and thought that they could never be equal or citizens until they abandoned their resguardos and communities, rejected their Indianness, and accepted Hispanization.[106] Caucano elites, led by Liberals, legally excluded many Indians who lived across the mountains around Tierradentro and in the Caquetá rain forest by declaring these areas territories where the normal laws of the Republic did not apply. Even when Liberals supported Indians' claims to their resguardos, they did so only by considering them inferior. State President Eliseo Payán said that Indians' protected status was "similar to that of minors, squanderers, the demented, and deaf-mutes."[107]

The continual attacks on Indians' property, communities, and ways of life helped unite many indigenous communities in the south and define what Indian would mean in the Republic. In 1866, the state government asked all local officials and indigenous cabildos to give their opinion on the compatibility of resguardos and the state constitution. Indians resoundingly answered that they wanted to keep their resguardos.[108] The village leaders lamented that, with individual propertyholding, "whites" could buy land for ridiculously low prices off of "Indians incapable of exactly discerning their true interests" by corrupting them with liquor or by calling in old debts.[109] While cabildos used a language of Indians' incompetence, the resguardos really protected individuals from the power of the landholding class, especially landlords' use of debt. The resguardos might be thought of as labor unions for smallholders, organizing farmers' collective interests against powerful merchants and hacendados. This constant harassment and persecution sharply delineated "blancos" from "indígenas."[110]

Indians also faced the problem of whites claiming that Indians were "more or less civilized" and, therefore, did not merit special laws, although this strategy was much more prevalent in the north than in the south.[111] In the north, settlers and speculators, hungry for land, accused Indians of having "made a complete fusion of the Indian race with the white and mestizo."[112] These accusations forced Indians to defend their "Indianness" and the cohesion of their communities.

The questioning by the state in the 1860s of the resguardos' future helped inspire a greater cohesiveness among the south's indigenous population. While before 1860 Indians had rarely united in petitions and lawsuits beyond the confines of a particular village or resguardo, large groups of Indians in the south now responded together. One petition was sent from many of the cabildos of the municipality of Obando—at least fifteen separate cabildos were represented under the office of an indigenous alcalde mayor. While the language retained much of the humble protestations of other petitions, it emphasized the importance of Indians' own local authority. The indigenous leaders stressed how they kept order over their communities and protected them from the invidious schemes of the "whites." They praised Law 90 (see chapter 4), especially as it allowed them "the important prerogative of we ourselves representing and defending our rights," instead of relying on others.[113] The state's challenge to Indians in 1866 marked the point at which the cabildos broke from an older discourse of deference and more forcefully evoked their independence while, more important, beginning to act in supralocal alliances to strengthen their political position.

Indians' new discourse emerged fully in 1873, after the state legislature passed yet another law abrogating Law 90 and ordering the resguardos' division. Indians from across the south gathered in Pasto to write to the legislature, chastising the representatives for not consulting the villages about the law and again exposing their communities to the possibility of losing their lands. The communalists expressed their frustration with the legislature and, noting the continued division of the Cauca between opposing political parties, warned: "If the mentioned law is put into effect or practice, we would find ourselves by necessity standing with the first who gave the shout of rebellion, as long as they assured us the repeal of the aforementioned law."[114]

Having threatened to side with the Conservatives in any future revolt, the Indians went on to suggest that such a turn of events need not come to pass if the Liberals acceded to their wishes: "We are convinced that the present legislators would not turn a deaf ear to the voice of more than twenty thousand inhabitants demanding the repeal of a law."[115] This moment marked an important change in the way in which the southern Indians related to the Cauca's powerful. The petition did not represent a complete break with the older discourse that I have called *popular indigenous conservatism* as it still contained professions of weakness, calls for justice, appeals to authority to perform its duties, and protestations of the importance of indigenous families and communities. Indians had responded favorably before to Conservatives' rhetoric and support of their resguardos, religion, and families; but now, like popular liberals and the Antioqueño migrants, they actively sought to bargain with the powerful, playing one party against the other.

Liberals responded, if somewhat halfheartedly. President Trujillo basically gutted the new law, returning Law 90 into effect, but also allowing the division of a resguardo if the majority of the community asked for it and permitting more outside interference by local authorities in Indian affairs.[116] However, the erosion of Indians' traditional allegiance to Conservatives, which had begun with Law 90 and the brutality of the 1860–63 civil war, now accelerated. The south's indigenous people, acting in a pan-village and regional alliance, had issued a declaration of independence. They would no longer simply react to Conservatives' occasional appeals; rather, they would make their own way in the dangerous waters of Colombia's politics. In these meetings of the south's Indians, the discourse and strategy that Quintín Lame and the founders of Colombia's modern Indian movement would employ in the twentieth century tentatively emerged.[117]

Discipline

During the 1860s, Liberals were confident that democracy's problems, such as overzealous political participation or race, would be solved by the creation of a disciplined citizenry. Liberals thought that plebeians might occasionally misbehave, owing to their misunderstanding of democracy, their lack of self-restraint (perhaps caused by their race or a generally inferior plebeian culture), or their irrationality. However, the party's vanguard assumed that it could discipline and educate the pueblo, make them understand the "true" meaning of democracy and their place as supporting players in the political system. Discipline would involve many institutions and processes: the Democratic Societies, penitentiaries, the National Guard, the church, the police, hospitals, economic development, and, most important by far, public schools.[118]

Education would resolve all the quandaries that republicanism and democracy had engendered. One Liberal noted that an educated populace "is much more necessary under the republican form" of government than under any other.[119] The government newspaper declared that education made people "capable of being citizens in a free and republican society."[120] Public primary schools would teach the masses to be citizens. The primary schools, at least those for boys, had classes on "the rights and obligations of citizens" and the "national and state constitutions," using a textbook called *Catecismo republicano*.[121] Education was also seen as the path to a powerful nation-state, following the examples of the United States and Prussia.[122]

Liberals devoted substantial resources and efforts to their project. They created a whole bureaucracy, probably the state's largest division, to administer the region's public schools. They tried time and again to make school attendance compulsory, although lack of resources and many subalterns' refusal to send their children to the classroom usually prevented enforcement.[123] They even established a normal school to train future teachers. In 1866, there were 234 public and private schools with 8,265 students between them.[124] By 1875, there were 139 public boys' schools and 31 public girls' schools with 6,634 male and 1,590 female students between them and 49 private boys' schools and 36 private girls' schools with 1,516 male and 831 female students between them. A total of 10,571 children were, thus, enrolled in 255 schools.[125] Given that the Cauca counted 142,610 children (70, 393 boys) between the ages of seven and twenty-one in 1879, a significant minority of Caucano males had access to primary schooling.[126] Although Liberals were generally quite suspicious of women's political participation, many urged primary education for girls so that they would be civilized enough to raise the future male citizen.[127]

Liberals seem to have had some success in teaching at least the basics of literacy. The *jefe municipal* of Obando Province, for example, claimed that 6,330 of the province's men and 1,335 of its women could read and write in 1865. If these figures are accurate, over 40 percent of men were literate.[128]

Education would also teach good habits of hard work, love of virtue, respect for the law, and recognition of legitimate authority. Schools would prevent crime: one Liberal described them as the "best preventative penal code."[129] Both Liberals and Conservatives held racist assumptions about Indians' and Afro-Colombians' work ethic (especially compared to Antioqueño migrants') but, with scientific racism still nascent, believed that education and development would foster habits of hard work and thrift instead of felonious deviance.[130] Like so many problems, the racial dilemma would be solved by education and economic development. The paper *La Unión* exhorted the state: "Found popular schools where the child of the poor man and the man of color learn to read and write at the side of the child of the rich and white, and you will have an enlightened pueblo, a pueblo educated in fraternity and learning."[131]

Schools and other institutions for instruction had two principal functions under the Liberal state, both designed to make the masses "rational." First, they would teach about rights and the meaning of republicanism so that plebeians could participate in politics wisely—that is, not be fooled by the church, the old patron, or other Conservative blandishments—and see in the nation and the Liberal Party their future.[132] Second, schools would discipline the masses, teach them their responsibilities and duties, so that they would not interpret their new rights in too radical a manner, would know their place behind Liberal leaders, and would contribute through their hard work to the economic modernity of Colombia.[133] The striking success of the first goal was matched by the resounding failure of the second. Discipline was supposed to solve the problems of labor unrest, disorder, and crime, but, by the 1860s, more elites began to suspect that democracy fostered in subalterns only a sense of entitlement and disobedience.

Indeed, by the 1870s, many Liberals were looking askance at the democratic and disciplinary project. They complained about the lack of interest that Liberal authorities displayed in cracking down on criminals and the party's willingness to accept former bandits into its fold.[134] Many Caucanos worried that the state was degenerating into "anarchy."[135] After the 1860–63 civil war, police forces simply did not exercise much control in the Cauca Valley. As one observer noted: "Immorality has deeply permeated the masses. The respect for property has almost completely disappeared. Robbery is the order of the day, the cancer of society."[136] Cattle theft remained endemic.[137]

Liberals began to suspect that the fierce sense of liberty that their lower-class allies harbored might hinder efforts at economic progress. Hacendados had no end of trouble managing their properties. One overseer protested that the "blacks . . . do not recognize at all the rights of the owners of these lands and threaten with death those that administer the hacienda."[138] Landowners near Cali complained that, while "before the revolution of 1860 people had a little respect for forests that were private property," now reserves were raided for wood with impunity.[139] A newspaper lamented the reluctance of the poor to submit themselves to laboring for others.[140] One writer described this reluctance as "our workers and peons' perversion of the sentiment of personal independence."[141] Indeed, on the coast, after emancipation and the economic collapse of mining, Afro-Colombians simply did not need elite Liberals any more and retreated into the bountiful and abundant lands of the tropical forests to live in relative independence. While the alliance between Afro-Caucanos and Liberals in the central valley would endure for some time still, the once-potent connections between popular and elite Liberals along the coast disintegrated.

All these concerns aggravated long-standing divisions in the Cauca's Liberal Party. Liberals were split nationally between a group called Radicals and their opponents.[142] Those disenchanted with Radicalism wanted a political project that would emphasize order and progress over regional power, popular participation, and a focus on rights. They began to support Rafael Núñez nationally (he promised more order), although he was not yet to win the presidency.[143] Liberals dissenting from the Radical wing seemed to be old Draconianos (who had always been more concerned with order; see chapter 4), Mosqueristas (who had joined the Liberals more out of political expedience than anything else and were wary of popular participation), and those worried that the Cauca's political excitation affected opportunities for capitalist development.[144] Various attempts were made at some type of alliance between Conservatives and Liberals worried about the region's Radical direction, but little came of these efforts in the short term.[145]

The Radicals and other Liberals with close ties to the popular classes, however, still had faith in their plebeian allies (even as they tried to focus more on citizens' responsibilities and less on citizens' rights). When even Liberal officials tried too hard to crack down on disorder, Radicals struck down local ordinances if they thought that such laws violated the pueblo's rights by preventing assemblies, persecuting vagrants, or restricting political speech.[146] The 1863 state constitution had even abolished the death penalty and limited imprisonment to ten years. Elites of all political stripes complained that juries routinely "acquit the most notorious criminals."[147] However, other Liberals defended the institution, noting that the carelessness of prosecutors also resulted in acquittals.[148] Generally, many Liberals remained reasonably confident in the republican system, future economic growth, and their ability to control the masses.

Liberals still believed that discipline would perfect the Cauca's republicanism. Schools were the principal agent, aided by the National Guard and Democratic Societies, in the project of moralizing the masses. A regulated police force would also exercise surveillance on the poor; but Liberals' reform of the police centered, not on cracking down on endemic cattle theft, but on encouraging constables to maintain cities' cleanliness and always be on the lookout for disease.[149] Finally, jails would reform the errant. Liberals complained that, at present, the jails were "schools of immorality," where the incarcerated simply honed their criminal skills.[150] They would, therefore, improve the penitentiaries, asserting that it was the function of "panópticos" to "to turn wayward men into good citizens."[151]

Yet Liberals' plans were not working, and the strain on the upper stratum of the party intensified. Plebeians seemed to absorb only what suited them in the schools and Democratic Societies and to pay no heed to disciplinary lessons. The party threatened to divide between those wishing to retreat from an alliance with the poor and more forcibly impose order and those still confident in the project begun in 1849. Only renewed Conservative threats helped Liberals at least temporarily set aside their differences in the face of yet another revolt.[152]

Conservative Reaction

Conservatives were pessimistic about the Cauca's future and the Liberals' project. What most worried and angered Conservatives (besides being out of power) was the Liberals' increasingly virulent attacks on the church, which, for Conservatives, was the only remaining institution standing between the Cauca and complete anarchy. After 1863, Liberals began to attack the property and prerogatives of the church, expropriating land and buildings, eliminating religious orders, and forcing the clergy to sign oaths of loyalty to the state.[153] Some clerics sought a more conciliatory line with the Liberal government, but the Vatican (perhaps the most influential foreign power in the Cauca) quickly rebuked them. Pope Pius IX chastised the bishop of Popayán for signing away the rights and prerogatives of the church while negotiating with the Liberals in 1863 and demanded that he both reexamine his conscience and consult with the archbishop in Bogotá before making any more decisions.[154] In the 1870s, the Caucano church took an extremely antagonistic line toward the Liberal government, refusing to cooperate on any matter.[155] Anger over issues of confiscation of property and interference of the Liberal government in church affairs had been festering among the clergy for years, but, in the 1870s, controversy over public education intensified the conflict.[156]

Conservatives were wary of Liberals' pedagogical plans. Republican-oriented education would not discipline the pueblo; rather, its emphasis on rights would only incite the masses to commit more democratic excesses. Only a pedagogy based on religion could hope to restrain the masses and make them "useful citizens."[157] Conservatives maintained that religious education combated, not only ignorance, but also disorder and class antagonisms.[158]

Conservatives began to actively protest Liberal education laws, especially the requirement that parents send their children to school. They asserted that the law violated constitutional guarantees of freedom of instruction and freedom of religion, but what most raised their ire was that the legislation contradicted "parental authority": "Head of his family by both natural and civil law, only the father has the power to rule his family as he sees fit, and no one is able to do that better than he to whom God has given domestic supremacy."[159]

The Liberal education system undermined the foundation of the Conservative citizen by appropriating some of the power of the father as master of his family. Forced school attendance was also wrong because children's teachers would not necessarily be of the same faith as the children's parents and might, therefore, attempt to shape children's thinking differently than their parents would.[160] (Indeed, this was Liberals' goal: to create "rational"—but still religious—citizens out of the superstitious and barbarous masses.) Particularly noxious was the creation of the "vigilance commissions" that would ensure that parents sent their children to school. In a letter to the state constitutional convention, Pasto's municipal council lamented the power of these commissions to "penetrate into the heart of the domestic home," warning that they would "become a horrible instrument of persecution and tyranny." The council also accused the commissions of making a mockery of "the most holy prerogatives of the free man."[161] A mammoth petition, signed by over two thousand people, accompanied the letter from the municipal council.[162] Other petitions made similar demands, including that parents should be able to select the public school teachers they wanted.[163] The bishop of Pasto warned that his flock was "ready to make any sacrifice . . . to defend the cause of God."[164] Across the Cauca, parish priests preached against the perfidy of the public schools. Bishops even threatened the excommunication of parents who sent their children to public schools.[165]

Of course, schools were unpopular for other reasons. Conservatives remonstrated that the high taxes required to support such ambitious education plans would unduly burden the poor. Plebeians specifically detested such taxes being used to pay teachers who were often incompetent. They also resented the loss of children's contribution to the agricultural labor force that school attendance represented.[166] Liberals further angered Indians by allowing towns to seize parts of the resguardos, rent them out, and use the funds thus raised to found schools.[167]

Conservatives took advantage of popular discontent to mobilize potential supporters actively and directly. They had appealed to the poor only haphazardly in the past, but they now looked to imitate Liberals by establishing more structured and permanent links with the lower classes. As the disaffected started to talk among themselves about the possibilities of a revolt, one plotter opined that, while Conservatives enjoyed much sympathy in the center and north of the valley, past conflicts had shown that these sympathies did not necessarily translate into support on the battlefield. He argued that Conservatives must organize and rally their potential allies by spreading their ideas and vilifying Liberals.[168] Conservatives knew that they did not enjoy the same close relationship with their popular followers that their elite adversaries had with popular liberals. The solution, a direct response to the Democratic Societies, was the Catholic Societies.[169]

The Catholic Societies began as a way to organize religious education for those boycotting the public schools. Women formed their own auxiliaries, focusing on education for young women and providing charity for the sick.[170] Conservatives did not necessarily initiate the societies with an eye to strengthening the party, but many took advantage of them to do just that. They thought "we will gain much" by fomenting the poor's discontent with secular education.[171] Conservatives urged their followers to establish the clubs, not just in the larger cities, but in villages too. The Catholic Societies sprang up in towns and villages across the state; clubs were active in Bolívar, Buga, Cali, Candelaria, Cartago, Dolores, Florida, Jamundí, Jimena, Palmira, Pasto, Pradera, Popayán, Riosucio,

Roldanillo, San Pablo, Sipí, Silvia, Tadó, Tambo, Timbío, Toro, Totoró, Vijes, and Yotoco.[172]

By 1875, parents had begun to boycott public schools in large numbers; the resistance was strongest in the north and among the Antioqueño migrants. Around Cartago, two schools' attendance dropped from 150 boys and 80 girls to 37 boys and 21 girls.[173] Liberals tried to compromise by allowing religious education to be conducted in the schoolhouses after classes were over, but this move found little support among the populace or the church hierarchy. Liberals complained that the Caucano clergy was the most vociferous in attacking public education of any in Colombia.[174] For their part, Conservatives increased their denunciations of Liberals, focusing on secular, public education, but including all the Liberals' past attacks on religion and the church.[175]

Rumors of a general revolt inspired by fears of religious persecution swept the Cauca from 1872.[176] Although the Democratic Societies in Cali, Palmira, and Buga had been increasingly active throughout the 1860s and 1870s, Liberals began to try to reenergize their clubs in small towns as well to counter the Catholic Societies.[177] In 1876, the revolt would finally come in the form of the bloodiest civil war that Colombia had experienced since Independence.

Anxious Republicans

Throughout the 1860s and early 1870s, most Liberals remained confident of the future of the republican experiment. Colombia, alongside the United States, would lead the New World into an era of republican freedom, leaving Europe (with the exception, perhaps, of young Italy) to stew in its own decadent despotism or revolutionary chaos.[178] Democracy, race, and order may have been preoccupations, but Liberals still believed that they had positioned Colombia in the vanguard of nation-states on the way to economic and political modernity.[179] More worrisome than disorder from below was the threat of Conservative reaction felt by Colombia's Liberals and all those of the "modern Liberal spirit"—a threat shared by their fellows in the Northern United States in that country's Civil War and Mexico's patriots battling against an imposed monarchy.[180] If they could fend off the Conservatives, eventually the republican system, reinforced with moralizing schooling, would resolve the problem of discipline.

Conservatives and a significant number of upper-class Liberals did not share the Radicals' sangfroid. In their eyes, crime was rampant. Lawlessness went unpunished. Anarchy reigned. Popular liberals were making more and more demands on the state for land reform, and Indians seemed less willing to play a subservient role. Instead of encouraging development, republicanism seemed to be hampering it. However, before any project to address these problems could be formulated, popular and elite Conservatives, outraged over Liberals' attacks on religion and the family, launched a revolt.

In the 1870s, popular republicans of all types, liberal and conservative, felt their status as free citizens threatened. Popular liberals feared that, without the land reforms that would make them propertyholders, they would never escape the power of the landlord and achieve true equality. Popular conservatives worried both about elite Liberals' efforts to create a rational citizen class through public education that appeared to undermine their patriarchal authority and about the increasing disorder that threatened the stability and viability of their smallholdings. On the other hand, elites felt threatened by the increasing demands of the poor and the disorder that democracy had wrought. The Liberal project had created immense strains at all levels of Caucano society. The triumph of democracy seemed to sow the seeds of its own dissolution.

6 Failure of Discipline:

The Suppression of Popular Politics,

1875–1886

The general impression is that the bourgeoisie in the nineteenth century
were relatively confident about the peasants.
—MICHEL FOUCAULT, *Power/Knowledge*

In 1875, Liberals again faced a Conservative revolt and again defeated it only with the help of their popular liberal armies. Their victory would be short-lived, however, as the culture of political bargaining tore at the Liberal Party's fragile unity. Popular liberals demanded radical land reform in exchange for their sacrifices in the past war, but most elites had no intention of ceding control of the resource that underlaid the class system in the Cauca. If popular liberals were greatly disappointed in their allies' failure to accede to their wishes, their unmet demands frightened many Liberal elites. Worse still, the Cauca presented a very worrisome picture in general: crime went unchecked; the economy stagnated; property was insecure.

Nor were elites alone in their disillusionment. Smallholders, especially many Antioqueño migrants, also questioned the future of the Liberal experiment. Small farmers and ranchers feared the growing lawlessness of the region and the threat that Liberalism—seemingly beholden to the valley's landless popular classes—posed to religion, family, and property, the foundations of popular smallholder republicanism. Many smallholders, formerly Liberals, now allied themselves with either the Conservatives or the Independents, the new order-and-progress-oriented Liberal faction.

The Independents sought to regenerate a Colombia and a Cauca that they saw as decadent and to control lower classes whom they viewed as degenerate.

Independents thought that Radical Liberals had erred in granting so much political space to popular groups. Independents allied both with Conservatives and with many popular republicans to sharply restrict the forms and extent of popular political participation. Economic modernity supplanted political modernity as the centerpiece of the Independents' project. The Radicals' program of discipline had failed. Independents and Conservatives imagined a much harsher regime of order that would physically punish dissenters, morally reform corrupted plebeians, and rein in the culture of political bargaining. Republicanism would survive, but democracy, at least as understood by many popular republicans, would die.

The 1876–1877 Civil War

Nineteenth-century Caucanos and subsequent historians have seen the 1876–77 civil war as a religious conflict as well as yet another partisan battle.[1] Disputes about secular education had exacerbated long-standing divisions over the role of the church in society and politics. While principally a bid by Conservatives to regain the power that they saw Liberals monopolizing through electoral fraud, the contest was also a religious war. The Catholic Societies served as the basis for organizing troops during the rebellion.[2] Conservatives began to refer to themselves as the Catholic Party, and their battalions bore names such as Pio IX.[3] Priests actively participated in the war, exhorting men to join the rebels and even enlisting in the armies themselves. During the war, Conservative troops attacked public school buildings, destroying the books and desks.[4]

The rebellion's locus and strength were in the northern half of the state. While relying on their traditional support among many of the valley's smallholders, Conservatives also counted on the backing of the Antioqueño migrants in the northern hills.[5] Soldiers from Antioquia State enrolled in Conservative armies, and these recruits from their homeland no doubt encouraged some migrants to side with the rebels.[6] While piety motivated many settlers and other small farmers to defend the church, popular conservatives had other, more material reasons for enlisting. In the Cauca Valley and the northern hills, mestizo peasants and Antioqueño migrants felt increasingly threatened by popular liberals. The conflation of Afro-Caucanos and the Liberal Party disturbed many Antioqueños, sure of their own racial superiority. Increasing disorder also played a role, as it threatened the viability of smallholdings. Liberals' attacks on religion undermined settlers' identity as padres de familia, threatening their position as masters of their families, their citizenship in the republic, and their landholding, as all of these were based on family life. Finally, some Antioqueño settlers and other popular conservatives joined the armies hoping to gain access to land (including Indians' resguardos) as a reward for their service.[7]

A Conservative commander gloated about how quickly his compatriots were raising troops in the north and center of the state. Around Palmira, nine hundred men volunteered in one day, and, across the north, twenty-three hundred men had enlisted.[8] Smallholders and especially many Antioqueño migrants swelled the rebellion's ranks. A Liberal warned that his party's own Antioqueño allies were not trustworthy: "These villages are all of Antioqueño origin, and those that call themselves Liberals are only Liberals of convenience in whom the government cannot place any confidence."[9] Indeed, while in the 1850s and 1860s migrants had joined the Liberal Party, by the 1870s the wisdom of that alliance must have been much less clear to many. Some villages, like María, seemed to remain largely Liberal, but many others joined the Conservative rebellion.[10]

Surprisingly, Conservatives relied less on support for their revolt in the south, in spite of the Catholic Societies' success there.[11] Indians no longer trusted Conservatives, and, given Liberals' grudging acceptance of resguardos in the south, many indigenous communities contributed little to the rebellion. More Indians joined the Liberals voluntarily than had in past wars, but most indigenous soldiers seemed to be conscripts, further aggravating difficult Liberal-Indian relations.[12]

As the local conflict exploded into a national civil war, the fractious Liberal Party quickly united to face the Conservative threat. Troops from Cali, Buga, Palmira, and Santander formed the backbone of the Liberal armies. Liberals had reactivated or invigorated Democratic Societies across the state in preparation for the coming conflict, and, once again, these troops served them well.[13] Just before the war, Palmira's famed Democratic Society held an assembly with over a thousand attendees.[14] David Peña prepared Cali's Democratic Society for battle, drilling hundreds of men every Saturday.[15] The state president lauded Cali's enthusiasm, referring to Peña's soldiers as "the armed Democratic Society."[16] As in past wars, Conservatives denigrated Liberal troops as "multitudes of blacks and mulattoes,"[17] and they bragged (incorrectly) that their opponents could raise at most four thousand men, from the "low class of society."[18]

Also, as in past conflicts, Liberals lauded the commitment of their lower-class allies: "Cali's battalions, five in all, are the Democratic Societies in arms, and they bring to the battle, not only their physical force, but the profound conviction and courage obtained from the voices of passionate orators during the tumultuous weekly meetings of the club."[19] Liberals offered enticements to recruits, promising better wages and rations and, Conservatives claimed, the looting of enemy properties.[20] Popular liberals, out of fear of a Conservative resurgence and with hopes to win further rights and rewards for their military service, ensured the Liberals' victory.

The revolt began in the Liberal heartland of Palmira, a strategic error for Conservatives. While many smallholders supported the uprising, this was still the Liberal Party's stronghold, and the rebels suffered a quick defeat. The rebels seemed to enjoy success everywhere else, however, and, with their impressive network of Catholic Societies, soon controlled the entire south and north of the state, leaving only parts of the central valley and a few coastal towns under Liberal control.

Conservatives had high hopes, given the Catholic Societies' strength and their large armies, but these were quickly dashed. In August 1876, at the Battle of Los Chancos, an outnumbered Liberal army (over three thousand men) soundly defeated the Conservative force (over five thousand troops, and perhaps as many as sixty-five hundred). An observer noted that, in the history of Colombia's civil wars, so "bloody" a battle had never been seen.[21] Unreliable statistics reported over a thousand Conservative dead and wounded, with Liberal casualties half that.[22] Not surprisingly, many soldiers went home after the victory, preventing Liberals from taking full advantage of their battlefield triumph.[23]

The war would drag on for another six months, but Conservatives had little hope for further success. Most of the war in the Cauca was fought in the northern valley and mountains, although a few important battles took place around Popayán. By the end of the war, Liberals had over six thousand troops marshaled to take the fight into Antioquia; in general, troop mobilizations were much larger than in past conflicts.[24] The land could not easily support so many soldiers, and their depredations angered the smallholders over whose properties the armies passed.

For elites, however, the most frightening aspect of the war was not the daily expropriations of property (legal and otherwise) but events that occurred in Cali around Christmas 1876. In December, Conservative citizens rose up in Cali and seized the city.[25] The surprise attack shocked Liberals as most of their standing armies were far to the north. David Peña, still marshaling troops in the valley, rushed back to Cali, attracting volunteers as he went. Within a few days, he gathered two thousand soldiers from the surrounding countryside. Observers marveled at the foot soldiers' eagerness for the assault, noting their hatred of the enemy: "That pueblo has felt so deeply the Conservative and clerical talon about their necks."[26] Presumably, Afro-Caucanos' memory of 1854 was strong, and they feared Conservative reprisals against their friends and families. Conservatives noted with disgust that women joined the makeshift army's ranks too, eager to take part in any looting that might occur after the city fell.[27]

The troops stormed the city, first rousting out the rebels, then proceeding to pillage the town. The telegraph quickly spread news of the event across the nation. Rumors of hundreds of bodies strewn through the streets horrified Conservatives and Liberals alike.[28] While the precise number of dead was never determined, the figure of four hundred became widely repeated.[29] The soldiers targeted houses of prominent Conservatives, many of them former slave masters, breaking in doors and taking everything down to that day's bread. Gruesome accounts of torture circulated. One story related how the marauders poked out a septuagenarian's eyes, cut out his tongue, and hacked off his hands, before leaving him to die. Another noted that only his daughters saved the venerable Conservative patriarch Vicente Borrero from death by shielding his body from the assailants' blows with their own. Women were dragged from houses and raped.[30]

Liberals also suffered in the confusion, and the troops robbed many of the wealthy, regardless of their partisan affiliation. The soldiers also looted the churches, robbed the bank (scattering notes through the streets), and broke open merchants' shops. Observers claimed that, in the frenzy, the troops even killed one another.[31] The sack ended only as the pillagers carted the booty to their homes in the surrounding countryside.

Conservatives denounced Peña for allowing the massacre, even claiming that the general had promised the city to his troops, "offering them four hours of slaughter and three days of looting if they triumphed."[32] Elite Liberals threatened to castigate the looters, but they had no available (and dependable) army to send.[33] They could only assure themselves that the perpetrators would be punished eventually, after the war.[34]

The sack was popular liberals' revenge on the city's aristocracy and Conservatives. Soldiers also plundered in an attempt to recover back pay and rations that they had not received. While Conservatives decried the theft of the churches' monstrances, most of the soldiers seemed to seek clothes and foodstuffs, to take back to their families. In an effort to satisfy his troops, Peña demanded money to pay them, and the state government hastily assembled rations. To add insult to injury, local officials even declared the stolen banknotes' use legal, augmenting the ire of the city's merchants.[35]

Many Liberals demanded the castigation of the offenders, but they could not risk alienating much-needed troops with hostile inquiries. The sack of Cali was, therefore, doubly depressing for many elite Liberals. Of course, they lamented the loss of life and property, the economic setback that this loss represented, and the soldiers' worrisome lack of partisan discrimination while looting (although some said that only Conservatives suffered attacks). Perhaps more threatening, however, was the impotence of the Liberal Party, beholden to its subaltern troops, and, therefore, unable to do anything at all about the sack except to promise that, after the war, things would change.

Popular Liberals Demand Their Due

The war had united a fractious Liberal Party, but its was a Pyrrhic victory. The party's greatest fault line had always been subalterns' political role and the concessions offered to them. Immediately after the war, the party began to divide again between Radicals (who controlled the state) and Independents. To secure their triumph, Liberals had relied as never before on their popular allies, who now demanded recognition for their wartime sacrifices. Cali's plundering and the general destruction of the war had only exacerbated elite Liberals' unease with the alliance. Popular liberals' subsequent demands would rip the party apart.

Bargaining had cemented popular and elite Liberals' relationship. While never entertaining identical understandings of republicanism or liberalism, the two camps had managed to find enough common ground in their respective conceptions of society and politics to make deals over many aspects of Caucano life. Land, however, had always been a problem. Liberals had made a concession by championing the ejidos, against their own ideological dictates, but had balked at even considering the broader problem of landed property in the valley. Popular liberals had long chafed under the haciendas' monopoly of the valley's soil, openly challenging it during the zurriago and, when possible, thereafter. In the 1860s and 1870s, some middling Liberals had proposed modest land reforms, but, on the whole, the ruling class had managed to suppress such a contentious issue. After 1877, it could do so no more.

Popular liberals began to demand the land denied them so long. Throughout the recent conflict, soldiers had continually ransacked haciendas, obtaining some loot while challenging the existence of such grand properties. After the war, former troops began to ask that the haciendas expropriated from Conservatives be divided and redistributed.[36] Elites could ignore this clamoring, but they could not so easily disregard the claims of Colombia's most powerful Democratic Society.

Soon after the war's end, Cali's Democratic Society demanded that the state resolve the land question and finally give popular liberals the economic and social equality for which they had sacrificed so much. The petitioners began by asking for back pay and rations and for pensions for all the widows and orphans created by the war. They cited the many battles in which they had fought, noting that they were often outnumbered and outgunned. They reminded the state that veterans had saved it from the Conservative threat, from "the enemies of liberty." Then they made a startling request. They asked for the "abolition of land rents," for the right to settle any unused land (haciendas maintained massive uncultivated reserves) in the Cauca as long as doing so did not "gravely harm another," and for the right to collect wood from any forests in the state. They noted:

> Although this may seem an extravagant request, it is not, if one weighs the criterion of justice, considering that those individuals, born here or elsewhere, who have promptly presented themselves to defend their country have the perfect right to live in the Cauca under the expressed terms [presented in the petition]. How can one think it just that those who have come every time to defend this soil that saw them born against the repeated and unjust invasions from Antioquia, invasions aided by those who call themselves the owners of the greater part of the Cauca's land, live without a home?[37]

The petitioners protested the injustice of the defeated rebels still enjoying "their immense lands." Then they closed with a plea: "Land cannot be occupied to such an extent that the other members of the community are deprived of the means of subsistence or are obligated to be the slaves of those feudal lords who do not admit onto their supposed properties any but those individuals who implicitly sell their personal independence, that is to say, their conscience and liberty, in order to be the peons and tributaries of an individual and to cease to be citizens of a free people."[38]

The response from the state to such an astonishing petition was decidedly muted. The secretary of government profusely thanked the club's members for their valiant service and agreed that they would receive their pay immediately. As to land, he equivocated, noting that it was a "grave and delicate question" that the congress would have to consider.[39] The Radical government owed popular liberals too much simply to reject the request outright. It also knew that subalterns were highly agitated, organized, and, after the war, well armed.

David Peña moderated popular liberals' demands somewhat in the bill that he presented to the state congress, but his measure was still quite radical. His suggested law exempted the poor from paying any land rents for five years. It also allowed those who did not have land to use any not already cultivated (up to three hectares, seven to eight acres) without paying rent to the owner for a similar period. Finally, it permitted the poor to extract wood from forests for construction or fuel. He proposed that government bonds be issued to landowners to cover their lost income.[40] Peña's law openly challenged the rule of landed private property and threatened the viability of the Cauca's hacienda complex, which remained the economic foundation of the region's ruling class.

Surprisingly, the land bill actually passed the first debate in the state legislature. Privately, elites reacted with dismay to Peña's legislation, calling it "disguised communism."[41] Publicly, they exercised more discretion. The legislative commission created to study the proposal lauded Peña for his "constant effort to help the Caucano people." The commission also recognized that "citizens" have a right to expect the legislature to "improve their difficult condition" after their sacrifices in the war. However, it explained, the state could neither afford nor enforce the law's provisions. Only near the end of the report did the commission reveal its fundamental distaste for the bill, warning of the "dangerous results of accustoming a part, perhaps the most numerous part, of society to use someone else's property without the obligation to remunerate him." The commission also chided the legislature that it should not pass the law simply to please popular liberals, under the assumption that the national Supreme Court would abrogate it later, as such a disappointment would only further rile the landless.[42]

Although elites rejected the land bill, they tried to assuage popular liberals with some small favors. They annulled all land rents or interest owed on loans that had accumulated during the period of the war.[43] Liberals had worried throughout the war about securing rations and pay for their troops, partly to prevent desertion, partly to prevent looting. After the war, commanders hounded the state government to make good on the back pay owed to soldiers. Some Liberals even proposed the unheard-of solution of raising taxes on the wealthy to pay the troops. An observer noted that plebeians supported the tax vociferously, crowding the galleries to demand (unsuccessfully) its passage. In spite of the tax's failure, Liberals did continue seizing Conservatives' properties to pay their troops. Although the state remunerated veterans, pensions for widows and orphans were less forthcoming, adding to popular liberals' sense of abandonment.[44]

Nature aggravated popular liberals' disappointment over the land bill and compounded their misery. From the spring of 1878, on the heels of the war's devastation, the valley suffered under both drought and locusts while food prices soared. Rice quadrupled its usual price; plantains sold at eight times the norm.[45] Famine spread across the land. Many families were reduced to eating once a day, if at all, and people began to starve to death.[46] Cali's Democratic Society asked the local government to remove all taxes on foodstuffs, which, given the failure of the land bill and the impending elections, the Radicals agreed to do. Furthermore, the club petitioned the state to buy food from abroad or in Panama and to resell it at moderate prices.[47] The Cauca's Radicals pushed the national government to approve twenty-five thousand pesos to be used for food relief in the region. Liberals accused President Julián Trujillo, an Independent opposed to Cauca's Radicals, of delaying sending the money, at the cost of hundreds of lives.[48] They lamented that hunger had turned many formerly proud soldiers into mendicants, forced to beg using "the hated word 'my master.' "[49] While famine can be a great motivator, it can suppress popular action as well, as individuals once joined together in a political project by necessity devote all their efforts to simply staying alive.[50]

Liberals did what they felt they could within the confines of their class and ideological position, but they had denied popular liberals' dreams of land ownership. They thought that they were just rejecting an economic request, but, as Cali's Democratic Society's petition illustrated, their refusal to alter the hacienda system struck both at the entire system of political bargaining and at popular liberals' political status. Popular liberals had served valiantly in yet another civil war and expected their allies to recognize and compensate them for their sacrifices. Bargaining was well established, as even the land bill's opponents acknowledged that returning soldiers had a right to expect the state to better their lot. By not rewarding the veterans, Liberals repudiated both the culture of bargaining and the basis of their alliance. Also, by rejecting land reform, elite Liberals struck a harsh blow to popular liberals' sense of citizenship. Popular liberals knew that they could never achieve true equality without the social and economic independence that land provided, knew that they would never be true equals while under the thumb of the hacendados as tenants or day laborers. Without land, they would never be "citizens of a free people."

Poverty and Progress

While popular liberals' disillusionment with their party grew, the Cauca's elites also began to doubt the wisdom of their decades-old alliance with the valley's poor. The Independents faction, already growing before the war, afterward further coalesced from those Liberals dissatisfied with plebeian political participation and influence in Caucano politics. The combination of the chaos that the war had engendered and popular liberals' demands galvanized Independents to act and greatly increased their appeal among many popular groups. For many elites and subalterns alike, the Cauca seemed to be degenerating into anarchy, with religion, families, and property all under constant threat.

The brutality and carnage of the past civil war, especially the sack of Cali, left an indelible imprint on many Caucanos' psyches. Reports of the city's ordeal spread far and wide, further confirming many Colombians' perceptions that the Cauca had completely succumbed to anarchy. For many elites, the sack of Cali was yet another sign of the need for a social and political regeneration. A Liberal described the depradations as a disgrace to both "civilization and the great Liberal Party," evidence of the "barbarism of this wretched land."[51] Conservatives compared it to "the horrors of the French Revolution" or the Paris Commune.[52] Cali was not an isolated incident; Conservative families reported assaults by Liberal troops wherever the armies had moved.[53] Some elites fretted that the popular classes and their Radical allies wanted to destroy the rule of property, one reporting that a Liberal had responded to a woman objecting to soldiers' thefts by saying: "The benefit of the revolution is to trample the aristocracy . . . and raise up democracy."[54]

Elites' darkest fears about the dangers of democracy seemed to be materializing. The assault on Conservative property and families had been bad enough, but Liberals also remembered how even their own had suffered during the war. Conservatives had always warned that one day Liberals' allies would not bother to distinguish between the two parties, and it seemed to many of the elite that that day had arrived. The powerful began to worry about their ability to control their popular allies in war and the consequences of continued conflict in the Cauca.[55]

The war had been brutal, especially in the north. Even Liberals regretted the massive devastation of cattle herds by the marauding armies, whether by legal requisition or by outright theft.[56] Looting, which had always accompanied warfare, was particularly widespread. Soldiers of the Parra Battalion from the valley ransacked the Arboledas' Japio hacienda. They pillaged the mansion, burned some buildings, and made off with all the tools and all but four head of cattle (which a neighbor had hidden).[57] While many Liberals despised Sergio Arboleda, the rebellion's leader, the ruin of so valuable a property no doubt gave many pause. An observer lamented the widespread devastation: "The cases of mass, brutal destruction of rural properties, large and small, are innumerable."[58]

Soldiers not only attacked large haciendas but looted small farms as well.

Again, the north, where so many battles were fought, suffered the most. Soldiers took over a hundred cattle from the migrant village of Palestina alone.[59] In San Francisco, the mayor decried the behavior of soldiers returning to the valley from the campaign: "They go about robbing whatever they find and killing too." He asked permission to set up a local militia to fend off the state's own soldiers.[60] Another local Liberal described the devastation of the smallholders' villages: "All the male livestock and two-thirds of the breeding stock have been consumed [by the soldiers], their [the villagers'] mares have disappeared, and many of their agricultural plantings were destroyed."[61] Observers especially accused troops from the valley of committing depredations, and racism played some role here as many of these troops were Afro-Caucanos soldiering in a region dominated by "white" or "mestizo" immigrants.[62] Lower-class smallholders, more and more disillusioned with the Cauca's lack of order, increasingly blamed the Liberal Party.

Even after the war had ended, the disorder and Liberal attacks on property continued. During the fighting, the state expropriated considerable amounts of Conservative property to pay for the conflict's costs, including produce from rebellious cacao and tobacco plantation owners in the northern valley. However, the Radicals, desperate to recoup losses and pay their agitated soldiers, continued to expropriate Conservative property after the war was over. Instead of using the proceeds simply to enrich Liberal Party cronies, as often assumed, the Radicals also needed the money to placate their subaltern allies, and there is evidence that they did distribute some properties to subalterns. Indeed, Independents and Conservatives claimed that Radicals offered confiscated land to their popular allies in exchange for continued support. Conservatives warned that, if plebeians grew accustomed to taking the wealthy's land, they "would be increasingly eager to invade any fields, not considering whether they are friend's or enemy's."[63] While popular liberals were disappointed by the failure of Peña's land bill, elites of all stripes shuddered at the Radicals' attacks on landed property.[64]

The property confiscations violated the tacit understanding of Colombian civil wars, an understanding that dictated that, after the conflict had ended, property would once again become sacrosanct. During warfare, expropriations and other excesses might be necessary, but such depredations should end immediately with the peace. Traditionally, even defeated elites could expect compensation for damages to their properties. Radicals' expropriations in the Cauca threatened the cohesiveness of the region's elites, who, even if divided along party lines, were still a class of and for themselves. The Radicals were setting a very dangerous precedent, which, if followed in subsequent civil wars, might destroy the upper class's economic dominance.

Perhaps even more worrisome than the official confiscations was the spread of disorder and attacks on haciendas after the war. The war seemed, not to have ended, but simply to have continued on, with plebeians attacking properties and stealing cattle as they did during times of conflict. Hacendados complained that their properties enjoyed no security whatsoever. Armed bands roamed the countryside, many of them formerly loyal Liberals from the past campaign. Cattle theft was so widespread and disorder so endemic that newspapers claimed that the central valley was becoming a "wilderness" and that farmers refused to plant crops for fear of theft.[65] "The owners of cattle" offered to pay for troops to pursue the bandits if the government would not do so.[66] In the cities, robbery was ubiquitous and went unpunished. One hacendado argued that "property is disappearing totally in the Cauca."[67] Elites in general feared that social conflict was escaping partisan bounds and becoming a "social war" or, worse, a "race war."[68] Elites' fear and hatred of Afro-Caucanos seemed to be growing, encouraged by the new discourse of scientific racism, and inflamed in the Cauca by Cali's sack and other moments when blacks and mulattoes challenged whites (or the rich). One Conservative warned of the coming complete destruction of the elite class: "The first victims . . . are the Conservatives, but later they will also be the Liberals of order."[69] Class and partisan conflict had often combined in curious ways, but elites worried that now social conflict—viewed through an increasingly racist lens—threatened to overwhelm their whole class.

While, in the 1850s, elites had quavered at "communism," now "anarchy" became the upper classes' great fear.[70] After the war, authorities declared themselves "impotent" to prevent the continuous cattle theft.[71] Other elites said that Radicals turned a blind eye to their subaltern allies' crimes.[72] The propertied, Liberal and Conservative, bemoaned that they could not seek redress in the courts as juries would simply absolve any popular liberal bandits.[73] Conservatives began to emigrate, fleeing persecution by both popular and elite Liberals; some claimed that as many as three thousand Caucanos sought refuge in Ecuador after the war.[74] Another Conservative asked Sergio Arboleda to help him get a job in Bogotá, where there were "not so many blacks, so many mobs."[75] This exodus scared many elite Liberals, who took it as further proof that anarchy was destroying the social and economic fabric of the region.

The chronic disorder dimmed any hopes that Liberals had of developing the Cauca economically while also besmirching their claims of political modernity. Liberals rued the horrible failure of discipline. One lamented: "Men give themselves up to vice and women to prostitution because in the Cauca they have lost the tradition of honorable labor." The only thing that would save the land from a "social war" was to give employment to the populace.[76] Liberals complained about plebeians' unwillingness to labor and the "demoralization of the masses accustomed to life in the army camps."[77]

Many Liberals began seriously to doubt the efficacy of their disciplinary project, a program centered on creating orderly citizens through education, the National Guards, and political inclusion. Now, jobs and development, before only one part of Liberals' disciplinary schema, became the central hope for salvation. Development, not republican education, would moralize the masses.[78] Instead of political modernity creating economic progress, economic progress would now quell the disorder that politics had wrought. A newspaper approvingly noted that, when people are working, "no one thinks about politics."[79]

Elites did have one hope—that a railroad connecting the port of Buenaventura with the river valley would bring the development that would, in turn, discipline the lower classes.[80] A newspaper noted that "true civilization" was impossible without railroads and steamships.[81] Many Independents invested in the concern, and work began in 1878. But, to build a railroad, order was needed —to reassure investors and prevent disruption of work on the tracks. Worse, ungrateful laborers refused to work on the project, owing to the low wages offered and fear of getting sick in the tropical lowlands. Rumors also circulated that, in order to get jobs on the project, workers had to promise to vote Independent.[82] Conservatives warned that the railroad would never succeed unless a way was found to bring order to the region.[83]

The promised economic flourishing of the Cauca had never come to pass. Exports from the region's two ports—Buenaventura and Tumaco—were minuscule compared to those from Colombia's other points of entry. Only tobacco and coffee (farmed on a very small scale in the Cauca compared to eastern Colombia) involved any substantial capital outlays, as most other products (resins or cinchona bark) were simply harvested from natural resources.[84] However, even what little success the region enjoyed began to erode as tobacco prices collapsed in the 1870s. Cinchona exports also stagnated in the Cauca, and prices were low, owing to poor quality control and destruction of the forests.[85] While the Atlantic economic system played a significant role in these fluctuations, elites also asserted that investment enjoyed no "guarantees" owing to the Cauca's constant disorder.[86]

To aggravate the situation further, the boatmen who ferried goods between Buenaventura and the Cauca Valley went on "strike."[87] At the behest of the city's merchants, local officials in Buenaventura tried to break the strike, claiming that the strikers harassed other boatmen, preventing them from working. Cali's Democratic Society supported the boatmen, reminding the state that the strikers were "defenders and loyal servants of the government" while the merchants were "Conservatives."[88] The state arrested many of the strikers, charging them with rioting and impeding public authority. In spite of popular liberals' entreaties, the state insisted on trying the men, although the case was moved to the more sympathetic Cali, where a jury acquitted at least some of the boatmen.[89]

The outcome made no one happy. The case further intensified the strain between elite and popular liberals as the state had insisted on prosecuting the men to please development-minded elites. The boatmen had warned the president that "a dark cloud will fall over your administration" if he did not help them.[90] However, the acquittals only confirmed the bankruptcy of the judicial system in the minds of those Caucanos already preoccupied with the region's economic and political direction.

Radicals were caught in a dilemma. With Independents threatening to seize power from them, they needed to appease Caucanos concerned with order and political quiescence. Radicals certainly had no sympathy for crime or disorder, but any strong actions against bandits or cattle thieves would anger many popular liberals, already made desperate by famine. The Radical president refused to help former soldiers charged with banditry even though the veterans claimed that they were being persecuted by local officials as punishment for sustaining the Liberal cause in the past war.[91] Radicals hoped to show solidarity with popular liberals after the land bill's failure, but any movement in that direction would further alienate Independents and other popular republicans. Independents worried about the unseemly bargaining necessary to maintain ties with Liberals' popular allies, claiming that democracy had degenerated into "egoism, libertinism, and vileness."[92]

The situation in the Cauca was dreadful—from almost everyone's perspective. Drought devastated the valley's agriculture, and the resulting famine wracked the poor. The economy of the region seemed near complete collapse. Elites and smallholders feared the constant disorder and threats to their property and families. Migrants were still upset over the devastation that the war had brought to their farms and the continued antagonism between Liberals and the church. Conservatives said that the locusts were a punishment sent to castigate "the red heretics."[93] To top it all off, earthquakes shook the land, and the Puracé volcano erupted, bad omens all. Many elite and popular republicans were eager to remake the Cauca's political landscape, even at the risk of sundering the Liberal Party.

Through 1878 and early 1879, the Radical government of Modesto Garcés stumbled along a path of trying to appease some popular groups while not frightening elites—satisfying neither, and, moreover, failing to restore any semblance of order to the region. The Independents began to gather strength and openly challenged the Radicals in the 1879 state presidential contest, championing Ezequial Hurtado against the Radicals' Manuel Sarria. Independents shuddered at Radicals' political appointments across the state (officials too sympathetic to popular liberals, such as David Peña) and doubted that they would be allowed to participate fully in elections. They complained that Garcés was persecuting Independents and would use any fraud to get his successor, Sarria, elected.[94]

The Independents' main concerns centered around order and progress. The Independents had drawn their adherents from all the Liberal factions upset with Radicals and wary of popular liberals, especially old Mosqueristas, but also many Liberals preoccupied with the Cauca's increasing lawlessness.[95] The two most important Caucano Independents were Julián Trujillo and Eliseo Payán, each representing a different constituency.[96]

Trujillo was part of the same generation of young lawyers as Payán; however, he had always been a follower of Mosquera. An astute military strategist, he contributed to Liberal victories in the 1860–63 civil war and the 1865 revolt. He was the commander in chief of Liberal forces in the south during the 1876–77 civil war, and his success in that conflict not only made him a war hero but also propelled him into the national presidency in 1878. Trujillo represented the Mosquerista Liberal faction that had joined the Cauca's Liberals when Mosquera converted in the late 1850s. Unlike Caucano Liberals in the early 1850s, Mosqueristas were established economically and socially. Mosquera, of course, was one of the region's largest landholders and the scion of a powerful, aristocratic family. Trujillo owned the important Las Cañas hacienda near Cali and was a major investor in the Buenaventura railroad.[97] Mosquera and his followers had been willing to use popular allies, but they always remained wary of popular liberals' influence and designs.

Eliseo Payán, of humble origin, had been a founding member of the Cauca's Liberal Party when that party enjoyed little support from the region's powerful.[98] He had helped forge the initial alliance between popular and middling Liberals. However, by the 1860s and 1870s, Payán and his fellows had begun to enjoy the fruits of power—Payán held the state presidency from 1863 to 1867 and invested in a Buenaventura road project. Payán's trajectory was emblematic of those of many young lawyers and bureaucrats who had established close ties to popular liberals in the 1850s. As did Bogotá's Liberals in the mid-1850s, middling Caucano Liberals in the 1860s and 1870s forged bonds with the region's powerful families, involving themselves in business interests and becoming large landholders. Caucano Liberals had evolved from young upstarts, desperate for allies in order to confront the ruling Conservative aristocracy, to become the dominant political and social class in the region.[99] Their positions of power and their material success, or at least the hope of future economic gains, realigned their ideological precepts and their views concerning their popular liberal allies.

Independents' political and economic positions strongly affected their politics as they hoped to restrict political excitation in favor of order and economic development. They feared the increasing anarchy, disorder, threat to families, and lack of respect for property that had engulfed the valley. They detested the "demagogy and exaggerated pretensions" of popular liberals.[100] Independents lamented the continual politicization of Caucano society and the unseemly disorder that elections continually brought.[101] The faction began to coalesce in a number of political societies, which, while seeking some popular support, made clear their intention to restrain subalterns and prevent their "corruption."[102] The Democratic Societies began to split in two, between the Radicals and the Independents. Most popular liberals in the valley were not sympathetic to the Independents' program, although the intricacies of the elites' divisions probably confused some subalterns.[103]

While not appealing to the valley's most ardent popular liberals, Independents garnered great support among all classes of society in the north after the war.[104] Radicals had angered many plebeians by seeking to restrict public religious functions, but Independents promised to respect the church. Liberals also exacerbated popular discontent by passing a new law requiring children's attendance at public schools.[105] Independents provided an appealing political alternative to migrants who had long identified with the Liberal Party but had grown increasingly suspicious of Radicalism. Antioqueños who had been Liberals seemed to side with the Independents, who, while still nominally Liberal, championed a program proclaiming the virtues of religion, order, and progress —a program that echoed the discourse of popular smallholder republicanism. The constant disorder of the preceding years did nothing to allay smallholders' fears or endear the Radicals to them.[106] Independents lobbied for the settlers' support, playing on their fears by accusing Radicals of desiring to take their lands and redistribute them to the "communist" Democratic Societies and of seeking to undermine religion and marriage.[107] Finally, Julián Trujillo, the Independents' leader, had great appeal as a military hero.

The Radicals responded to the Independent challenge ineffectually, partly because many of their former stalwarts had defected to the new faction. State President Garcés, desperate to please elite and middling Caucanos demanding pacification, ordered Cali's jefe municipal David Peña to tone down his popular rhetoric, prosecuted the boatmen during their strike, and appointed Independents to powerful positions in the state militia.[108] Under threat from Garcés, and weakened by illness, Peña issued a circular calling on Liberals to end their attacks on Conservatives and promising more order.[109] Garcés had to walk a fine line between reassuring elites that he would rein in popular liberals and convincing popular liberals that he still represented them. He satisfied neither group.

While Radicals felt that they could not cater to their Afro-Colombian allies without further alienating other elites, some thought that they might turn to Indians for popular support. Jorge Isaacs, the famed novelist, at the time serving in the state government, ordered local officials to be considerate of Indians, protect them from hacendados' abuses, and end "feudal" oppression. He explained his motives: "The time has arrived to prove in the towns of the state's south, by the effective protection that the government will give to Indians, that the Liberal Party, liberator in all the nation of slaves of the African race, will also make free, perfectly free, people of the Indian race. It will protect them, educate them, diffusing civilization and well-being in their villages." He assured his comrades that they would enjoy "the gratitude of the protected race."[110] Isaacs hoped that the Liberal Party could establish the same relationship with Indians that it had with Afro-Colombians. There is evidence that Liberals did side with Indians in some local disputes and allow them to occupy Conservative properties seized during and after the war.[111] Yet events moved too fast to enable a solid alliance between Radicals and Indians to coalesce.

Meanwhile, the Radicals suffered yet another cruel blow. David Peña's sickness worsened. The great Liberal general went to his deathbed, writing a final message to the Radical Garcés begging him to maintain "the sacred respect for popular rights." He closed his "last farewell" with a plea for the party to look after his beloved Caleños: "I especially entrust to you the pueblo of Cali, pueblo of heroes, of active democrats who for many years have lent such important services to the republic."[112] Peña died soon afterward, on 26 May 1878. The state newspaper claimed that over six thousand people attended his funeral.[113] With his death, popular liberals lost their strongest leader, their most fervent advocate, and the most eloquent interlocutor between popular and elite liberals. Peña's celebration of Cali's popular liberals, his exhortation that the party's leaders not abandon them, might well have been the eulogy for the alliance between elite and popular liberals in the Cauca.

The presidential elections of 1879 widened the division in the Liberal Party between Independents supporting Ezequial Hurtado and Radicals supporting Manuel Sarria. The opposing popular societies began to attack each other, rhetorically and physically.[114] In the valley, most popular liberals threw their support to the Radicals and Sarria, although the failure of the Radical government to procure land reform must have tempered their enthusiasm.[115] Radicals warned that the Independents planned to ally themselves with Conservatives.[116] Many popular republicans, however, did not heed the Radicals and, along with a majority of elite Liberals, supported the Independents and Hurtado.[117]

Independents began to ask that national troops be sent to the Cauca to restore order, proposing that the national government abandon federalism and the idea that the states were sovereign entities. They claimed that popular liberals were stealing arms from federal stores, thus giving the army the grounds that it needed to intefere in the state.[118] In March 1878, popular liberals, many Afro-Colombian, did appear to raid the local armory in Santander. They also attacked and killed several Indians on election day to prevent them from voting. In April, Cali's Radicals seized weapons from the national depot. Some popular liberals threatened a revolt if their candidate, Sarria, were not elected state president.[119]

The Independents had a distinct advantage as one of their own, Julián Trujillo, had won the national presidency in 1878. Trujillo did not hide his true sympathies: "The conservation of public peace is today the supreme necessity . . . in order to reestablish the harmony of social relations and so that there is order, security, and repose."[120] And he began to make peace with the church—easing restrictions, restoring funds, and allowing priests to return to their parishes—a necessity both for a future alliance with Conservatives and for social control. He demanded that Caucanos return expropriated land to Conservatives and protect "the right of property."[121] Trujillo made it clear that he would look kindly on any move to oust Radicals from the state's government.

The Independents made their move in the spring of 1879, convinced that the Radicals would not let them win the presidential elections. Eliseo Payán led the coup d'état. One commentator noted that Payán's army was "composed largely of Conservatives."[122] Many young men from the valley's prominent Conservative families did join his forces. During the coup, Conservatives who had fought in the 1876–77 civil war now sided with their old enemies, the Independents, against the Radicals.[123] However, much of Payán's support came from smallholders in the valley and the northern hills, including many Antioqueño migrants.[124] Many smallholders had sided with the Conservatives in the last war, but other popular liberals, loyal to their party and its past support of their interests, had not. Now, however, these popular smallholder republicans joined with the Independents—at least nominally still Liberals—who shared their fears of disorder, their support of the church, and their desire for landed property's security. The stalwart Maríans, bastion of Liberalism in the north, contributed two battalions to the Independents.[125] One commander lauded his troops, whom he thought fought to "defend their political faith, their home, their property, and their good name."[126] Eliseo Payán extolled his volunteers as "the propertyholder, the padre de familia, the worker who lives by the fruit of his labor."[127]

The national troops recently stationed in the Cauca also joined Payán and the Independents, claiming that Radical forces had illegally seized federal arms in Cali, had destroyed federal property by damaging the telegraph, and had attacked the national troops themselves. Radicals excoriated Trujillo for sending national troops to support the coup, but he defended the move as necessary to restore order and recover federal arms.[128]

The only important battle to take place during the coup was fought in the valley on 21 April 1879, with the Independents winning decisively. The Independents' armies vastly outnumbered the Radicals' forces.[129] By June, except for some guerrilla activity, the Independents had triumphed and controlled the state. In April, Eliseo Payán installed himself as the Cauca's provisional ruler (later, Ezequial Hurtado was declared the winner of the disputed 1879 elections and became state president). The Radicals' defeat was swift, the battles small, casualties few.[130] Perhaps Radicals were caught off guard, but most knew that conflict with the Independents was nigh, hence their earlier assaults on the armories. Of course, Independents enjoyed great support from elites and plebeians concerned with order and property. No doubt, if the war had been prolonged, the Independents' popular allies would have served them well.

Why had the Radicals collapsed? Certainly, the weight of national troops played a role, but this is hardly a sufficient explanation. I propose that popular liberals simply did not rally to Liberal banners as they had in 1851, 1860, 1865, 1876, and numerous other small conflicts. Perhaps Radicals simply did not have the time to marshal their forces, but some leaders seemed to fear calling up popular liberals lest it create more disorder.[131] More likely, I think, is that many popular liberals declined to fight this battle—in part because of fatigue caused by drought, pestilence, and famine, but also because David Peña, the intermediary between those above and those below, was dead and no one had taken his place. While their exact mind-set is unknown, popular liberals must also have been somewhat disillusioned with Radicals, with the breaking of the boatmen's strike, Liberals' attempts at a discourse of order, and, most important, the failure of the land bill. Radicals had turned their backs on their allies, and, when they needed popular support to save their skins one last time, many subalterns were not so eager to bleed for uncertain gains in order to secure a victory for their elite commanders once again.

The Regeneration

The Independents' coup was not simply a bid for power; they had a project for reforming Caucano society and politics that they called the Regeneration. Soon after the Independents seized control of the state, a prominent Independent summed up the primary goal of their program: "Now that the epoch of the Regeneration has come there is much work to be done in order to make the masses understand what real and true liberty and democracy are."[132] The Regenerators had many plans for the region: strengthening the central state and state power in general; restoring order; securing property; reemphasizing religion as a basis of the polity; and promoting economic growth and an export-based economy. However, while their project had many motivations and goals, the effort to retake control of the meanings and practice of politics expressed in the quotation offered above was paramount. The end point of the Regeneration was order and progress, but this could be accomplished only by severely reducing the political space open to subalterns.

Events in the Cauca reflected larger national divisions of the Liberal Party. Radicals controlled the central highlands and Bogotá, although they had largely abandoned their popular allies and ruled through significant electoral fraud. Nationally, Independents arose to oppose Radicals' monopoly of power, their failed economic policies, and the anarchic disorder of federalism and doctrinaire liberalism. Julián Trujillo broke the Radicals' hold on national executive power in 1878. However, the most influential national Independent leader was Rafael Núñez, who became president in 1880. The Cauca's Independents appropriated Núñez's national slogan: "Regeneration or Catastrophe."[133] However, while looking to Núñez for national leadership, Cauca's Independents pioneered and prefigured much of the discourse and political policies of the Regeneration.

The word regeneration had been used throughout the nineteenth century in Colombia to describe new political projects, but, by the 1870s, it became associated with Conservatives' and Independents' plans to promote quiescence, order, and progress. They described their project as a "social and economic regeneration."[134] Payán announced: "The question of the day is entirely social and is involved with nothing less than saving the Cauca and Colombia from the most abominable anarchy."[135] The north's political elite saluted this goal of reining in popular politics, asking for a "complete reform in the system of government."[136] During the coup, one officer signed his letters "Viva the Regeneration! Viva the Independent National Army! Viva the security of our families!"[137]

The Independents claimed that there were three bases of society—religion, family, and property—all linked together: religion formed the family, through which property passed through the generations. These institutions were central to the Regeneration's program, and Independents promised that they would protect and promote them against the threats of the corrupted masses and their middling allies.[138] These same concerns, not coincidentally, also formed the bedrock of smallholder popular republicanism. One observer remarked how the coup saved Cali from "ignorant and semibarbarous men" who had supported the Radicals and, with them, practiced "terrorism, filling families with fear, paralyzing commerce, blocking every source of progress and well-being" under their rule of "anarchy."[139] Independents replaced liberty, equality, and fraternity with some variation of "peace, order, and fraternity," or "peace, industry, and work."[140]

The regeneration of family, property, and religion would also lead to economic development, which would, in turn, engender further political quiescence. Economic progress demanded order, however, which Independents planned to achieve by cracking down on crime, increasing the power of the state, and making peace with Conservatives. Independents needed Conservatives as allies against the Radicals, of course, but they also hoped that an alliance would help avoid any future military contests that would necessitate turning again to plebeians for aid. Avoiding future mobilizations of the popular classes was especially important to Independents since none of their goals could be accomplished without sharply restricting the culture of political bargaining and subalterns' access to the public, political realm.

The Independents set to work immediately, with Payán nullifying all laws passed by the legislature since 1877. This act was principally aimed at establishing a rapprochement with Conservatives and the church. Payán sought to woo his old enemies, returning properties that the Radicals had confiscated during the 1876–77 civil war and afterward. An Independent approvingly noted that this measure would ensure that everyone knew that, even in times of war, "property is inviolable."[141] Conservatives too applauded the Independents' actions, Sergio Arboleda's son exclaiming: "Those victories are worth much more to us than those that we would have obtained on the fields of battle in the past revolution."[142]

Reconciliation with the church was central to the project and was especially popular with subaltern conservatives.[143] Payán nullified the law of religious inspection and allowed all exiled priests to return to the Cauca. Independents also returned to the church properties that had once housed charitable institutions, with the hope that the religious orders would reopen them.[144] There would continue to be conflict between church and state, but, generally, relations were amicable, and the church became a major supporter of the Regeneration. The church would be central in teaching "the impassible limits of human liberty so that this liberty will be rational and civilized." Religion would also shore up "respect for the individual, property, and the family"—all bases of the Independents' project.[145]

With property rights now somewhat more secure and the church hierarchy mollified, Independents turned their attention to the Cauca's most pressing problem: the extreme disorder of the countryside, which prevented economic development. Local officials urged the state government to make harsh punishment of criminals the new regime's priority. Cali's mayor complained that many of his constituents were "savages who respect neither life, nor the decorum of families, nor property." He blamed the masses' degeneration on "demagogy" and the "propagandists of corruption," which he hoped the Regeneration would subdue.[146] Numerous petitioners encouraged Payán to use a "firm hand" in restoring order.[147] In Cali, elites organized a new police force.

Independents promised that fighting crime would be one of their chief concerns. The state president urged courts to prosecute criminals diligently and asked that the legislature not commute sentences for any reason as pardons encouraged crime and "diminished bit by bit the prestige of authority."[148] Legislators argued that, in the past, the state had been too free with pardons, "making almost negligible the established and imposed punishments." This custom had only created more crime and anarchy. The congressmen demanded that "the full weight of justice fall on bad citizens."[149] A Conservative paper argued that the leniency of the penal system had destroyed all security in Colombia, that "the presumption of being the most free nation in the world" had reduced Colombians "almost to the level of barbarians."[150] The state attorney general demanded a reform of the system of jury trials as these often led to "notorious criminals" being set free; he urged that only judges be allowed to rule over cases involving serious crimes.[151] Radicals, for their part, protested that the courts were sentencing people to over ten years' imprisonment, which was unconstitutional.[152]

Many Caucanos assumed that the Regeneration would usher in economic development and prosperity. However, they knew that they had to overcome a number of problems—the region's chronic disorder, the lack of respect for private property rights, and the unwillingness of the poor to submit themselves to labor for others. By harshly punishing criminals, state authorities hoped to bring stability and to force the masses to recognize property rights. Independents assumed that greater respect for property would be the Regeneration's foundation and pave the way for development.[153]

Equally difficult was the problem of labor. The Regenerators planned to "inculcate in the masses the habit of labor."[154] Independents blamed the Cauca's prostration on the "laziness" of its inhabitants.[155] A paper chastised Caucanos for their refusal to submit to work for others. One argued that, if hunger existed in the Cauca, it was due to nothing more than the sloth and shiftlessness of the masses, who refused to work: "The Cauca's proletarian classes had better remember that, in the Old World, families die of hunger owing to lack of work; . . . that to be admitted as a laborer in any factory, to earn a salary that, usually, the owner fixes, you need a certificate of good conduct and many recommendations."[156] Elite Caucanos lamented that they did not exercise the type of power that they imagined Europeans wielded over their working class, but the Regeneration aimed to do what it could to increase landlords' control vis-à-vis their workers. The state newspaper lauded the hardworking north, where everyone had "dedicated themselves to labor," especially compared to the desolation of the river valley.[157] Conservatives urged that vagrancy be considered a crime again and that the state actively enforce work contracts between employers and laborers.[158] In Cali, the local government cracked down on begging. Mendicants now needed a license, issued by the chief of police only if the applicant could prove an injury or a disability that prevented work. Begging without a license or fabricating an injury could result in jail time or forced labor.[159]

Independents got a small taste of success in September 1880 with the first run, albeit only three miles, of the Buenaventura to Cali railroad under construction. Another boost came when a British firm completed a submarine telegraph cable between Buenaventura and Panama in October 1882. The government did what it could to promote agriculture, awarding bonuses to those planting coffee trees. Papers claimed that agriculture, ranching, and mining were slowly recovering.[160] Julián Trujillo, replaced in the national presidency by Rafael Núñez in 1880, still thought that economic development, particularly the railroad, would pacify the "anarchic elements" in the Cauca. Núñez was less confident in such predictions and, to maintain order, sent even more national troops into the region, including a battalion from Antioquia.[161] Núñez had less faith in Trujillo's modernization argument, believing that only direct force and the legal exclusion of plebeians from politics could save Colombia from the excesses of democratic republicanism.

Punishment and Exclusion versus Discipline

Like Núñez, most Independents doubted that economic development alone would moralize the masses. Rather, they believed that only strict control over plebeians would bring the peace and tranquility necessary to attract and protect capital. The Regenerators saw Colombia's democratic republican experiment as a failure, and they proposed radically restricting subalterns' access to the political realm. Elites would have to curtail the culture of bargaining to lessen plebeians' influence, harshly punish and control any agitators, and legally and institutionally limit subalterns' role in politics.

The constant negotiation necessitated by endless political contests had to end. Endemic civil wars not only hurt the economy, by creating instability, but corrupted the masses as well, the lower classes usually preferring "to entertain themselves for a while on the fields of battle with a Remington rifle" than submit to labor.[162] Elites argued that the constant disorder, revolutions, and anarchy prevented economic development as capital feared disruptions or confiscation and workers refused to submit themselves to toil. Hard work would also distract plebeians from "sterile political discussions."[163] Elites worried that constant warring had ruined subalterns, who, accustomed to the comparatively free rein of the military campaign, would not be content with laboring on haciendas or plantations. War had made plebeians believe that they could get away with anything, as looting and attacks on the enemy would be considered a "political crime" and, therefore, not punished.[164]

Independents criticized the culture of bargaining, claiming that the Radicals had used public funds to keep plebeians satiated (referring to the disbursements during the famine), and warned that, when the funds ran out, the Radicals "would point to other people's property and tell [the pueblo] that it belongs to them by the right of sovereignty." Independents attacked both the reality of bargaining—especially subalterns' claimsmaking concerning land—and the discourse of rights that underlay it.[165] In 1878, a newspaper condemned the Democratic Societies for encouraging their members to expect welfare from the state, which was insolvent anyway.[166] Independents claimed that Radicals had taught plebeians only "laziness" instead of "work, activity, and honor."[167]

Soon after the coup, State President Ezequial Hurtado attacked part of the linchpin of the region's culture of bargaining. Traditionally, after any war, the winners pardoned their own soldiers for any crimes that they may have committed while under arms (mainly looting)—a necessary trade-off to gain popular support in combat. However, Hurtado refused to pardon his own soldiers: "The impunity offered to delinquents as compensation for services sadly necessary overturns all notions of justice and is an immoral threat to the great honorable mass of society."[168]

Restricting republican bargaining was only part of a larger attempt to depoliticize the Cauca's inhabitants. Generally, Independents expressed a strong desire to reduce citizens' political investment. Conservatives had warned that popular forces would escape elites' control and need to be forcibly subdued: "The monster that has reared its head in the Cauca is neither Liberal, nor Conservative, neither monarchist, nor republican; if today it has assumed a political name for its work, tomorrow it will take another, or none at all."[169] Conservatives had long claimed that the Cauca's problems were caused by what one of their number referred to as "fifty years of demoralizing and perverting the hearts and minds" of the masses.[170] They dreamed of sharply reducing popular politics. Another wished that the legislature would decrease the frequency of elections, "remove the right to vote from those who do not merit it," and "extinguish partisan hatreds" and the love of political conflict.[171]

Independents hoped that plebeians would just forget about politics, return to their fields and labors, and leave the public sphere to their social superiors. An Independent paper, referring to popular liberals, celebrated the reduced influence of the "machete wielders of the pueblo that in other times have been the owners and lords of lives and haciendas."[172] On assuming the state presidency in 1883, Eliseo Payán said: "We need to have more peace, more industry, more labor, and less politics . . . keeping in mind that liberty and order are politically synonymous."[173] Order, not democracy or even republicanism, was to be the watchword of the day. One Independent declared the necessity of a government that would "attend only to the salvation of order, even at the cost of a dictatorship."[174] Another feared the possibility of a popular uprising, which he referred to as a "republican plague."[175] For a political culture steeped in republicanism, this rhetoric was wildly unorthodox but a heresy that many were now willing to consider in the face of popular pressure. Eliseo Payán said that disorder had reached such extremes, economic prostration had sunk to such depths, "that the path of the dictator is considered justifiable as the way to obtain order and peace."[176]

The Independents found a voice in the aptly named newspaper El Ferrocarril (The Railroad), which, in its opening issue, explained: "Our goal is to reconstruct, civilize, and restrain."[177] The paper asserted that it would try to avoid political discussions as these only "poison the soul, prostitute every good sentiment, and will soon drive us to misery, demoralization, and barbarism."[178] El Ferrocarril praised the English, who, while obsessed with politics in Cromwell's time, now turned their attention to industry while "politics remained the charge of a limited portion of individuals who had made a special study of that subject." The paper exhorted plebeians to leave governing to the political class and "devote themselves to useful occupations."[179] This was the Regeneration's project: returning politics to the control of the few.

Since it was impossible to remove plebeians from politics completely, the Regenerators strove to moralize and discipline them as much as possible. However, this civilizing mission was somewhat different than that undertaken by the Radicals, relying much more on brute force, punishment, and religion than on the "rationalization" of the masses. Instead of disciplining the masses so that they overcame their unruly passions to embrace hard work and an orderly republicanism, the Cauca's elites would force plebeians to work and exclude them from a political realm that they were too uncivilized to enter.

Education, although still important, would now focus on combating "demoralization" and on "inculcating work habits," instead of on creating active and knowledgeable citizens.[180] Religion would be the new basis for education, the resource with which to "moralize" the poor.[181] A writer warned of the consequences of secular education: "Eliminate God from the schools, . . . and you will have the Paris Commune."[182] Generally, the state gave councils of padres de familia much authority in regulating local schools (a move popular with many smallholder republicans). After the coup, 6,707 children in the state's schools had classes on "religion," while only 136 took courses on "rights and duties of the citizen."[183] Eliseo Payán wanted a reorganization of the education system, which he saw as, at present, forming "citizens only for politics and war."[184] In Cali, schools sought to teach "rules and notions of courtesy, morality, good behavior, and hygiene." Teachers were also carefully to review with their charges all the laws of the city and the punishments for breaking them as well as "inculcate in pupils' hearts the respect due authorities."[185]

Independents turned their attention to popular culture as well, urging that the dances of the "people of color" be outlawed.[186] Towns banned games of chance favored by the poor; in 1887, Cali's governor banned gaming as it discouraged the poor from seeking work. Some elites claimed that the constant holidays and festivals generated only laziness and disorder.[187] The national government urged all states to ban bullfights and cockfights. The state ordered local officials to prosecute drunkards.[188] If education failed to improve the masses' conduct, perhaps legal proscription would work better.

Elites sought to reform jails as well, which were notoriously insecure. Subalterns regularly broke compatriots out of prison.[189] Independents demanded "effective punishments" to reduce crimes and warned that, without them, the propertied would have to resort to "lynching."[190] New prison regulations spoke, not of reforming convicts, but only of the various additional punishments that jailers could inflict. One paper demanded the termination of the practice of suspending prisoners' sentences owing to their supposed moral reform while in jail.[191] The Independents engaged in a prison-construction spree, building or reinforcing jails in Cali, Cartago, Obando Municipality, Pasto, Toro, Tuluá, and Túquerres. The Independent penal program found its greatest expression in the establishment of a prison on Gorgona Island off the Cauca's Pacific Coast in 1883.[192] Instead of the Radicals' Benthamite dream of moralizing and disciplining offenders, now prisoners would simply be banished, removed from society.

Elites also sought to restrict the role of local militias, replacing them with a professional army. By 1878, the budget of the national army allowed for the maintenance of three thousand men in peacetime, a force much larger than had been maintained in previous years. This expansion took place under Secretary of War Ezequial Hurtado, soon to be president of the Cauca. Trujillo also pushed through a new military school, which hoped to bring in foreign instructors to professionalize the army. By 1880, the army could maintain a force of five thousand men in peacetime, a massive increase over the 450-man national peacetime army of the 1850s.[193] National troops were now regularly stationed in the Cauca, welcomed by many as a force of order. When budget shortfalls threatened the removal of these troops, local elites offered to pay the balance to ensure that the soldiers remained. The professional army came to be seen as a stabilizing force, one balancing the unruly and unreliable local militias.[194] While relying on the national government, Cauca State also sought to replace local militias with its own permanent, professional army that would protect "property," ensure order, and guard prisons.[195]

However, the Regeneration's program of depoliticizing the masses did not rely only on somehow disciplining plebeians more effectively; it also included a number of concrete proposals to restrict subalterns' access to political space. Soon after their victory, Independents targeted elections. Newspapers complained that elections brought nothing but disorder and chaos. El Ferrocarril denigrated elections as a "tempest that threatens every enterprise."[196] The paper argued that the Cauca's frequent electoral contests were just part of a broader problem of overpoliticization: "Citizens have accustomed themselves to live in the public plazas, engaging in nothing but politics . . . and abandoning their work, with great harm to themselves and public wealth."[197] The people must forget about politics and the "partisan spirit" and dedicate themselves to labor. Fewer elections and more work would moralize the poor, reduce crime, and prevent revolutions. If Radicals had failed in making elections safe for republicanism, then Independents would simply restrict the opportunities that plebeians had to misuse the franchise. Independents extended the term of the state president from two years to four in order to reduce the number of elections. Caucano Independents urged the national government to follow suit and extend the national president's term as well.[198] Independents also wanted to restrict the suffrage, at the minimum establishing literacy requirements, although this would have to wait a few years.[199] In 1883, the state ordered the fining or arrest of any armed person who came near polling places, banning an important way in which subalterns participated in elections.[200]

Many elites had always looked with apprehension at the vast political repertoire that subalterns employed. After the coup, plebeian political activity came under increasingly strident attack. The Regenerators first targeted demonstrations. Independents applauded 1879's Christmas festivities, noting that, unlike in previous years, political disruption and shouting between different factions did not mar the occasion.[201] In Buga, a local ordinance banned unruly demonstrations, ordering fines or jail for those who disturbed the public peace.[202] In 1883, the state government reminded local officials to disband any public gathering that threatened the peace, basically outlawing any demonstration that met with the state's disapproval.[203] The demands that local authorities prevent political demonstrations were so intense that Radicals sympathetic to plebeians felt obliged to defend their position, reminding Caucanos that "those disorders are guaranteed in our constitution" and that demonstrations had been taking place since 1849.[204] For many elites, that was exactly the problem; both the constitution and the political culture inaugurated in 1849 needed changing.

But the part of the subalterns' political repertoire that Independents most dearly wanted to restrict was the radical Democratic Societies. Many elites had been eager to rein in the clubs for some time. Mosquera, never sympathetic to popular participation, suggested that Colombia follow the example of the United States and carefully restrict freedom of association.[205] He worried that Cali's society corrupted the state militia and denigrated it as a "club of communists."[206] Independents, formally sympathetic to and allied with the Democratic Societies, now claimed that the clubs were "degenerating."[207] In Pasto, residents protested that Liberals were meeting in a secret society called *The Serpent* and urged the government to forcibly disband the club immediately.[208] Independents jailed members of a Serpent society in San Vicente.[209]

In 1882, Radical Liberals tried to rally and formed the Society of Public Welfare in Cali with the promise to defend their principles in every way, "even on the battlefield."[210] The state's secretary of government responded severely: "I cannot accept as legitimate the principle that a part of the associated resolve, by themselves, to carry the defense of their ideas to the battlefield." He warned that warfare was the prerogative only of the state and that any disorder would be dealt with harshly.[211] Other Radicals reported harassment by local authorities when they tried to reorganize Democratic Societies. In Popayán, a local official gathered an informal posse to dissolve that city's club, under the pretext of arresting some of its members on outstanding warrants. The society reminded the state that the "liberty to associate" was still guaranteed by the constitution.[212] The Independent jefe municipal kindly offered the service of the local police to help ensure that Cali's Society of Public Welfare's meetings went smoothly and did not disturb public order.[213] The state president chastised the societies as a threat to order and progress and accused them of plotting to revolt.[214]

The state government forbade, in May 1882, public employees to join any "popular society" that involved itself in elections.[215] Middling public employees had been important interlocutors between popular liberals and the party, and Independents hoped to break this link. In October of the same year, the state exploited an outbreak of smallpox to prohibit all assemblies, conveniently at the time of upcoming state presidential elections. Independents also declared a state of emergency in Palmira in order to suspend constitutional rights and influence the elections.[216] It seems that Radicals made another attempt to rally popular forces in late 1882, but Independents quickly crushed their efforts and used these activities as an excuse to further repress the Democratic Societies, whom the state blamed for any disturbance.[217]

In 1883, Buga's local government prohibited any gathering of armed citizens or any assembly that threatened public order. In the same year, the state government ordered officials to disband any assembly that disturbed the public peace, with force if necessary. The government further instructed local authorities to arrest any assembly of more than four people, armed or not, if it was suspected that they might commit some type of crime sometime in the future.[218] Caucano elites applauded the 1886 national constitution's restrictions on freedom of assembly, claiming that troublemakers could no longer plot revolts in "the clubs and popular associations."[219] Independents had outlawed the Democratic Societies, in fact, if not in name.

Liberal elites in the 1860s and 1870s had not harbored illusions that democracy and republicanism were unproblematic, as recalcitrant popular conservatives and uncontrollable popular liberals had continually showed them. However, they had expected discipline to solve all these problems, rationalizing the poor, civilizing them, making them morally and intellectually fit to participate productively in politics. But discipline had failed. The masses participated in politics surely enough, but they refused to do so in an orderly manner or to fulfill their obligations as hardworking citizens. For many Liberals, the failure of discipline also necessarily meant the failure of democracy. Since the masses refused to accept discipline, these Liberals felt that they had to abandon the democratic experiment, castigate unruly subalterns, and reduce the political space open to all plebeians. Liberals had lost their faith in the peasants and landless poor as potential democratic citizens.

Conclusion

The Regeneration's project did not proceed smoothly. Conservatives still felt excluded from power, and some even talked of another revolt. Calmer voices warned them that past revolts had failed and had led only to more violence, corruption of the masses, partisan hatreds, and economic stagnation.[220] Disorder and crime continued in the Cauca, of course, although punishments were far harsher. Radicals tried somewhat to rally in 1882, but succeeded only in further uniting Independents and Conservatives.[221] The national Conservative directorate ordered its party's members to vote for Independents unless the Conservative candidate proper stood a chance of winning.[222] A few Independents, including Julián Trujillo, were disenchanted with the hard line taken by national president Rafael Núñez, but they were a minority. Most elites supported Núñez, who won the presidency again in 1884, and his policies.[223]

In 1885, Radicals engaged in a national revolt to attempt to regain power by force. Although some of the Cauca's Radicals participated in the movement, the region was not at all the center of the conflict, in sharp contrast to past civil wars. Cauca's Radicals made an attempt at resurgence, but they had already been defeated by Independents and Conservatives over the previous few years. Popular liberals around Cali, Palmira, and Santander did seem eager to overthrow the Independents and hated Conservatives.[224] However, they lacked elite support to help them organize, and they were now isolated politically from broader national events, so little came of their effort. The war in the Cauca ended quickly, most of the fighting the result of invasions from forces beyond the state.[225] In 1879, Radicalism suffered defeat because of popular liberals' disillusionment; in 1885, it fell because of the weakness of middling and elite mediators and their inability to organize popular forces. The war only strengthened the Regeneration by further uniting Independents and Conservatives.[226]

The Liberal Party had completely shattered in the late 1870s. First, a significant number of elites abandoned it to pursue a vision of politics in which plebeians played a greatly diminished role. These Independents felt that the Cauca's republican political experiment had failed, resulting in anarchy and economic stagnation. Second, many popular smallholder republicans—migrants and other small farmers—abandoned the party too, allying with either Conservatives or Independents. Radicalism and the disorder with which it became associated seemed to threaten religion, families, and property—popular smallholder republicans' very economic, political, and social lives. The Independents, whose program stressed the protection of those supposed pillars of society, held great appeal. Finally, popular liberals lost their traditional political strength. This was due in part to their abandonment by some middling sectors who became Independents and in part to the deaths of the party's most active agents who connected with the poor. However, it seems that many popular liberals also ceased to see the Liberal Party as their own after it utterly failed to support calls for land reform. The differences between elite and popular liberalism—always present but subdued either by political or economic concessions or by Conservative threat—emerged to break the once-powerful alliance.

Independents took advantage of the Radicals' collapse to attack the Cauca's political culture. They sought to secure property, restore order, and foment development by reducing plebeians' political space. They harshly punished deviants and used religious education to moralize the poor. They hampered subalterns' ability to politically bargain by emphasizing professional armies over militias. They directly restricted plebeians' political activities by reducing the number of elections, forbidding disorderly demonstrations, and harassing Democratic Societies. For many Colombians, the Radicals' democratic and disciplinary experiments had failed, and the Regeneration would replace them with a sharply restricted republicanism that reined in subalterns' political participation. The program in the Cauca foreshadowed and made possible a broader, national regeneration that would fundamentally alter Colombia's political culture.

7 Conclusion:
Popular Republicans' Legacies

Do they think that men who have been able to enjoy the blessing of liberty
will calmly see it snatched away?
—TOUSSAINT L'OUVERTURE, Saint Domingue, 5 November 1797[1]

The 1885 civil war forced President Rafael Núñez to forge an even stronger bond with Conservatives, who would rule Colombia for almost the next half century. In 1886, the Regenerators codified their program in a new constitution that dramatically restricted the previous decades' democratic experiment. As the ruling class closed legal, institutional, and traditional methods of political participation, subalterns had fewer and fewer avenues available through which to pursue their goals and enter the political sphere. In general, Colombia's reigning political elites turned away from trying to incorporate a disciplined citizenry, instead focusing their efforts on ruling over recalcitrant subjects. Colombia, once at the vanguard of political innovation in the Atlantic World, retreated from democratic republicanism and all the risks that it entailed. However, nineteenth-century struggles over republicanism would endure in legacies bequeathed to the Colombian state and nation.

The 1886 Constitution

The defeat of the Cauca's Radicals between 1879 and 1885 had great import beyond the immediate region. The Cauca was central owing to its importance in propping up the national Liberal Party both electorally and militarily. The Cauca had been the nexus of the great civil wars of the mid-nineteenth century—1851,

1860–63, 1876–77—and the region was the bastion of Liberalism. In these civil wars, thanks to a strong alliance with popular liberals, Caucano Liberals consistently defeated Conservatives—in spite of their enemies' great wealth and considerable popular support. If the Liberal Party did not exercise the same dominance in the region as it did in the eastern highlands of Santander and Boyacá, Caucano armies still ensured Liberals' national victories. During the 1876–77 civil war, congressman warned that, if the Cauca fell, Liberalism as a whole was doomed throughout the nation.[2] The 1879 coup neutralized Caucano popular liberal armies, which played a much smaller role in subsequent civil conflicts.

However, the importance of the Cauca extended beyond just securing any one political faction's base of power. The region also served as an example of the need for, and the possibilities entailed by, the Regeneration. Colombians of all political factions saw the Cauca as key to changing the nation-state's direction since outsiders thought it the region most contaminated by popular politics and anarchy.[3] One Independent wrote to Payán: "I am convinced that the battle of 21 April 1879 [during the Independents' coup] saved not just the interests of the Cauca but those of all the republic."[4]

The Regeneration is usually understood as a national project fulfilled under the reign of Rafael Núñez in the 1880s, although the Caucano Julián Trujillo had taken some important initial steps. However, the Caucano local project not only enabled the national effort by defeating Radicalism but also foreshadowed it. After 1879, the region's Independents and Conservatives embraced the Regeneration's political discourse—religion, order, family, development—and acted on these tenets. The Cauca was seen as the most disorderly and politicized of all of Colombia's states, yet elites there seemed to have had some success in closing down the vibrant political culture of earlier years. An Independent paper proclaimed: "If in some parts of the Republic they have the idea that the Cauca is only a territory populated by barbarians, the entire nation also knows that those barbarians have been the first to open the road to the social regeneration."[5]

After the 1885 civil war and Conservatives' ascension, the project of the Regeneration accelerated. Independents and Conservatives had for some time been eager to correct the deficiencies of the Radicals' 1863 constitution. Trujillo had proposed reforming the national constitution in 1879, after the successful coup in the Cauca. In 1880, Núñez won the legal right to intercede in the internal conflicts of the sovereign states to secure order if a state legislature or executive requested his help, basically ending the right to local revolt that the parties had enjoyed.[6] Local elites in the Cauca also pushed for reform of the national constitution.[7] The old Radical constitution had led only to "anarchy."[8] Many desired a more centralized government in order to distance power from plebeian influence. In general, elites realized that the state needed to be much stronger if the Regeneration were to succeed.[9] Sergio Arboleda proposed a constitution that established a state religion, restricted access to public office (he envisioned a senate made up of "the most distinguished men of the country"), favored centralization, limited freedom of association, and reinstated the death penalty. He also wanted citizenship to be contingent on owning property but feared the reaction to such a restriction given Caucanos' jealous protection of their historical rights.[10]

Although written by others, the 1886 constitution adhered closely to Arboleda's plan. The document was much more centrist than the 1863 constitution was, terminating the states' sovereignty (the president would appoint regional governors), and giving great power to the national executive. The executive's term of office was now six years (up from two), and representatives served four years (also previously two), reducing the number of elections considerably. The Catholic Church would control public education.[11] The death penalty was reinstated, including for the crimes of arson and banditry, thereby targeting plebeian malefactors who challenged property rights. The president had the power to suspend many rights if necessary to suppress disturbances. The constitution struck directly at popular liberals in Article 47: "All popular political organizations of a permanent character are forbidden."[12]

The document redefined citizenship, limiting it to males over the age of twenty-one who had means of support or gainful employment. In addition, this citizenship permitted voting only in local elections. To cast ballots for representatives to the national congress and for presidential electors, one also needed to be literate and have an annual income of at least five hundred pesos (or fifteen hundred pesos' worth of property).[13] However, the constitution, and the Regeneration in general, struck more deeply at popular republicans' conception of citizenship than just through these important legal restrictions. The Regeneration attacked the very soul of popular citizenship—the idea of belonging to the nation and the right to call on the state—by seeking to reduce plebeians' ability to enter politics.[14] The new constitution and political order were only nominally democratic, with society's hierarchy now strictly encoded and the limitation of subaltern political participation now institutionally and legally enforced. Caucano elites applauded the new constitution and the orderly future that it promised. One speaker exulted that no more would "conspirators hatch their plots in broad daylight, in the clubs and popular associations, . . . and neither would licentiousness, demagogy, and anarchy—disguised under the beautiful concept of liberty—continue poisoning the political organism of the nation."[15]

Usually, the Regeneration is understood as the result of elite factionalism (positively as Conservative triumph or negatively as a betrayal of Liberalism) or, perhaps, as a laudable project to strengthen the Colombian state and ensure "national unification" after the anarchy resulting from the Radicals' federalism.[16] A similar interpretation stresses the reaction against federalism in favor of a more orderly centralism with a strong national state.[17] As important as centralism was to the Regeneration, it was, I think, more of a means than an end for the Caucano elite—one tool, among many, to accomplish the goals of reducing plebeians' political participation, increasing order, and fomenting development.[18]

The Regeneration has also been seen as largely economically oriented, a reaction to the collapse of tobacco and quinine exports or a step (or a retrogression) in the process of the formation of a national bourgeoisie.[19] I would agree that both these factors were powerful elements of the Regeneration, but, in the Cauca, elites thought that no such economic renaissance would be possible without restraining the region's highly politicized lower class. First, they needed a working class forced to seek wage labor and not constantly challenging elite prerogatives or agitating for land. Second, they required social peace to encourage investment, especially if they hoped to attract foreign capital. Democracy and capitalism, at least in the Cauca, seemed from the upper class's point of view a poor mix.

In general, I would argue that the Regeneration's project was much more socially oriented than interpretations centered on high politics or economics have allowed.[20] When Independents and Conservatives sought to remake Colombia to save it from anarchy and strengthen state power, they acted with an eye to reducing the past decades' popular political participation. Subalterns' appropriation of the political sphere and their reframing of republicanism led to the supposed disorder and anarchy that the Regenerators hoped to terminate. While the Regeneration had many goals beside restricting popular politics, its architects saw limiting subalterns' political repertoire as key to obtaining those goals.

Colombia in the Atlantic World

Before the Regeneration, Colombia was as "democratic" and republican as any nation-state in the Atlantic World. Colombia's political system and political culture were part of a shared Atlantic political community including other regions of Latin America, the United States, and republican Europe. Indeed, the contention of one branch of modernization theory that Latin America's political underdevelopment led to its economic underdevelopment simply does not hold for Colombia.[21] During the Regeneration, Caucano notables argued the reverse, that Colombia's disorderly political modernity prevented economic modernization. The reasons for Colombia's economic development, or lack thereof, are legion, but, at least politically, nineteenth-century Colombia swam in the same currents as the Atlantic World's most economically dynamic societies.

Why did democracy flourish in Colombia? Again, there is no one answer, but I would like to propose that the necessity of elites to turn to subalterns for political and military support, owing either to internal division or to an external threat, greatly increased the inclusion of subalterns in the nation and the possibilities for a democratic opening. Subalterns did not just react to elites—they would adeptly appropriate democracy and republicanism as their own. Yet they usually needed an opportunity to do so. I would like briefly to compare Colombia with other postcolonial American nation-states to reflect on popular politics' importance in these societies' histories. We can imagine a spectrum that runs from an internally consolidated and unified upper class facing no external threats (or strong internal pressure from below) to an elite highly internally divided or forced to deal with foreign invasion or occupation.

In the nineteenth-century Americas, Brazil anchored one pole of the spectrum. Independence occurred with little popular participation, and, while the Brazilian ruling class experimented with democracy through the 1830s, republican and slave revolts soon deterred it. Under the monarchy, elites avoided serious division or even the necessity of at least mouthing the virtues of democratic republicanism. In the 1880s, abolition and republicanism seemed momentarily to open the possibilities for greater subaltern participation, but elites quickly overcame their differences to fortify oligarchic control. Ruling over the largest slave society in the New World, the Brazilian upper class had long ago learned that the mobilization of popular forces was something to be avoided at all costs.[22]

Colombia would reside near the other end of the spectrum. Elites needed subalterns for any political project, in part owing to their partisan division and the weak state. Even the Regeneration, designed to reduce popular mobilization, was possible only because of the support of many members of the lower classes. Subalterns in general had significant access to the public political sphere.

The much-studied cases of Cuba and Mexico provide counterparts. In Mexico, a lengthy and violent independence struggle, partisan division, and foreign invasion all contributed to permit a massive mobilization of popular forces, which scholars have mined in many of the pioneering works on popular politics.[23] Cuba resembled Brazil until the late nineteenth century, when the struggles over abolition and independence offered many opportunities for popular political life. These movements resulted in a new republic, which, in spite of being under the influence of an increasingly racist U.S. protectorate, was much more democratic, especially for Afro-Cubans. Afro-Cubans had constituted the majority of the patriot armies, breaking open national political life and making a return to nineteenth-century oligarchic rule impossible.[24]

These nineteenth-century struggles paved the way for continued popular mobilization throughout the twentieth century. Elites in Mexico, Colombia, and Cuba had to continually accommodate in some ways their popular classes. Mexico did so via its institutionalized revolution, Colombia via its stable electoral system, and Cuba via the communist Revolution.

The middle of this range would no doubt see many other Latin American states and the U.S. South during Reconstruction. In the antebellum South, a fairly united elite class, enjoying the support of many poor whites, supported slavery and excluded free African Americans from politics. After the war, Republicans needed support in the South against the defeated planter class and turned to the Union army, carpetbaggers, upcountry poor whites, urban artisans, and the freedpeople.[25] The exigencies that the Republicans faced in ruling a conquered area and their political struggles with resurgent Democrats created an opening, seized by the new African American citizens, for a momentary democratization of Southern politics and life. Eric Foner asserts: "Alone among the nations that abolished slavery in the nineteenth century, the United States, within a few years of emancipation, clothed its former slaves with citizenship rights equal to those of whites."[26]

Of course, the United States was not exceptional in this regard. In fact, it lagged behind Colombia and other New World nation-states. Across the Americas, when elites turned to subalterns in times of crisis, subalterns seized those opportunities to claim a place for themselves in their nations' politics, democratizing states that often had been only nominally republican. Not just Europeans or North Americans, but people across the Atlantic World created and made meaningful for themselves rights, citizenship, republicanism, and democracy.[27]

The 1886 constitution marked an important diversion in Colombia's political trajectory away from broader subaltern incorporation. Yet many American states seemed to follow a similar path. Across the Atlantic World, conservatives enjoyed a resurgence of power in the late nineteenth century as elites reacted against increasing popular political participation. The failure of Reconstruction in the U.S. South, the Porfiriato in Mexico, and Colombia's Regeneration were different faces on a similar project, depending on the particular intricacies in each society of increased racial division, popular support for projects of political restriction, and economic development.

The rise of scientific racism and an increasing racial division among the lower classes facilitated the restriction of popular politics throughout the Atlantic World. Southern racist terror (mostly against African Americans, but also against white "collaborators"), epitomized by the Ku Klux Klan, solidified whites against Reconstruction in the South, while increasing Northern racism led to disinterest in events beyond the Mason-Dixon line.[28] Racism's triumph ushered in segregation and the almost complete exclusion of African Americans from Southern political life. A similar reaction against blacks and mulattoes' participation engulfed Cuba after Independence, culminating in the 1912 massacre. However, the legacies of Afro-Cubans' contribution to nation building, their continued political pressure, and the necessities of partisan struggle all prevented the marginalization of blacks and mulattoes in national politics.[29] In Colombia, popular liberalism's equation with Afro-Colombians frightened both upper-class Liberals and many Antioqueño smallholders. In the increasingly racist Atlantic World, under the spell of scientific racism and social Darwinism, racial fears and policies played a great role in elites' abilities to restrict further popular mobilization.

In Mexico, the Southern United States, and Colombia, elites succeeded in restricting popular politics only with the support of segments of the lower classes. Often, as in the case of the U.S. South or Colombia, racial fears drove popular conservatives to support restrictions in democracy across the board. Partisan loyalty also eased elites' projects. Porfirio Díaz, a war hero, came to power initially with the support of many of central Mexico's popular liberals, including those of Emiliano Zapata's hometown of Anenecuilco. While the Porfiriato suppressed popular mobilization to a remarkable degree, it used its popular liberal origins as an important legitimating mechanism.[30]

Variations in economic development also greatly affected the amount of resources that elites were able to devote to the task of ensuring their projects' long-term success. In the United States, the increasing influence of big business within the Republican Party lessened that party's enthusiasm for active intervention in the South. Northern business interests, confronting increasingly volatile labor relations, began to look less favorably on popular democracy in general.[31] With increased foreign investment and economic growth, the Mexican state under the Porfiriato enjoyed considerable resources, which it used to repress its former popular allies and to solidify its lengthy hold on power. In contrast, the Cuban state and elites, suffering through the booms and busts of the sugar industry, and delegitimized owing to continuing U.S. intervention, had much less power and currency. Similarly, while Colombia enjoyed somewhat more economic stability after the Regeneration, the plantation class did not control coffee production to a great degree, and its control over the countryside remained weak.[32] Despite the best efforts of the Regenerators, the state remained debilitated, and continued division once again forced elites to turn to popular support in the War of a Thousand Days (1899–1902). In all areas, as with the Independents in Colombia, new ideas and examples of industrialization, progress, and imperialism influenced elites, prompting them to rethink the nature of their societies.[33] Economic development seemed to demand political order while providing the resources to strengthen the state against popular influence.

Of course, within these broader efforts to restrict democracy, elite retrenchment took distinct forms in different states. In Colombia, this restriction of popular politics involved an important shift in elites' utilization of what Foucault called *the political technology of the body*—the ways in which power studies, normalizes, and disciplines a populace.[34] Colombia's elites had grown disenchanted with the "modern" system of disciplining the poor, which relied on the diffuse and continual surveillance and correction of the masses by means of the indirect (and superficially beneficial) exercise of power. While not abandoning the methods of control championed during the triumph of liberalism, the state would increasingly rely on the more traditional use of direct force and political exclusion to coerce and control its subjects.

The retreat from unrestricted adult male suffrage was the most striking signification of this shift, but still only a part of a much broader process. Voting had not satiated the masses' desire for political participation but only encouraged more demands and disorder. Therefore, the new constitution restricted the suffrage, retreating from the time (after 1853) when Colombia surpassed most Atlantic societies, including the United States, in suffrage rights.[35] Republican education had failed to discipline subalterns and teach them their duties and place in the nation, having only encouraged them to pursue their rights and make the nation their own. Religious education would make the poor understand the divine architecture of society's hierarchies and the emptiness of pursuing power in the fleeting material world. Popular militias had not co-opted subalterns into voluntarily keeping order in the state; rather, they had given them the training and arms to challenge elites more efficaciously. Professional armies would reduce the clout of the unruly poor and punish malefactors. Panopticons were supposed to have morally reformed deviants and made them good citizens again but had only released "criminals" back into society. A prison island would isolate prisoners from society, while the death penalty would demonstrate the power of the state and the futility of challenging it. Finally, freedom of the press and popular associations, the vehicles for creating an orderly republican citizenry who willingly participated in their own rule, had been the greatest disappointment. Now the state would carefully monitor or directly suppress newspapers and popular associations to prevent plebeians' further corruption.[36] If plebeians would not be disciplined, they would simply be punished or excluded from the political realm.

Colombia had, since 1849, experimented avidly with the new theories of discipline—in which social control generally was exercised more subtly through schools, armies, (nominally) reformist prisons, hospitals, reformed mental-health institutions, and (at times) labor unions—part of a shared elite project in the Atlantic World. North Atlantic states seemed successfully to "discipline" the majority of their populations through the new institutions of state power, although recalcitrant dissenters or minorities were often still violently punished and excluded. Yet the modern state's technologies of power—which Foucault saw as being ushered in by the French Revolution, but which were probably developed across the revolutionary Atlantic World—had utterly failed Colombia's elites. They had tried them, to a degree rivaling, if not surpassing, their employment by their sister republics, but the results were increasingly unsatisfactory. To an impressive degree, Colombia's elites reduced their reliance on these "new" technologies of power in favor of a simpler politics of exclusion and more comfortable older institutions—the army, the church, and direct (as opposed to diffuse) state power.

Democracy Undone

Elites' lack of confidence regarding their ability to discipline the masses was part of a broader transmogrification of Colombia's political culture. The Cauca had been a place where subalterns had multiple and varied means of asserting themselves politically, a vast repertoire that they used, often successfully, to make government more responsive to their concerns. Perhaps more important, Caucano elites had to bargain with subalterns and, at least nominally (if not to a greater degree), include them in the political sphere. For all the differences in power (which were vast), subalterns had become part of the nation.

Along with much recent scholarship, I have hoped to show here how subalterns' political ideas and practices influenced the development of the nineteenth-century Colombian nation. Popular republicans helped create the Colombian nation (and, to some extent, the weak Colombian state) by reframing elite discourse about the nation-state to suit their interests. They took an elite construct and altered it as best they could—given their limited access to wealth and power—in order to position themselves within the nation. They called on the state to serve them, brought it into their local conflicts, and expected it to respond to their demands. Much more so than intellectuals or bureaucrats did, they breathed life into the Colombian nation and defined what it meant to be a Colombian citizen.

Subaltern contributions to nation building cannot be overemphasized. Subalterns entered the nation through contention and claimsmaking, not pacifism. They acted with words, by reframing republicanism, and with deeds. They voted, argued, marched, petitioned, struck, boycotted, chastised, assaulted, fought, and died. By doing so, they completely altered Colombia's political culture, making it far more democratic than it would have been. Action and disorder created democracy and meaningful republicanism, as scholars charting Latin America's political development would do well to remember.[37] While many elites saw the Cauca as the most disorderly Colombian region, we might, given the connotations that order had assumed by the 1870s, interpret this critique as implying that the Cauca was also the most democratic.[38] The desire for order, promoted by the Regenerators (and supported by many fearful plebeians), restricted this democracy.

The Regeneration sought to rein in subalterns' power to imagine, call on, and act within the nation; yet I do not want to suggest that elites completely succeeded in this goal. They did not, as the nineteenth century bequeathed a culture of very politicized subalterns to the twentieth. There are many factors determining the course of twentieth-century Colombian history and Colombia's stable electoral system. One aspect not usually mentioned, however, is the strength, durability, and viability of nineteenth-century popular republicanism. Subalterns' embrace of republicanism was their legacy to Colombian history.

Subalterns usually practiced politics (and nation building) by acting in some sort of alliance with middling or upper-class allies. Throughout the nineteenth century, including the Regeneration, Colombia's elites were too weak to pursue any significant political project without the support of some subalterns. Therefore, it is impossible to understand the course of Colombian politics without investigating how elites won popular support, why subalterns supported an elite faction, and the bargaining that these alliances entailed. Popular politics evolved uniquely in different local environments, preventing many broad generalizations (although Afro-Colombians did often seem to embrace popular liberalism). Unfortunately for theorists and model builders, but fortunately for archive-haunting historians, popular politics can be understood only by exploring the local social history of its subaltern actors. Nevertheless, across Colombia, the nineteenth century begot intense popular identification with the two political parties, a legacy that would only strengthen in the early twentieth century.

Some might anachronistically criticize subalterns for not pursuing their own independent political organization, thus circumventing the inevitable betrayal by their elite allies (which Indians constantly faced and Afro-Colombians felt most brutally between 1877 and 1879). Besides being counterfactual, this argument also denies the important gains that subalterns did make with their allies: from such concrete matters as slavery's abolition, the protection of resguardos, and migrants' securing public land to the discursive triumph of inclusion in the national imaginary. Unlike the countries of the North Atlantic, where increasing racism eroded possibilities for cross-race mobilizing, Colombia displayed an impressive and powerful alliance between mostly white elite Liberals and mostly black and mulatto popular liberals.[39]

While often acting in a coalition with members of other classes, the lower class itself was internally divided. Subalterns acted, not for their class, but for identities built on race, culture, economic location (particularly the idiosyncrasies of landholding—communal, individual, tenant, day laborer, etc.), geography, and, increasingly, partisan affiliation.[40] This legacy of subalterns' identity politics was even codified in the 1991 constitution, which gave special political rights and representation to Indians and (less clearly) Afro-Colombians. While Indians' political affiliation changed drastically in the twentieth century, Afro-Colombians are generally still ardent Liberals—in the Cauca, Liberal politicians still remind voters which party abolished slavery.[41]

The story of popular republicanism in the Cauca makes evident the importance of studying the divisions, racial and otherwise, that mark and often corrupt relations, not only between rich and poor, but among subalterns as well. I have tried to uncover the reasons why different popular republicans chose the politics they did. While it would be arrogant to fault subalterns' political decisions in the nineteenth century, given the forces arrayed against them, I think that some reflection is warranted. Subalterns' divisions were understandable, but those divisions entailed costs as well. Antioqueño migrants and other smallholders had comprehensible reasons for turning against popular liberals in the 1870s, and, while they could not have foreseen the results, their actions would also cost them as the new constitution limited their political space as well. Popular republicans' divisions, especially those based on race, enabled the Regeneration to restrict and denigrate all subaltern politics, although Afro-Colombians would suffer the most.

However, immediately following the inauguration of the Regeneration, some popular republicans seemed to enjoy some benefits. Certainly, Indians and smallholders, especially veterans of the 1876–77 religious civil war, generally viewed the renewed strength of the Catholic Church as a positive development. The state also rewarded popular allies by passing legislation favoring smallholders in their quest for public lands and securing Indians' resguardos.[42] The situation was very different for the Cauca's popular liberals, as the state monopolized aguardiente production, raised the hated aguardiente taxes, and put further restrictions and rents on the ejidos.[43] Assisted by the introduction of barbed wire, the Regenerators took control of the valley from popular liberals, strengthening property rights and attracting foreign investment. The Cauca finally entered the world market, and the land over which popular liberals had struggled for so long would be covered with a sea of green sugarcane, waiting, along with hundreds of disillusioned workers, to be consumed by the mills.[44]

Besides becoming cane cutters, Afro-Colombians faced another fate. The Regeneration was also a racial construction. The social Darwinism of the late nineteenth century—combined with the Cauca's own local history of racism and of the conflation of liberalism and blackness—convinced many that Afro-Colombians had no place in a future oriented toward order and progress. Blacks and mulattoes—especially in discourse, if not in reality—would be pushed to the margins of the Colombian nation and state, isolated geographically and ideologically from the rest of the polity.[45] Afro-Colombians would never again play such a dominant role in the region's politics. In general, fewer opportunities to enter the public, political realm, to participate in the life of the nation, and to find some redress for their concerns were available to them in the early twentieth century than in the nineteenth.[46]

Elite Liberals also paid a price for their racism, their unwillingness to accommodate popular liberals' visions, and their retreat from promoting a politicized citizenry. Caucano Liberals had been unbeatable (when not divided) for thirty years, but they would suffer severe decline during the 1880s. In their own party, leadership and power passed to other areas of Colombia. Nationally, Liberals' division over their relationship with the popular classes doomed the party to suffer Conservative rule until the 1930s. While elites as a class won much in the Regeneration, Liberals as a party lost their powerful political organization in the Cauca.

Popular republicanism as a whole also lost much of its previous influence. I have discussed the important contribution that popular republicans made to Colombia's political culture; yet equally important is what was lost. The Regeneration gutted many of the most radical and democratic aspects of popular republicanism. Popular republicanism had always been a public discourse developed in alliance and collusion with other classes. However, even this public discourse (perhaps a very poor reflection of subalterns' actual beliefs), a discourse in direct conversation with the powerful, was too radical for Colombia's late-nineteenth-century capitalists and state builders. Some middling Liberals had championed a much more socially just vision of society, a vision that included in meaningful ways their lower-class allies. However, the majority of elite Colombians abandoned these ideals out of class and racial fears. Much of popular republicanism (especially popular liberalism, but also popular indigenous conservatism and popular smallholder republicanism) was excised by the state from political life during the Regeneration. While it is important to recognize the role of subalterns in nation formation, scholars must exercise care that their histories do not become positivist stories of state making.[47] Indeed, popular republicanism's fate also suggests the failure or limits of the nation-state as a vehicle for popular politics.

In the short term, the Regeneration actually benefited many plebeians, perhaps not surprisingly, given that many subalterns were important allies in securing the project's success. Yet, in the long term, all subalterns suffered from the restrictions that the Regeneration imposed and from the greater political resources that elites now possessed owing to a somewhat stronger state apparatus. The nation as a whole would also suffer (although subalterns would bear the brunt of this) as Colombian politics became increasingly violent over the course of the next century. The increasing violence that was the unwanted offspring of the Regeneration reaped a much harsher toll on subalterns' lives than even the most bloody of the nineteenth century's conflicts.

Contentious Colombians

The Regeneration's project both succeeded and failed. With coffee, Colombia finally found a relatively stable export commodity, produced with the great participation (if not always to the great benefit) of numerous small farmers, including the smallholders of the northern Caucano hills. In the Cauca Valley, elites triumphed to a remarkable degree in transforming the landscape to their liking, as cane fields dominated the land. Popular liberals' quest for land in the valley was unequivocally denied. Caucano elites had created at least a sufficient veneer of control to attract foreign investment and to reinforce property rights. While disorder would continue, private property was much more secure than it had been in the 1860s and 1870s.

Of course, the Regeneration utterly failed in depoliticizing the country or preventing civil wars, and Colombia would face its most grueling crisis to date in the War of a Thousand Days, although the Cauca was not the center of this conflict. The nineteenth century's legacy was highly active and politicized lower classes, which had become irrevocably accustomed to having their voices heard. What the Regeneration did accomplish was to limit the institutional and legal avenues through which subalterns could pursue politics. The result was a significant change in subalterns' repertoire of politics and their relations to the nation-state.

Violence had always been a part of the political repertoire, but only one tool among many; however, in the twentieth century, it would become more central. Before the Regeneration, popular republicans had recourse to violent actions and, at times, used them to great effect in changing the political scene. However, violent action—usually channeled as partisan, rather than only social, conflict—was only a very small part of the repertoire, compared with all the other alternatives that subalterns regularly employed to enter the political sphere. Even in warfare, the act of service was more important than the fighting and killing proper. The power of popular politics emerged out of subalterns' political community and collective action, not essentially through violence.[48] Nineteenth-century Colombia was marked, not by its mass violence, but by its lack thereof. Subalterns did not enter into rebellions against the state or engage in long-running jaqueries (the zurriago was directed against, not hacendados generally, but Conservative hacendados) or millenarian movements. On the other hand, elites did not have the power to conduct sustained social war (except briefly in 1854) against their own peoples, a situation in sharp contrast to that in Mexico, Brazil, Chile, or Argentina, where state armies regularly marched against their own. Claimsmaking existed everywhere in nineteenth-century Latin America, but, in Colombia, it was channeled via a republican political culture. Colombia's much-talked-of "culture of violence" simply did not exist in the nineteenth century. However, the ordeal that presently wracks the country is at least in part the legacy of a highly politicized citizenry's continual efforts to enter the public, political sphere. When the Regeneration closed down many ways in which subalterns practiced politics, it forced them to adopt new, and increasingly violent and extralegal, methods.[49]

Another misconception is that the Colombian nation had always been weak, threatened by regionalism, illegitimacy, and an ineffectual state. Actually, the mid-nineteenth-century Colombian nation was incredibly strong. Across the republic, subalterns of distinct ethnic groups, classes, regions, and cultures regularly identified themselves as part of the nation and as citizens within it.

This was due, not to any special project by elites (except, perhaps, one by part of the Liberal Party), but to subalterns' efforts to democratize the nation through their political participation. However, they participated by seeking to enter politics "legitimately"—although, of course, they fought endlessly with elites over what constituted legitimate political action. Nevertheless, this political participation gave the nation legitimacy and currency. Subalterns refrained from entering into their own rebellions, jaqueries, or millenarian movements, not because they were content or depoliticized, but because they had found other promising outlets through which to enter the political realm.

This dynamic nineteenth-century democracy often seems unknown to or ignored by current policymakers in both Colombia and the United States—the assumption seems to be that Colombia lacks a history of democratic practices and political culture. By erroneously assuming that no democratic base exists with which to address the contemporary crisis, policymakers focus on strengthening the state rather than democratic civil society. Thus, the U.S. Plan Colombia seems to repeat the experience of the nineteenth-century Regeneration, in which a vibrant political culture was restricted in favor of a more powerful state.[50] If the past is any guide, such a strategy will only further weaken Colombia's now-fragile democracy, leaving recourse to violence as the only avenue through which to pursue political change.

In the nineteenth century, the Regeneration managed to partially delegitimize and weaken the powerful nation imagined by popular republicans. As the Regeneration redefined citizenship to exclude most subalterns and the state reconfigured itself in opposition to mass political participation, the nation lost some of its hard-won currency. Colombia's republicans would remain politicized but would exercise their politics more and more outside institutional boundaries and increasingly against the state. At the end of the long nineteenth century, the Colombian state was stronger, but the nation became, in the process of creating this stronger state, decidedly much less vital to and legitimate for the vast majority of Colombian people than it had been fifty years earlier.

Notes

A list of abbreviations used in references to archival sources can be found on pp. 237–38.

1 A Social History of Politics

1 Franco V., *Apuntamientos para la historia*, 1:94–110; quotation from Jorge Quijano and Thirty-seven Others to Julián Trujillo, 30 April 1877, AGN, SR, FLM, t. 155, p. 330.

Unless otherwise noted, all translations are mine. I have not corrected the orthography of nineteenth-century sources except for obvious typographic errors. I have updated the spelling of place-names, except in the titles of works.

2 El *Montañes*, 1 Feb. 1876; Simón [Arboleda] to T. C. de Mosquera, Coconuco, 14 Feb. 1859, ACC, SM, #36,041.

3 Throughout this book I use *Colombia* in place of the various designations used in the nineteenth century—except in quotations.

4 Although Bushnell recognizes that new research may reveal such conclusions to be overstated, his synthesis of modern Colombian history exemplifies this trend. For example: "Yet the political framework directly touched the lives and affairs of only a small minority of the population" (Bushnell, *The Making of Modern Colombia*, 74; see also 65–66, 78, 93–95, 116). For his challenge to explore clientelism further, see Bushnell, "Assessing the Legacy of Liberalism," 285.

In his classic El *café en Colombia*, Marco Palacios recognized that an often-overlooked difference between the Conservative and the Liberal Parties was their relationship with subaltern classes (see Palacios, El *café en Colombia*, 29). However, in a more recent survey, he takes a more traditional view, seeing political history as the ebb and flow of elite factionalism in a Colombia seemingly "immune to the democratic virus" (Palacios, *Entre la legitimidad*, 36; see also 15).

See also Colmenares, *Partidos políticos*, 24–30; McGreevey, *Economic History*, 75–77, 96; Tirado Mejía, *Aspectos sociales*, 37–38; Delpar, *Red against Blue*, 39 41, Fals Borda, *Historia doble*, vol. 2; Valencia Llano, *Estado Soberano del Cauca*, 14–16, 44, 59–60, 127; and Lynch, *The Spanish American Revolutions*, 347–51. Valencia Llano's more recent essays show much more concern with popular politics (see, e.g., "La guerra de 1851"). Fernán E. González González recognizes that the Liberal Party served briefly as a vehicle to express popular sentiment, but he generally views nineteenth-century politics as largely clientelist (see González González, *Para leer la política*, 1:33–40).

5 This scholarship has grown too large to cite inclusively, but see esp. Mallon, *Peasant and Nation*; and Joseph and Nugent, eds., *Everyday Forms of State Formation*.

Most of the new work on Colombia concerns urban artisans: Gutiérrez Sanín, *Curso y discurso*; Aguilera Peña and Vega Cantor, *Ideal democrático*; Sowell, *The Early Colombian Labor Movement*; Pacheco, *La fiesta liberal*; Valencia Llano, "La guerra de 1851"; Zambrano, "Algunas formas de sociabilidad"; Stoller, "Liberalism and Conflict"; Deas, "La política en la vida cotidiana," and "*Del poder y la gramática*," 209–18; and Jiménez, "La vida rural cotidiana."

6 A very influential evocation of this process is Gabriel García Márquez's magisterial *One Hundred Years of Solitude*.

7 An important exception is Ada Ferrer's *Insurgent Cuba*, an insightful study of Afro-Cuban popular politics. I also found her remonstration about the use of racial labels very provoking. She prefers *black* and *mulatto* to other categories (see Ferrer, *Insurgent Cuba*, 10–12), but I still have chosen to use *Afro-Colombian* to refer to people of African descent, although at times I will use *black* and *mulatto* as well. Colombians themselves are now employing *Afro-Colombiano*. Also, employing *Afro-Colombian* is simply more aesthetically pleasing than having continually to refer to *blacks and mulattoes* (while using only *black* is often inaccurate). Similarly, I have translated the Spanish *indígena* as *Indian*, primarily for stylistic reasons (please read *Indian* as *indígena*, not *indio*, as the two were not synonymous in nineteenth-century Colombia).

8 I contrast this style of republican bargaining with the more traditional popular action described by E. P. Thompson as prevailing in England through the 1750s. Thompson delineates three features of this older style: its anonymity; the employment of countertheater with often-hidden symbolism; and the crowd—quick to dissipate—as its principal agent. See Thompson, *Customs in Common*, 66–71. See also Tilly, *Popular Contention*, 1–105; and Tarrow, *Power in Movement*, 31–78. For the importance of bargaining, see Markoff, *The Abolition of Feudalism*.

9 According to Stern ("The Age of Andean Insurrection," 76), imagery linked to "an Andean- or Inca-led social order," found by scholars in Peruvian and Bolivian indigenous peoples' national visions, seems to have faded (or never existed) for the Cauca's Indians by the 1850s.

10 Roseberry, "Hegemony and the Language of Contention," 361. See also Thompson, *Customs in Common*. I follow Roseberry in understanding Gramsci's conception of hegemony as being more political and material and less ideological. See Gramsci, *Selections from the Prison Notebooks*.

11 Mallon, "Time on the Wheel," 340. The concept of hegemony is, I think, more useful than the concepts *political culture* and *public sphere* as *hegemony* strongly implies power relations, while employing *political culture* alone may at times occlude power.

12 Scott sees discourse in the public sphere as largely for show and devoid of meaning, especially to subalterns, yet it seems to me that hegemonic political culture defines and limits the actions and discourse of both elites and subalterns. See Scott, *Domination*. See also Habermas, *The Theory of Communicative Action*.

13 I have not sought to write subalterns' story, nor would I presume to do so, even if the sources made that possible. I have merely tried to present how subalterns participated in politics and how they publicly represented their own political ideas. The concern of subaltern studies with the feasibility (or even the desirability) of appropriately representing subalterns' history and ideas so often assumes that the only discourse that matters is the private, hidden text. However, subalterns regularly engage in public political activities. The realities of power relations, of course, restrict and taint these activities, masking subalterns' own representation of politics. Yet,

for the historian, it is often the public discourse (warped as it is) that is the most interesting as this is what most affected (and was affected by) the power relations that form the core of much political and social history. See Beverley, *Subalternity*; Mallon, "Promise and Dilemma"; and Spivak, "Can the Subaltern Speak?" Guha himself noted that one of the principal efforts of subaltern studies was to explore the interactions of the dominant, subaltern, and middle groups and their competing (and, at times, colluding) conceptions of the nation. See Guha, "On Some Aspects."

14 On social bargaining, see Jiménez, *Struggles on an Interior Shore*.

15 Gramsci as quoted in Kurtz, "Hegemony and Anthropology," 106.

16 Marx, "The Eighteenth Brumaire of Louis Bonaparte."

17 Guha, "On Some Aspects," 37, 44.

18 Pablo Arosemena to Julián Trujillo, Juan de D. Ulloa, and B. Reinales, Bogotá, 1 April 1882, in Reinales, *Ferrocarril del Cauca*, 51. See also Hyland, "The Secularization of Credit," 136.

19 Comisión Corográfica, *Jeografía*, 354; James M. Eder to Secretary of State William H. Seward, Buenaventura, 24 Oct. 1868, in U.S. State Department, *Dispatches*.

20 Emigdio Palau in *Alcance a la Gaceta núm. 300* (Popayán), 15 Aug. 1869.

21 Valdivia Rojas, "Mapas de densidad de población."

22 Figures for 1843 taken from *Estadística jeneral de la Nueva Granada*, 22, 45, 52, 92, 97. Figures for 1870 taken from *Boletín Industrial*, 5 Oct. 1873. See also Melo, "Las vicisitudes del modelo liberal," 120.

23 Reinales, *Informe*, app.

24 See Zambrano, "Historiografía sobre los movimientos sociales," 147–81.

25 James M. Eder to Secretary of State William H. Seward, Buenaventura, 24 Oct. 1868, in U.S. State Department, *Dispatches*.

26 Rappaport, *The Politics of Memory*, 31–60; Jaramillo Uribe, "La población indígena de Colombia."

27 Mosquera, *Memoria*, 141; *Gaceta Oficial del Cauca*, 10 July 1866.

28 Comisión Corográfica, *Jeografía*, 323, 333, 339.

29 Pérez, *Jeografía*, 273, 297, 368; Correa González, "Intergración socio-económica," 20.

30 Tovar Pinzón, "La lenta ruptura," 101–2.

31 Urrutia M. and Arrubla, eds., *Compendio de estadísticas históricas*, table 8; for children, AGN, SR, FM, t. 1, pp. 342, 354, 431, 437; AGN, SR, FGV, t. 216, pp. 494–500.

32 Castellanos, *La abolición*, 86.

33 J. B. González, Popayán, 19 Sep. 1877, ACC, AM, pq. 138-34.

34 Appelbaum, *Muddied Waters*, 9–11, 33–40.

35 Mejía Prado, *Origen del campesino*; Escorcia, *Sociedad y economía*, 40–44.

36 Escorcia, *Sociedad y economía*, 45–75.

37 *El Sentimiento Democrático*, 31 May 1849.

38 Avelino Vela to Secretary of Government, Ipiales, 28 April 1865, ACC, AM, pq. 92-83; Samper, *Ensayo aproximado sobre la jeografía*, 28.

39 Comisión Corográfica, AGN, SR, FLM, t. 143, p. 17.

40 Comisión Corográfica, BN, libro 397, p. 11; Comisión Corográfica, AGN, SR, FLM, t. 142, p. 12.

41 Escorcia, "Haciendas"; The Undersigned Colombian Citizens and Members of the Democratic Society of Palmira to President, Palmira, 21 June 1868, INCORA, t. 7, p. 492.

42 Pérez, *Jeografía*, 277; Mejía Prado, *Origen del campesino*, 87–142.

43 Comisión Corográfica, *Jeografía*, 95; Comisión Corográfica, AGN, SR, FLM, t. 142, p. 12.

44 Comisión Corográfica, AGN, SR, FLM, t. 143, p. 17.

45 Comisión Corográfica, *Jeografía*, 337; José Francisco Vela to Secretary of Government, Ipiales, 27 June 1866, ACC, AM, pq. 94-40; Jefe Municipal, Popayán, 15 June 1866, ACC, AM, pq. 94-54; Friede, *El indio en lucha*.

46 Villegas and Restrepo, *Resguardos*, 45–49; Rappaport, *The Politics of Memory*, 101–12.

47 Rafael Diago, Popayán, 20 Oct. 1853, ACC, AM, pq. 54-1; *Gaceta Oficial*, 1 Dec. 1870; Joaquín Gárcez, Túquerres, 15 Sep. 1849, ACC, AM, pq. 46-6.

48 AGN, SR, FM, t. 1, pp. 146, 149, 155, 182bis, 355, 437; AGN, SR, FM, t. 2, pp. 194, 195, 473, 779; "Lista nominal de los esclavos cimarrones," Cali, 2 Jan. 1852, AHMC, t. 82, p. 597; Zuluaga and Bermúdez, *La protesta social*, 37–102.

49 Comisión Corográfica, *Jeografía*, 85, 89, 93, 103, 107.

50 Ibid., 323–24, 336; Governor of Atrato Province to Secretary of the Treasury, Quibdó, 1 March 1859, ACC, AM, pq. 73-39.

51 Pérez, *Jeografía*, 307.

52 Jesus M. López S. to General Superintendent of Public Instruction, Cartago, 21 Nov. 1877, ACC, AM, pq. 135-49; *Gaceta Oficial del Cauca*, 30 Oct. 1866.

53 The Undersigned Residents of Fraternidad Parish to Jefe Político, Cali, 22 July 1853, AHMC, t. 124, p. 500.

54 *Registro Oficial*, 29 April 1876.

55 Samper, *Ensayo aproximado sobre la jeografía*, 28; Pérez, *Jeografía*, 370.

56 Helguera, "Antecedentes sociales," 57.

57 *Estadística de Colombia*, 115–16.

58 For general economic history of the Cauca, see Colmenares, *Cali*, and *Historia*; Escorcia, *Sociedad y economía*; and Valencia Llano, *Empresarios y políticos*. For Colombia in general, see Ocampo, ed., *Historia económica de Colombia*; and Ann Twinam, *Miners, Merchants, and Farmers*.

59 Díaz de Zuluaga, *Oro, sociedad y economía*; Colmenares, *Cali*.

60 Hyland, "The Secularization of Credit," 95–120; Salvador C. de Guzmán to Circuit Judge, Popayán, 11 Nov. 1870, ACC, EC, #2714.

61 *El Republicano*, 1 Dec. 1867; Samper, *Ensayo aproximado sobre la jeografía*, 27.

62 McGreevey, *Economic History*, 217–43.

63 Comisión Corográfica, BN, libro 397, p. 16; Saffray, *Viaje a Nueva Granada*, 226.

64 Gregorio Arboleda, Popayán, 1 Jan. 1875, ACC, AM, pq. 133-80.

65 Sergio Arboleda, Japio, 14 Sep. 1867, ACC, FA, #26, p. 1; Primitivo Chaux and Henrique Chaux to President, Popayán, 1 Sep. 1882, ACC, AM, pq. 161-25; *Gaceta Oficial*, 1 Dec. 1870.

66 Rafael Caicedo to Municipal President, [Cali?, 1847/1848?], AHMC, t. 101, p. 676; Vicente Javier Arboleda to Tomás Cipriano de Mosquera, Popayán, 11 April 1855, BLAA, #558.

67 Escorcia, "Haciendas," 121–27; *Los Principios*, 26 June 1874; LeGrand, *Frontier Expansion*, 63–90.

68 Belisario Zamorano to Salvador Camacho R., Cali, 1 Nov. 1878, AGN, SA, FSCR, caja 13-175, p. 44.

69 Palacios, *El café en Colombia*, 71, 101, 189.

70 Mariano del Campo Larraondo to S. D., Quilichao, 3 Oct. 1848, BN, libro 165, p. 354; McGreevey, *Economic History*, 146–81.

71 José Gregorio Fernández to T. C. de Mosquera, Panamá, 28 Sep. 1852, ACC, SM, #28,406.

72 The Undersigned Colombians and Foreigners to President, Tumaco, 30 Aug. 1878, INCORA, t. 14, p. 947.

73 Ocampo, *Colombia y la economía mundial*, 255–300.

74 McGreevey, *Economic History*, 71.

75 Samper, *Ensayo aproximado sobre la jeografía*, attached table.

76 *Estadística de Colombia*, 32, 101, 105; Melo, "Las vicisitudes del modelo liberal," 120.

2 Popular Republicanism

1 The quotation that I use as the title of this chapter is taken from the opening line of a petition: Citizens of the State and Residents of Caldas Municipality to President, Bolívar, 5 July 1868, ACC, AM, pq. 99-14.

2 Fighting continued in the region until 1824. Bushnell, *The Making of Modern Colombia*, 50–73; McFarlane, *Colombia before Independence; Earle, Spain and the Independence of Colombia.*

3 Zuluaga Ramírez, *Guerrilla y sociedad*, 67–72, 83, 116–19, and "Clientelismo y guerrillas," 128–31; Hamnett, "Popular Insurrection," 309–25; Hernández de Alba, *Libertad de los esclavos*, 47–48.

4 López Garavito, *Historia de la hacienda*, 197; Uribe de Hincapié and Alvarez, *Poderes*, 289–91.

5 Melo, "Las vicisitudes del modelo liberal," 120, 152.

6 See Castellanos, *La abolición*, 62; Earle, "The War of the Supremes"; Lobato Paz, "Caudillos y nación"; González González, *Para leer la política*, 2:83–161; Escorcia, *Sociedad y economía*, 82–84.

7 A note on capitalization: Owing to the loosely organized nature of the parties, it is often difficult to ascertain membership. Nevertheless, elite and middling actors usually left enough records to allow one to refer to them as *Liberals* or *Conservatives*. At times, popular actors may also have considered themselves party members, but, given their own reframing of the parties and the difficulty in ascribing membership, I refer to them as *popular liberals* or *popular conservatives* (or some variation thereof, as this chapter details). The adjectives *conservative* and *liberal* refer to political philosophies as opposed to political parties. For the history of the parties in general, see Delpar, *Red against Blue.*

8 Uribe-Uran, *Honorable Lives*, 127–28.

9 Escorcia, *Sociedad y economía*, 111–16; Lobato Paz, "Caudillos y nación," 199–207; Helguera, "Antecedentes sociales," 61. For Colombia as a whole, see Safford, "Social Aspects of Politics" (Safford notes that, unlike in most of Colombia, in the Cauca the Conservatives were clearly economically more powerful than the region's Liberals); Helguera, "The First Mosquera Administration," 226–67; Uribe-Uran, *Honorable Lives*, 4–5, 82–85, 122–23, 126–28, 135–37, and "Rebellion of the Young Mandarins"; Delpar, *Red against Blue*, 23; Bushnell, *The Making of Modern Colombia*, 92–95; and Colmenares, *Partidos políticos*, 21–49 (in contrast to Safford, Colmenares proposes that Liberals represented an incipient civilian bourgeoisie).

10 Gibson, *The Constitutions of Colombia*, 160–62.

11 Jaramillo Uribe, *El pensamiento colombiano*, 112–48; König, *En el camino*, 189–502; Molina, *Las ideas liberales*, 17–52. More broadly, see Andrews, "Spanish American Independence"; Roig, "El siglo XIX latinoamericano"; and Lempérière, "Reflexiones."

12 See Helg, "The Limits of Equality"; Lasso, "Race and Republicanism."

13 Castellanos, *La abolición*, 65; Hamnett, "Popular Insurrection," 304.

14 Colmenares, "Castas," 144.

15 López, *Mensaje del Presidente de la Nueva Granada*, 1; Zamorano, *Bosquejo biográfico*, 4–5; Mercado, *Memorias*, xiv–xv.

16 *La Unión*, 7 Feb. 1864.

17 Ibid.

18 *Estadística de Colombia*, 59.

19 Vicente Cárdenas to Governor, [Popayán?], Aug. 1848, ACC, AM, pq. 44-6.

20 Register of Slaves in Barbacoas Province, 31 Dec. 1851, AGN, SR, FM, t. 2, p. 857.

21 Lasso, "Haiti as an Image of Popular Republicanism."

22 Valencia Llano, *Luchas sociales y políticas*; Zambrano, "Las sociabilidades modernas," and "Algunas formas de sociabilidad"; Aguilera Peña and Vega Cantor, *Ideal democrático*; Deas, "La presencia de la política nacional."

23 Edward Said has rightly criticized authors such as Joseph Conrad for imagining that all significant action, history, and culture originate in the West and for granting no independence or integrity to Asians, Africans, or Latin Americans. While he notes how Conrad can imagine no response to the West's power, Said assumes that response will emanate from some indigenous, non-Western wellspring. However, I propose that, in nineteenth-century Colombia, subalterns responded by seizing the language and tools of Atlantic (not Western) republicanism for their own ends. See Said, *Culture and Imperialism*, xvii–xx, 165–66.

24 One problem is that writers rarely identified themselves; the handwriting of a petition is often different from that of any of the signatures (many signatories signed with an X or had someone sign for them), and usually no notation exists of who actually wrote the petition. See Granados García, "Algunos aspectos de la cultura política popular."

25 For example, the municipality of Obando, on the border with Ecuador and with a large Indian population, had 36,270 inhabitants in 1864. The *jefe municipal* asked the census taker to record literacy rates too: 7,665 people (6,330 men and 1,335 women) could read and write. While the number may be exaggerated, Obando was also very poor and without the educational centers of Cali or Popayán. *Gaceta Oficial del Cauca*, 10 July 1866; Jefe Municipal of Obando to Secretary of Government, Ipiales, 28 April 1865, ACC, AM, pq. 92-83.

26 For opposing views, see Spivak, "Can the Subaltern Speak?" and Scott, *Domination*.

27 The historiography of the Antioqueño migration is probably Colombia's largest, next to studies of *la violencia*. See, e.g., Parsons, *Antioqueño Colonization*; Palacios, *El café en Colombia*; Santa, *La colonización antioqueña*; Valencia Llano, *Colonización*; and Uribe de Hincapié and García, "La espada," 77–107.

28 Residents of Toro Municipality to President of the Senate, Riosucio, 28 Feb. 1874, AC, C, 1874, vol. IV, p. 141.

29 Gregorio Arcila and over 340 Others to Deputies of the Constitutional Assembly, n.p., n.d., received 30 Oct. 1857, ACC, AM, pq. 64-41.

30 Until 1853, most tenants, not being propertyholders, would not have been citizens. Gibson, *The Constitutions of Colombia*, 160–62.

31 Residents of Nuevo Salento to Senators and Representatives, Nuevo Salento, 25 Jan. 1865, AC, C, 1865, vol. I, p. 175.

32 "Proyecto de decreto," Bogotá, 13 March 1869, AC, C, 1869, vol. II, p. 129.

33 "Proyecto de Lei," [1857?], ACC, AM, pq. 64-36. These rules were not simply imposed on settlers, who stated that they would accept them "with much pleasure." Residents of Finlandia to Senate and House of Representatives, Finlandia, 1 March 1884, AC, C, 1884, vol. V, p. 252.

34 Francisco A. Ospina to Secretary of the Treasury, Salento, 5 March 1884, AGN, SR, FB, t. 4, p. 192.

35 LeGrand, *Frontier Expansion*; Palacios, *El café en Colombia*; Jiménez, *Struggles on an Interior Shore*.

36 For example, Paulo Emilio Mora and Five Others to Secretary of the Treasury, Salento, 1 March 1884, AGN, SR, FB, t. 4, p. 294.

37 LeGrand, *Frontier Expansion*, 14–17; Botero Villa, *Adjudicación*.

38 Residents of the Aldea de María to Representatives, Aldea de María, 4 April 1853, AC, C, 1853, Petitciones, p. 369; Residents of Santa Rosa to Senators and Representatives, Santa Rosa, 22 Feb. 1856, AC, C, 1856, Solicitudes, p. 349; Residents of San Francisco to President, San Francisco, 17 Nov. 1864, AGN, SR, FMI, t. 38, p. 611.

39 Residents of Pereira to Judge of the Quindío Circuit, Pereira, 18 Oct. 1868, INCORA, t. 13, p. 933.

40 Appelbaum, *Muddied Waters*; Uribe de Hincapié and Alvarez, *Poderes*, 47; Roldán, *Blood and Fire*, 35–40; Uribe de Hincapié and García, "La espada."

41 Residents of the Villa de María to State President, Villa de María, 26 May 1872, ACC, AM, pq. 116-20.

42 Residents of Riosucio to Deputies of the Constitutional Assembly, Riosucio, 27 Aug. 1857, ACC, AM, pq. 64-41.

43 Residents of the Aldea de Cerillos to Senators and Representatives, Cerillos, 19 March 1851, AC, S, 1851, vol. VI, p. 419.

44 Citizens and Residents of the Aldea de María to Legislators, María, 20 Feb. 1855, AC, C, 1855, vol. VI, p. 156.

45 The number of petitions asking for roads to be built or simply citing proximity to a road as reason enough for a new village's success is legion. For example, Residents of Villa Rica to Governor, Villa Rica, 20 Oct. 1863, ACC, AM, pq. 90-50.

46 Residents of Boquía to Senators and Representatives, Boquía, 26 Jan. 1859, AC, C, 1860, vol. XIX, p. 12.

47 Residents of Finlandia to Senate and House of Representatives, Finlandia, 1 March 1884, AC, C, 1884, vol. V, p. 252.

48 *Ordenanzas espedidas por la Cámara Provincial*, 16.

49 *Gaceta Oficial*, 28 May 1870.

50 Gibson, *The Constitutions of Colombia*, 43, 82–83, 162, 201, 227, 281.

51 *Ordenanzas espedidas por la Lejislatura Provincial . . . 1856*, 9; Escovar, *Alegato*, 6.
   On the importance of family and religion, see Gutiérrez de Pineda, *Familia y cultura*, 355–402; Appelbaum, "Remembering Riosucio," 42–45, 57–58; and Farnsworth-Alvear, *Dulcinea in the Factory*.

52 For example, Residents of San Francisco to Governor, San Francisco, 19 Oct. 1858, ACC, AM, pq. 71-2; Rafael Meléndez and 57 Others to Deputies, Cartago Viejo, 29 Sep. 1857, ACC, AM, pq. 64-41.

53 Residents of Boquía to Senators and Representatives, Boquía, 23 April 1853, AC, C, 1853, vol. VIII, p. 329.

54 Residents of Cabal Parish to Representatives and Senators, Cabal, 1 March 1849, AC, S, 1849, vol. II, p. 175.

55 Residents of Nuevo Salento District to President, Salento, 1 Sep. 1883, AGN, SR, FB, t. 4, p. 283.

56 See Joseph and Nugent, eds., *Everyday Forms of State Formation*.

57 Residents of the Aldea de María to Senators and Representatives, María, 30 Jan. 1855, AC, S, 1858, vol. XII, p. 188.

58 Residents of Boquía to Senators and Representatives, Boquía, 23 April 1853, AC, C, 1853, vol. VIII, p. 329.

59 The Assembly of Padres de Familia of the Aldea de Chinchiná to Legislators, n.p., n.d., received 2 Feb. 1856, AC, C, 1856, vol. IV, p. 20.

60 Governor and Alcaldes of the Parcialidad of Pitayó to Governor, Popayán, 24 Nov. 1858, ACC, AM, pq. 67-19.

61 Indians of Toribio, San Francisco, and Tacueyó to Governor, Toribio, 25 May 1868, ACC, AM, pq. 101-60.

62 Cabildo de Indígenas of Túquerres to President of the Legislature, Túquerres, 26 July 1871, ACC, AM, pq. 112-15.

63 Cabildos Pequeños de Indígenas of Túquerres, Cumbal, Guachucal, Muellamuez, Sapuyes, Guaitarilla, Ospina, Yascual, Mallama, and Imués to Deputies of the Legislature, Túquerres, 14 Aug. 1877, ACC, AM, pq. 137-18.

64 Cabildos Pequeños de Indígenas of Túquerres, Sapuyes, Imués, Ospina, Cumbal, Guachucal, Muellamuez, Yascual, and Puerres to Deputies of the Legislature, Pasto, 19 July 1875, ACC, AM, pq. 133-75.

65 Blassingame, The Slave Community, 223–48; Genovese, Roll, Jordan, Roll, 113–58; Scott, Domination. Scott and Genovese offer different points of view, of course, as Scott completely rejects the concept of "hegemony" while Genovese allows that the acting of deference may have lasting psychological and political effects.

66 The Cabildos Pequeños de Indígenas of Guachucal and Muellamuez to Governor, Guachucal, 4 Oct. 1852, ACC, AM, pq. 53-56.

67 Vocales of the Pequeño Cabildo of Riosucio District to Governor, Riosucio, 1 Aug. 1869, ACC, AM, pq. 105-74.

68 Pequeño Cabildo de Indígenas of Riosucio District to Tómas Sipriano [sic] Mosquera, Riosucio, 13 Feb. 1863, ACC, SM, #45,290.

69 Cabildo Pequeño de Indígenas of Túquerres to Alcalde, Túquerres, 5 Oct. 1852, ACC, AM, pq. 53-56.

70 Juan Ipia, Alcalde Indígena of Paniquitá, to Governor, Popayán, 15 March 1850, ACC, AM, pq. 48-57.

71 Cabildo de Indígenas of Caldono to Governor, Caldono, 19 Nov. 1853, ACC, AM, pq. 55-85.

72 Governors of the Parcialidades of Riosucio, Anserma Vieja, and Guática to Governor [sic], Riosucio, 29 March 1869, ACC, AM, pq. 105-74. Protestations of respect were so common that they were almost pro forma, and, hence, I do not want to make too much of them. However, as I noted, while migrants and popular liberals also paid their respects, they did so much less vociferously and often did not do so at all.

73 For the language of petitions in colonial Colombia, see Garrido, Reclamos y representaciones.

74 Cabildo de Indígenas of Caldono to Governor, Caldono, 19 Nov. 1853, ACC, AM, pq. 55-85.

75 Juan Ipia, Alcalde Indígena of Paniquitá to Governor, Popayán, 15 March 1850, ACC, AM, pq. 48-57.

76 Bushnell, The Making of Modern Colombia, 78, 93–95; Lynch, The Spanish American Revolutions, 347–49; and Hobsbawm, The Age of Revolution, 121.

77 Cabildo Pequeño de Indígenas of Yascual to President of the Provincial Legislature, Túquerres, 8 Oct. 1852, ACC, AM, pq. 48-4.

78 Testimony of Governor Bautista Pechene, Popayán, 18 Aug. 1856, ACC, AM, pq. 62-45.

79 Governors of Pitayó, Jambaló, and Quichaya to Governor, Jambaló, 1 Aug. 1859, ACC, AM, pq. 74-51.

I propose that, more so than Indians in other areas of Latin America, Indians in the Cauca had some success in integrating Indian identity and universalizing republican citizenship. See Thurner, *From Two Republics to One Divided*, 146–52; and Gould, *To Die in This Way*, 11–15, 285.

80 Members of the Cabildo Pequeño de Indígenas and Adults of the Village of Sibundoy to State President, Sibundoy, 8 Nov. 1874, ACC, AM, pq. 129-45.

81 The Cabildo Pequeño de Indígenas de Santiago de Pongo to Deputies, Santiago de Pongo, 8 Aug. 1869, ACC, AM, pq. 103-3.

82 Governor and Alcalde of Quichaya to Governor, Popayán, 1 April 1853, ACC, AM, pq. 55-85.

83 Cabildo Pequeño de Indígenas of Cumbal to State President, Ipiales, 12 April 1871, ACC, AM, pq. 108-32.

84 Cabildo de Indígenas of Caldono to Governor, Caldono, 19 Nov. 1853, ACC, AM, pq. 55-85.

85 The Cabildo Pequeño de Indígenas of Santiago de Pongo to Deputies, Santiago de Pongo, 8 Aug. 1869, ACC, AM, pq. 103-3. Because Caquetá was a territory, the people living there did not have the same rights as those living in the states.

86 This lack of "tribal" affiliations may reflect a gap between public discourse and private consciousness, but, while Indians did not discursively declare themselves as belonging to groups larger than the village or differentiate themselves culturally from other Indians (except for "savage" Indians), they did act together at times.

87 Alcaldes Mayores of Túquerres and Ipiales Cantones, Along with All the Pequeños Cabildos de Indígenas of the Provinces, to President of the Provincial Legislature, Túquerres, 17 Sep. 1848, ACC, AM, pq. 44-39.

88 Governor and Cabildo Pequeño de Indígenas of Pancitará to Governor, Pancitará, 24 Aug. 1850, ACC, AM, pq. 48-57.

89 Governors of Pitayó, Jambaló, and Quichaya to Governor, Jambaló, 1 Aug. 1859, ACC, AM, pq. 74-51.

90 The Indian Bosses of the Aldea de Coconuco to Alcalde, Coconuco, 1 Aug. 1860, ACC, AM, pq. 80-70.

91 Members of the Cabildo Pequeño de Indígenas and Adults of the Village of Sibundoy to State President, Sibundoy, 8 Nov. 1874, ACC, AM, pq. 129-45.

92 The Cabildo de Indígenas of Guachucal and Colimba to Legislators, Guachucal, 12 Aug. 1873, ACC, AM, pq. 124-60.

93 Citizens and Residents of Silvia Parish to Senators and Representatives, Silvia, 19 March 1852, AC, S, 1852, vol. IV, p. 137 (ellipses in original; emphasis added).

94 Inhabitants of Riosucio District to Deputies of the State Legislature, Riosucio, 27 June 1875, ACC, AM, pq. 130-17. See also Appelbaum, "Remembering Riosucio."

95 Cabildos Pequeños de Indígenas of Guachucal and Muellamuez to Governor, Guachucal, 4 Oct. 1852, ACC, AM, pq. 53-56.

96 Cabildo de Indígenas of Ipiales to President, Ipiales, 1 Oct. 1863, AGN, SR, FMI, t. 66.

97 Vocales of the Pequeño Cabildo of Riosucio District to Governor, Riosucio, 1 Aug. 1869, ACC, AM, pq. 105-74.

98 Pequeño Cabildo of Cumbal to State President, Cumbal, 29 July 1871, AGN, SR, FMI, t. 82, p. 986.

99 Pequeño Cabildo of Túquerres to President of the Legislature, Túquerres, June 1869, ACC, AM, pq. 103-3.

100 Pequeño Cabildo de Indígenas of Genoy to President of the Legislature, Pasto, 15 Aug. 1877, ACC, AM, pq. 137-18.

101 Indian Alcalde Mayor of Obando Municipality (with Signers from the Parcialidades of Potosí, Mayasquer, Yaramal, Cumbal, Guachucal, Muellamuez, Colimba, Carlosama, Caserio de Pastas, Pupiales, Anfelima, Girón, Iles, Ospina, and Puerres) to Secretary of State Government, Ipiales, 4 March 1866, ACC, AM, pq. 94-54.

102 Alcaldes Mayores of Túquerres and Ipiales Cantones . . . to President of the Provincial Legislature, Túquerres, 17 Sep. 1848, ACC, AM, pq. 44-39.

103 For example, Governor de Indígenas of the Parcialidad of Tacueyó to Corregidor, Tacueyó, 28 Feb. 1866, ACC, AM, pq. 94-54.

104 Chapa Parcialidad to Vocales of the Municipality, Popayán, 24 March 1866, ACC, AM, pq. 94-40.

105 Pequeños Cabildes de Indígenas of Túquerres, Obando, and Pasto to Deputies of the State Legislature, Pasto, 29 July 1873, ACC, AM, pq. 124-60.

106 Governor of the Indians of Guachicono to Governor, Popayán, 24 Feb. 1855, ACC, AM, pq. 60-61.

107 Cabildo Pequeño de Indígenas of Guachavéz to Deputies, Pasto, 6 Oct. 1856, ACC, AM, pq. 61-6.

108 Governor of Indígenas of Polindará to Governor, Popayán, 1855 (full date illegible), ACC, AM, pq. 60-56.

109 See, e.g., Smith, *Livelihood and Resistance;* Mallon, *Peasant and Nation;* and Stern, *The Secret History of Gender.*

110 Indian Alcalde Mayor of Obando Municipality . . . to Secretary of State Government, Ipiales, 4 March 1866, ACC, AM, pq. 94-54.

111 Alcalde Mayor de Indígenas of Túquerres Cantón to President of the House of Representatives, Túquerres, 30 Dec. 1848, AC, C, 1849, vol. IX, p. 184.

112 Appelbaum, "Remembering Riosucio."

113 Sewell, *Work and Revolution in France;* Lempérière, "Reflexiones," 49–56.

114 Villegas and Restrepo, *Resguardos,* 30–31, 45–49.

115 Pequeño Cabildo de Indígenas of Mocondino to State President, Pasto, 18 Feb. 1866, ACC, AM, pq. 94-54.

116 For an extended discussion of Democratic Societies, see chapter 3 below.

117 Juan de Dios and María Concepcion Larraondo to President of the Cabildo, Cali, 19 May 1853, AHMC, t. 124, p. 515.

118 Inhabitants of the San Julián Hacienda to Governor, San Julián, 15 Oct. 1853, ACC, AM, pq. 55-92.

119 Bautista Feijoo to Governor, Caloto, 8 April 1854, ACC, AM, pq. 75-84.

120 Hilario Hurtado to Judge, Popayán, 16 Feb. 1845, ACC, EC, #4031.

121 The Undersigned, in the Majority Former Slaves, to President, Barbacoas, 6 Nov. 1852, AGN, SR, FGV, t. 179, p. 341.

122 Residents of the Micay River and Parish to Legislators, Micay, 23 Feb. 1853, AC, S, 1853, vol. VI, p. 262.

123 Residents of San Juan to Senators and Representatives, [n.p., 1852?], AC, S, 1852, vol. II, p. 19.

124 The Bogas [Boatmen] of the Dagua River to State President, Cali, 15 May 1878, ACC, AM, pq. 144-64.

125 Inhabitants of the San Julián Hacienda to Governor, San Julián, 15 Oct. 1853, ACC, AM, pq. 55-92.

126 Residents of Cali to Provincial Legislature, Cali, 17 Sep. 1849, in *El Sentimiento Democrático,* 27 Sep. 1849.

127 Colombian Citizens to Secretary of the Treasury, Villa de Bao, 20 Aug. 1883, AGN, SR, FB, t. 4, p. 274.

128 Residents of Tumaco to President, Tumaco, 30 Aug. 1878, INCORA, t. 14, p. 947.

129 La Sociedad Democrática de Cali, *Mentir con descaro*. See also *Ariete*, 2 March 1850.

130 *El Republicano*, 22 Dec. 1867.

131 Residents of Quilcacé Aldea to Municipal Vocales, Quilcacé, 14 Feb. 1864, ACC, AM, pq. 88-54.

132 José M. Castro to Jefe Municipal, Popayán, 14 Sep. 1867, ACC, AM, pq. 97-8.

133 The Bogas of the Dagua River to State President, Cali, 15 May 1878, ACC, AM, pq. 144-64.

134 Citizens and Residents of Caldas Municipality to President, Bolívar, 5 July 1868, ACC, AM, pq. 99-14.

135 Citizens and Residents of La Cruz to President, La Cruz, 8 July 1868, ACC, AM, pq. 99-14.

136 Miguel Guerrero and Others to State President, Cali, 25 Oct. 1875, ACC, AM, pq. 130-18.

137 Fermín Pretel to the Cabildo, Cali, 19 April 1853, AHMC, t. 124, p. 512.

138 Vicente Javier Arboleda to Tomás Cipriano de Mosquera, Popayán, 11 April 1855, BLAA, #558.

139 Gabriel Lalinde to State President, Popayán, 9 Oct. 1869, ACC, AM, pq. 105-74.

140 The Undersigned Colombian Citizens and Active Members of the Democratic Society of Palmira to President, Palmira, 21 June 1868, INCORA, t. 7, p. 492. See also *El Pensamiento Popular*, 22 July 1852.

141 Residents of Quilcacé Aldea to Municipal Vocales, Quilcacé, 14 Feb. 1864, ACC, AM, pq. 88-54.

142 Pioquinto Diago, for Himself and in the Name of His Friends, to State President, Popayán, 7 Feb. 1878, ACC, AM, pq. 144-64.

143 The Bogas of the Dagua River to State President, Cali, 15 May 1878, ACC, AM, pq. 144-64.

144 Camilo Salamendro and Manuel María Rivera to Governor, Cali, 5 April 1852, AHMC, t. 120, p. 419.

145 *Observaciones para servir a la historia*, 1. See also Gutiérrez Sanín, *Curso y discurso*, 49–56.

146 The Masked Ones to Sergio Arboleda, n.p., n.d., ACC, FA, #866. See also Taussig, *The Devil and Commodity Fetishism*, 54–55.

147 Residents of Tumaco to President, Tumaco, 30 Aug. 1878, INCORA, t. 14, p. 947.

148 The Bogas of the Dagua River to State President, Cali, 15 May 1878, ACC, AM, pq. 144-64.

149 See, e.g., Rafael Reyes to Sergio Arboleda, Bogotá, 16 Oct. 1885, ACC, FA, #1,525; and Manuel María [Mosquera] to Tomás [Cipriano Mosquera], Popayán, 15 May 1877, ACC, SM, #57,555. The latter reports such shouting by "negros and mulattos" in Popayán.

150 Colombian Citizens to Secretary of the Treasury, Villa de Bao, 20 Aug. 1883, AGN, SR, FB, t. 4, p. 274.

151 Citizens of Colombia to the Municipality, Cali, 29 May 1863, AHMC, t. 150, p. 556.

152 In 1866, a partial census of the Cali ejido listed 166 plots of land. Of these, women controlled 74 (45 percent), and most of these women had children. Two-parent households controlled only 26 plots (16 percent). Single men or multiple owners controlled the remaining plots. See AHMC, t. 126, p. 293.

153 Testimony of M. Ruiz, La Cruz, 4 June 1868, ACC, AM, pq 99-14; Ramon Bermudes and 13 Others to Senators and Representatives, Cali, 15 April 1853, AC, S, 1853, vol. VI, p. 169; *El Estado de Guerra*, 9 Jan. 1877; *El Espectador: Dios, Relijion i Libertad*, 6 Feb. 1862; Cabal, *Contestacion al inmundo pasquín*, 15.

154 Chambers, *From Subjects to Citizens*; Hunefeldt, *Liberalism in the Bedroom*; Dore, "One Step Forward."

155 The Undersigned Members of the Democratic Society of Cali to State President, Cali, 1 June 1877, ACC, AM, pq. 137-7.

156 Ibid.

157 The weakness of the state and the importance of regionalism are two of the organizing themes of Safford and Palacios's *Colombia*. Other scholars go further. Cristina Rojas de Ferro ("Identity Formation," 220) asserts: "Nineteenth-century Colombians did not invent a nation."

158 Anderson, *Imagined Communities*. Partha Chatterjee (*The Nation and Its Fragments*, 3–13) critiques Anderson's assertion that Europeans and Americans produced the original versions of imagined communities that other areas would borrow. Chatterjee's concern is to uncover how Asian and African nationalism sought to create a modern national culture that was not Western. I examine how Colombian subalterns appropriated the tools of nationalism and republicanism and refashioned them to suit their own purposes.

3 Republican Bargaining

1 José Hilario López, Presidential Address, Bogotá, 1 April 1849, AC, S, 1849, vol. V, p. 181.

2 *Ariete*, 3 Aug. 1850.

3 Mercado, *Memorias*, xcv.

4 Matéus, *Informe*, 10; Alaix, *No sin desconfianza*, 23.

5 Hernández de Alba, *Libertad de los esclavos*.

6 AGN, SR, FM, t. 1, pp. 143, 171, 344, 434, 437, 603.

7 AGN, SR, FM, t. 1, p. 150.

8 AGN, SR, FM, t. 2, p. 331; J. N. Montero, Barbacoas, 15 Sep. 1850, ACC, AM, pq. 48-37.

9 J. N. Montero to Secretary of Foreign Relations, Barbacoas, 20 Dec. 1849, AGN, SR, FM, t. 1, p. 580.

10 José Esteban Raposeño to Governor, Quilichao, 1 Oct. 1849, ACC, AM, pq. 47-77.

11 Report of Jefe Político, Almaguer, 21 May 1849, AGN, SR, FM, t. 1, p. 227.

12 *Ariete*, 13 July 1850.

13 J. N. Montero to Secretary of Foreign Relations, Barbacoas, 28 Feb. 1851, AGN, SR, FM, t. 1, p. 587; Carlos Gómez to Secretary of Foreign Relations, Buga, 10 Feb. 1851, AGN, SR, FM, t. 1, p. 588.

14 Bosch, *Reseña histórica*, 30–31.

15 Reports of Manuel S. Muñoz, Caloto, 5, 10, 21 May, 15 July 1848, ACC, AM, pq. 45-67bis; Bautista Feijoo to Governor, Caloto, 15 June 1848, ACC, AM, pq. 45-67bis.

16 *El Sentimiento Democrático*, 12 July 1849; Residents of Cali to President, Cali, 19 March 1851, AGN, SR, FP, t. 7, p. 501.

17 *La Unión*, 8 June 1848; José Rafael Troyano to President, Cali, 2 Nov. 1849, AGN, SR, FP, t. 6, p. 99; Julio Arboleda to Intendente, Popayán, 19 Aug. 1849, ACC, AM, pq. 62-45.

18 Bautista Feijoo to Governor, Caloto, 6 May 1849, ACC, AM, pq. 47-84; José Rafael Troyano to Parish Judge, Cali, 3 April 1850, AGN, SR, FG, t. 12, p. 161; 500 Signatures to Provincial Legislature, Cali, 17 Sep. 1849, in *El Sentimiento Democrático*, 27 Sep. 1849.

19 Law of 3 June 1848, Barbacoas, ACC, AM, pq. 44-47; *Ordenanzas de la Cámara Provincial*, 7, 43–48.

20 Bautista Feijoo, Caloto, 15 Jan. 1849, ACC, AM, pq. 47-84bis.

21 *Ordenanzas de la Provincia del Chocó*, 4.

22 Mercado, *Memorias*, xi–xii.

23 Ibid., xiv–xv; Bosch, *Reseña histórica*, 28; *El Republicano*, 8 Dec. 1851.

24 Comisión Corográfica, [early 1850s], BN, libro 397, pp. 11, 16.

25 Mercado, *Memorias*, lvii.

26 Bosch, *Reseña histórica*, 9–12; Vicente Borrero to Jefe Político, Cali, 22 May 1848, AHMC, t. 104, p. 458.

27 Bushnell, *The Making of Modern Colombia*, 92–104.

28 Vicente Borrero to Tomás Cipriano de Mosquera, Cali, 22 Dec. 1849, ACC, SM, #26,426; Mercado, *Memorias*, xxxi; Safford, "Social Aspects of Politics," 360–61.

29 J. N. Nuñez Conto to José H. López, Cali, 26 Jan. 1850, AGN, SA, FJHL, caja 2-1, p. 70.

30 Escorcia, *Sociedad y economía*, 59–61, 110–22. Escorcia ("La formación de las clases sociales," 93) also notes that, even though many prominent Conservative politicians came from this same middling strata, they enjoyed the patronage and power of the region's prominent families. See also Uribe-Uran, *Honorable Lives*, 4–5, 82–86, 122–26.

31 González Toledo, *El General Eliseo Payán*, 9; Mercado, *Memorias*; Zamorano, *Bosquejo biográfico*, 2; Arboleda, *Diccionario*; Jaramillo Uribe, *El pensamiento colombiano*, 173–80.

32 Molina, *Las ideas liberales*, 1–127; Jaramillo Uribe, *El pensamiento colombiano*, 103–349.

33 At times, Cali's club counted over a thousand members; Cali had nowhere near so many artisans. In the early 1850s, Cali Cantón counted only 19,277 people, of which only 1,160 were "suitable to bear arms." Comisión Corográfica, [early 1850s], BN, libro 397, p. 16; *El Sentimiento Democrático*, 29 Nov., 6 Dec. 1849. Much work remains to be done on the Democratic Societies outside Bogotá, but some authors suggest that they had limited appeal beyond artisans along the coast and in Santander. Fals Borda, *Historia doble*, vol. 2; and Stoller, " 'Democracy in SanJil.' "

34 Mercado, *Memorias*, xxxi. Conservatives described the Democratic Society's members as from the "most abject, ignorant, and miserable class." *Ariete*, 23 March 1850.

35 Arboleda, "El Misóforo," 347–48; *Ariete*, 3 Aug. 1850.

36 *El Sentimiento Democrático*, 3, 31 May, 14, 21 June 1849.

37 Ramón Martínez L. to José H. López, Buga, 24 Feb. 1850, AGN, SA, FJHL, caja 2-3, p. 189.

38 AGN, SR, FGV, t. 216, p. 481; AGN, SA, FJHL, caja 5-6, p. 419; AGN, SR, FGV, t. 216, p. 489; AGN, SR, FGV, t. 216, p. 491; AC, C, 1852, vol. I, p. 47; AC, C, 1854, vol. V, p. 68.

39 ACC, AM, pq. 49-76; ACC, AM, pq. 51-67; ACC, FA, #1,505; ACC, AM, pq. 53-77.

40 Mercado, *Memorias*, xliii; *El Hombre*, 10 July 1852.

41 Ramón M. Orejuela to Tomás C. de Mosquera, Hacienda Rosalía, 3 Feb. 1853, ACC, SM, #28,960.

42 José Joaquín Carvajal to José Hilario López, Buga, 17 March 1850, AGN, SA, FJHL, caja 2-3, p. 212; Pacheco, *La fiesta liberal*, 106–11; Hunt, *Politics, Culture, and Class*, 52–86.

43 Fals Borda, *Historia doble*, 2:97a–98a.

44 J. N. Montero to Secretary of Foreign Relations, Barbacoas, 12 Feb. 1851, AGN, SR, FM, t. 1, p. 603.

45 Ramón Mercado, Narciso Riascos, Manuel Antonio Vernaza, et al., AHMC, t. 114, p. 478.

46 Manuel José Castrillón to José Hilario López, Popayán, 22 Oct. 1850, AGN, SA, FJHL, caja 4-16, p. 1391.

47 *El Cernícalo*, 22 Sep. 1850.

48 Bosch, *Reseña histórica*, 13–14.

49 *El Ciudadano*, 3 June 1848.

50   El Ciudadano, 17 June 1848.

51   Julio Arboleda to T. C. de Mosquera, Popayán, 7 Jan. 1849, ACC, SM, #26,383.

52   Vicente Borrero to Tomás Cipriano de Mosquera, Cali, 22 Dec. 1849, ACC, SM, #26,426.

53   Ibid. Conservatives had founded elite-oriented clubs before. See Lobato Paz, "Caudillos y nación," 194.

54   Jorge J. Hoyos to Tomás C. Mosquera, Palmira, 4 Jan. 1850, ACC, SM, #27,558. Conservatives also started societies in Pasto and Popayán. ACC, FA, #1,505; El Patriota, 15 March 1848.

55   Eusebio Borrero to T. C. de Mosquera, Hacienda Limones, 21 Dec. 1849, ACC, SM, #26,427.

56   M. M. Alaix to José Hilario López, Popayán, 13 Nov. 1850, AGN, SA, FJHL, caja 4-18, p. 1575.

57   El Sentimiento Democrático, 26 July 1849; El Pueblo, 15 Sep. 1850.

58   Guillermo Molina to President of the Cabildo, Cali, 10 Jan. 1853, AHMC, t. 124, p. 520.

59   Ariete, 10 Aug. 1850.

60   Ramón Mercado to José Hilario López, Cali, 25 Jan. 1851, AGN, SA, FJHL, caja 5-2, p. 142.

61   El Sentimiento Democrático, 12 July 1849.

62   Residents of Cali to Provincial Legislature, Cali, 17 Sep. 1849, in El Sentimiento Democrático, 27 Sep. 1849.

63   La Unión, 8 June 1848.

64   Melo, "Las vicisitudes del modelo liberal," 148; ACC, AM, pq. 50-15.

65   El Sentimiento Democrático, 13 Sep. 1849.

66   The Undersigned Residents of Buenosaires Parish to Jefe Político, Buenosaires, 29 [sic] Oct. 1852, ACC, AM, pq. 53-77.

67   Bautista González, 5 Oct. 1852, ACC, AM, pq. 53-77.

68   Narciso Tello, Santander, 9 Oct. 1852, ACC, AM, pq. 53-77.

69   El Sentimiento Democrático, 21 June 1849.

70   AGN, SR, FG (Buenaventura), t. 13, p. 255.

71   El Clamor, 7 Oct. 1850.

72   Ordenanzas espedidas por la Cámara Provincial, 12.

73   Ariete, 2 March 1850.

74   El Sentimiento Democrático, 6 Dec. 1849; El Hombre, 26 June, 10 July 1852.

75   El Pensamiento Popular, 22 July 1852.

76   El Pueblo, 24 Oct. 1850.

77   AHMC, t. 119, p. 348; Díaz Aparicio, Los ejidos, 58; Espinosa Jaramillo, La saga de los ejidos, 232–36.

78   Fermín Pretel to Cabildo, Cali, 19 April 1853, AHMC, t. 124, p. 512.

79   José Joaquín Reies to President of the Cabildo, Cali, 20 June 1853, AHMC, t. 124, p. 517.

80   Juan A. García to the Cabildo, Cali, 4 Jan. 1852, AHMC, t. 56, p. 278.

81   López Garavito, Historia de la hacienda, 98.

82   Vicente [Arboleda] to Tomás C. de Mosquera, Popayán, 9 Jan. 1850, ACC, SM, #27,357.

83   El Pensamiento Popular, 22 July 1852.

84   González, "El proceso de manumisión," 334; Jaramillo Uribe, "La controversia jurídica."

85   Mercado, Memorias, xxxi.

86   El Clamor Nacional, 22 March 1851.

87   José Hilario López, Bogotá, 1 March 1851, AC, C, 1851, vol. IV, p. 97.

88   La Unión, 15, 22 May 1848.

89   M. M. Alaix to José H. López, Popayán, 26 Nov. 1850, AGN, SA, FJHL, caja 4-19, p. 1683.

90 Ibid.

91 José María Calero to Governor, Buenaventura, 17 Jan. 1852, AGN, SR, FGV, t. 178, p. 732.

92 Juan Antonio Delgado to José Hilario López, Cali, 14 Feb. 1852, AGN, SA, FJHL, caja 7-2, p. 69.

93 Ramón Mercado to José María Calero, Cali, 21 Feb. 1852, AGN, SR, FGV, t. 178, p. 732.

94 J. N. Montero to Secretary of Foreign Relations, Barbacoas, 7 Jan. 1852, AGN, SR, FGV, t. 179, p. 169.

95 Carlos Gómez to Secretary of Foreign Relations, Buga, 10 Feb. 1851, AGN, SR, FM, t. 1, p. 588.

96 José Velasco to Secretary of Foreign Relations, Barbacoas, 14 Oct. 1852, AGN, SR, FGV, t. 179, p. 146; The Landowners of Barbacoas Cantón to Secretary of Foreign Relations, Barbacoas, 16 Aug. 1852, AGN, SR, FGV, t. 179, p. 147.

97 Ramón M. Orejuela to Tomás C. de Mosquera, Hacienda Rosalía, 28 Jan. 1852, ACC, SM, #28,529.

98 Vicente Camilo Fontal to Governor, Almaguer, 1 Aug. 1852, ACC, AM, pq. 53-77.

99 Vicente Camilo Fontal to Cocitizens, Almaguer, 1 Jan. 1852, ACC, AM, pq. 53-77.

100 J. N. Montero to Secretary of Foreign Relations, Barbacoas, 7 Jan. 1852, AGN, SR, FGV, t. 179, p. 171.

101 Ramón M. Orejuela to Tomás C. de Mosquera, Hacienda Rosalía, 3 Feb. 1853, ACC, SM, #28,960.

102 Vicente Cárdenas to T. C. de Mosquera, Popayán, 10 Jan. 1849, ACC, SM, #26,470.

103 Arboleda, "El Misóforo," 347–48, 358.

104 Alaix, No sin desconfianza, 54.

105 El Pensamiento Popular, 1 July 1852.

106 El Clamor Nacional, 19 April 1851.

107 Ariete, 10 Aug. 1850.

108 J. A. Mallarino to Tomás C. de Mosquera, Cali, 7 Dec. 1850, ACC, SM, #27,613.

109 Ariete, 27 April 1850.

110 Ibid.; R. Mercado to José Hilario López, Cali, 18 Jan. 1851, AGN, SA, FJHL, caja 5-2, p. 90.

111 El Clamor Nacional, 19 April 1851.

112 Ramón Caldas to President of the Cabildo, Cali, 15 May 1851, AHMC, t. 113, p. 473; Saffray, Viaje a Nueva Granada, 216.

113 Members of the Democratic Society to Municipal Deputies, Cali, 26 June 1868, AHMC, t. 154, p. 67. This reference is, obviously, from a later date, but circumstantial evidence suggests that meetings had long taken place in the gallera.

114 El Hombre, 10 July 1852.

115 Ramón Mercado to José Hilario López, Cali, 18 Jan. 1851, AGN, SA, FJHL, caja 5-2, p. 90.

116 Jefe Político to Alcalde, Cali, 17 Dec. 1850, AHMC, t. 138, p. 185; Bosch, Reseña histórica, 36–37; Pacheco, La fiesta liberal, 141–61.

117 Mercado, Memorias, lviii.

118 El Clamor Nacional, 8 Feb. 1851.

119 José Joaquín Carvajal to José Hilario López, Buga, 8 Nov. 1849, AGN, SA, FJHL, caja 1bis-11, p. 551.

120 Bosch, Reseña histórica, 35.

121 Unknown to José Hilario López, Cali, 15 Feb. 1851, AGN, SA, FJHL, caja 5-3, p. 234.

122 Ibid.; El Clamor Nacional, 8 Feb., 22 March 1851; Miguel Saa to Governor, Cali, 5 May 1851, AHMC, t. 120, p. 611.

123 Some Miserable People to Tomás C. de Mosquera, Cali, 9 Aug. 1851, ACC, SM, #28,252.

124 Bernandino Torres Z. to José Hilario López, Cali, 11 Feb. 1851, AGN, SA, FJHL, caja 5-3, p. 217.

125 Antonio Matéus, Palmira, 30 March 1851, AGN, SR, FGV, t. 216, p. 484; Mercado, *Memorias*, lv–lvii, lxvii.

126 La Sociedad Democrática de Cali, *Mentir con descaro*, 1.

127 *Observaciones para servir a la historia*, 1.

128 Antonio Matéus, Palmira, 30 March 1851, AGN, SR, FGV, t. 216, p. 484.

129 Carlos Gómez, Palmira, 14 Feb. 1851, AGN, SR, FGV, t. 216, p. 475.

130 La Sociedad Democrática de Cali, *Mentir con descaro*, 1.

131 *Observaciones para servir a la historia*, 1.

132 R. Mercado to Secretary of Government, Cali, 24 Jan. 1851, AGN, SR, FGV, t. 165, p. 799; La Sociedad Democrática de Cali, *Mentir con descaro*, 1.

133 Mercado, *Memorias*, li–liii.

134 El *Hombre*, 10 July 1852; Guha, "The Prose of Counter-Insurgency."

135 Ramón M. Orejuela to Tomás C. de Mosquera, Hacienda Rosalía, 1 Aug. 1851, ACC, SM, #28,148.

136 El *Clamor Nacional*, 19 April 1851.

137 Unsigned draft, New York, 26 Sep. 1852, ACC, SM, #28,521.

138 Vicente Javier Arboleda to Tomás [Mosquera], Popayán, 18 Feb. 1853, ACC, SM, #28,651.

139 José Joaquín Carvajal to José Hilario López, Buga, 8 Nov. 1849, AGN, SA, FJHL, caja 1bis-11, p. 551.

140 Los Verdaderos Constitucionalistas, *A los liberales de la provincia*, 1.

141 Vicente [Arboleda] to Tomás C. de Mosquera, Popayán, 9 Jan. 1850, ACC, SM, #27,357.

142 Testimony of Fernando Pontón, Caloto, 22 Oct. 1852, AGN, SR, FGV, t. 182, p. 45.

143 *Ariete*, 19 Jan. 1850.

144 Alcalde Mayor de Indígenas of Túquerres Cantón to President of the House of Representatives, Túquerres, 30 Dec. 1848, AC, C, 1849, vol. IX, p. 184.

145 Alcaldes Mayores of Túqerres and Ipiales Cantones to President of the Provincial Legislature, Túquerres, 17 Sep. 1848, ACC, AM, pq. 44-39.

146 Joaquín Garcés, Túquerres, 15 Sep. 1850, ACC, AM, pq. 48-25; Joaquín Garcés, Túquerres, 15 Sep. 1849, ACC, AM, pq. 46-6.

147 Ramón M. Aroila, Pasto, 13 Oct. 1852, ACC, AM, pq. 53-66.

148 Rafael Diago, Popayán, 20 Oct. 1853, ACC, AM, pq. 54-1.

149 Ibid.

150 Governor Vicente Cárdenas to Jefe Político, [Popayán], June 1848, ACC, AM, pq. 44-16.

151 The Landowners of Barbacoas Cantón to Secretary of Foreign Relations, Barbacoas, 16 Aug. 1852, AGN, SR, FGV, t. 179, p. 147.

152 El *Hurón*, 1 May 1851.

153 R. Diago to José Hilario López, Popayán, 28 Dec. 1853, AGN, SA, FJHL, caja 9-1, p. 64. Local political control was another national factor. Safford and Palacios, *Colombia*, 205–6.

154 Arboleda, "El Misóforo," 336; *Las Máscaras*, 21 Nov. 1850.

155 Burbano, Astorquiza, et al., *Ciudadano Presidente de la República*; The Residents of Popayán to Senators and Representatives, Popayán, 7 March 1848, AC, C, 1850, vol. XI, p. 259.

156 Vicente Cárdenas to Sergio Arboleda, Pasto, 7 Nov. 1850, ACC, FA, #1,505.

157 El Clamor Nacional, 8 Feb. 1851.

158 El Cernícalo, 22 Sep. 1850.

159 J. N. Montero to Secretary of Government, Barbacoas, 26 June 1851, AGN, SR, FGV, t. 165, p. 706.

160 Boletín Democrático, 12 July 1851.

161 J. N. Montero to Secretary of Government, Barbacoas, 10 May 1852, AGN, SR, FGV, t. 179, p. 243.

162 El Pueblo, 1 Sep. 1850.

163 El Hurón, 1 May 1851.

164 Mercado, Memorias, lxxiii.

165 Manuel A. Tello to Governor, Quilichao, 27 April 1851, ACC, AM, pq. 50-50.

166 Mercado, Memorias, lxxvi.

167 Carlos Gómez to Governor of Popayán Province, Buga, 13 July 1851, ACC, AM, pq. 51-67; Bosch, Reseña histórica, 43–44.

168 Luis Espinosa, Jan. 1851, ACC, FA, #846, p. 2.

169 Taussig, The Devil and Commodity Fetishism, 48.

170 Laureano López to Governor, Popayán, 3 Nov. 1851, ACC, AM, pq. 51-67.

171 The Undersigned Landowners to the Provincial Legislature, Pasto, 20 Sep. 1852, ACC, AM, pq. 53-70; Boletín Político i Militar, 20 July 1851.

172 Escorcia, Sociedad y economía, 134.

173 Boletín Democrático, 12 July 1851.

174 ACC, FA, #988.

175 Contestacion al folleto del Jeneral Franco.

176 ACC, FA, #988.

177 The Undersigned, in the Majority Ex-Slaves to President, Barbacoas, 6 Nov. 1852, AGN, SR, FGV, t. 179, p. 341.

178 Residents of San Juan to Senators and Representatives, n.p., n.d., AC, S, 1852, vol. II, p. 19.

179 El Cauca (Cali), 19 Nov. 1857.

180 Boletín Democrático, 18 July 1851.

181 Palacios, El café en Colombia, 29.

182 Mehta, Liberalism and Empire, 51–64, 115–23, 159–66.

183 Members of the Democratic Society to Deputies of the Provincial Legislature, Cali, 1 Sep. 1850, AHMC, t. 109, p. 303.

184 Las Máscaras, 26 Sep. 1850.

185 The Undersigned, Citizens and Residents of Silvia Parish, to Senators and Representatives, Silvia, 19 March 1852, AC, S, 1852, vol. IV, p. 155.

186 Gibson, The Constitutions of Colombia, 162.

187 Arboleda, "El Misóforo," 318–24, 342–44.

188 El Clamor Nacional, 19 April 1851.

189 Bosch, Reseña histórica, 7.

190 Juan Antonio Arturo, Pasto, 20 Oct. 1853, ACC, AM, pq. 54-26.

191 Vicente Cárdenas to Sergio Arboleda, Pasto, 3 Aug. 1850, 23 Jan., 7 Feb., 12 Dec. 1851, ACC, FA, #1,505; Olano, Opúsculo, 1.

192 El Cernícalo, 22 Aug. 1850.

193 Las Máscaras, 7 Nov. 1850.

194 We the Undersigned to the Examining Committee, Cali, 14 May 1848, AHMC, t. 101, p. 681; Response of Examining Committee, 18 May 1848, AHMC, t. 101, p. 684.

195 Camilo Salamendro and Manuel María Rivera to Governor, Cali, 5 April 1852, AHMC, t. 120, p. 419.

196 Gutiérrez Sanín makes a similar point about the pueblo acting as arbiter of who was a citizen, thereby ensuring the integrity of politics, although we differ on exactly how the pueblo imagined itself and its relation to its upper-class allies. See Gutiérrez Sanín, Curso y discurso. See also Tarrow, Power in Movement, 75–78.

197 José Hilario López, Bogotá, 1 March 1851, AC, C, 1851, vol. IV, p. 97.

198 Miguel María Borrero Durán to Tomás C. Mosquera, Cali, 20 Oct. 1850, ACC, SM, #27,399.

199 Eusebio Borrero to T. C. de Mosquera, Hacienda Limones, 21 Dec. 1849, ACC, SM, #26,427.

200 Pombo and Guerra, Constituciones de Colombia, 8, 10.

201 Matéus, Informe, 4.

202 R. Mercado to President, Cali, 7 Oct. 1852, AGN, SR, FGV, t. 179, p. 10.

203 Safford and Palacios (Colombia, 135) argue that, in the first half of the nineteenth century, "gentlemen" dominated politics.

4 The Limits of Elite Power

1 Rainborough quoted in Thompson, The Making of the English Working Class, 23.

2 Rafael Diago, Popayán, 20 Oct. 1853, ACC, AM, pq. 54-1.

3 Cabildo de Indígenas of Caldono to Governor, Caldono, 19 Nov. 1853, and Governor and Alcalde of Quichaya to Governor, Popayán, 1 April 1853, ACC, AM, pq. 55-85.

4 Villegas and Restrepo, Resguardos, 36–44; Curry, "The Disappearance of the Resguardos Indígenas."

5 ACC, AM, pq. 53-56.

6 The Members of the Cabildo Pequeño de Indígenas of Guachucal Parish and the Vice-Parish of Muellamuez to Governor, Guachucal, 4 Oct. 1852, ACC, AM, pq. 53-56.

7 Pequeño Cabildo of Indians of Túquerres to Parish Alcalde, Túquerres, 5 Oct. 1852, and Cabildo Pequeño of Indians to Parish Alcalde, Cumbal, 2 Oct. 1852, ACC, AM, pq. 53-56.

8 AHMC, t. 125, pp. 358–73; Escorcia, Sociedad y economía, 140–41.

9 Arboleda, Historia contemporánea, 6:269–70.

10 ACC, AM, pq. 54-36.

11 Antonio J. Chaves to the Legislature, Túquerres, 7 Oct. 1854, ACC, AM, pq. 57-45.

12 Bushnell, The Making of Modern Colombia, 111–14; Colmenares, Partidos políticos, 155–88.

13 Testimony of Eustaquio Urrutia and Captain Miguel Astudillo, Popayán, 18 April 1854, AGN, SR, FGV, t. 201, pp. 64, 65. For the Caribbean Coast, see Fals Borda, Historia doble, 2:121a–122a.

14 El Sur, 20 Aug. 1854.

15 Scarpetta, El grito de un republicano, 1.

16 Manuel de J. Quijano to Secretary of Government, Popayán, 12 April 1854, AGN, SR, FGV, t. 201, p. 26.

17 José Hilario López, Popayán, 18 June 1854, AGN, SA, FJHL, caja 9-5, p. 85.

18 I would suggest that the Draconiano/Gólgota divide is not very useful in explaining Liberals' actions outside Bogotá. Better results can be obtained by examining which Liberals had

stronger ties to the popular classes over time, which in the Cauca was not always the Draconianos, many of whom would join the Conservative reaction against the Radicals (supposedly former Gólgotas) in the 1870s (see chapter 5).

19 Testimony of Miguel Dueñas, Popayán, 11 April 1854, AGN, SR, FGV, t. 201, p. 27.

20 Ramón M. Orejuela to Tomás C. de Mosquera, Barbacoas, 30 May 1854, ACC, SM, #31,796; Toribio María Malo to Governor, Silvia, 12 May 1854, ACC, AM, pq. 58-85; J. M. Mosquera to Secretary of Government, Popayán, 28 Oct. 1854, AGN, SR, FGV, t. 201, p. 116; José de Obaldía to Miguel Saturino Uribe, Ibagué, 30 Aug. 1854, ACC, SM, #31,761; La Paz: Periódico Oficial, 24 March 1855.

21 Antonio Matéus to Commander of Torres Column, Palmira, 25 June 1854, AGN, SR, FGV, t. 201, p. 100; Holguín, Noticia histórica; Safford and Palacios, Colombia, 213–14.

22 José M. Cañadas to José Hilario López, Cali, 25 Sep. 1854, AGN, SA, FJHL, caja 9-7, p. 172.

23 Cabal, Contestacion al inmundo pasquín, 12–13.

24 José de Obaldía to José Hilario López, Ibagué, 18 Oct. 1854, AGN, SA, FJHL, caja 9-8, p. 249.

25 Ibid.

26 Zamorano, Bosquejo biográfico, 6–7.

27 Uribe-Uran, Honorable Lives, 149–54.

28 Some scholars at least imply that, like Liberals in Bogotá, many of the Cauca's Liberals used the alliance with Conservatives to crush dangerous populist movements, thus ending popular political mobilization in Colombia for decades. See Pacheco, La fiesta liberal, 170–91; Zambrano, "Algunas formas de sociabilidad," 164–74; Gutiérrez Sanín, Curso y discurso, 15–16; König, En el camino, 493–502; Fals Borda, Historia doble, 2:116a; and Stoller, " 'Democracy in SanJil.' "

29 M. M. Mallarino to Secretary of the Treasury, Cali, 6 Oct. 1854, AGN, SR, FG, t. 14, p. 713; M. M. Mallarino to Secretary of the Treasury, Cali, 23 Nov. 1854, AGN, SR, FG, t. 15, p. 135.

30 M. Quijano to Governors of Pasto and Neiva Provinces, n.p., 17 Sep. 1854, ACC, AM, pq. 56-1, p. 207. For banditry, see Guha, Elementary Aspects, 77–108.

31 Judicial Report, Popayán, 21 May 1855, ACC, AM, pq. 60-62.

32 Juan Antonio Delgado to José Hilario López, Cali, 25 Sep. 1854, AGN, SA, FJHL, caja 9-7, p. 173.

33 Vicente Cárdenas to Sergio Arboleda, Pasto, 31 Aug. 1854, ACC, FA, #1,505.

34 Ordenanzas espedidas por la Lejislatura Provincial . . . 1854, 24–27; Gaceta del Cauca, 29 Aug. 1858; ACC, AM, pq. 59-32; Tomás Velasco to Secretary of Government, Santander, 30 Oct. 1858, ACC, AM, pq. 67-19.

35 ACC, AM, pq. 58-82.

36 M. M. Mallarino to Jefe Político, Cali, 4 Jan. 1854, AHMC, t. 128, p. 269.

37 Jefe Político to Governor, Popayán, 28 June 1854, ACC, AM, pq. 58-84; El Cauca (Cali), 20 Aug. 1857.

38 José de Obaldía [citing Sergeant Major Valdez] to Miguel S. Uribe, Ibagué, 30 Aug. 1854, ACC, SM, #31,761.

39 ACC, AM, pq. 59-40.

40 El Republicano, 17 Sep. 1858.

41 Arboleda, El clero, 22–23; Castro C., "Caridad."

42 El Cauca (Cali), 24 Sep. 1857.

43 Manuel Antonio Arboleda to Constitutional Assembly, Popayán, 23 Oct. 1857, ACC, AM, pq. 64-41.

44 El Republicano, 17 Sep. 1858; El Cauca (Cali), 13 Aug. 1857–21 Jan. 1858.

45 *Constitucion i leyes*, 20–22.

46 *Gaceta Oficial del Cauca*, 4 Oct. 1857.

47 *Gaceta Oficial del Cauca*, 17 Oct. 1857.

48 M. M. Buenaventura to Governor, Cali, 21 March 1857, ACC, AM, pq. 65-69.

49 Jorge J. Hoyos to Mariano Ospina, Popayán, 15 Dec. 1857, BN, libro 189, p. 359; Miguel Mazorra to Governor, Bolívar, 20 June 1855, ACC, AM, pq. 60-61.

50 Urrutia, Ospina, Monzón, et al., *Defensa del "Luto nacional,"* 1.

51 Testimony of Serafín Quijano and Pablo Jaramillo, Caloto, 4 Feb. 1857, ACC, EC, #337.

52 Members of the Cabildo to Senators and Representatives, [place illegible but near Supía], 6 Feb. 1855, AC, S, 1855, vol. VI, p. 615.

53 V. M. [Vicente Mosquera] to Tomás [Mosquera], Popayán, 21 Sep. 1853, ACC, SM, #28,880.

54 Vicente Javier Arboleda to Tomás Cipriano de Mosquera, Popayán, 11 April 1855, BLAA, #558.

55 Unsigned to Joaquín García, Japio, 24 April 1857, ACC, FA, #24, p. 1.

56 Sergio Arboleda, Japio, 4 Sep. 1857, ACC, FA, #140, p. 7; Correa González, "Integración socio-económica," 340–416.

57 Tomás M. Mosquera to Tomás C. de Mosquera, Buenosaires, 15 March 1859, ACC, SM, #36,668.

58 Unsigned to Joaquín García, Japio, 24 April 1857, ACC, FA, #24, p. 1.

59 Joaquín García to Sergio Arboleda, Santander, 19 July 1857, ACC, FA, #1,514.

60 T. C. de Mosquera to President of the Senate, Popayán, 17 Jan. 1859, ACC, SM, #36,672; Jorge J. Hoyos to Mariano Ospina, Buenaventura, 25 March 1859, BN, libro 189, p. 363.

61 Jorge J. Hoyos to Mariano Ospina, Popayán, 15 Dec. 1857, BN, libro 189, p. 359.

62 *El Cauca* (Cali), 14 Jan. 1858.

63 Helguera, "The First Mosquera Administration," 39.

64 Ibid., 40–48.

65 Fidel Calero to Tomás C. de Mosquera, Palmira, 4 Sep. 1859, ACC, SM, #36,188; Jorge H. Isaacs to Tomás C. de Mosquera, Cali, 2 April 1859, ACC, SM, #36,584.

66 Juan N. Aparicio to Tomás C. de Mosquera, Buga, 3 April 1859, ACC, SM, #36,015.

67 Pablo Meza to Parish Cabildo, Cali, 2 April 1857, AHMC, t. 139, p. 267.

68 José M. Chicaíza to Mariano Ospina, Pasto, 7 June 1859, BN, libro 322, p. 374.

69 J. M. Bustamente to Mariano Ospina, Cartago, 15 Sep. 1859, BN, libro 210, p. 97.

70 Jorge J. Hoyos to Mariano Ospina, Buenaventura, 25 March 1859, BN, libro 189, p. 363.

71 David Peña to Governor, Cali, 19 July 1859, ACC, SM, #36,899.

72 Tomás M. Mosquera to Tomás C. de Mosquera, Buenosaires, 15 March 1859, ACC, SM, #36,668.

73 Residents of Cali Province to Governor, Cali, 30 July 1859, ACC, AM, pq. 71-15.

74 David Peña to Governor, Cali, 19 July 1859, ACC, SM, #36,899.

75 Manuel Joaquín Otero to T. C. de Mosquera, Cali, 19 Aug. 1859, ACC, SM, #36,809.

76 Manuel José González to Mariano Ospina, Cali, 10 June 1859, BN, libro 210, p. 114.

77 Residents of Cali Province to Governor, Cali, 30 July 1859, ACC, AM, pq. 71-15.

78 T. C. de Mosquera, Popayán, 11 Aug. 1859, ACC, AM, pq. 74-48.

79 T. C. de Mosquera to President of the Senate, Popayán, 2 Sep. 1859, ACC, AM, pq. 74-56.

80 *Gaceta del Cauca*, 23 Aug., 29 Oct. 1859.

81 Mercado, *Memorias*, xxv, xxvi.

82 P. A. Herrán to Mariano Ospina, New York, 18 July 1859, BN, libro 189, p. 142.

83 Pedro Prías to Tomás Cipriano de Mosquera, Buga, 14 April 1859, ACC, SM, #36,868; M. M. Buenaventura to Tomás C. de Mosquera, Cali, 7 May 1859, ACC, SM, #36,160.

84 *Gaceta del Cauca*, 29 Oct. 1859. For a different interpretation, see Findji and Rojas, *Territorio*, 68–69.

85 Governor of Atrato Province to Secretary of the Treasury, Quibdó, 1 March 1859, ACC, AM, pq. 73-39; Appelbaum, "Whitening the Region," 631–52.

86 Residents of Riosucio to Deputies of the Constitutional Assembly, Riosucio, 27 Aug. 1857, ACC, AM, pq. 64-41; Valencia Llano, *Colonización*; Appelbaum, *Muddied Waters*, 52–79.

87 Uribe de Hincapié and García, "La espada," 86–87.

88 LeGrand, *Frontier Expansion*, 33–90.

89 For example, Pedro J. Carrillo to Mariano Ospina Rodríguez, Cartago, 18 April 1859, BN, libro 194, p. 45.

90 Residents of the Aldea de María to Senators and Representatives, María, 30 Jan. 1855, AC, S, 1858, vol. XII, p. 188; Aldea de María, *Declaraciones*, 1.

91 Venancio Salazar to T. C. de Mosquera, María, 13 March 1863, ACC, SM, #45,036. Marco Palacios mentions the conflict (but not the bargaining [see below]) in *El café en Colombia*, 320–23. Similarly, see Valencia Llano, *Colonización*, 131–45.

92 Arana, *Aldea de María*; Escovar, *Alegato*.

93 The Undersigned Citizens to Legislators, María, 20 Feb. 1855, AC, C, 1855, vol. VI, p. 156; Residents of the Aldea de María to Representatives, María, 4 April 1853, AC, C, 1853, Peticiones, p. 369.

94 N. Perinal to Ramón M. Arana, Bogotá, 5 Sep. 1859, ACC, SM, #36,915.

95 Antonio Matéus to Secretary of Government, Buga, 27 Jan. 1854, AGN, SR, FGV, t. 197, p. 54; Escovar, *Alegato*, 19–20.

96 R. M. Arana to Tomás C. de Mosquera, María, 15 June 1859, ACC, SM, #36,025.

97 R. M. Arana to Tomás C. de Mosquera, María, 13 Sep. 1859, ACC, SM, #36,026.

98 T. C. de Mosquera to Miguel Quijano, Popayán, 25 Aug. 1859, ACC, FA, #344, p. 1.

99 *Gaceta del Cauca*, 12 Feb. 1859.

100 R. M. Arana to Tomás C. de Mosquera, María, 25 Oct. 1859, ACC, SM, #36,028.

101 R. M. Arana to Tomás C. de Mosquera, María, 22 Nov. 1859, ACC, SM, #36,029.

102 Ramón A. Palau to Tomás C. de Mosquera, Boquía, 23 Oct. 1859, ACC, SM, #36,828.

103 Pablo Marulanda to Senators and Deputies, Santander, 1 Aug. 1863, ACC, AM, pq. 85-79.

104 Rafael Torres, Bogotá, 15 Feb. 1860, AGN, SR, FB, t. 1, p. 57.

105 Pedro J. Carrillo to Mariano Ospina, Cartago, 11 Aug. 1859, 2 Dec. 1859, BN, libro 194, pp. 51, 58.

106 The Municipal Corporation of Chinchiná District to Governor, María, 15 July 1863, ACC, AM, pq. 85-79.

107 Vicente Bueno to Secretary of Government, Cartago, 16 Oct. 1862, ACC, AM, pq. 83-16; Palacios, *El café en Colombia*, 317–40.

108 Pedro Carrillo to President Mariano Ospina, Unión, 13 June 1859, BN, libro 194, p. 47; various petitions in BN, libro 210, pp. 86–92, and ACC, AM, pq. 74-51.

109 T. C. Mosquera to Deputies of the Convention, Rionegro, 16 Feb. 1863, AC, S, 1863, vol. IV, p. 146.

110 "Decreto," Rionegro, 29 April 1863, AC, S, 1863, vol. V, p. 112.

111 R. Rosales to Municipal Corporation of María, Popayán, 27 Sep. 1863, ACC, AM, pq. 85-79.

112 The Undersigned Residents of the Aldea de María to Senators and Representatives, María, 15 Feb. 1854, AC, C, 1854, vol. V, p. 267; Venancio Salazar to T. C. de Mosquera, María, 13 March 1863, ACC, SM, #45,036. While some of the settlers were originally from other parts of the Cauca, most came from Antioquia.

113 T. C. de Mosquera, Popayán, 1 July 1859, ACC, AM, pq. 74-48. For Mexico, Peter Guardino (*Peasants*, 96–100, 113–27, 178–210) has shown how federalism became a popular cause. However, in the Cauca, other subaltern concerns were paramount, and popular liberals probably saw federalism as a means to an end rather than as a goal in itself.

114 José Tomás del Carmen to Governor, Popayán, 16 March 1855, ACC, AM, pq. 60-60.

115 Francisco González to Governor, Santander, 20 March 1855, ACC, AM, pq. 60-60.

116 Jorge J. Hoyos to Mariano Ospina, Buenaventura, 25 March 1859, BN, libro 189, p. 363; José V. López to Mariano Ospina, Cali, 21 May 1859, BN, libro 210, p. 129.

117 José V. López to Mariano Ospina, Cali, 26 Oct. 1859, BN, libro 210, p. 134.

118 J. M. Bustamente to Mariano Ospina, Cartago, 15 Sep. 1859, BN, libro 210, p. 97.

119 Cayetano Delgado to Tomás C. de Mosquera, Buga, 14 Sep. 1859, ACC, SM, #36,349; Provincial Governor to Secretary of Government, Buga, 21 March 1859, ACC, AM, pq. 76-112.

120 Jorge J. Hoyos to Mariano Ospina, Buenaventura, 12 Sep. 1859, BN, libro 189, p. 383.

121 Manuel José González to Mariano Ospina, Cali, 21 Dec. 1859, BN, libro 210, p. 127.

122 "Diario Histórico del Ejército Unido de Antioquia y Cauca," n.d., ACC, FA, #63, p. 235. A *zambo* was a person of both African and Indian descent.

123 Johnson, *Santander*, 63, 101; Zamorano, *Bosquejo biográfico*, 8–12; Valencia Llano, *Estado Soberano del Cauca*, 13.

124 Eliseo Payán to Secretary of Government, Naranja, 17 Jan. 1861, ACC, AM, pq. 81-2; Juan N. Cobo to Secretary of Government, Popayán, 7 Feb. 1861, ACC, AM, pq. 82-38; El Espectador: Dios, Relijion i Libertad, 23, 30 Jan. 1862.

125 Ospina, *Informe*, 9.

126 Unsigned to Reto A. Martínez, Inzá, 31 Aug. 1860, ACC, FA, #65, p. 1; The Residents of Caldono to Deputies to the State Convention, n.p., n.d., ACC, AM, pq. 116-20.

127 Mosquera, *T. C. de Mosquera*, 1; *Boletín Oficial*, 20 Jan., 24 July 1862.

128 Findji and Rojas, *Territorio*, 73, 81–87.

129 Governor of the Indians of Quichaya to Commander in Chief of Militias, Popayán, 5 Oct. 1860, ACC, AM, pq. 78-44; Marcelino Rodríguez to Governor, Silvia, 15 Sep. 1861, ACC, AM, pq. 82-27.

130 Daniel Mosquera to Governor, Tambo, 18 Aug. 1861, ACC, AM, pq. 82-27.

131 José Rojas Garrido to Governor of Cauca, Medellín, 30 Dec. 1862, ACC, AM, pq. 84-44.

132 Cabal, *Contestacion al inmundo pasquín*, 15; El Espectador: Dios, Relijion i Libertad, 6 Feb. 1862.

133 "Diario Histórico del Ejército Unido de Antioquia y Cauca," n.d., ACC, FA, #63, p. 235.

134 *La Voz de la Juventud*, 12 Nov. 1861.

135 [Sergio Arboleda], n.p., n.d., ACC, FA, #180, p. 4.

136 José V. López to Mariano Ospina, Cali, 21 May 1859, BN, libro 210, p. 129.

137 See Tirado Mejía, *Aspectos sociales*, 37–38; Bushnell, *The Making of Modern Colombia*, 94; Jaramillo Castillo, "Guerras civiles"; and Fals Borda, *Historia doble*, 2:62b–76b, 191. For opinions closer to my own, see Deas, "Poverty, Civil War, and Politics"; and Earle, ed., *Rumours of Wars*.

138 *Los criminales, al presidio*, 1.

139 Luis Acero to Secretary of Government, Palmira, 28 April 1863, ACC, AM, pq. 98-22.

140 Tomás María Mosquera to Tomás C. de Mosquera, Santander, 28 May 1860, BLAA, #558.

141 Manuel José González to Sergio Arboleda, Cali, 11 March 1862, ACC, FA, #437, p. 1.

142 Bushnell, *The Making of Modern Colombia*, 118–20; Delpar, *Red against Blue*, 2–14; Pinzón, *Historia del conservatismo*, 213. James William Park (*Rafael Núñez*, 20–23, 37–46) stresses federalism and regionalism (among elites) in his analysis of the war.

143 Cristina Rojas (*Civilization and Violence*, 160) forwards an interpretation that rejects the importance of such bargaining. She argues that nineteenth-century economic and political systems in the Cauca were characterized by "a culture of terror."

5 The Triumph of Democracy

1 AC, C, 1857, vol. IV, p. 30.

2 Guy P. C. Thomson notes that only Colombia was as thorough as Mexico in breaking with the colonial era during their respective periods of Liberal reform. See Thomson with LaFrance, *Patriotism, Politics, and Popular Liberalism*, xiii.

3 For an excellent overview of this period's political history, see Valencia Llano, *Estado Soberano del Cauca*.

4 Eliseo Payán, Popayán, 15 July 1863, ACC, AM, pq. 85-81.

5 Restrepo Piedrahita, ed., *Constituciones de la primera República liberal*, 923–49.

6 Ibid.

7 AHMC, t. 153, p. 417.

8 Bushnell, "Voter Participation," 242–46, 248.

9 AGN, SR, FCP, t. IV, p. 634; ACC, AM, pq. 90-42.

10 See González González, *Para leer la política*, 1:97–99; Valencia Llano, *Estado Soberano del Cauca*, 190–99; and Graham, *Patronage and Politics*, 101–45. Bushnell (*Política y sociedad*, 29–35) has stressed that, in the 1850s, elections were important, although he sees the era of Liberal reform as vitiating this. For a new perspective, see Posada-Carbó, ed., *Elections before Democracy*; and Annino, ed., *Historia de las elecciones en Iberoamérica*.

11 For example, The Undersigned Residents of Silvia and Indians of Ambaló to Governor, Silvia, 8 Aug. 1856, ACC, AM, pq. 62-45; *El Cauca* (Cali), 20 Aug. 1857; *Gaceta Oficial*, 13 Nov. 1869.

12 AC, S, 1857, vol. V; Bushnell, "Voter Participation," 237–49.

13 Deas, "La política en la vida cotidiana," 282; Jiménez, "La vida rural cotidiana," 197–98; Markoff, "Really Existing Democracy."

14 *Gaceta Oficial del Cauca*, 13 July 1867.

15 *Los Principios*, 12, 26 Dec. 1873.

16 *Gaceta Oficial*, 17 July 1869.

17 T. C. de Mosquera to Miguel Quijano, Popayán, 25 Aug. 1859, ACC, FA, #344, p. 1.

18 The Municipal Corporation of Chinchiná to Governor, María, 15 July 1863, and response, Popayán, 27 Sep. 1863, ACC, AM, pq. 85-79.

19 Simón Arboleda to T. C. de Mosquera, Coconuco, 14 Feb. 1859, ACC, SM, #36,041.

20 Pedro José Piedrahíta to T. C. de Mosquera, Cali, 12 March 1859, ACC, SM, #36,922; *El Montañés*, 1 Feb. 1876.

21 For example, Vicente Cárdenas to Sergio Arboleda, Quito, 2 Nov. 1878, ACC, FA, #1,506; Tomás M. Mosquera to Tomás C. de Mosquera, Buenosaires, 17 Feb. 1859, ACC, SM, #36,666.

22 Rafael [Arboleda] to T. C. de Mosquera, Popayán, 19 April 1876, ACC, SM, #56,918.

23 For example, The Undersigned Voters to Governor, Popayán, 10 Dec. 1850, ACC, AM, pq. 48-57.

24 The Undersigned Residents of Silvia and Indians of Ambaló to Governor, Silvia, 8 Aug. 1856, ACC, AM, pq. 62-45.

25 José M. Correa to Tomás C. de Mosquera, Roldanillo, 9 April 1859, ACC, SM, #36,291; *El Demócrata: Organo del Partido Liberal Independiente*, 13 March 1879.

26 Vicente Cárdenas to Sergio Arboleda, Pasto, 17 April 1856, ACC, FA #1,506; *Gaceta Oficial del Cauca*, 22 Dec. 1866.

27 Andrés Cerón to Salvador Camacho Roldán, Popayán, 19 Oct. 1870, AGN, SA, FSCR, caja 6-59, p. 9.

28 See Tilly, "Contentious Repertoires," *The Contentious French*, 380–98, and *Popular Contention*, 1–105. See also Tarrow, *Power in Movement*, 39–47; Thompson, *Customs in Common*, 66–71; and Sabato, *La política en las calles*. David Sowell ("Repertoires of Contention") has also examined political repertoires in Colombia, but he focuses on one aspect of the repertoire (urban riots), sees more continuity between the nineteenth century and the colonial era, and emphasizes the liberalization of economic patterns as a driving force sparking unrest.

29 Bosch, *Reseña histórica*, 50. See also C. Conto to Aquileo Parra, Popayán, 7 Aug. 1877, BLAA, #295; and *El Guaitara*, 20 Sep. 1864.

30 See chapter 6. See also Bautista Feijoo to Provincial Governor, Caloto, 6 May 1849, ACC, AM, pq. 47-84.

31 James M. Eder to Secretary of State William Seward, Buenaventura, 24 Oct. 1868, in U.S. State Department, *Dispatches*. In Panama, confrontations between popular politics and imperial power were more common. See McGuinness, "In the Path of Empire."

32 The Undersigned Citizens of Caldas Municipality to State President, Bolívar, 5 July 1868, ACC, AM, pq. 99-14.

33 Fermín Pretel to Members of the Town Council, Cali, 19 April 1853, AHMC, t. 124, p. 512; LeGrand, *Frontier Expansion*, 63–68.

34 Unos de Yervarrucia, *Mentir con descaro*, 1.

35 Pedro José Piedrahíta to District Judge, Cali, 12 June 1858, AHMC, t. 143, p. 469.

36 M. A. Scarpetta to Secretary of Government, Palmira, 21 March 1867, ACC, AM, pq. 96-1.

37 Tilly, "Contentious Repertoires," 268–70.

38 Juan Antonio Arturo, Pasto, 20 Oct. 1853, ACC, AM, pq. 54-26.

39 For example, Jesus López to Secretary of Government, Cartago, 17 April 1863, ACC, AM, pq. 85-88; *La Voz del Pueblo: Organo de la Sociedad Democrática*, 21 Nov. 1878.

40 Sociedad Democrática de Palmira, *Estatuto*, 9, 12, 15, 16; *El Sentimiento Democrático*, 6 Dec. 1849.

41 Sociedad Democrática de Palmira, *Estatuto*, 9, 13, 15.

42 *Boletín de la Sociedad Democrática*, 5 June 1867; Rafael de la Pedroza to Secretary of Government, Cali, 28 Nov. 1878, ACC, AM, pq. 144-61.

43 *El Sentimiento Democrático*, 6 December 1849.

44 Carlos Gómez to Secretary of Government, Buga, 10 Dec. 1851, AGN, SR, FGV, t. 216, p. 549.

45 Gabriel Lalinde to State President, Popayán, 9 Oct. 1869, ACC, AM, pq. 105-74.

46 For example, Democratic Society of Cali to the Municipal Government, Cali, 3 Feb. 1867, AHMC, t. 153, p. 401; *El Estandarte Liberal*, 15 May 1878.

47 Sociedad Democrática de Palmira, *Estatuto*, 3, 4.

48 Tilly, "Contentious Repertoires," 270–76.

49 César Conto, Popayán, 1 July 1865, ACC, AM, pq. 90-48; *El Sufragio*, 10 Feb. 1873; José Hilario López, Bogotá, 1 March 1851, AC, C, 1851, vol. IV, p. 97.

50 *El Cauca* (Cali), 13 Aug. 1857; *Ariete*, 6 Oct. 1849.

51 Pedro José Piedrahíta to T. C. de Mosquera, Cali, 12 March 1859, ACC, SM, #36,922.

52 *El Montañes*, 1 Feb. 1876.

53 *Constitucion i leyes*, 56–58.

54 *El Cauca* (Cali), 14 Jan. 1858.

55 *El Sentimiento Democrático*, 26 July 1849; *El Pueblo*, 15 Sep. 1850.

56 *Ariete*, 10 Aug. 1850.

57 Peña was described as a "mulato claro" in a private letter, and, in his biography, allusions are made to Africa. See, respectively, Pedro José Piedrahíta to T. C. de Mosquera, ACC, SM, #36,933; and Zamorano, *Bosquejo biográfico*.

58 Democratic Society of Cali to State President, Cali, 19 July 1877, ACC, AM, pq. 137-7; Ramírez, *General David Peña*.

59 Jorge J. Hoyos to Mariano Ospina, Popayán, 15 June 1858, BN, libro 189, p. 369; Arboleda, *Diccionario*, 474–75; Valencia Llano, "Gamonales y bandidos."

60 The Undersigned Members of the Democratic Society to State President, Cali, 14 Oct. 1866, ACC, AM, pq. 65-67.

61 *El Caucano*, 21 May 1863.

62 The Undersigned Colombian Citizens, Members of the Democratic Society, to President, Palmira, 21 June 1868, INCORA, t. 7, p. 492.

63 *El Caucano*, 21 May 1863.

64 For example, José del Carmen Castillo, Juan de los Santos Cuabí, and Victoriano Rialpe to President, Tumaco, 12 Dec. 1875, INCORA, t. 10, p. 49.

65 For example, The Pequeño Cabildo of Indians of Mocondino to State President, Pasto, 18 Feb. 1866, ACC, AM, pq. 94-54.

66 *Ariete*, 26 Jan. 1850.

67 *Ariete*, 20 Oct. 1849; *Baluarte*, 1 March 1850; *El Pueblo*, 15 Aug. 1850; Alaix, *No sin desconfianza*, 23.

68 *El Republicano*, 15 March 1868.

69 *La Unión*, 26 March 1865.

70 Carlos Gómez to Secretary of Foreign Relations, Buga, 10 Feb. 1851, AGN, SR, FM, t. 1, p. 588.

71 Ramón Mercado to President, Cali, 7 Oct. 1852, AGN, SR, FGV, t. 179, p. 10.

72 José Felipe Caicedo to Jefe Municipal, Quilcacé, 13 March 1876, ACC, AM, pq. 133-80.

73 Jesus López to Secretary of Government, Cartago, 17 April 1863, ACC, AM, pq. 85-88; P. A. Herrán to Mariano Ospina, Washington, D.C., 2 July 1858, BN, libro 189, p. 77.

74 *El Clamor Nacional*, 19 April 1851.

75 José V. López to Mariano Ospina, Cali, 3 June 1859, BN, libro 210, p. 132.

76 Vicente Cárdenas to Sergio Arboleda, Quito, 19 Nov. 1878, ACC, FA, #1,506.

77 *El Caucano*, 6 Aug. 1863.

78 Bobbio, *Liberalism and Democracy*. See also Williams, *Keywords*, 93–98.

79 *El Republicano*, 23 Jan. 1869.

80 Samper, *Ensayo sobre las revoluciones políticas*, 266–67, 292–300; Appelbaum, *Muddied Waters*, 9–11; Safford, "Race, Integration, and Progress"; Graham, ed., *The Idea of Race*; Arocha, "Inclusion," 77.

81 Arboleda, *El clero*, 15, and *Rudimentos*, 18.

82 *Ariete*, 20 Oct. 1849; Special Commission to Consider Constitutional Reform, Cali, 26 Sep. 1855, AC, C, 1856, vol. II, p. 279.

83 Arboleda, *El clero*, 15.

84 *Ariete*, 2 March 1850.

85 *Ariete*, 27 July 1850.

86 José V. López to Mariano Ospina, Cali, 21 May 1859, BN, libro 210, p. 129.

87 For example, Manuel María Mosquera to Tomás [Mosquera], Popayán, 15 May 1877, ACC, SM, #57,555; J. N. Montero to Secretary of Foreign Relations, Barbacoas, 7 Jan. 1852, AGN, SR, FGV, t. 179, p. 171.

88 Jorge J. Hoyos to Mariano Ospina, Buenaventura, 25 March 1859, BN, libro 189, p. 363.

89 Pedro José Piedrahíta to T. C. de Mosquera, Cali, 12 March 1859, ACC, SM, #36,922.

90 *El Caucano*, 20 Aug. 1863. See also Ferrer, *Insurgent Cuba*, 10–12.

91 *Los Principios*, 5 May 1876.

92 *La Unión*, 23 Oct. 1864.

93 *El Montañes*, 15 Feb. 1876. See also McGuinness, "In the Path of Empire."

94 *El Pueblo*, 15 Aug. 1850.

95 Cabal, *Contestacion al inmundo pasquín*, 14–15.

96 Unknown to José Hilario López, Cali, 15 Feb. 1851, AGN, SA, FJHL, caja 5-3, p. 234; Arboleda, "El Misóforo," 347–51.

97 *El Espectador: Dios, Relijion i Libertad*, 2 Oct. [1862] (the date actually printed on the paper is 1852, but this is an error); "Diario Histórico del Ejército Unido de Antioquia y Cauca," n.d., ACC, FA, #63, p. 235.

98 For example, José J. Lemos to Governor, Silvia, 30 May 1854, ACC, AM, pq. 58-84; Carlos Holguín to Sergio Arboleda, Manizales, 30 Jan. 1877, ACC, FA, #1,515.

99 See Escorcia, *Sociedad y economía*, 89.

100 Pedro José Piedrahíta to T. C. de Mosquera, Cali, 14 May 1859, ACC, SM, #36,933.

101 Manuel González to Mariano Ospina, Cali, 21 Dec. 1859, BN, libro 210, p. 127.

102 See, more generally, Conrad, *Nostromo*, 59, 174. For Cartagena, see Long, "Popular Liberalism and Civil War."

103 For one exception, see *El Ferrocarril*, 8 March 1878.

104 For work on contemporary identity, see Friedemann and Arocha, *De sol a sol*; Arocha, "Inclusion"; Wade, *Blackness*; and Maya, "Los Afrocolombianos."

105 Anselmo Soto Arana and E. León to Deputies, Popayán, 9 Sep. 1871, ACC, AM, pq. 112-2.

106 Safford, "Race, Integration, and Progress."

107 Eliseo Payán, Popayán, 1 July 1865, ACC, AM, pq. 90-49.

108 See multiple petitions in ACC, AM, pq. 94-54.

109 Indian Alcalde Mayor of Obando Municipality (with Signers from the Parcialidades of Potosí, Mayasquer, Yaramal, Cumbal, Guachucal, Muellamuez, Colimba, Carlosama, Caserío de Pastas, Pupiales, Anfelima, Girón, Iles, Ospina, and Puerres) to Secretary of State Government, Ipiales, 4 March 1866, ACC, AM, pq. 94-54; The Indigenous Cabildos of Guachucal and Colimba to Legislators, Guachucal, 12 Aug. 1873, ACC, AM, pq. 124-60.

110 For example, The Indians and Members of the Pequeño Cabildo of Túquerres to President of the Legislature, Túquerres, June 1869, ACC, AM, pq. 103-3.

111 The Undersigned Members of the Cumbal Town Council to President of the Legislature, Cumbal, 24 July 1871, ACC, AM, pq. 112-15. By the 1890s, those hungry for Indian land began to use this strategy more frequently in the south too. See Rappaport, *Cumbe Reborn*, 30–36.

112 The Undersigned Residents of Riosucio District to Deputies, Riosucio, 27 June 1875, ACC, AM, pq. 130-17. See also Appelbaum, "Whitening the Region," 645–62.

113 Indian Alcalde Mayor of Obando Municipality . . . to Secretary of State Government, Ipiales, 4 March 1866, ACC, AM, pq. 94-54.

114 Members or Vocales of the Pequeños Cabildos de Indígenas of Túquerres, Obando, and Pasto to Deputies of the State Legislature, Pasto, 29 July 1873, ACC, AM, pq. 124-60.

115 Ibid.

116 Registro Oficial, 25 Oct., 1 Nov., 6 Dec. 1873.

117 For the modern movements, see Friedemann, "Niveles contemporáneos de indigenismo"; and Rappaport, The Politics of Memory, 112–16. It should be noted, however, that these works make no connection between modern and nineteenth-century movements.

118 See Foucault, Discipline and Punish.

119 Belisario Zamorano to Secretary of Government, Cali, 23 Jan. 1866, ACC, AM, pq. 94-40. See also Mehta, Liberalism and Empire, 190–201.

120 Registro Oficial, 23 Feb. 1874.

121 Gaceta Oficial del Cauca, 9 June 1866; Pinzón, Catecismo republicano.

122 President of the Democratic Society to Legislature, Cali, 16 Aug. 1877, ACC, AM, pq. 137-15.

123 Gaceta Oficial del Cauca, 8 Sep. 1866, 6 July 1867; Quijano, Informe, 12.

124 Gaceta Oficial del Cauca, 1 July 1867.

125 B. Reinales, Popayán, 8 July 1875, ACC, AM, pq. 130-7.

126 Registro Oficial, 3 July 1875.

127 Benjamín Pereira, Popayán, 8 July 1871, ACC, AM, pq. 112-10.

128 Avelino Vela to Secretary of Government, Ipiales, 28 April 1865, ACC, AM, pq. 92-83.

129 Quijano, Informe, 4. See also El Imparcial, 25 Nov. 1857; El Volcán, 15 Feb. 1850.

130 Foción Mantilla to Salvador Comacho Roldán, Popayán, 16 Oct. 1878, AGN, SA, FSCR, caja 9-104, p. 7; Benjamín Pereira, Popayán, 8 July 1871, ACC, AM, pq. 112-10.

131 La Unión, 14 Feb. 1864. See also, more generally, Rausch, La educación durante el federalismo; and Cacua Prada, Historia de la educación en Colombia.

132 Juan Antonio Arturo, Pasto, 20 Oct. 1853, ACC, AM, pq. 54-26; El Caucano, 15 Oct. 1863.

133 Vicente Camilo Fontal to Conciudadnos, Almauguer, 1 Jan. 1852, ACC, AM, pq. 53-77.

134 Unos liberales independientes, Uno i diez i ocho, 1; Los Principios, 31 July 1874; Registro Oficial, 25 Dec. 1875.

135 Los Principios, 31 March 1876.

136 Manuel W. Carvajal to Secretary of Government, Palmira, 1 April 1863, ACC, AM, pq. 86-104.

137 Provincial Government of Cali to the Municipal Corporation, Cali, 20 June 1863, AHMC, t. 150, p. 515.

138 Gabriel Lalinde to State President, Popayán, 9 Oct. 1869, ACC, AM, pq. 105-74.

139 Miguel Guerrero and 6 Others to State President, Cali, 25 Oct. 1875, ACC, AM, pq. 130-18.

140 Los Principios, 18 Sep. 1874; Valencia Llano, Estado Soberano del Cauca, 145.

141 El Republicano, 22 Dec. 1867.

142 Valencia Llano, Estado Soberano del Cauca; Park, Rafael Núñez; Sowell, The Early Colombian Labor Movement, 56–128.

143 The Undersigned Citizens to State President, Popayán, 19 Aug. 1875, ACC, AM, pq. 130-18; El Telégrafo, 25 March 1875.

144 Rafael [Arboleda] to Tomás [Mosquera], Popayán, 1 March 1876, ACC, SM, #56,912; Valencia Llano, Estado Soberano del Cauca, 27; Park, Rafael Núñez, 176–77.

145 Sergio Arboleda and Abraham Garcés, Bogotá, 26 March 1873, ACC, FA, #345, p. 1; Los Principios, 24 Oct. 1873.

146 Manuel W. Carvajal to Secretary of Government, Palmira, 13 April 1863, ACC, AM, pq. 86-104; César Conto, Popayán, 1 July 1865, ACC, AM, pq. 90-48.

147 Joaquín Aguilar to Secretary of Government, Túquerres, 1 May 1865, ACC, AM, pq. 92-74.

148 M. Scarpetta to Secretary of Government, Palmira, 16 May 1865, ACC, AM, pq. 92-73.

149 Benjamín Pereira, Popayán, 8 July 1871, ACC, AM, pq. 112-10.

150 Gaceta Oficial del Cauca, 6 July 1867.

151 Reinales, Informe, 34. Bentham's influence was considerable in Colombia. See Uribe-Uran, Honorable Lives, 108–13; and Jaramillo Uribe, El pensamiento colombiano, 149–72.

152 C. Conto to Aquileo Parra, Popayán, 19 April 1876, BLAA, #295.

153 González González, Poderes enfrentados, 167–245; Hyland, "The Secularization of Credit."

154 Pope Pio IX to Bishop of Popayán, San Pedro de Roma, 30 Nov. 1863, ACC, FA, #655, p. 1.

155 Carlos, Bishop de Popayán, to Priest of Popayán, Popayán, 28 March 1875, ACC, AM, pq. 133-80.

156 B. Reinales, Popayán, 8 July 1875, ACC, AM, pq. 130-7; Mosquera, Mensaje, 5–8.

157 Bermúdez, Pastoral, 1.

158 Los Principios, 21 Oct. 1873, 16 Jan. 1874.

159 The Pasto Municipal Corporation to State Constitutional Convention, Pasto, 11 July 1872, ACC, AM, pq. 116-17.

160 Bermúdez, Pastoral, 1; Los Principios, 14 Nov. 1873, 20 Feb. 1874.

161 The Pasto Municipal Corporation to State Constitutional Convention, Pasto, 11 July 1872, ACC, AM, pq. 116-17.

162 The Undersigned Residents of Pasto Municipality to State Constitutional Convention, Pasto, 20 July 1872, ACC, AM, pq. 116-17.

163 Petitions in ACC, AM, pq. 116-17.

164 Bishop of Pasto to Vicar of the Diocese, Pasto, 20 Nov. 1872, in Lemos, Informe, 14–15.

165 Quindío District Delegate to Superintendent of Public Instruction, Cartago, 1 Dec. 1875, ACC, AM, pq. 124-96; Avelino Vela to Superintendent of Public Instruction, Ipiales, 25 Jan. 1876, ACC, AM, pq. 133-77.

166 José María Muños to Jefe Municipal, Rioblanco, 16 Feb. 1869, ACC, AM, pq. 103-27; The Undersigned Members of the Indian Parcialidad of Coconuco to Jefe Municipal, Popayán, 22 July 1870, ACC, AM, pq. 112-18.

167 José Quintano to Jefe Municipal, Paniquitá, 31 Aug. 1871, ACC, AM, pq. 113-39.

168 Carlos Dorronsoro to Sergio Arboleda, Buga, 24 Sep. 1875, ACC, FA, #1,511.

169 Unsigned manuscript, 9 March 1873, ACC, FA, #357, p. 1. Catholic Societies had existed in the 1830s, as largely elite affairs. See Uribe-Uran, Honorable Lives, 120.

170 Vicente Cárdenas to Sergio Arboleda, Pasto, 9 March 1876, ACC, FA, #1,506; Los Principios, 31 March 1876.

171 M. A. Sanclemente to Sergio Arboleda, Buga, 12 Dec. 1875, ACC, FA, #1,525.

172 ACC, SM, ##56,911, 57,316; AGN, SR, FLM, t. 197, p. 204; ACC, FA, ##1,506, 1,511, 1,525; ACC, AM, pq. 132-59; Los Principios, 28 Jan.–19 May 1876.

173 Quindío District Delegate to Superintendent of Public Instruction, Cartago, 1 Dec. 1875, ACC, AM, pq. 124-96.

174 Julián Trujillo, Popayán, 1 July 1875, ACC, AM, pq. 130-9.

175 *Los Principios*, 17 March 1876.

176 P. Santacoloma to Municipal Chief of Barbacoas, Túquerres, 13 Nov. 1872, ACC, AM, pq. 119-72; Carlos Dorronsoro to Sergio Arboleda, Buga, 24 Sep. 1875, ACC, FA, #1,511.

177 See ACC, AM, pqs. 135-46, 130-18.

178 *El Caucano*, 3 Nov. 1864; *La Unión*, 30 Oct. 1864.

179 *La Unión*, 23 Oct. 1864; *El Republicano*, 16 May 1868; Markoff, "Really Existing Democracy," 52–57. For a dissenting view, see Rojas de Ferro, "Identity Formation."

180 *El Caucano*, 21 Jan. 1864; *Gaceta Oficial del Cauca*, 10 Aug. 1867.

6 Failure of Discipline

1 President of the Democratic Society to Secretary of Government, Santander, 17 May 1876, ACC, AM, pq. 135-46; Franco V., *Apuntamientos*; González González, *Poderes enfrentados*, 235–45; Palacios, *Entre la legitimidad*, 43–47.

2 Pompeyo Guzmán to Commander in Chief, n.p., 17 Sep. 1876, AGN, SR, FLM, t. 197, p. 204.

3 President of the Catholic Society to Sergio Arboleda, Buga, 22 April 1876, ACC, FA, #1,525; César Conto, Popayán, 1 July 1877, ACC, AM, pq. 137-27.

4 Manuel Sarria to Commander in Chief, Popayán, 19 July 1876, AGN, SR, FLM, t. 195, p. 10; C. Conto to Aquileo Parra, Popayán, 7 Aug. 1877, BLAA, #295.

5 Miguel A. Palau to Commander in Chief, María, 20 Oct. 1876, ACC, FA, #1,523; *Registro Oficial*, 12 May 1877.

6 [César Conto] to President, Buga, 4 Sep. 1876, ACC, AM, pq. 134-43.

7 Pompeyo Guzmán to Commander in Chief, n.p., 17 Sep. 1876, AGN, SR, FLM, t. 197, p. 204.

8 Miguel A. Palau to Commander in Chief, María, 20 Oct. 1876, ACC, FA, #1,523.

9 Agustín Patiño to Tomás C. de Mosquera, Villa María, 15 May 1876, ACC, SM, #57,262.

10 The Undersigned Residents of the Villa de María to State President, Villamaría, 13 Oct. 1877, ACC, AM, pq. 141-8.

11 Jefe Municipal, Barbacoas, 10 Aug. 1876, BLAA, #1, p. 70.

12 M. Muse to Vicente Guzmán, Calderas, 8 Jan. 1877, ACC, AM, pq. 118-72.

13 César Conto, Popayán, 1 July 1877, ACC, AM, pq. 137-27; Democratic Societies' petitions in ACC, AM, pq. 135-46.

14 Rafael [Arboleda] to T. C. de Mosquera, Popayán, 31 May 1876, ACC, SM, #56,922.

15 Rafael [Arboleda] to T. C. de Mosquera, Popayán, 14 June 1876, ACC, SM, #56,924.

16 César Conto, Popayán, 1 July 1877, ACC, AM, pq. 137-27.

17 Carlos Holguín to Sergio Arboleda, Manizales, 30 Jan. 1877, ACC, FA, #1,515.

18 Miguel A. Palau to Commander in Chief, María, 20 Oct. 1876, ACC, FA, #1,523.

19 *El Estado de Guerra*, 9 Jan. 1877.

20 Miguel A. Palau to Commander in Chief, María, 20 Oct. 1876, ACC, FA, #1,523.

21 [César Conto] to President, Buga, 4 Sep. 1876, ACC, AM, pq. 134-43.

22 Ibid.; Franco V., *Apuntamientos*, 1:108.

23 Julián Trujillo to Tomás C. de Mosquera, Cartago, 14 Oct. 1876, ACC, SM, #57,353.

24 General Santos Acosta to Marceliano Vélez, n.p., n.d., BLAA, #702.

25 For an extended, if very biased, account, see Sinisterra, *El 24 de diciembre*.

26 *El Estado de Guerra*, 9 Jan. 1877.

27 Sinisterra, El 24 de diciembre, 8. Conservative women, who had always used religion as their entrée into the public sphere, also participated in the war. A mob of conservative women and children demonstrated in Popayán, demanding the release of an arrested priest. Manuel Sarria to Commander in Chief of the Army of the Cauca, Popayán, 19 July 1876, AGN, SR, FLM, t. 195, p. 10.

28 M. D. Martínez to Secretary of the Treasury, Palmira, 25 Dec. 1876, AGN, SR, FLM, t. 194, p. 410.

29 Franco V., Apuntamientos, 1:311; Palacios, Apuntaciones, 77; M. M. Mosquera to Tomás [C. de Mosquera], Popayán, 10 Jan. 1877, BLAA, #558.

30 "Relacion de los sucesos de Cali," 30 Dec. 1876, ACC, FA, #440, p. 1; Sinisterra, El 24 de diciembre, 11–84.

31 "Relacion de los sucesos de Cali," 30 Dec. 1876, ACC, FA, #440, p. 1; Sinisterra, El 24 de diciembre, 11–84; Palacios, Apuntaciones, 77.

32 "Relacion de los sucesos de Cali," 30 Dec. 1876, ACC, FA, #440, p. 1.

33 M. Garcés to Commander in Chief, Cartago, 25 Dec. 1876, AGN, SR, FLM, t. 194, p. 409.

34 M. D. Martínez to Secretary of the Treasury, Palmira, 25 Dec. 1876, AGN, SR, FLM, t. 194, p. 410.

35 "Relacion de los sucesos de Cali," 30 Dec. 1876, ACC, FA, #440, p. 1; M. Garcés to Commander, Cartago, 25 Dec. 1876, AGN, SR, FLM, t. 194, p. 409.

36 [T. C. de Mosquera] to Aquileo Parra, Cali, 28 Sep. 1877, ACC, SM, #57,579.

37 The Democratic Society of Cali to State President, Cali, 1 June 1877, ACC, AM, pq. 137-7.

38 Ibid.

39 M. Sarria to Cali's Democratic Society, Popayán, 18 July 1877, ACC, AM, pq. 137-7.

40 David Peña, Popayán, 9 Aug. 1877, ACC, AM, pq. 137-30.

41 J. B. González to Julián Trujillo, Popayán, 2 Aug. 1877, AGN, SC, caja 94-346, p. 18,565.

42 Ramón Cerón, Popayán, 14 Aug. 1877, ACC, AM, pq. 137-30.

43 Registro Oficial, 1 Sep. 1877.

44 Belisario Zamorano to Chief General, Cali, 21 Sep. 1877, AGN, SR, FLM, t. 195, p. 260; C. Conto to Aquileo Parra, Popayán, 7 Aug. 1877, BLAA, #295; La Voz del Pueblo: Organo de la Sociedad Democrática, 29 Aug. 1878.

45 El Ferrocarril, 4 [Oct.] 1878 (the month actually printed on the paper is September, but this is an error).

46 C. de la Cadena to Salvador Camacho Roldán, Cali, 11 Oct. 1878, AGN, SA, FSCR, caja 6-61, p. 18; Registro Oficial, 19 Oct. 1878.

47 President of the Democratic Society to the Municipal Council, Cali, 1 March 1878, AHMC, t. 162, p. 59; President of the Democratic Society to State President, Cali, 23 Sep. 1877, ACC, AM, pq. 137-7.

48 Herrera Olarte, La administracion Trujillo, 41.

49 La Voz del Pueblo: Organo de la Sociedad Democrática, 3 Oct. 1878.

50 Scheper-Hughes, Death without Weeping, 65–215.

51 M. D. Martínez to Secretary of the Treasury, Palmira, 25 Dec. 1876, AGN, SR, FLM, t. 194, p. 410.

52 "Relacion de los sucesos de Cali," 30 Dec. 1876, ACC, FA, #440, p. 1; El Ferrocarril, 14 Feb. 1878.

53 Joaquín [Mosquera] to Tomás [Mosquera], n.p., 1 May 1877, ACC, SM, #57,544.

54 Manuel María [Mosquera] to Tomás [Mosquera], Popayán, 15 May 1877, ACC, SM, #57,555.

55 J. Trujillo to Tomás C. de Mosquera, Medellín, 17 July 1877, ACC, SM, #57,702.

56 Tulio Gómez to Commandant, Cartago, 14 Oct. 1876, AGN, SC, caja 94-348.

57 Inventory of Japio Hacienda, ACC, FA, #27, p. 1.

58 J. Mosquera to Tomás [Mosquera], Popayán, 24 Jan. 1877, ACC, SM, #57,540.

59 District Mayor to Commander in Chief, Palestina, 14 Jan. 1877, AGN, SR, FLM, t. 197, p. 177.

60 José M. Villegas to Commander in Chief, San Francisco, 16 April 1877, AGN, SR, FLM, t. 197, p. 253.

61 Jesus M. López S. to General Superintendent of Public Instruction, Cartago, 25 April 1877, ACC, AM, pq. 135-49.

62 J. M. Navarrete to Julián Trujillo, Neiva, 9 April 1877, AGN, SC, caja 94-346, pp. 18, 554.

63 The Undersigned Colombians Now Immigrants in Ecuador to Senators and Representatives, Quito, 1 March 1878, AC, S, 1878, vol. V, p. 67; Vicente Cárdenas to Sergio Arboleda, Quito, 29 Jan. 1878, ACC, FA, #1,506; Registro Oficial, 30 Jan. 1878, 24 April 1880.

64 The Undersigned Members of the Liberal Party, Pasto, 1 May 1878, AC, S, 1878, vol. V, p. 78.

65 El Estandarte Liberal, 17 Oct. 1878; Registro Oficial, 29 April 1876, 22 Feb. 1878; El Ferrocarril, 2 Aug., 13 Sep., 8 Nov. 1878; Foción Mantilla to Salvador Camacho Roldán, Popayán, 16 Oct. 1878, AGN, SA, FSCR, caja 9-104, p. 7.

66 Registro Oficial, 22 Dec. 1877.

67 I. V. Martínez to Tomás C. de Mosquera, Hacienda Paraíso, 7 June 1877, ACC, SM, #57,514.

68 For "social war," see Alejandro Micolta to Eliseo Payán, Cali, 26 April 1876, ACC, FA, #314, p. 4; for "race war," see Manuel María [Mosquera] to Tomás [Mosquera], Popayán, 15 May 1877, ACC, SM, #57,555.

69 Manuel María [Mosquera] to Tomás [Mosquera], Popayán, 15 May 1877, ACC, SM, #57,555.

70 See, e.g., Los Principios, 31 March 1876; El Correo de la Costa, 1 June 1879; El 21 de Abril, 18 May 1879; and Park, Rafael Núñez, 207.

71 Aníbal Micolta to Secretary of Government, Cali, 20 Sep. 1878, ACC, AM, pq. 140-no legajo.

72 The Undersigned Colombians Now Immigrants in Ecuador to Senators and Representatives, Quito, 1 March 1878, AC, S, 1878, vol. V, p. 67.

73 Joaquín [Mosquera] to Tomás [Mosquera], n.p., 1 May 1877, ACC, SM, #57,544.

74 The Undersigned Colombians Now Immigrants in Ecuador to Senators and Representatives, Quito, 1 March 1878, AC, S, 1878, vol. V, p. 67.

75 Estanislao Navia to Sergio Arboleda, Palmira, 8 April 1878, ACC, FA, #1,521.

76 Alejandro Micolta to Eliseo Payán, Cali, 26 April 1876, ACC, FA, #314, p. 4.

77 C. de la Cadena to Salvador Camacho Roldán, Cali, 1 Nov. 1878, AGN, SA, FSCR, caja 6-61, p. 14.

78 Julián Trujillo to Salvador Camacho Roldán, Cali, 1 Oct. 1880, AGN, SA, FSCR, caja 13-163, pp. 4–5; El Ferrocarril, 14 Feb. 1878.

79 El Ferrocarril, 15 Nov. 1878.

80 J. Trujillo to Tomás C. de Mosquera, Medellín, 4 Dec. 1877, ACC, SM, #57,701.

81 El Ferrocarril, 14 Feb. 1878.

82 El Ferrocarril, 13 Sep., 22 Nov. 1878.

83 Vicente Cárdenas to Sergio Arboleda, Quito, 2 Nov. 1878, ACC, FA, #1,506.

84 Estadística de Colombia, 32, 101, 105; Valencia Llano, Empresarios y políticos, 141–246; Ocampo, Colombia y la economía mundial, 303-395.

85 Valencia Llano, "Los proyectos económicos," 2–13.

86 Alfonso [Arboleda] to Sergio Arboleda, Japio, 23 July 1878, ACC, FA, #447, p. 12.

87 The Undersigned Caucano Citizens and Boatmen of the Dagua River to State President, Cali, 16 May 1878, ACC, AM, pq. 141-38.

88   President of the Democratic Society to Secretary of Government, Cali, 9 May 1878, ACC, AM, pq. 141-38.

89   Report of Circuit Judge, Buenaventura, 1 June 1878, ACC, AM, pq. 141-38.

90   The Bogas of the Dagua River to State President, Cali, 15 May 1878, ACC, AM, pq. 144-64.

91   Pioquinto Diago and Friends to State President, Popayán, 7 Feb. 1878, ACC, AM, pq. 144-64.

92   El Montañes, 1 Feb. 1876.

93   El Estandarte Liberal, 8 May 1878.

94   Various Residents of Cali to State President, Cali, 15 Jan. 1879, ACC, AM, pq. 141-16; J. Trujillo to Tomás C. de Mosquera, Medellín, 4 Dec. 1877, ACC, SM, #57,701.

95   Herrera Olarte, La administracion Trujillo, 21; La Voz del Pueblo: Organo de la Sociedad Democrática, 10 Oct. 1878; Valencia Llano, Estado Soberano del Cauca, 226–59.

96   Flórez Gallego, Modernidad política, 43–47.

97   Valencia Llano, "Los proyectos económicos," 15.

98   González Toledo, El General Eliseo Payán, 9.

99   Valencia Llano, "Los proyectos económicos," 13–30; Uribe-Uran, Honorable Lives, 149–54; Palacios, El café en Colombia, 83.

100 Juan de D. Ulloa to Tomás C. de Mosquera, Cali, 23 Nov. 1877, ACC, SM, #57,711; Belisario Zamorano to Salvador Camacho Roldán, Cali, 18 Oct. 1878, AGN, SA, FSCR, caja 13-175, p. 42.

101 Foción Mantilla to Salvador Camacho Roldán, Popayán, 4 Dec. 1878, AGN, SA, FSCR, caja 9-104, p. 1; Guillermo [Pereira] to Salvador Camacho Roldán, Popayán, 29 May 1878, AGN, SA, FSCR, caja 10-129, p. 1.

102 La Sociedad La Unión Filantrópica to Julián Trujillo, Túquerres, 28 Jan. 1878, AGN, SC, caja 94-349.

103 Manuel María [Mosquera] to Tomás [Mosquera], Popayán, 15 May 1877, ACC, SM, #57,555.

104 Benjamín Núñez to T. C. de Mosquera, Cali, 9 Aug. 1878, ACC, SM, #57,808; El Demócrata: Organo del Partido Liberal Independiente, 30 Jan. 1879.

105 J. B. González to Julián Trujillo, Popayán, 2 Aug. 1877, AGN, SC, caja 94-346, p. 18,565; Registro Oficial, 7 Oct. 1877.

106 El Estandarte Liberal, 22 Aug. 1878.

107 La Voz del Pueblo: Organo de la Sociedad Democrática, 14 Nov. 1878.

108 Modesto Garcés to Tomás C. de Mosquera, Popayán, 2 Nov. [1877], ACC, SM, #57,036. (The year actually given is 1876, but this is an error.)

109 Juan de D. Ulloa to Tomás C. de Mosquera, Cali, 23 Nov. 1877, ACC, SM, #57,711.

110 Registro Oficial, 8 Dec. 1877.

111 Vicente Cárdenas to Sergio Arboleda, Quito, 29 Jan. 1878, ACC, FA, #1,506.

112 David Peña to State President, Cali, 15 May 1878, ACC, AM, pq. 144-61.

113 Registro Oficial, 1 June 1878.

114 The Sarrista Democratic Society to State President, Popayán, 24 Nov. 1878, ACC, AM, pq. 141-38.

115 El Estandarte Liberal, 24 July 1878; El Elector, 20 Oct. 1878.

116 La Voz del Pueblo: Organo de la Sociedad Democrática, 22 Aug. 1878.

117 El Estandarte Liberal, 22 Aug. 1878; Valencia Llano, Estado Soberano del Cauca, 248.

118 E. Hurtado to Secretary of Government, Bogotá, 29 Nov. 1878, ACC, AM, pq. 144-61; [T. C. de Mosquera] to Aquileo Parra, Cali, 28 Sep. 1877, ACC, SM, #57,579.

119 Foción Mantilla to Salvador Camacho Roldán, Popayán, 4 Dec. 1878, AGN, SA, FSCR, caja 9-104,

p. 1; Residents of Santander to Secretary of the Treasury, Santander, 4 March 1879, ACC, AM, pq. 141-16.

120 Julián Trujillo to Senators and Representatives, Bogotá, 27 April 1878, AC, C, 1878, vol. XIV, p. 12.

121 Julián Trujillo to Senators and Representatives, Bogotá, 11 May 1878, AC, S, 1878, vol. III, p. 12.

122 Francisco Escobar to Salvador Camacho Roldán, Cali, 6 May 1879, AGN, SA, FSCR, caja 7-80, p. 20.

123 Bautista Feijoo to Sergio Arboleda, Caloto, 7 March 1883, ACC, FA, #1,513.

124 Sergeant Major to Commander of First Division, Palmira, 23 April 1879, ACC, AM, pq. 147-60.

125 M. D. Camacho to Jefes Municipales, Cartago, 10 May 1879, ACC, AM, pq. 147-61.

126 B. Reinales to Jefe Civil y Militar, Palmira, 23 April 1879, ACC, AM, pq. 147-60.

127 Rejistro Oficial, 31 May 1879.

128 Julián Trujillo to Senators and Representatives, Bogotá, 14 April 1879, AC, S, 1879, vol. IX, p. 46.

129 Rejistro Oficial, 31 May 1879.

130 El Ferrocarril, 2 May 1879.

131 Rafael de la Pedrosa to State President, Popayán, 25 Aug. 1879, ACC, AM, pq. 150-94.

132 Juan E. Ulloa to Salvador Camacho Roldán, Palmira, 19 June 1879, AGN, SA, FSCR, caja 13-166, p. 6.

133 La Voz del Pueblo: Organo de la Sociedad Democrática, 5 Dec. 1878.

134 El Ferrocarril, 10 May 1878.

135 El 21 de Abril, 18 May 1879.

136 La Municipalidad de Quindío, Proposicion n. 161, 1.

137 For example, Commander of Second Brigade to Commander in Chief, near Caloto, 27 April 1879, ACC, AM, pq. 147-60.

138 El Estandarte Liberal, 24 July 1878; El Ferrocarril, 10 Dec. 1880.

139 Pacífico Orejuela to Eliseo Payán, n.p., [1879], ACC, AM, pq. 147-62.

140 El Ferrocarril, 17 Oct. 1879; El Cauca (Popayán), 6 Aug. 1883.

141 Alejandro Micolta to Deputies, Popayán, 7 Sep. 1879, ACC, AM, pq. 146-3.

142 Alfonso [Arboleda] to Sergio Arboleda, Popayán, 14 May 1879, ACC, FA, #447, p. 44.

143 El Estandarte Liberal, 5 June 1878; The Undersigned Citizens to Senators and Representatives, Jamundí, 1 Feb. 1880, AC, S, 1880, vol. VI, p. 246.

144 AHMC, t. 163, p. 518; Castro C., "Caridad," 77–80.

145 El Ferrocarril, 10 Dec. 1880.

146 Juan de la Cruz Escobar B. to Jefe Municipal, Cali, 9 Oct. 1879, ACC, AM, pq. 150-94.

147 Rejistro Oficial, 29 April 1879; 250 Residents of Pasto to State President, Pasto, 18 Feb. 1880, ACC, AM, pq. 152-51.

148 Ezequial Hurtado to Deputies, Popayán, 19 Sep. 1879, ACC, AM, pq. 146-1.

149 Enrique Muñoz to Deputies, Popayán, 26 Aug. 1881, ACC, AM, pq. 157-62.

150 El Conservador, 21 March 1882.

151 Valencia C., Informe, 26–27.

152 El Montaraz, 3 Sep. 1881.

153 Julián Trujillo, Bogotá, 1 Feb. 1879, AC, S, 1879, vol. IX, p. 1; El Cauca (Popayán), 9 June 1883.

154 Alfonso [Arboleda] to Sergio Arboleda, Japio, 15 Oct. 1879, ACC, FA, #447, p. 73.

155 El Ferrocarril, 12 March 1880.

156 *El Ferrocarril*, 1 Oct. 1880.

157 *Registro Oficial*, 30 March 1878.

158 Bautista Feijoo to Sergio Arboleda, Caloto, 7 March 1883, ACC, FA, #1,513.

159 *El Ferrocarril*, 2 Jan. 1880.

160 *El Ferrocarril*, 8 Oct. 1880.

161 Julián Trujillo to Salvador Camacho Roldán, Cali, 1 Oct. 1880, AGN, SA, FSCR, caja 13-163, pp. 4-5.

162 *El Ferrocarril*, 30 May 1879.

163 Francisco Marulanda to Julián Trujillo, Popayán, 20 Nov. 1880, AGN, SC, caja 93-342, pp. 18, 184.

164 *El Conservador*, 21 March 1882; Pablo Saavedra to Representatives, Toro, 16 Feb. 1881, AC, C, 1881, vol. IX, p. 44; *La Epoca*, 7 Sep. 1883.

165 *El Estandarte Liberal*, 17 Oct. 1878.

166 *El Ferrocarril*, 13 Sep. 1878.

167 *El Estandarte Liberal*, 17 Oct. 1878.

168 Ezequial Hurtado to Deputies, Popayán, 19 Sep. 1879, ACC, AM, pq. 146-1.

169 The Undersigned Colombians Now Immigrants in Ecuador to Senators and Representatives, Quito, 1 March 1878, AC, S, 1878, vol. V, p. 67.

170 Vicente Cárdenas to Sergio Arboleda, Quito, 2 Sep. 1878, ACC, FA, #1,506.

171 Alfonso [Arboleda] to Sergio Arboleda, Japio, 15 Oct. 1879, ACC, FA, #447, p. 73.

172 *El Cauca* (Popayán), 1 Sep. 1883.

173 *El Cauca* (Popayán), 6 Aug. 1883.

174 Foción Mantilla to Salvador Camacho Roldán, Popayán, 4 Dec. 1878, AGN, SA, FSCR, caja 9-104, p. 1.

175 Guillermo [Pereira] to Salvador Camacho Roldán, Popayán, 29 May 1878, AGN, SA, FSCR, caja 10-129, p. 1.

176 *Rejistro Oficial*, 1 May 1880.

177 *El Ferrocarril*, 14 Feb. 1878.

178 *El Ferrocarril*, 17 Oct. 1879.

179 *El Ferrocarril*, 7 Nov. 1879.

180 *Rejistro Oficial*, 25 July 1879.

181 *Rejistro Oficial*, 1 May 1880.

182 *El Ferrocarril*, 6 Aug. 1880.

183 Arboleda, *Informe*, 18.

184 *Rejistro Oficial*, 1 May 1880.

185 Núñez, *Decreto*, 1.

186 *El Correo de la Costa*, 16 March 1879.

187 *El Ferrocarril*, 12 March 1880.

188 *Registro Oficial*, 15 June 1883, 19 Nov. 1885.

189 Elias Ospina to State President, Buga, 3 Oct. 1878, ACC, AM, pq. 144-61.

190 *El Ferrocarril*, 26 July, 2 Aug. 1878.

191 *El Cauca* (Popayán), 25 Aug. 1883.

192 *El Cauca* (Popayán), 3 Nov. 1883.

193 *Rejistro Oficial*, 31 July 1880.

194 Joaquín Valencia to Sergio Arboleda, Popayán, 3 Dec. 1884, ACC, FA, #1,529; *Registro Oficial*, 19 Aug. 1882.

195 *Registro Oficial*, 1 Sep. 1883.

196 *El Ferrocarril*, 24 Jan. 1879.

197 *El Ferrocarril*, 16 May 1879.

198 *El Cauca* (Popayán), 10 Nov. 1883.

199 Valencia C., *Informe*, 35.

200 *Registro Oficial*, 1 Sep. 1883.

201 *El Ferrocarril*, 2 Jan. 1880.

202 *Registro Municipal*, 15 Aug. 1882.

203 *Registro Oficial*, 25 Aug. 1883.

204 Rafael de la Pedroza to Secretary of Government, Cali, 14 Nov. 1878, ACC, AM, pq. 144-61.

205 [T. C. de Mosquera] to Aquileo Parra, Cali, 28 Sep. 1877, ACC, SM, #57,579.

206 T. C. de Mosquera to Aquileo Parra, Popayán, 17 Oct. 1877, ACC, SM, #57,581.

207 *El Estandarte Liberal*, 5 Sep. 1878.

208 Residents of Pasto to State President, Pasto, 18 Feb. 1880, ACC, AM, pq. 152-51.

209 *Rejistro Oficial*, 10 July 1880.

210 Society of Public Welfare [*Salud Pública*] to State President, Cali, 6 Oct. 1882, ACC, AM, pq. 161-25.

211 W. Jordan to Society of Public Welfare, Popayán, 17 Oct. 1882, ACC, AM, pq. 161-25.

212 Members of the Democratic Society to State President, Popayán, 15 Nov. 1882, ACC, AM, pq. 161-25.

213 *Registro Oficial*, 4 Nov. 1882.

214 Ezequial Hurtado, Popayán, 1 July 1883, ACC, AM, pq. 162-17.

215 *Registro Oficial*, 12 May 1882.

216 *Registro Oficial*, 7 Oct., 9 Dec. 1882.

217 Hurtado, *Mensaje*, 7–11.

218 *Registro Oficial*, 26 May, 25 Aug., 8 Sep. 1883.

219 *El Cauca* (Popayán), 16 Oct. 1886.

220 *El Ferrocarril*, 10 Sep. 1880.

221 Henrique Grizales to Julián Trujillo, Popayán, 3 Nov. 1882, AGN, SC, caja 94-345, p. 20,723.

222 Conservative Directorate, Bogotá, 7 Aug. 1882, ACC, FA, #479, p. 31.

223 Alejandro Ontaneda to Julián Trujillo, Pasto, 5 Oct. 1882, AGN, SC, caja 94-347, p. 18,402; *La Epoca*, 7 Sep. 1883; *El Cauca* (Popayán), 9 June 1883.

224 Juan E. Ulloa to Eliseo Payán, Palmira, 29 Jan. 1885, ACC, AM, pq. 168-15; Residents of Caloto to State President, Caloto, 16 May 1885, ACC, AM, pq. 174-63.

225 Flórez Gallego, *Modernidad política*, 47.

226 Carlos Dorronsoro to Sergio Arboleda, Buga, 4 April 1885, ACC, FA, #1,511.

7 Popular Republicans' Legacies

1 L'Ouverture quoted in James, *The Black Jacobins*, 196.

2 T. C. de Mosquera, J. W. Quijano W., and Pablo Diago to President, Bogotá, 22 July 1876, AGN, SR, FMI, t. 13, p. 455. A similar process must have occurred on the Caribbean Coast as an area

with a strong popular liberal tradition became Núñez's base for the Regeneration. See Lasso, "Race and Republicanism"; and Posada-Carbó, *The Colombian Caribbean*, 236–37.

3 Rafael Reyes to Sergio Arboleda, Bogotá, 16 Oct. 1885, ACC, FA, #1,525; Julián Trujillo to Senators and Representatives, Bogotá, 14 April 1879, AC, S, 1879, vol. IX, p. 46.

4 B. Reinales to Jefe Civil y Militar, Palmira, 23 April 1879, ACC, AM, pq. 147-60.

5 *El 21 de Abril*, 18 May 1879. See also Valencia Llano, *Estado Soberano del Cauca*, 167; and Flórez Gallego, *Modernidad política*, 45.

6 *El Ferrocarril*, 19 Sep. 1879; *Rejistro Oficial*, 12 June 1880.

7 See petitions in ACC, AM, pq. 168-7.

8 M. A. Sanclemente to Secretary of Government, Buga, 22 April 1885, ACC, AM, pq. 168-7.

9 Alfonso [Arboleda] to Sergio Arboleda, Japio, 9 Sep. 1884, ACC, FA, #445, p. 18.

10 Sergio Arboleda, [1885], ACC, FA, #464, pp. 1, 5.

11 González González, *Poderes enfrentados*, 255–60.

12 Gibson's translation. Gibson, *The Constitutions of Colombia*, 321; see also 318, 320, 344.

13 Gibson, *The Constitutions of Colombia*, 316, 341–42.

14 Aguilera Peña and Vega Cantor, *Ideal democrático*, 159–61.

15 *El Cauca* (Popayán), 16 Oct. 1886.

16 Bushnell, *The Making of Modern Colombia*, 143, 140–48. See also Liévano Aguirre, *Rafael Núñez*; Leal and Díaz, "La Regeneración"; Park, *Rafael Núñez*, 266, 270; and Flórez Gallego, *Modernidad política*, 17–42. In general, see Flórez Gallego, "Discusiones recientes"; Safford, "Acerca de las interpretaciones socioeconómicas"; Vélez, "La Regeneración"; and Deas, Safford, and Palacios, "La Regeneración," 51–94.

17 In his excellent study of elite politics and its factions, Valencia Llano (*Estado Soberano del Cauca*, 141–55, 248–53, 260–79) argues this point, but he claims that Caucano Independents did not approve of the Regeneration's antidemocratic elements. Malcolm Deas (Deas, Safford, and Palacios, "La Regeneración," 51–74, 86–89) also stresses Núñez's desire for order after the chaos of Radical federalism. Luis Eduardo Nieto Arteta (*Economía y cultura*, 293–320) stresses centralism but also the importance of the collapse of exports. See also Vélez, "La Regeneración," 12–19, 46–47.

18 Many Independents were federalists. *El Cauca* (Popayán), 15 Oct. 1883.

19 Bergquist, *Coffee and Conflict*, 3–17; Bustamente, *Efectos económicos*. Fernando Guillén Martínez (*La Regeneración*, 15–16, 22, 23–42) sees the export crises as weakening the clientelist bonds that defined Colombian politics to such an extent that elites had to come together to make a new state powerful enough to continue clientelist politics, control urbanized masses, and attract foreign investment.

20 The notion of the Regeneration closest to my own is suggested in Urrego, "La noción de ciudadanía," 657–62. See also Palacios, *El café en Colombia*, 35–40. Mario Aguilera Peña and Renán Vega Cantor (*Ideal democrático*, 157–68) also stress the social-control aspects of the Regeneration, although they tend to see the project as anticapitalist.

21 See Worcester, "The Spanish-American Past." See also Rueschemeyer, Stephens, and Stephens, *Capitalist Development and Democracy*. The authors contend that twentieth-century capitalism would create democracy (which would then transform capitalism), assuming that democracy did not exist in nineteenth-century Latin America.

22 Costa, *The Brazilian Empire*, 1–23, 53–77, 243–46; Andrews, *Afro-Latin America*; Graham, *Patronage and Politics*.

23 See esp. Mallon, *Peasant and Nation*, 23–62; and Guardino, *Peasants*, 44–68, 110–42.

24 Ferrer, *Insurgent Cuba*; Scott, *Slave Emancipation in Cuba*.

25 Foner, *Reconstruction*, 291–307.

26 Ibid., 279.

27 Cooper, Holt, and Scott, *Beyond Slavery*, 11–26.

28 Foner, *Reconstruction*, 524–63.

29 Fuente, *A Nation for All*. See also Scott, "Fault Lines, Color Lines, and Party Lines." For a more pessimistic view, see Helg, *Our Rightful Share*.

30 Mallon, *Peasant and Nation*, 247–75.

31 Foner, *Reconstruction*, 488–99, 575–87; Oestreicher, "The Two Souls of American Democracy."

32 Jiménez, *Struggles on an Interior Shore*.

33 Hobsbawm, *The Age of Empire*.

34 Foucault, *Discipline and Punish*, 26. See also Foucault, *Power/Knowledge*, 134–65. I argue that the Regeneration was not only the exclusion of formerly useful plebeian allies after victory—as Mallon (*Peasant and Nation*, 247–75) details for Mexico—but a reaction against the whole political culture that allowed their inclusion in the first place.

35 Keyssar, *The Right to Vote*.

36 *Registro Oficial*, 15 March 1884.

37 I refer here to the fetishization of order in Collier and Collier, *Shaping the Political Arena*.

38 Much comparative work remains to be done on popular politics throughout Colombia. How did popular politics develop in regions of less racial diversity, in areas dominated by one party, or under the pressure of U.S. imperialism? See Johnson, *Santander*; McGuinness, "In the Path of Empire"; and Fals Borda, *Historia doble*, vol. 2.

39 Ada Ferrer (*Insurgent Cuba*, 3) claims that, in the nineteenth century, Cuban patriot armies were "unique in the history of the Atlantic World" owing to their integration. However, Caucano armies, while perhaps not to the impressive extent of Cuban armies, were an even earlier example of at least a partially integrated (and potent) force. For earlier movements, see Linebaugh and Rediker, *The Many-Headed Hydra*.

40 Somers, "Narrativity, Narrative Identity, and Social Action."

41 This latter observation is drawn both from personal experience and from Taussig, *The Devil and Commodity Fetishism*, 67–69.

42 LeGrand, *Frontier Expansion*, 14–18, 29–32, 83–87; Rappaport, *The Politics of Memory*, 93, 143.

43 Rafael de la Pedrosa to State President, Popayán, 25 Aug. 1879, ACC, AM, pq. 150-94; ACC, AM, pq. 150-91; *Artículos del "Correo del Cauca*," 1–7, 44; AHMC, t. 163, pp. 208, 459.

44 Friedemann and Arocha, *De sol a sol*, 202; Taussig, *The Devil and Commodity Fetishism*, 39–139; Mejía Prado and Moncayo Urrutia, "Origen y formación."

45 Wade, *Blackness*; Appelbaum, "Remembering Riosucio," 275, 326–27. John Green ("Left Liberalism and Race") notes that, while twentieth-century left liberalism in Colombia proudly championed a mestizo identity, it was much more circumspect about representing Afro-Colombians.

46 This was also part of a broader process in Latin America. See Andrews, *Afro-Latin America*.

47 Beverley and Sanders, "Negotiating with the Disciplines"; Beverley, *Subalternity*.

48 Arendt, *On Violence*.

49 Urrego, "La noción de ciudadanía," 661–62; Deas and Gaitán Daza, *Dos ensayos especulativos*, 197–205.

50 For other critiques of Plan Colombia, see Estrada Álvarez, ed., *Plan Colombia*.

Notes to Chapter 7   235

Abbreviations

Archives

AC   Archivo del Congreso (Bogotá)
  C   Cámara
  S   Senado

ACC   Archivo Central del Cauca (Centro de Investigaciones
      Históricas "José María Arboleda Llorente") (Popayán)
  AM   Archivo Muerto
  EC   Archivo de "El Carnero," Sala República
  FA   Fondo Arboleda
  SM   Sala Mosquera

AGN   Archivo General de la Nación (Bogotá)
  SA   Sección Academia Colombiana de Historia
    FJHL   Fondo José Hilario López
    FSCR   Fondo Salvador Camacho Roldán
  SC   Sección Colecciones, Fondo Enrique Ortega Ricaurte, Serie Generales y Civiles
  SR   Sección República
    FB   Fondo Ministerio de Fomento - Baldíos
    FC   Fondo Congreso
    FCP   Fondo Censos de Población
    FG   Fondo Gobernaciones
    FGV   Fondo Gobernaciones Varias
    FLM   Fondo Libros Manuscritos y Leyes Originales
    FM   Fondo Manumisión
    FMI   Fondo Ministerio de lo Interior y Relaciones Exteriores
    FP   Fondo Particulares

AHMC   Archivo Histórico Municipal de Cali, Archivo del Concejo Municpal (Cali)

BLAA   Biblioteca Luis Angel Arango, Sala de Manuscritos (Bogotá)

BN   Biblioteca Nacional, Fondo Manuscritos (Bogotá)

INCORA   Archivo del Instituto Colombiano de la Reforma Agraria, Bienes Nacionales (Bogotá)

General

car.   *carpeta*
pq.   *paquete*
t.   *tomo*

Bibliography

Published Primary Sources

Alaix, M. M. *No sin desconfianza en mis propias fuerzas me propongo refutar la carta que el señor Julio Arboleda ha publicado en el número 9.° de "El Misóforo."* Popayán: n.p., 1850. Work is untitled; "title" given here is first line of text.

Aldea de María. *Declaraciones a que se refiere la hoja anterior.* N.p., 1854.

Arana, R. M. *Aldea de María.* Bogotá: Imprenta de Echeverría Hermanos, 1859.

Arboleda, Gregorio. *Informe del Superintendente de Instruccion Pública Primaria del Estado del Cauca.* Popayán: Imprenta del Estado, 1880.

Arboleda, Julio. "El Misóforo, número noveno—Popayán 27 de noviembre de 1850." In *Prosa de Julio Arboleda: Jurídica, política, heterodoxa y literaria,* 307–59. Bogotá: Banco de la República, 1984.

Arboleda, Sergio. *El clero puede salvarnos i nadie puede salvarnos sino el clero.* Popayán: Imprenta de Colejio Mayor, 1858.

——. *Rudimentos de geografía, cronología e historia: Lecciones dispuestas para la enseñanza elemental de dichos ramos en el seminario conciliar de Popayán.* Bogotá: Imprenta de El Tradicionista, 1872.

Artículos del "Correo del Cauca." N.p., n.d.

Bermúdez, Carlos. *Pastoral del Ilustrísimo Señor Obispo de Popayán, Doctor Carlos Bermúdez.* Popayán: Imprenta de J. Clímaco Rivera, 1869.

Bosch, Manuel Joaquín. *Reseña histórica de los principales acontecimientos políticos de la ciudad de Cali, desde el año de 1848 hasta el de 1855 inclusive.* 1856. Cali: Centro de Estudios Históricos y Sociales "Santiago de Cali," 1996.

Burbano, Miguel, Juan Ignacio Astorquiza, et al. *Ciudadano Presidente de la República.* Pasto: Imprenta de Pastor Enríquez, 1850.

Cabal, Miguel. *Contestacion al inmundo pasquín titulado "La revolucion del Cauca."* Cali: Imprenta de Hurtado, 1866.

Cervantes, P. P. *Observaciones a los "Apuntamientos para la historia de la guerra de 1876 a 1877" escritos por el señor Constancio Franco V.* Bogotá: n.p., 1877.

Comisión Corográfica. *Jeografía física i política de las provincias de la Nueva Granada.* Vol. 2. Bogotá: Banco de la República, 1959.

Constitucion i leyes del Estado Soberano del Cauca sancionadas en 1857, precedidas de la constitucion política para la Confederacion Granadina. Bogotá: Imprenta de Echeverría Hermanos, 1858.

Contestacion al folleto del Jeneral Franco titulado "A la nacion i al gobierno." Popayán: Imprenta de Hurtado, 1852.

Los criminales, al presidio. [Cali]: Imprenta de Nicolás Pontón i Compañia, n.d.

Los Editores. *Documentos curiosos, escojidos de entre otros muchos que se interceptaron últimamente, en el Cauca, a los rebeldes Canal, Arboleda, Enao i compañeros.* Bogotá: Imprenta del E. de Cundinamarca, 1862.

Escovar, Avelino. *Alegato fundado los derechos del pueblo de María a las tierras de "La Florida" cuestionados por el Señor Marcelino Palacios ante el Superior Tribunal del Cauca.* Bogotá: Imprenta de Echeverría Hermanos, 1857.

Estadística de Colombia. Pt. 2, *Comercio esterior—esportacion, importacion, cabotaje i movimiento marítimo.* Bogotá: Imprenta de Medardo Rivas, 1876.

Estadística jeneral de la Nueva Granada. Pt. 1. Bogotá: Imprenta de J. A. Cualla, 1848.

Franco V., Constancio. *Apuntamientos para la historia: La guerra de 1876 i 1877.* 2 vols. Bogotá: Imprenta de la Epoca, 1877.

Gibson, William Marion. *The Constitutions of Colombia.* Durham: Duke University Press, 1948.

González Toledo, Aureliano. *El General Eliseo Payán: Vicepresidente de la República.* Bogotá: Imprenta de "La Luz," 1887.

Herrera Olarte, José. *La administracion Trujillo: Juicio histórico.* Bogotá: Imprenta de Gaitán, 1880.

Holguín, Carlos. *Noticia histórica del orijen, formacion i campaña de la columna Torres.* Cali: Imprenta de Velasco, 1854.

Hurtado, Ezequial. *Mensaje del Presidente constitucional del Estado Soberano del Cauca a la Legislatura de 1883.* Popayán: Imprenta del Estado, 1883.

Lemos, Francisco E. *Informe del Secretario de Gobierno del Estado Soberano del Cauca a la Legislatura en sus sesiones ordinarias.* Popayán: Imprenta del Estado, 1873.

López, José Hilario. *Mensaje del Presidente de la Nueva Granada al Congreso Constitucional de 1852.* Bogotá: Imprenta del Neo-Granadino, 1852.

Mallarino, M. M. *Carta dirijida al Señor Dr. Ramón Mercado.* Cali: Imprenta de Velasco, 1854.

Matéus, Antonio. *Informe del Gobernador de la Provincia del Cauca a la Lejislatura Provincial; constitucion i ordenanzas espedidas por ella en el año de 1853.* Bogotá: Imprenta del Neo-Granadino, 1854.

Mercado, Ramón. *Memorias sobre los acontecimientos del Sur, especialmente en la Provincia de Buenaventura, durante la administración del 7 de marzo de 1849. 1853.* Cali: Centro de Estudios Históricos y Sociales "Santiago de Cali," 1996.

Mosquera, T. C. de. *Memoria sobre la geografía, física y política de la Nueva Granada.* New York: Imprenta de S. W. Benedict, 1852.

——. *T. C. de Mosquera, Gobernador del Estado Soberano del Cauca, i Presidente de los Estados Unidos de Colombia, as sus conciudadanos.* Bogotá: Imprenta de la Nación, 1861.

——. *Mensaje del Presidente del Estado Soberano del Cauca a la Legislatura de 1873.* Popayán: Imprenta del Estado, 1873.

——. *Ojeada sobre la situacion política y militar de Colombia.* Bogotá: Imprenta de Echeverría Hermanos, 1878.

La Municipalidad de Quindío. Proposicion n. 161. Cartago: Imprenta de J. Pio Durán, 1879.

Núñez, Benjamín. *Decreto sobre educacion social y urbanidad.* Cali: n.p., 1881.

Observaciones para servir a la historia de la administracion del 7 de marzo, i especialmente en lo que concierne a la polémica promovida por el Arzobispo de Bogotá con relacion a algunas disposiciones lejislativas recientemente puestas en ejecucion. Bogotá: Imprenta del Neo-Granadino, 1851.

Olano, Antonio. *Opúsculo sobre la espulsion de los Jesuitas.* Popayán: Imprenta de la Universidad, 1850.

Ordenanzas de la Cámara Provincial de Popayán, 1849. Popayán: Imprenta Democrática, 1849.

Ordenanzas de la Provincia del Chocó expedidas en el año de 1849. Novita: Imprenta de Nicolás Hurtado, 1849.

Ordenanzas espedidas por la Cámara Provincial del Cauca en sus sesiones ordinarias de 1852. N.p., [1852?].

Ordenanzas espedidas por la Lejislatura Provincial del Cauca: 1854. Bogotá: Imprenta del Neo-Granadino, 1855.

Ordenanzas espedidas por la Lejislatura Provincial del Cauca en sus sesiones de 1856. Bogotá: Imprenta de Francisco Torres Amaya, n.d.

Ospina, Mariano. *Informe del Presidente de la Confederacion Granadina.* Bogotá: n.p., 1861.

Palacios, Belisario. *Apuntaciones histórico-geográficas de la actual Provincia de Cali.* Cali: Imprenta de Eustaquio Palacios, 1889.

Palau, Francisco A. *Resumen histórico de los hechos patrióticos i recomendables que se han ejecutado en esta provincia desde las elecciones populares de 1853 hasta el 4 de diciembre de 1854.* Cali: Imprenta de Velasco, 1855.

Partido Conservador de Colombia. *Constitucion, acuerdos y resolucion expedidos por la Convencion Nacional del Partido Conservador de Colombia.* Bogotá: Nicolás Pontón, 1879.

Pedrosa, M. E. *Alcance a la Reseña histórica.* Cali: Imprenta de Velasco, 1857.

Pérez, Felipe. *Jeografía física i política de los Estados Unidos de Colombia.* Vol. 1, *Comprende la jeografía del distrito federal i las de los estados de Panamá i el Cauca.* Bogotá: Imprenta de la Nación, 1862.

Pinzón, Cerbeleón. *Catecismo republicano para instruccion popular.* Bogotá: Imprenta de "El Mosaico," 1864.

Pombo, Manuel Antonio, and José Joaquín Guerra. *Constituciones de Colombia.* Vol. 4. Bogotá: Biblioteca Banco Popular, 1986.

Quijano, Manuel de J. *Informe del Director de la instruccion pública primaria del Estado Soberano del Cauca al Presidente del mismo.* Popayán: Imprenta del Estado, 1873.

Reinales, B. *Informe del Secretario de Gobierno a la Lejislatura del Estado en sus sesiones ordinarias de 1869.* Popayán: Imprenta del Colejio Mayor, 1869.

———. *Ferrocarril del Cauca: Documentos relacionados con esta obra.* Bogotá: Imprenta de Vapor de Zalamea Hermanos, 1882.

Restrepo Piedrahita, Carlos, ed. *Constituciones de la primera República liberal, 1855–1885.* Vol. 4. Bogotá: Universidad Externado de Colombia, 1985.

Saffray, Charles. *Viaje a Nueva Granada.* Bogotá: Biblioteca Popular de Cultura Colombiana, 1948.

Samper, José María. *Ensayo aproximado sobre la jeografía i estadística de los ocho estados que compondrán el 15 de septiembre de 1857 la Federacion Neo-Granadina.* Bogotá: Imprenta de "El Neo-Granadino," 1857.

———. *Ensayo sobre las revoluciones políticas y la condicion social de las repúblicas colombianas (Hispano-Americanas); con un apéndice sobre la orografía y la poblacion de la Confederacion Granadina.* 1861. Bogotá: Universidad Nacional de Colombia, 1969.

Scarpetta, M. *El grito de un republicano.* Cali: Imprenta de Velasco, 1854.

La Sociedad Democrática de Cali. Mentir con descaro. Cali: Imprenta de Velasco, 1851.

Sociedad Democrática de Palmira. *Estatuto de la Sociedad Democrática de Palmira, aprobado definitivamente en la sesion del día 19 de mayo de 1868.* Bogotá: Imprenta de Echeverría Hermanos, 1868.

Unos Caucanos. *Los tratados con Mosquera.* Bogotá: Imprenta de "El Mosaico," 1860.

Unos de Yervarrucia. *Mentir con descaro*. Cali: Imprenta de Hurtado, 1869.

Unos liberales independientes. *Uno i diez i ocho*. Cali: Imprenta de Hurtado, 1864.

Urrutia, Manuel, Mázimo Ospina, J. Rafael Monzón, et al. *Defensa del "Luto nacional."* Barbacoas: n.p., 1856.

U.S. State Department. *Dispatches from United States Consuls in Buenaventura, Colombia: 1867–1885*. Washington, D.C.: National Archives, 1948. Microfilm, unpaginated.

Valencia C., Miguel. *Informe del Procurador General del Estado Soberano del Cauca en el año de 1883*. Popayán: Imprenta del Estado, 1883.

Los Verdaderos Constitucionalistas. *A los liberales de la provincia*. Popayán: Imprenta Democrática, 1853.

Zamorano, Belisario. *Bosquejo biográfico del Jeneral David Peña*. Cali: Imprenta de Eustaquio Palacios, 1878.

Secondary Sources

Aguilera Peña, Mario, and Renán Vega Cantor. *Ideal democrático y revuelta popular: Bosquejo histórico de la mentalidad política popular en Colombia, 1781–1948*. Bogotá: Fondo Editorial Instituto María Cano, 1991.

Anderson, Benedict. *Imagined Communities: Reflections on the Origin and Spread of Nationalism*. London: Verso, 1991.

Andrews, George Reid. "Spanish American Independence: A Structural Analysis." *Latin American Perspectives* 44 (winter 1985): 105–32.

——. *Afro-Latin America, 1800–2000*. New York: Oxford University Press, in press.

Annino, Antonio, ed. *Historia de las elecciones en Iberoamérica, siglo XIX: De la formación del espacio político nacional*. Buenos Aires: Fondo de Cultura Económica, 1995.

Appelbaum, Nancy. "Remembering Riosucio: Race, Region, and Community in Colombia, 1850–1950." Ph.D. diss., University of Wisconsin—Madison, 1997.

——. "Whitening the Region: Caucano Mediation and 'Antioqueño Colonization' in Nineteenth-Century Colombia." *Hispanic American Historical Review* 79 (November 1999): 631–67.

——. *Muddied Waters: Race, Region, and Local History in Colombia, 1846–1948*. Durham: Duke University Press, 2003.

Arboleda, Gustavo. *Diccionario biográfico y genealógico del antiguo Departamento del Cauca*. Bogotá: Biblioteca Horizontes, 1962.

——. *Historia contemporánea de Colombia*. 12 vols. Bogotá: Banco Central Hipotecario, 1990.

Arendt, Hannah. *On Violence*. New York: Harcourt, Brace, and World, 1969.

Arocha, Jaime. "Inclusion of Afro-Colombians: Unreachable National Goal?" *Latin American Perspectives* 25 (May 1998): 70–89.

Bergquist, Charles. *Coffee and Conflict in Colombia, 1886–1910*. Durham: Duke University Press, 1986.

Beverley, John. *Subalternity and Representation: Arguments in Cultural Theory*. Durham: Duke University Press, 1999.

Beverley, John, and James Sanders. "Negotiating with the Disciplines: A Conversation on Latin American Subaltern Studies." *Journal of Latin American Cultural Studies* 6 (November 1997): 233–57.

Blassingame, John W. *The Slave Community: Plantation Life in the Antebellum South*. Rev. ed. New York: Oxford University Press, 1979.

Bobbio, Norberto. *Liberalism and Democracy*. London: Verso, 1990.

Botero Villa, Juan José. *Adjudicación, explotación y comercialización de baldíos y bosques nacionales: Evolución histórico-legislativa, 1830–1930*. Bogotá: Banco de la República, 1994.

Bushnell, David. "Voter Participation in the Colombian Election of 1856." *Hispanic American Historical Review* 51 (May 1971): 237–49.

———. *Política y sociedad en el siglo XIX*. Tunja: Universidad Pedagógica y Tecnológica, 1975.

———. *The Making of Modern Colombia: A Nation in Spite of Itself*. Berkeley and Los Angeles: University of California Press, 1993.

———. "Assessing the Legacy of Liberalism." In *Liberals, Politics, and Power: State Formation in Nineteenth-Century Latin America*, ed. Vincent C. Peloso and Barbara A. Tenenbaum, 278–300. Athens: University of Georgia Press, 1996.

Bustamente, Darío. *Efectos económicos del papel moneda durante la Regeneración*. Bogotá: Editorial Carreta, 1980.

Cacua Prada, Antonio. *Historia de la educación en Colombia*. Bogotá: Academia Colombiana de Historia, 1997.

Castellanos, Jorge. *La abolición de la esclavitud en Popayán, 1832–1852*. Cali: Universidad del Valle, 1980.

Castro C., Beatriz. "Caridad y beneficencia en Cali, 1848–1898." *Boletín Cultural y Bibliográfico* 27, no. 22 (1990): 67–80.

Chambers, Sarah C. *From Subjects to Citizens: Honor, Gender, and Politics in Arequipa, Peru, 1780–1854*. University Park: Pennsylvania State University Press, 1999.

Chatterjee, Partha. *The Nation and Its Fragments: Colonial and Postcolonial Histories*. Princeton: Princeton University Press, 1993.

Collier, Ruth Berins, and David Collier. *Shaping the Political Arena: Critical Junctures, the Labor Movement, and Regime Dynamics in Latin America*. Princeton: Princeton University Press, 1991.

Colmenares, Germán. *Partidos políticos y clases sociales*. Bogotá: Universidad de los Andes, 1968.

. "Castas, patrones de poblamiento y conflictos sociales en las provincias del Cauca, 1810–1830." In *La independencia: Ensayos de historia social*, by Germán Colmenares, Zamira Díaz de Zuluaga, José Escorcia, and Francisco Zuluaga, 137–80. Bogotá: Instituto Colombiano de Cultura, 1986.

———. *Cali: Terratenientes, mineros y comerciantes, siglo XVIII*. Bogotá: Tercer Mundo, 1997.

———. *Historia económica y social de Colombia*. Vol. 2, *Popayán, una sociedad esclavista, 1680–1800*. Bogotá: Tercer Mundo, 1997.

Conrad, Joseph. *Nostromo: A Tale of the Seaboard*. 1904. New York: Penguin, 1990.

Cooper, Frederick, Thomas C. Holt, and Rebecca J. Scott. *Beyond Slavery: Explorations of Race, Labor, and Citizenship in Postemancipation Societies*. Chapel Hill: University of North Carolina Press, 2000.

Correa González, Claudia María. "Intergración socio-económica del manumiso caucano, 1850–1900." Trabajo de Grado, Universidad de los Andes, 1987.

Costa, Emilia Viotti da. *The Brazilian Empire: Myths and Histories*. Chicago: Dorsey, 1985.

Curry, Glenn. "The Disappearance of the Resguardos Indígenas of Cundinamarca, Colombia, 1800–1863." Ph.D. diss., Vanderbilt University, 1981.

Deas, Malcolm. "Poverty, Civil War, and Politics: Ricardo Gaitán Obeso and His Magdalena River Campaign in Colombia, 1885." *Nova Americana* 2 (1979): 263–303.

———. "La presencia de la política nacional en la vida provinciana, pueblerina y rural de Colombia en el primer siglo de la república." In *La unidad nacional en América Latina: Del regionalismo a la nacionalidad*, ed. Marco Palacios, 149–73. Mexico City: El Colegio de México, 1983.

———. "Del poder y la gramática," y otros ensayos sobre historia, política y literatura colombiana. Bogotá: Tercer Mundo Editores, 1993.

———. "La política en la vida cotidiana repúblicana." In *Historia de la vida cotidiana en Colombia*, ed. Beatriz Castro Carvajal, 271–90. Bogotá: Grupo Editorial Norma, 1996.

Deas, Malcolm, and Fernando Gaitán Daza. *Dos ensayos especulativos sobre la violencia en Colombia.* Bogotá: FONADE, 1995.

Deas, Malcolm, Frank Safford, and Marco Palacios. "La Regeneración y la Guerra de los Mil Días." In *Aspectos polémicos de la historia colombiana del siglo XIX: Memoria de un seminario*, 51–94. Bogotá: Fondo Cultural Cafetero, 1983.

Delpar, Helen. *Red against Blue: The Liberal Party in Colombian Politics, 1863–1899.* University: University of Alabama Press, 1981.

Díaz Aparicio, Omar. *Los ejidos: Desde Alfonso el Sabio en Castilla hasta nuestros días en Cali.* Cali: Imprenta Departamental del Valle, 1992.

Díaz de Zuluaga, Zamira. *Oro, sociedad y economía: El sistema colonial en la Gobernación de Popayán, 1533–1733.* Bogotá: Banco de la República, 1994.

Dore, Elizabeth. "One Step Forward, Two Steps Back: Gender and the State in the Long Nineteenth Century." In *Hidden Histories of Gender and the State in Latin America*, ed. Elizabeth Dore and Maxine Molyneux, 3–32. Durham: Duke University Press, 2000.

Earle, Rebecca, ed. *Rumours of Wars: Civil Conflict in Nineteenth-Century Latin America.* London: Institute of Latin American Studies, 2000.

———. *Spain and the Independence of Colombia, 1810–1825.* Exeter: University of Exeter Press, 2000.

———. "The War of the Supremes: Border Conflict, Religious Crusade, or Simply Politics by Other Means?" In *Rumours of Wars: Civil Conflict in Nineteenth-Century Latin America*, ed. Rebecca Earle, 119–34. London: Institute of Latin American Studies, 2000.

Escorcia, José. "Haciendas y estructura agraria en el Valle del Cauca, 1810–1850." *Anuario Colombiano de Historia Social y de la Cultura* 10 (1982): 119–38.

———. *Sociedad y economía en el Valle del Cauca.* Vol. 3, *Desarrollo político, social y económico, 1800–1854.* Bogotá: Biblioteca Banco Popular, 1983.

———. "La formación de las clases sociales en el periódo de la independencia." In *La independencia: Ensayos de historia social*, by Germán Colmenares, Zamira Díaz de Zuluaga, José Escorcia, and Francisco Zuluaga, 69–110. Bogotá: Instituto Colombiano de Cultura, 1986.

Espinosa Jaramillo, Gustavo. *La saga de los ejidos: Crónica legal, siglos XIII al XX.* Cali: Universidad Santiago de Cali, 1997.

Estrada Álvarez, Jairo, ed. *Plan Colombia: Ensayos críticos.* Bogotá: Universidad Nacional de Colombia, 2001.

Fals Borda, Orlando. *Historia doble de la costa.* 4 vols. Bogotá: Carlos Valencia Editores, 1981.

Farnsworth-Alvear, Ann. *Dulcinea in the Factory: Myths, Morals, Men, and Women in Colombia's Industrial Experiment, 1905–1960.* Durham: Duke University Press, 2000.

Ferrer, Ada. *Insurgent Cuba: Race, Nation, and Revolution, 1868–1898.* Chapel Hill: University of North Carolina Press, 1999.

Findji, María Teresa, and José María Rojas. *Territorio, economía y sociedad Páez.* Cali: Universidad del Valle, 1985.

Flórez Gallego, Lenin. "Discusiones recientes en torno a Núñez y a la Regeneración." *Historia y Espacio* 2 (May 1983): 43–55.

———. *Modernidad política en Colombia: El republicanismo en el Valle del Cauca, 1880–1920.* Cali: Universidad del Valle, 1997.

Foner, Eric. *Reconstruction: America's Unfinished Revolution, 1863–1877*. New York: Harper and Row, 1988.

Foucault, Michel. *Discipline and Punish: The Birth of the Prison*. New York: Vintage, 1977.

——. *Power/Knowledge: Selected Interviews and Other Writings, 1972–1977*. New York: Pantheon, 1980.

Friede, Juan. *El indio en lucha por la tierra*. Bogotá: Editorial Espiral, 1944.

Friedemann, Nina S. de. "Niveles contemporáneos de indigenismo en Colombia." In *Indigenismo y aniquilamiento de indígenas en Colombia*, by Juan Friede, Nina S. de Friedemann, and Dario Fajardo, 15–37. Bogotá: Universidad Nacional de Colombia, 1975.

Friedemann, Nina S. de, and Jaime Arocha. *De sol a sol: Génesis, transformación y presencia de los negros en Colombia*. Bogotá: Planeta, 1986.

Fuente, Alejandro de la. *A Nation for All: Race, Inequality, and Politics in Twentieth-Century Cuba*. Chapel Hill: University of North Carolina Press, 2001.

García Márquez, Gabriel. *One Hundred Years of Solitude*. New York: Harper and Row, 1970.

Garrido, Margarita. *Reclamos y representaciones: Variaciones sobre la política en el Nuevo Reino de Granada, 1770–1815*. Bogotá: Banco de la República, 1993.

Genovese, Eugene D. *Roll, Jordan, Roll: The World the Slaves Made*. New York: Vintage, 1976.

González, Margarita. "El proceso de manumisión en Colombia." In *La nueva historia de Colombia*, ed. Dario Jaramillo Agudelo, 217–340. Bogotá: Instituto Colombiano de Cultura, 1976.

González González, Fernán E. *Para leer la política: Ensayos de historia política colombiana*. 2 vols. Bogotá: CINEP, 1997.

——. *Poderes enfrentados: Iglesia y estado en Colombia*. Bogotá: CINEP, 1997.

Gould, Jeffrey L. *To Die in This Way: Nicaraguan Indians and the Myth of Mestizaje, 1880–1965*. Durham: Duke University Press, 1998.

Graham, Richard, ed. *The Idea of Race in Latin America, 1870–1940*. Austin: University of Texas Press, 1990.

——. *Patronage and Politics in Nineteenth-Century Brazil*. Stanford: Stanford University Press, 1990.

Gramsci, Antonio. *Selections from the Prison Notebooks*. Edited by Quintin Hoare and Geoffrey Nowell-Smith. New York: International, 1971.

Granados García, Aimer. "Algunos aspectos de la cultura política popular en el Gran Cauca, 1880–1910." In *El siglo XIX: Bolivia y América Latina*, ed. Rossana Barragán, Dora Cajías, and Seemin Qayum, 663–77. La Paz: Muela del Diablo Editores, 1997.

Green, John. "Left Liberalism and Race in the Evolution of Colombian Popular National Identity." *The Americas: A Quarterly Review of Inter-American Cultural History* 57 (July 2000): 95–124.

Guardino, Peter. *Peasants, Politics, and the Formation of Mexico's National State: Guerrero, 1800–1857*. Stanford: Stanford University Press, 1996.

Guha, Ranajit. *Elementary Aspects of Peasant Insurgency in Colonial India*. Delhi: Oxford University Press, 1983.

——. "On Some Aspects of the Historiography of Colonial India." In *Selected Subaltern Studies*, ed. Ranajit Guha and Gayatri Chakravorty Spivak, 37–44. New York: Oxford University Press, 1988.

——. "The Prose of Counter-Insurgency." In *Selected Subaltern Studies*, ed. Ranajit Guha and Gayatri Chakravorty Spivak, 45–86. Oxford: Oxford University Press, 1988.

Guillén Martínez, Fernando. *La Regeneración: Primer frente nacional*. Bogotá: Carlos Valencia Editores, 1986.

Gutiérrez Azopardo, Ildefonso. *Historia del negro en Colombia*. 4th ed. Bogotá: Editorial Nueva América, 1994.

Gutiérrez de Pineda, Virginia. *Familia y cultura en Colombia: Tipologías, funciones y dinámica de la familia.* Bogotá: Instituto Colombiano de Cultura, 1975.

Gutiérrez Sanín, Francisco. *Curso y discurso del movimiento plebeyo.* Bogotá: El Áncora Editores, 1995.

Habermas, Jürgen. *The Theory of Communicative Action.* Boston: Beacon, 1984.

Hamnett, Brian R. "Popular Insurrection and Royalist Reaction: Colombian Regions, 1810–1823." In *Reform and Insurrection in Bourbon New Granada and Peru,* ed. John R. Fisher, Allan J. Kuethe, and Anthony McFarlane, 292–326. Baton Rouge: Louisiana State University Press, 1990.

Helg, Aline. *Our Rightful Share: The Afro-Cuban Struggle for Equality, 1886–1912.* Chapel Hill: University of North Carolina Press, 1995.

——. "The Limits of Equality: Free People of Colour and Slaves during the First Independence of Cartagena, Colombia, 1810–15." *Slavery and Abolition* 20 (August 1999): 1–30.

Helguera, J. León. "The First Mosquera Administration in New Granada: 1845–1849." Ph.D. diss., University of North Carolina, Chapel Hill, 1958.

——. "Antecedentes sociales de la revolución de 1851 en el sur de Colombia (1848–1849)." *Anuario Colombiano de Historia Social y de la Cultura* 5 (1970): 53–63.

Hernández de Alba, Guillermo. *Libertad de los esclavos en Colombia.* Bogotá: Editorial ABC, 1956.

Hobsbawm, Eric. *The Age of Revolution, 1789–1848.* Cleveland: World, 1962.

——. *The Age of Capital, 1848–1875.* New York: Vintage, 1975.

——. *The Age of Empire, 1875–1914.* New York: Vintage, 1987.

Hunefeldt, Christine. *Liberalism in the Bedroom: Quarreling Spouses in Nineteenth-Century Lima.* University Park: Pennsylvania State University Press, 2000.

Hunt, Lynn. *Politics, Culture, and Class in the French Revolution.* Berkeley and Los Angeles: University of California Press, 1984.

Hyland, Richard Preston. "The Secularization of Credit in the Cauca Valley, Colombia, 1851–1880." Ph.D. diss., University of California, Berkeley, 1979.

James, C. L. R. *The Black Jacobins: Toussaint L'Ouverture and the San Domingo Revolution.* New York: Vintage, 1963.

Jaramillo Castillo, Carlos Eduardo. "Guerras civiles y vida cotidiana." In *Historia de la vida cotidiana en Colombia,* ed. Beatriz Castro Carvajal, 291–309. Bogotá: Grupo Editorial Norma, 1996.

Jaramillo Uribe, Jaime. *El pensamiento colombiano en el siglo XIX.* Bogotá: Editorial Temis, 1964.

——. "La controversia jurídica y filosófica librada en la Nueva Granada en torno a la liberación de los esclavos y la importancia económica-social de la esclavitud en el siglo XIX." *Anuario Colombiano de Historia Social y de la Cultura* 4 (1969): 63–86.

——. "La población indígena de Colombia en el momento de conquista y sus transformaciones posteriores." In *Ensayos sobre historia social colombiana,* 89–161. Bogotá: Imprenta Nacional, 1969.

Jiménez, Michael. "La vida rural cotidiana en la República." In *Historia de la vida cotidiana en Colombia,* ed. Beatriz Castro Carvajal, 161–203. Bogotá: Grupo Editorial Norma, 1996.

——. *Struggles on an Interior Shore: Wealth, Power, and Authority in the Colombian Andes.* Durham: Duke University Press, in press.

Johnson, David Church. *Santander, siglo XIX: Cambios socioeconómicos.* Bogotá: Carlos Valencia Editores, 1984.

Joseph, Gilbert, and Daniel Nugent, eds. *Everyday Forms of State Formation: Revolution and the Negotiation of Rule in Modern Mexico.* Durham: Duke University Press, 1994.

Keyssar, Alexander. *The Right to Vote: The Contested History of Democracy in the United States.* New York: Basic, 2000.

246   Bibliography

König, Hans-Joachim. *En el camino hacia la nación: Nacionalismo en el proceso de formación del estado y de la nación de la Nueva Granada, 1750–1856*. Bogotá: Banco de la República, 1994.

Kurtz, Donald V. "Hegemony and Anthropology: Gramsci, Exegeses, Reinterpretations." *Critique of Anthropology* 16, no. 2 (1996): 103–35.

Lasso, Marixa. "Haiti as an Image of Popular Republicanism in Caribbean Colombia: Cartagena Province (1811–1828)." In *The Impact of the Haitian Revolution in the Atlantic World*, ed. David P. Geggus, 176–90. Columbia: University of South Carolina Press, 2001.

———. "Race and Republicanism in the Age of Revolution, Cartagena, 1795–1831." Ph.D. diss., University of Florida, 2002.

Leal, Francisco, and Oscar Díaz. "La Regeneración y la formación del estado nacional." *Historia y Espacio* 3 (January–December 1987): 269–305.

LeGrand, Catherine. *Frontier Expansion and Peasant Protest in Colombia, 1830–1936*. Albuquerque: University of New Mexico Press, 1986.

Lempérière, Annick. "Reflexiones sobre la terminología política del liberalismo." In *Construcción de la legitimidad política en México en el siglo XIX*, ed. Brian Connaughton, Carlos Illades, and Sonia Pérez Toledo, 35–56. Zamora: El Colegio de Michoacán, 1999.

Liévano Aguirre, Indalecio. *Rafael Núñez*. Bogotá: Editorial Cromos, 1944.

Linebaugh, Peter, and Marcus Rediker. *The Many-Headed Hydra: Sailors, Slaves, Commoners, and the Hidden History of the Revolutionary Atlantic*. Boston: Beacon, 2000.

Lobato Paz, Luis Eduardo. "Caudillos y nación: Sociabilidades políticas en el Cauca, 1830–1860." Tesis de Magister, Universidad del Valle, 1994.

Long, Gary. "The Dragon Finally Came: Industrial Capitalism, Radical Artisans, and the Liberal Party in Colombia, 1910–1948." Ph.D. diss., University of Pittsburgh, 1995.

———. "Popular Liberalism and Civil War in Nineteenth-Century Colombia: Historical Roots of Labor's Radical Ideology in the Twentieth Century." Paper presented at the Fourteenth Latin American Labor History Conference, Duke University, 3 May 1997.

López Garavito, Luis Fernando. *Historia de la hacienda y el tesoro en Colombia, 1821–1900*. Bogotá: Banco de la República, 1992.

Lynch, John. *The Spanish American Revolutions, 1808–1826*. New York: Norton, 1986.

Mallon, Florencia E. "The Promise and Dilemma of Subaltern Studies: Perspectives from Latin American History." *American Historical Review* 99 (December 1994): 1491–1515.

———. *Peasant and Nation: The Making of Post-Colonial Mexico and Peru*. Berkeley and Los Angeles: University of California Press, 1995.

———. "Time on the Wheel: Cycles of Revisionism and the 'New Cultural History.'" *Hispanic American Historical Review* 79 (May 1999): 331–51.

Markoff, John. *The Abolition of Feudalism: Peasants, Lords, and Legislators in the French Revolution*. University Park: Pennsylvania State University Press, 1996.

———. "Really Existing Democracy: Learning from Latin America in the Late 1990s." *New Left Review* 223 (May–June 1997): 48–68.

Marx, Karl. "The Eighteenth Brumaire of Louis Bonaparte." In *The Marx-Engels Reader*, ed. Robert C. Tucker, 594–617. New York: Norton, 1978.

Maya, Adriana. "Los Afrocolombianos: Memoria, poder y derechos territoriales." Paper presented at the conference of the Latin American Studies Association, Miami, 16–18 March 2000.

McFarlane, Anthony. *Colombia before Independence: Economy, Society, and Politics under Bourbon Rule*. Cambridge: Cambridge University Press, 1993.

McGreevey, William Paul. *An Economic History of Colombia, 1845–1930*. Cambridge: Cambridge University Press, 1971.

McGuinness, Aims. "In the Path of Empire: Land, Labor, and Liberty in Panamá during the California Gold Rush, 1848–1860." Ph.D. diss., University of Michigan, 2001.

Mehta, Uday Singh. *Liberalism and Empire: A Study in Nineteenth-Century British Liberal Thought*. Chicago: University of Chicago Press, 1999.

Mejía Prado, Eduardo. *Origen del campesino vallecaucano: Siglo XVIII y siglo XIX*. Cali: Universidad del Valle, 1996.

Mejía Prado, Eduardo, and Armando Moncayo Urrutia. "Origen y formación del ingenio azucarero industrializado en el Valle del Cauca." *Historia y Espacio* 3 (1987): 53–107.

Melo, Jorge Orlando. "Las vicisitudes del modelo liberal (1850–1899)." In *Historia económica de Colombia* (4th ed.), ed. José Antonio Ocampo, 119–72. Bogotá: Tercer Mundo Editores, 1994.

Mina, Mateo [Michael Taussig]. *Esclavitud y libertad en el Valle del Río Cauca*. Bogotá: Publicaciones de la Rosca, 1975.

Molina, Gerardo. *Las ideas liberales en Colombia*. Vol. 1, 1849–1914. Bogotá: Tercer Mundo Editores, 1988.

Nieto Arteta, Luis Eduardo. *Economía y cultura en la historia de Colombia*. Medellín: Editorial La Oveja Negra, 1942.

Ocampo, José Antonio, ed. *Historia económica de Colombia*. 4th ed. Bogotá Tercer Mundo Editores, 1996.

——. *Colombia y la economía mundial, 1830–1910*. Bogotá: Tercer Mundo Editores, 1998.

Oestreicher, Richard. "The Two Souls of American Democracy." In *The Social Construction of Democracy, 1870–1990*, ed. George Reid Andrews and Herrick Chapman, 118–31. New York: New York University Press, 1995.

Pacheco, Margarita. *La fiesta liberal en Cali*. Cali: Ediciones Universidad del Valle, 1992.

Palacios, Marco. *El café en Colombia, 1850–1970: Una historia económica, social y política*. Mexico City: El Colegio de México, 1983.

——. *Entre la legitimidad y la violencia, Colombia, 1875–1994*. Bogotá: Grupo Editorial Norma, 1995.

Park, James William. *Rafael Núñez and the Politics of Colombian Regionalism, 1863–1886*. Baton Rouge: Louisiana State University Press, 1985.

Parsons, James J. *Antioqueño Colonization in Western Colombia*. Rev. ed. Berkeley: University of California Press, 1968.

Pinzón, Martín Alonso. *Historia del conservatismo*. Bogotá: Ediciones Tercer Mundo, 1979.

Posada-Carbó, Eduardo. *The Colombian Caribbean: A Regional History, 1870–1950*. Oxford: Clarendon, 1996.

——, ed. *Elections before Democracy: The History of Elections in Europe and Latin America*. New York: St. Martin's, 1996.

——. "Limits of Power: Elections under the Conservative Hegemony in Colombia, 1886–1930." *Hispanic American Historical Review* 77 (May 1997): 245–79.

Ramírez, Francisco E. *General David Peña*. Bogotá: Imprenta Nacional, 1938.

Rappaport, Joanne. *The Politics of Memory: Native Historical Interpretation in the Colombian Andes*. Cambridge: Cambridge University Press, 1990.

——. *Cumbe Reborn: An Andean Ethnography of History*. Chicago: University of Chicago Press, 1994.

Rausch, Jane M. *La educación durante el federalismo: La reforma escolar de 1870*. Bogotá: Instituto Caro y Cuervo, 1993.

Roig, Arturo Andrés. "El siglo XIX latinoamericano y las nuevas formas discursivas." In El pensamiento latinoamericano en el siglo XIX, 127–40. Mexico City: Instituto Panamericano de Geografía e Historia, 1986.

Rojas de Ferro, Cristina. "Identity Formation, Violence, and the Nation-State in Nineteenth-Century Colombia." Alternatives 20 (April–June 1995): 195–224.

———. Civilization and Violence: Regimes of Representation in Nineteenth-Century Colombia. Minneapolis: University of Minnesota Press, 2002.

Roldán, Mary. Blood and Fire: La Violencia in Antioquia, Colombia, 1946–1953. Durham: Duke University Press, 2002.

Roseberry, William. "Hegemony and the Language of Contention." In Everyday Forms of State Formation: Revolution and the Negotiation of Rule in Modern Mexico, ed. Gilbert M. Joseph and Daniel Nugent, 355–66. Durham: Duke University Press, 1994.

Rueschemeyer, Dietrich, Evelyne Huber Stephens, and John D. Stephens. Capitalist Development and Democracy. Chicago: University of Chicago Press, 1992.

Sabato, Hilda. La política en las calles: Entre el voto y la movilización, Buenos Aires, 1862–1880. Buenos Aires: Sudamericana, 1998.

Safford, Frank. "Social Aspects of Politics in Nineteenth-Century Spanish America: New Granada, 1825–1850." Journal of Social History 5 (spring 1972): 344–70.

———. "Acerca de las interpretaciones socioeconómicas de la política en la Colombia del siglo XIX: Variaciones sobre un tema." Anuario Colombiano de Historia Social y de la Cultura 13–14 (1985–1986): 91–151.

———. "Race, Integration, and Progress: Elite Attitudes and the Indian in Colombia, 1750–1870." Hispanic American Historical Review 71 (February 1991): 1–33.

Safford, Frank, and Marco Palacios. Colombia: Fragmented Land, Divided Society. New York: Oxford University Press, 2002.

Said, Edward W. Culture and Imperialism. New York: Knopf, 1993.

Santa, Eduardo. La colonización antioqueña: Una empresa de caminos. Bogotá: Tercer Mundo Editores, 1993.

Scheper-Hughes, Nancy. Death without Weeping: The Violence of Everyday Life in Brazil. Berkeley and Los Angeles: University of California Press, 1992.

Scott, James C. Domination and the Arts of Resistance: Hidden Transcripts. New Haven: Yale University Press, 1990.

Scott, Rebecca J. Slave Emancipation in Cuba: The Transition to Free Labor, 1860–1899. Princeton: Princeton University Press, 1985.

———. "Fault Lines, Color Lines, and Party Lines: Race, Labor, and Collective Action in Louisiana and Cuba, 1862–1912." In Beyond Slavery: Explorations of Race, Labor, and Citizenship in Postemancipation Societies, by Frederick Cooper, Thomas C. Holt, and Rebecca J. Scott, 61–106. Chapel Hill: University of North Carolina Press, 2000.

Sewell, William H., Jr. Work and Revolution in France: The Language of Labor from the Old Regime to 1848. Cambridge: Cambridge University Press, 1980.

Sinisterra, Manuel. El 14 de diciembre de 1876 en Cali. Cali. Impresa de Manuel Sinisterra, 1919.

Smith, Gavin. Livelihood and Resistance: Peasants and the Politics of Land in Peru. Berkeley and Los Angeles: University of California Press, 1989.

Somers, Margaret R. "Narrativity, Narrative Identity, and Social Action: Rethinking English Working-Class Formation." Social Science History 16 (winter 1992): 591–630.

Sowell, David. *The Early Colombian Labor Movement: Artisans and Politics in Bogotá, 1832–1919.* Philadelphia: Temple University Press, 1992.

——. "Repertoires of Contention in Urban Colombia, 1760s–1940s: An Inquiry into Latin American Social Violence." *Journal of Urban History* 24 (March 1998): 302–36.

Spivak, Gayatri Chakravorty. "Can the Subaltern Speak?" In *Marxism and the Interpretation of Culture,* ed. Cary Nelson and Lawrence Grossberg, 271–313. Urbana: University of Illinois Press, 1988.

Stern, Steve J. "The Age of Andean Insurrection, 1742–1782: A Reappraisal." In *Resistance, Rebellion, and Consciousness in the Andean Peasant World, Eighteenth to Twentieth Centuries,* ed. Steve J. Stern, 34–93. Madison: University of Wisconsin Press, 1987.

——. *The Secret History of Gender: Women, Men, and Power in Late Colonial Mexico.* Chapel Hill: University of North Carolina Press, 1995.

Stoller, Richard J. "Liberalism and Conflict in Socorro, Colombia, 1830–1870." Ph.D. diss., Duke University, 1991.

——. "'Democracy in SanJil': Liberal Ideology and Artisan Protest in Northeastern Colombia, 1850–1855." Pennsylvania State University, Schreyer Honors College, 1995. Typescript.

Tarrow, Sidney. *Power in Movement: Social Movements, Collective Action, and Politics.* Cambridge: Cambridge University Press, 1994.

Taussig, Michael T. *The Devil and Commodity Fetishism in South America.* Chapel Hill: University of North Carolina Press, 1980.

Thompson, E. P. *The Making of the English Working Class.* New York: Vintage, 1966.

——. *Customs in Common.* New York: New Press, 1991.

Thomson, Guy P. C., with David G. LaFrance. *Patriotism, Politics, and Popular Liberalism in Nineteenth-Century Mexico: Juan Francisco Lucas and the Puebla Sierra.* Wilmington: SR, 1999.

Thurner, Mark. *From Two Republics to One Divided: Contradictions of Postcolonial Nationmaking in Andean Peru.* Durham: Duke University Press, 1997.

Tilly, Charles. *The Contentious French.* Cambridge: Belknap, 1986.

——. "Contentious Repertoires in Great Britain, 1758–1834." *Social Science History* 17 (summer 1993): 253–80.

——. *Popular Contention in Great Britain, 1758–1834.* Cambridge: Harvard University Press, 1995.

Tirado Mejía, Alvaro. *Aspectos sociales de las guerras civiles en Colombia.* Bogotá: Instituto Colombiano de Cultura, 1976.

Tovar Pinzón, Hermes. "La lenta ruptura con el pasado colonial (1810–1850)." In *Historia económica de Colombia* (4th ed.), ed. José Antonio Ocampo, 87–117. Bogotá: Tercer Mundo Editores, 1994.

Twinam, Ann. *Miners, Merchants, and Farmers in Colonial Colombia.* Austin: University of Texas Press, 1982.

Uribe de Hincapié, María Teresa, and Jesus María Alvarez. *Poderes y regiones: Problemas en la constitución de la nación colombiana, 1810–1850.* Medellín: Universidad de Antioquia, 1987.

Uribe de Hincapié, María Teresa, and Clara Inés García. "La espada de las fronteras." In *Colombia: País de regiones,* ed. Fabio Zambrano, 1:77–107. Bogotá: CINEP, 1998.

Uribe-Uran, Victor M. "Rebellion of the Young Mandarins: Lawyers, Political Parties, and the State in Colombia, 1780–1850." Ph.D. diss., University of Pittsburgh, 1993.

——. *Honorable Lives: Lawyers, Family, and Politics in Colombia, 1780–1850.* Pittsburgh: University of Pittsburgh Press, 2000.

Urrego, Miguel Angel. "La noción de ciudadanía bajo la Regeneración: Colombia, 1880–1900." In *El* siglo XIX: Bolivia y América Latina, ed. Rossana Barragán, Dora Cajías, and Seemin Qayum, 651–62. La Paz: Muela del Diablo Editores, 1997.

Urrutia M., Miguel, and Mario Arrubla, eds. *Compendio de estadísticas históricas de Colombia.* Bogotá: Universidad Nacional de Colombia, 1970.

Valdivia Rojas, Luis. "Mapas de densidad de población para el suroccidente: 1843 y 1870." *Historia y Espacio* 2 (June 1980): 102–10.

Valencia Llano, Albeiro. *Colonización, fundaciones y conflictos agrarios (Gran Caldas y norte del Valle).* Manizales: Gobernación de Caldas, 1994.

Valencia Llano, Alonso. *Estado Soberano del Cauca: Federalismo y regeneración.* Bogotá: Banco de la República, 1988.

——. "Los proyectos económicos de los regeneradores en el Valle del Cauca (1875–1890)." *Historia y Espacio* 4 (January 1990): 1–30.

——. *Empresarios y políticos en el Estado Soberano del Cauca, 1860–1895.* Cali: Universidad del Valle, 1993.

——. *Luchas sociales y políticas del periodismo en el Estado Soberano del Cauca.* Cali: Gobernación del Valle del Cauca, 1994.

——. "La guerra de 1851 en el Cauca." Paper presented at II Cátedra Anual de Historia, Bogotá, 22–24 October 1997.

——. "Gamonales y bandidos en el Estado Soberano del Cauca." Universidad del Valle, Department of History, 1997. Typescript.

Vélez, Humberto. "La Regeneración: ¿Algo más que un proyecto político?" In *Estudios sobre la Regeneración,* by Lenin Flórez G., Adolfo Atehortúa C., and Humberto Vélez R., 7–47. Cali: Imprenta Departamental del Valle, 1987.

Villegas, Jorge, and Antonio Restrepo. *Resguardos de indígenas, 1820–1890.* Medellín: Universidad de Antioquia, 1977.

Wade, Peter. *Blackness and Race Mixture: The Dynamics of Racial Identity in Colombia.* Baltimore: Johns Hopkins University Press, 1993.

Williams, Raymond. *Keywords: A Vocabulary of Culture and Society.* New York: Oxford University Press, 1983.

Worcester, Donald E. "The Spanish-American Past—Enemy of Change" (1969). In *Politics and Social Change in Latin America: Still a Distinct Tradition?* ed. Howard J. Wiarda, 31–39. Boulder: Westview, 1992.

Zambrano, Fabio. "Las sociabilidades modernas en la Nueva Granada, 1820–1848." *Cahiers des Amériques Latines* 10 (1990): 197–203.

——. "Historiografía sobre los movimientos sociales en Colombia: Siglo XIX." In *La historia al final del milenio: Ensayos de historiografía colombiana y latinoamericana,* 1:147–81. Bogota: Editorial Universidad Nacional, 1994.

——. "Algunas formas de sociabilidad en la Nueva Granada, 1780–1860." Universidad Nacional de Colombia, Department of History, 1996. Typescript.

Zuluaga Ramírez, Francisco U. "Clientelismo y guerrillas en el Valle del Patía, 1536–1811." In *La independencia: Ensayos de historia social,* by Germán Colmenares, Zamira Díaz de Zuluaga, José Escorcia, and Francisco Zuluaga, 111–36. Bogotá: Instituto Colombiano de Cultura, 1986.

——. *Guerrilla y sociedad en el Patía: Una relación entre clientelismo político y la insurgencia social.* Cali: Universidad del Valle, 1993.

Zuluaga Ramírez, Francisco, and Amparo Bermúdez. *La protesta social en el suroccidente colombiano: Siglo XVIII.* Cali: Universidad del Valle, 1997.

Newspapers

El 21 de Abril (Popayán)

Ariete (Cali)

Baluarte (Cali)

Boletín de la Sociedad Democrática (Cali)

Boletín Democrático (Cali)

Boletín Industrial (Buenaventura)

Boletín Oficial (Bogotá)

Boletín Político i Militar (Pasto)

El Cauca (Cali)

El Cauca (Popayán)

El Caucano (Cali)

El Cernícalo (Popayán)

El Ciudadano (Popayán)

El Clamor (Popayán)

El Clamor Nacional (Popayán)

El Conservador (Bogotá)

El Correo de la Costa (Buenaventura)

El Demócrata: Organo del Partido Liberal
    Independiente (Palmira)

El Elector (Tumaco)

La Epoca (Cali)

El Espectador: Dios, Relijion i Libertad (Pasto)

El Estado de Guerra (Bogotá)

El Estandarte Liberal (Cali)

El Ferrocarril (Cali)

Gaceta del Cauca (Popayán)

Gaceta Oficial (Popayán)

Gaceta Oficial del Cauca (Popayán)

El Guaitara (Pasto)

El Hombre (Cali)

El Hurón (Popayán)

El Imparcial (Popayán)

Las Máscaras (Pasto)

El Montañes (Barbacoas)

El Montaraz (Barbacoas)

El Patriota (Popayán)

La Paz: Periódico Oficial (Popayán)

El Pensamiento Popular (Cali)

Los Principios (Cali)

El Pueblo (Popayán)

Registro Municipal (Buga)

Registro Oficial (Organo del Gobierno del Cauca)
    (Popayán)

Rejistro Oficial (Organo del Gobierno del Estado)
    (Popayán)

El Republicano (Popayán)

El Sentimiento Democrático (Cali)

El Sufragio (Popayán)

El Sur (Popayán)

El Telégrafo (Palmira)

La Unión (Popayán)

El Volcán (Pasto)

La Voz de la Juventud (Popayán)

La Voz del Pueblo: Organo de la Sociedad Democrática
    (Cali)

Index

James E. Sanders is an assistant professor of history
at Utah State University.

Library of Congress Cataloging-in-Publication Data
Sanders, James E.
Contentious republicans : popular politics, race, and class
in nineteenth-century Colombia / by James E. Sanders.
Includes bibliographical references and index.
ISBN 0-8223-3234-5 (cloth : alk. paper)
ISBN 0-8223-3224-8 (pbk. : alk. paper)
1. Colombia—Politics and government—1832–1886.
2. Republicanism—Colombia—History—19th century.
3. Political participation—Colombia—History—19th
century. 4. Political culture—Colombia—History—19th
century. 5. Colombia—Race relations—Political aspects.
6. Social classes—Colombia—History—19th century.
I. Title.
F2276.S25 2004   986.1′05—dc22   2003016426